Rehabilitating Canada's armed forces to civilian life following World War II was a massive undertaking. The Veterans Charter, the program devised by the federal government to do this, promised to provide "opportunity with security" and was one of the building blocks of the Canadian welfare state. This collection of essays by some of Canada's leading historians explores the Charter's origins, history, and benefits as well as highlighting its role in the development of the Canadian welfare state and postwar society.

Desmond Morton sets the scene with a survey of the experiences of veterans of the Great War, who found much to fault in Ottawa's policies; Jeff Keshen looks at the very different experience of Canada's veterans of World War II. Dean Oliver examines the organization and administration of the return of Canadian soldiers from Europe after VE-day, and Don Ives examines the philosophy and program of the Veterans Charter. Focusing on specific benefits of the Charter, Michael Stevenson looks at issues surrounding the veterans' right to reinstatement in civil employment, Peter Neary deals with educational benefits made available through the Veterans Rehabilitation Act of 1945, and Terry Copp and Mary Tremblay examine the rehabilitation of veterans with psychiatric and physical disabilities. Taking a broader scope, James Struthers provides an insightful assessment of the construction of the Canadian welfare state, and Doug Owram offers a revisionist appraisal of Canadian society in the postwar era. J.L. Granatstein concludes the volume with a probing reflection on the meaning for Canadians of the veteran experience and of their country's participation in World War II.

The achievements of this generation of Canadian veterans are sometimes downplayed; this collection of essays puts their achievements on the historical record and pays tribute to their memory and accomplishments.

PETER NEARY is Professor of History and Dean of the Faculty of Social Science, University of Western Ontario.

J.L. GRANATSTEIN is Distinguished Research Professor of History Emeritus, York University, and Rowell Jackman Resident Fellow at the Canadian Institute of International Affairs. He has written many books on Canada's role in World War II.

The Veterans Charter and Post–World War II Canada

EDITED BY PETER NEARY
AND J.L. GRANATSTEIN

McGill-Queen's University Press
Montreal & Kingston · London · Buffalo

© McGill-Queen's University Press 1998
ISBN 0-7735-1678-6 (cloth)
ISBN 0-7735-1697-2 (paper)

Legal deposit first quarter 1998
Bibliothèque nationale du Québec

Printed in Canada on acid-free paper

McGill-Queen's University Press acknowledges the support of the Canada
Council for the Arts for its publishing program.

Canadian Cataloguing in Publication Data

Main entry under title:
    The Veterans Charter and post–World War II Canada
    Includes index.
    ISBN 0-7735-1678-6 (cloth)
    ISBN 0-7735-1697-2 (paper)
    1. Veterans – Legal status, laws, etc. – Canada. 2. World War, 1939–1945
    – Veterans – Canada. 3. Veterans – Government policy – Canada.
    4. Canada – Social conditions – 1945–1971.
    I. Neary, Peter, 1938–
    II. Granatstein, J.L., 1939–
    UB359.C2V48 1998   971.06
    C97-900898-0

This book was typeset by Typo Litho Composition Inc.
in 10/12 Baskerville.

To P.B. Waite
veteran of World War II
and historian of Canada

Contents

Tables and Figures

FIGURES

Abbreviations

D HIST	Directorate of History, Department of National Defence
DL	Department of Labour
DND	Department of National Defence
DNHW	Department of National Health and Welfare
DPNH	Department of Pensions and National Health
DRIC	Demobilization and Rehabilitation Information Committee
DSCR	Department of Soldiers' Civil Re-establishment
DVA	Department of Veterans Affairs
GACDR	General Advisory Committee on Demobilization and Rehabilitation
GAR	Grand Army of the Republic
GAUV	Grand Army of United Veterans
GWVA	Great War Veterans' Association
ICCR	Inter-departmental Co-ordinating Committee on Rehabilitation
MHC	Military Hospitals Commission
MSA	Military Service Act
NA	National Archives of Canada (Ottawa)
NATO	North Atlantic Treaty Organization
NCO	Non-commissioned Officer
NCCU	National Conference of Canadian Universities
NEC	National Employment Committee
NORAD	North American Air Defence Agreement
NRMA	National Resources Mobilization Act
NRMAs	Men enlisted under the National Resources Mobilization Act
NSS	National Selective Service
OAS	Old Age Security
OECD	Organization for Economic Cooperation and Development
PC	Privy Council
PCO	Privy Council Office
POW	Prisoner-of-war
PTSD	Post-traumatic stress disorder
RCAF	Royal Canadian Air Force
RCAMC	Royal Canadian Army Medical Corps
RCEA	Reinstatement in Civil Employment Act
RCN	Royal Canadian Navy
REL	Research Enterprises Limited
TLC	Trades and Labor Congress
UAW	United Auto Workers
VA	Veterans Administration (United States)
VAC	Veterans Affairs Canada (Charlottetown)
VE-day	Victory in Europe Day (8 May 1945)
VJ-day	Day marking the end of the war against Japan
VLA	Veterans' Land Act
WIB	Wartime Information Board
YMCA	Young Men's Christian Association

Preface

Work on this volume began with a conference at Windermere Manor Conference Centre, University of Western Ontario, 5–7 October 1995. For their financial support of the conference we are grateful to the Social Sciences and Humanities Research Council of Canada; Veterans Affairs Canada; the Faculty of Social Science, University of Western Ontario; and the Franklin and Eleanor Roosevelt Institute, Hyde Park, New York. We thank Alan Adlington, a veteran of World War II and a former president of the University of Western Ontario, for opening the conference with stirring memories of his life in the Great Depression and then as a serviceman and veteran. We are likewise grateful for the encouragement and help in organizing the conference to received from Robert Taylor of "Canada Remembers," the Government of Canada's program to commemorate the fiftieth anniversary of the end of World War II. For special help in preparing this volume we wish to thank Jock Bates of Winnipeg; Don Ives of Veterans Affairs Canada; Beverly Hughes of the Dean's Office, Faculty of Social Science, University of Western Ontario; Robert A. Young, Department of Political Science, University of Western Ontario; Philip Cercone and Joan McGilvray of McGill-Queen's University Press; Michael D. Stevenson and Daniel Robinson, two recent PH DS in Canadian history; and Carlotta Lemieux of London, Ontario, our inestimable editor.

The poll results in appendix 1 taken from the *Public Opinion Quarterly* are reprinted by permission of the University of Chicago Press; those taken from Canadian Institute of Public Opinion news releases are reprinted by permission of the Gallup Organization, Princeton. *Back to Civil Life* (revised 1 April 1946) is reprinted, with minor corrections, by permission of the Hon. Lawrence MacAulay, Secretary of State (Veterans).

Over the years, we have noted in our teaching that Canadian students often know about the American G.I. Bill of Rights (officially, Public Law 346, the Servicemen's Readjustment Act) but have never heard of their own country's Veterans Charter. We trust that this volume will change that.

Ian Alistair Mackenzie (1890–1949), Minister of Pensions and National Health, 1939–44, and Minister of Veterans Affairs, 1944–48. The inscription to William Lyon Mackenzie King reads: "To my Prime Minister with sincerest regards, Ian A. Mackenzie" (National Archives of Canada [NA], C-016784).

Walter Sainsbury Woods (1884–1960), Associate Deputy Minister, Department of Pensions and National Health, 1941–44, and Deputy Minister, Department of Veterans Affairs, 1944–50. He is seen here with his wife Elene Lucille Woods (1885–1960) in 1950 at the unveiling of his portrait by Milton Fowler Gregg (1892–1978), Minister of Veterans Affairs, 1948–50. The portrait, commissioned to mark Woods's retirement, was painted by Ernest Fosberry, RCA. Woods died in 1960 on 11 November. (*Veterans Affairs* 5, no. 6 [1950]: 1)

Robert England (1894–1985), author of *Discharged: A Commentary on Civil Re-establishment of Veterans in Canada* (Toronto: Macmillan 1943) (*Veterans Affairs* 3, no. 12 [1948]: 7)

Edward Dunlop (1919–1981), Casualty Rehabilitation Section, Department of Veterans Affairs, 1945–48 (Canadian Paraplegic Association, *Third Annual Report*, 1948, 13)

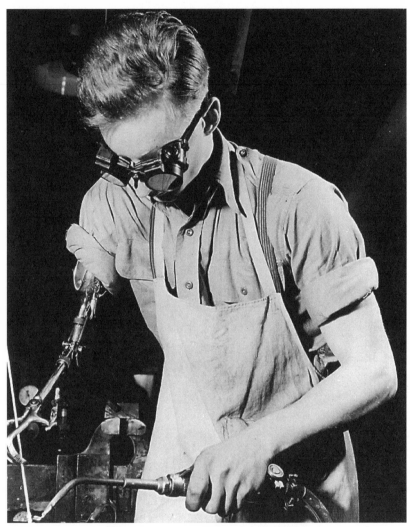

This veteran lost his right arm as the result of gunshot wounds. A dyer in a large textile plant before the war, he successfully retrained as a machinist (Veterans Affairs Canada, Ottawa, "Casualty Rehab. Case History 1946").

Disabled veteran L.A. Bradley at work in Edmonton ("R") district (Veterans Affairs
Canada, Ottawa, "Casualty Rehab. Case History 1946")

Jack Bryson (*left*), who served in the RCAF, being interviewed by an official of the Department of Veterans Affairs, Ottawa, September 1945 (NA, C-49384)

Patricia Hayes (*left*), who served in the RCAF, 1942–44, being interviewed by an official of the Department of Veterans Affairs, September 1945 (NA, PA-197729)

Provincial women supervisors of Canadian Vocational Training discuss plans for training ex-service women, at a conference in Ottawa convened by the Department of Labour. *Centre, at head of table:* Marion Margaret Graham (1903–95), Department of Labour; *standing on her left:* Dr Mary Dinsmore Salter (now Ainsworth) (b. 1 December 1913), Supervisor of Women's Rehabilitation, Department of Veterans Affairs; *seated, second from right:* Dr Olive Ruth Russell (1897–1979), Executive Assistant to the Director General of Rehabilitation, Department of Veterans Affairs (*Veterans Affairs* 1, no. 8 [1946]: 7)

Veterans' community apartments, former air force and army barracks, University of Saskatchewan, Saskatoon. The apartments were administered by the Saskatchewan Reconstruction Housing Corporation (NA, C-49393).

Student veterans at McGill University, Sir William Dawson College, St Johns, Quebec, February 1947. They are seen in the engineering drafting room (NA, C-49422).

Hinson MacLeod, a former bomber pilot with the RCAF, with his family in the veterans' apartment building at Acadia University, Wolfville, Nova Scotia, February 1947 (NA, PA-197732)

Stuart Trask addresses students at Acadia University, Wolfville, Nova Scotia, February 1947, about the December 1946 conference of student veterans (NA, C-49425).

Students learning typing at the Toronto Rehabilitation Centre, February 1945 (NA, PA-144884)

Clinton Anderson of Plaster Rock, New Brunswick, who served five years in the Canadian Army. He is seen here at the Maritime Forest Ranger School, Fredericton, New Brunswick (NA, PA-197733).

Learning to build a house at the Edmonton Rehabilitation School, March 1946. The school was located in the former drill hall of the Edmonton Exhibition (NA, PA-197731).

Cafeteria scene at the Training and Re-establishment Institute, Brockville, Ontario, June 1946. A meal cost twenty-five cents. Six months after it opened, the institute had an enrolment of more than six hundred veterans, both men and women, and a staff of eighty administering academic, commercial, and technical subjects (NA, PA-197734).

In the barbershop of the Training and Re-establishment Institute, Brockville, Ontario, June 1946 (NA, PA-197735)

Left to right: Walter S. Woods, Milton F. Gregg, and Veterans' Land Act Director Thomas John Rutherford (1893–1975) examine the model of a house typical of those being built for veterans, November 1949 (NA, PA-197736).

Aerial view of a Veterans' Land Act subdivision being built around the edges of the golf course at Roseland, near Windsor, Ontario, November 1949 (NA, PA-197737)

Veteran B.E. Stauth and his wife at work on the house they built near Windsor, Ontario, under the Veterans' Land Act program. In the background are their daughter Gail and her friend Karen Mann (NA, PA-197738).

Community centre built by veterans of the Veterans' Land Act subdivision of
Spring Valley near Ancaster, Ontario, November 1949 (NA, PA-197739)

Construction work on the Veterans' Land Act subdivision at Waterloo,
Ontario (NA, PA-197740)

The Veterans Charter and Post–World War II Canada

PETER NEARY

Introduction

Canada went to war in 1939 burdened with two bitter and interwoven legacies from the Great War of 1914–18. One was of conscription and the other of the alleged betrayal of those who had served overseas. Canadian nationhood, it has been argued, was born on the battlefields of France, but the "war to end all wars" also cost many lives, divided French-speaking and English-speaking Canadians as never before, and produced a generation of angry and disgruntled veterans. Many lessons were learned from all this, not least by William Lyon Mackenzie King, who led the country through World War II. In 1914, King turned forty and was in the political wilderness. Following the general election of 1908, he had been named to the Liberal government of Sir Wilfrid Laurier, but in 1911 that government had been turned out and King had suffered personal defeat in Waterloo North. Worse followed both for the party and for King himself. In 1917, after three hard years of war, the Liberal opposition in the House of Commons, still led by Laurier (who was now seventy-five), split over the issue of conscription of men for overseas service. For reasons of history and outlook, this course of action was bitterly opposed by the French-speaking majority of Quebec. The division in the Liberal ranks eventually led many (but by no means all) English-speaking Liberal members to cross the floor of the House to join the Tories in a "Union" government, which promoted equality of sacrifice in the war effort through conscription. Soon after the formation of the Union government, an election was called for 17 December 1917.

In the campaign leading up to this election, the Union propaganda machine advanced a stark choice: party or country, Quebec or Canada. "Quebec," the *Free Press* of London, Ontario, told its readers three days before the vote, "has 'scabbed' on the soldier. Quebec has 'scabbed' on the Red Cross. Quebec has 'scabbed' on the patriotic fund. Quebec has 'scabbed' on the victory loan ... Compulsion is the only means to bring Quebec into line. This is a British country. Quebec MUST obey its laws."[1] In sum, to vote Liberal was to be unpatriotic and unCanadian.

Given this blunt and uncompromising message, loyalty to Laurier carried a high price in Ontario in 1917. One of the Liberals who paid that price was Mackenzie King. King was a mixture of caution and ambition, and he certainly agonized over what to do in the conscription crisis. Ultimately, however, he stood as a Liberal candidate, this time in North York. Once again, both he and his party were soundly defeated. King's political career had reached its nadir in one of the greatest crises that had ever enveloped the country.

Yet as events unfolded, defeat in 1919 brought King lasting political benefits. Laurier died in 1919, and a national convention was called for August of that year to choose his successor. King won the leadership on the fourth ballot by defeating W.S. Fielding, who had supported the Union government, by 476 votes to 438. His razor-thin victory owed much to the great support he enjoyed among the Quebec delegates, who remembered his loyalty to Laurier in 1917. In every election he subsequently fought as leader of the Liberal Party, King carried Quebec handily.

Nevertheless, his early years as leader were turbulent, as the country made a rough passage from war to peace. King had to unify his own party while devising policies for the country in conditions of social and economic upheaval. The return of the Canadian armed forces from overseas was a messy operation, and veterans quickly became an unpredictable and sometimes alarming element in Canadian society. In 1919, two years after the Bolshevik revolution in Russia, Canada experienced a wave of strikes that terrified conservative elements in the country and provoked a hard response from Ottawa. Also in 1919, Ontario broke sharply with its political past by electing a farmer-labour government. In 1921 and 1922, respectively, farmer governments came to power in Alberta and Manitoba. When a national election was held in 1921, the Liberals won the largest number of seats but not a majority. King became prime minister but at the head of the country's first minority government. Second place, moreover, went not to the Conservatives but to the National Progressive Party, which fed on the multiple discontents of the time.

It was not until the mid-1920s that the normality and predictability craved by many Canadians, especially King, began to return to the country. Not surprisingly, the defeat, division, and disorder of the 1917–21 period made a deep and lasting impression on King and his generation of Canadians. What had occurred in those years over the interconnected issues of conscription and demobilization must never be allowed to happen in Canada again. This, then, was the legacy that shaped King's conduct of Canada's affairs during World War II and the plans his government laid for meeting the personnel needs of the armed forces and for demobilization and re-establishment once victory was won. This time around, moderation and planning would keep the country united and secure. Above all, King was determined as a wartime leader not to repeat the mistakes of the past.

How successful were King and his ministers after 1939 in achieving this objective? On conscription, King moved warily. In 1940, after the fall of France, he introduced the National Resources Mobilization Act (NRMA). This permitted the conscription of men, but only for service in Canada. When pressure mounted on the government to step up the war effort, King called a plebiscite for April 1942, seeking release for the government from its prior commitments restricting the methods of raising men for military service. The eight provinces with English-speaking majorities voted unequivocally in favour of this release, but Quebec voted massively against what the government wanted. This put King in a very awkward position indeed. His response was to amend the NRMA by Bill 80, which received assent on 1 August 1942, so as to remove the geographical limitation on where conscripts might be required to serve. Henceforth, they would serve on the same basis as volunteers in terms of their deployment. However, in practice and in response to the sensibilities of Quebec, the government was actually able to avoid ordering conscripts overseas until late 1944. The result was that only 2,463 were posted to Europe by the end of the war. Through brilliant manoeuvring, King had been able to avoid a repeat of the depths reached in the "khaki election" of 1917. Still, there was a price to national unity in his actions; another generation of French Canadians had learned at first hand, albeit less brutally, what it meant to be overruled on a fundamental issue by the English-speaking majority. King lost two ministers from Quebec on the conscription issue, and he failed to carry his Quebec members with him on Bill 80. Nevertheless, he won handily in Quebec in the general election of 1945, although he won only a bare majority nationally. On the other hand, the autonomist Maurice Duplessis had returned to power in Quebec in 1944. Moreover, many Quebecers may have supported King in 1945 not out of enthusiasm for him but because on the conscription issue his was the least objectionable of the national parties.

In contrast to what happened over conscription, the government's planning for a smooth postwar transition was straightforward and without rancour. The first step was taken on 8 December 1939 when, by order-in-council PC 4068½, a cabinet committee was appointed to study and make recommendations on the problems that would arise from the demobilization and discharge of members of the armed forces, both during and after the war. With the help of the General Advisory Committee on Demobilization and Rehabilitation, which eventually had fourteen subcommittees, this new unit set out to define the obligation of the government "to those whose lives were interrupted by their service to their Country."[2] A key event in this regard was the issuing on 1 October 1941 of PC 7633, the "Post-Discharge Re-establishment Order."[3] This order promised all veterans of World War II rehabilitation assistance and specified that military service would constitute insurable employment under the Unemployment Insurance Act of June 1940. These provisions represented a big step forward in veterans' benefits. In the case of the World War I generation, only disabled veterans had been eligible for rehabilitation benefits. Now everyone who served would qualify.

Devising the program that would fulfil the commitment to rehabilitation made in PC 7633 was the job of the Department of Pensions and National Health, which since 1928 had been administering veterans' benefits, including the running of a network of veterans' hospitals across the country. The division of powers in the Canadian federal system assigned hospitals (other than marine hospitals) to the provincial sphere of authority. But since World War I had been a national crusade, Ottawa had accepted a national responsibility to its victims. The hospitals were but one manifestation of this responsibility.

From 19 September 1939 to 12 October 1944 the Minister of Pensions and National Health was Ian Mackenzie, the member of parliament for Vancouver Centre and a veteran of the Great War. Mackenzie is best known in the historiography of World War II for the tough stand he took in favour of the evacuation of Japanese Canadians, but on veterans' matters he was a constructive force. Unquestionably, however, the chief architect of the program devised for Canadian veterans of the 1939–45 conflict was Walter S. Woods, who, from April 1941, was Associate Deputy Minister of Pensions and National Health with responsibility for the rehabilitation program for veterans. Woods (originally Sainsbury-Woods) had been born in England and had come to Canada at the age of twenty-one. He started out in the dominion doing farm work in Ontario; he then went to Manitoba, where he moved from farm labour to employment with the Canadian Pacific Railway, first in manual and then in clerical work. In 1911 he went to work for the Grand Trunk Pacific Railway as foreman of a hundred-man crew that laid track across the prairie. When the Great War started, he went overseas with the first Canadian contingent and was wounded in France in 1915. While he was overseas, his wife died and he was left a widower with two small sons. In the memorable year of 1919, he was president of the Calgary branch of the Great War Veterans' Association (GWVA). He remarried after the war and from 1919 to 1930 worked for the Soldier Settlement Board, an agency of the dominion government that administered a land settlement scheme for veterans. When Ottawa created the War Veterans' Allowance Board in 1930, Woods was named chairman. This board administered allowances to veterans who had served in a theatre of war and had become unemployable and destitute. Among veterans themselves this particular entitlement, which Woods helped invent, was known as the burnt-out pension.

Woods's reputation was of a self-made man with practical values and a broad experience of Canadian life. He liked to present himself as multifaceted: as someone who knew what was involved in earning a living in Canada because he had worked his way up in a new country; as someone who understood the point of view of serving members of the armed forces because he too had been in uniform; and as someone who appreciated the outlook and needs of ex-servicemen because he was one himself and had served the veterans' cause both in the GWVA and the public service. In sum, he saw himself as the right man for the big job implicit in PC 7633. Woods's philosophy of veterans' benefits derived from the "basic truth ... that the great majority of veterans would much rather work than receive relief in any form from the State."[4] Canada was obligated to provide long-term support for sick and disabled veterans and for the dependants of those who had died in the service of their country. Able-bodied veterans, however, would need only short-term help to compensate for service rendered, opportunities lost, and interrupted life. Given the means to make a fresh start, they would soon be looking after themselves and their families, and building up the country they had so gallantly come forward to defend. In short, what the able-bodied veterans of World War II would need to re-establish themselves was "OPPORTUNITY WITH SECURITY."[5]

In making their plans, Woods and his associates had to work within a set of constraints. Length of service would obviously have to be taken into account in awarding benefits. So too would the deeply felt difference between home service and overseas service and the great divide in the armed forces between volunteers and NRMA conscripts. Those who had served longer, gone overseas, and volunteered expected their accomplishments to be recognized in tangible benefits. The NRMA conscripts who were sent overseas in 1944 and 1945 constituted another category, which also had to be acknowledged in the benefit scheme. Likewise, the presence of women's units in the Canadian armed forces during World War II meant that provision would have to be made for both male and female veterans.

A legislative milestone in the development of Ottawa's plan was the passage in 1944 of the War Service Grants Act. This legislation provided for payment of a gratuity to all volunteers and to NRMA conscripts who served overseas. The amount of the gratuity would vary according to length of service, and a supplement was provided for service abroad. These provisions satisfied the expectation that both duration and location of service would be acknowledged in the benefit scheme. The gratuity would also, of course, give individuals money to spend as they saw fit. At the same time, eligibility for the gratuity would qualify a veteran for a re-establishment credit, the amount of which would be related to the amount of the gratuity. But whereas the gratuity would be paid out in cash, the re-establishment credit would be a sum against which bills for specified household and work-related charges could be submitted to the government for reimbursement. This benefit was designed to promote employment and domesticity, and therefore independence and reliability – which was what the government wanted. By definition, along with all this (though it was never stated) was a reassertion of the gender division of labour, which had been altered dramatically by wartime events. The gratuity and credit combination was the rehabilitation benefit taken by the vast majority of Canadian veterans of World War II, both male and female. It provided the means to "settle down" and facilitated the postwar baby boom.

A veteran might also qualify for the benefits of the Veterans' Land Act of 1942 or the educational and training benefits specified in the Veterans Rehabilitation Act of 1945. Unlike the provisions of the War Service Grants Act, the benefits provided under these acts were discretionary. In the case of education and training, a veteran had to be recommended by a counsellor, who was thus a powerful authority figure, the prevailing rhetoric of disinterested service notwithstanding. (In the United States, a contrasting scheme existed. There, under the benefits of the G.I. Bill of Rights, further education was an entitlement.)[6] In 1946 another discretionary benefit for those eligible for the gratuity was provided through the Veterans' Business and Professional Loans Act. Other benefits provided for World War II veterans, subject to various eligibility criteria, included the right to reinstatement in previous employment, preference for jobs listed with the National Employment Service, and, in the case of individuals who had served in a theatre of war, preference in civil service appointments. There were also medical benefits and a scheme of veterans' insurance. Finally, depending on individual circumstances, those who enlisted after 1939 were eligible for the benefits of the Pension Act and the War Veterans' Allowance Act. The Pension Act dated from 1919 but had been substantially amended over the years and was changed again in 1941 to meet radically new conditions. It applied to all Canadian veterans and had been administered from 1933 by the Canadian Pension Commission, which reported to Parliament through the Minister of Pensions and National Health. Eventually, the whole program of benefits worked out after 1939 and embodied in many statutes and regulations was designated the Veterans Charter. Its provisions were summarized and explained to rank-and-file members of the armed forces and veterans in the pamphlet *Back to Civil Life*, which was revised and reprinted as circumstances required. In his foreword, Ian Mackenzie wrote: "Canada's rehabilitation belief is that the answer to civil re-establishment is a job, and the answer to a job is fitness and training for that job."[7] In the same spirit, the main text of *Back to Civil Life* opened with the sentence: "The object of Canada's plan for the rehabilitation of her Armed forces is that every man or woman discharged from the forces shall be in a position to earn a living."[8]

To facilitate administration of the program, the Department of Pensions and National Health was abolished in 1944 and two new departments created: the Department of National Health and Welfare and the Department of Veterans Affairs (DVA). Ian Mackenzie became the first Minister of Veterans Affairs and Walter Woods the first deputy minister. In 1945, Woods went overseas and recruited thirty-four men from the armed forces to take senior positions in the new department and begin work immediately. He did this to promote fairness in hiring and to avoid the charge, which had often been heard in the past, that home service was an inside track to the best jobs in the country. The staff of DVA rose to 22,000 in February 1947, but by March 1951, in keeping with Woods's expectation, it had declined to approximately 15,500.

The department was organized into treatment, prosthetic, and rehabilitation services. It also ran a veterans' insurance scheme and the Veterans' Bureau, which helped veterans with pension claims through a chief pension advocate. The Canadian Pension Commission, the War Veterans' Allowance Board, and the Veterans' Land Act were administered separately but were the parliamentary responsibility of the Minister of Veterans Affairs. In administering the Veterans Charter, DVA worked closely with many other government departments in what Woods called "a combined operation." The Department of National Defence administered gratuities; the Department of Finance made the loans provided for in the Veterans' Business and Professional Loans Act; the Civil Service Commission was responsible for the civil service preference; and the National Employment Service of the Department of Labour handled the reinstatement of duly qualified veterans in civil employment and certified veterans to DVA for out-of-work benefits. Veterans who qualified for vocational training under the Veterans Rehabilitation Act attended classes run by Canadian Vocational Training, another branch of the Department of Labour. Universities interacted with DVA to mutual advantage through an advisory committee which the department established in 1945.

Before VE-day (8 May 1945), about 250,000 individuals had been discharged from the armed forces. In the calendar years 1945 and 1946, total discharges were 395,013 and 381,031, respectively. These numbers created a huge demand for the services DVA had on offer. To meet this demand, the department set up counselling centres across the country to advise veterans on the rehabilitation and other benefits available to them. Women veterans were counselled by women, and DVA emphasized the equality of male and female veterans under the Veterans Charter.[9] This, however, was somewhat misleading. While it is true that women veterans were equally eligible with men for almost all the benefits available, equality of opportunity did not mean equal treatment. Only 4.6 per cent of those who served in the armed forces in World War II were female and, not surprisingly, the benefits of the Veterans Charter were planned primarily with men in mind. Women certainly benefited, but within the framework of a program designed for men. This inevitably produced unequal outcomes, though the gains made by women under the Veterans Charter should not be underestimated. For example, a higher percentage of female than male veterans qualified for vocational training and support to attend university. Olive Ruth Russell, who directed the counselling operation for women, believed that female veterans should seize on the educational and training opportunities made available by the Veterans Charter to break out of female job ghettos. In practice, though, most women who took vocational training or went to university prepared themselves for jobs that were well established as being for females.

Spending on the programs of the Veterans Charter was substantial. By 31 March 1951, $469,065,790.34 had been paid out in gratuities to 961,975 men and women. Of this amount, $319,125,150.24 had gone to army veterans, $102,781,210.08 to air force veterans, and $47,159,430.02 to navy veterans, with an average payment of $488.00.[10]

To the same date, the government had paid out $267,794,786.47 under the re-establishment credit scheme.[11] In total, 1,827,298 applications (multiple claims could be made by a single individual) had been honoured, and the average sum paid per application had been $146.55.[12] On 31 March 1949, when Newfoundland became a province, the re-establishment credit scheme was extended retroactively to World War II veterans there (Newfoundlanders who had served in the Canadian forces were already eligible for this benefit but could receive it in full only if resident in Canada).[13]

During the war, Keynesian economic ideas took root in Ottawa, and it became conventional wisdom that the government would have to act to keep up the level of purchasing power at the end of the war if another catastrophe was to be avoided. Veterans' benefits dovetailed nicely with this understanding. In effect, they provided the enabling fiction for expenditure that almost everyone agreed would somehow have to be made. Added to this was the fact that Canadians' expectations about the future were heightened during the war and that many of the men and women in the forces dreamed of a life not only on civvy street but on easy street. The war was a crusade, those who enlisted were often told, not only to defeat Hitler but to build the Canada of their dreams. To press their case, members of the armed forces had a lobby in the Canadian Legion which a government could ignore only at its peril.

From the government's perspective, spending on veterans' benefits had distinct advantages over many other possible forms of expenditure. There was no political opposition to helping veterans; the amount that would have to be spent was both predictable and controllable; the recipients were a clearly defined group (despite the fact of "total" war, only those who had enlisted could benefit); and the payments would constitute an investment in Canadian youth that could be expected to pay dividends later on, as indeed they did. Unquestionably, the Veterans Charter drew its inspiration from the altruism and patriotism of the time, but it also helped meet an economic necessity, in which, perforce, status would count for more than citizenship. It likewise reinforced certain trends in the nascent Canadian welfare state, namely, that benefits would be hierarchical, competitive, and subject to complex eligibility criteria. The man and woman in uniform would benefit but not Rosie the Riveter or the tens of thousands of other civilians, male and female, who had served the war effort in field and factory. And, of course, within the ranks of the veterans themselves there would be many gradations of benefit. In the case of the Veterans Charter, the state was willing to undertake heavy short-term costs to avoid long-term dependency. The history of the Veterans Charter is also a reminder that, far from subverting self-reliance and property holding, state intervention has at times been crucial to their cultivation. At root perhaps, this is what much of the Canadian welfare state, of which the Veterans Charter was such an important building block, has been all about. At its core, the Veterans Charter was a conservative program for a conservative country.

Thanks to careful planning and the judicious expenditure of so much money, after 1945 there was no repetition in Canada of the social disorder that had followed the Great War. In fact, the exact opposite was the case. This time, the transition from war to peace was smooth, and the country went from strength to strength. In the good, grey 1950s, with Walter Woods happily retired in Vancouver, his work well and truly done, Canada came to enjoy the greatest prosperity it had ever known. Naturally, the political beneficiary of all this was the Liberal Party, which had guided the country from depression through war and into great good times. Mackenzie's King's departure from the political stage was therefore sweet. He retired from politics in 1948, leaving behind a party that was united and firmly entrenched in power. The contrast with the party he had inherited in 1919 and the problems he had faced in his early years as leader was striking.

On 4 September 1945, Charles Ritchie made the following entry in his diary: "Back to Ottawa on a train crowded with returning soldiers. Train after train travels across Canada from east to west laden with them, dropping them off by threes and fours at small towns and in their hundreds at the big cities. The train windows are crowded with their sunburned, excited faces. They lean out in their shirt-sleeves, whistling at the girls on the station platforms, making unflattering jokes about Mackenzie King."[14] In the same vein, Desmond Morton has written of King that after the events of 1917, "neither the soldiers not the future prime minister would ever understand each other."[15] This was undoubtedly true, but King had taken the measure of the military just the same.

The essays in this volume touch on many facets of the Veterans Charter and the time in which it figured so prominently in the life of Canada. Desmond Morton sets the scene with a survey of the troubled history of the veterans of the Great War, who found much to fault in Ottawa's policies. Jeff Keshen surveys the very different experience of Canada's veterans of World War II. Dean Oliver's subject is the organization and administration of the return of Canadian soldiers from Europe after ve-day. In 1918–19, the return of the Canadian Expeditionary Force from Europe had been so badly handled that there was violence in England among soldiers waiting to ship out. By contrast, demobilization proceeded smoothly and efficiently after World War II. As in so much else, the Canadian authorities had learned from the bitter lessons of the earlier conflict. The origins, philosophy, and program of the Veterans Charter are examined by Don Ives, while the issues that arose in relation to a particular benefit, the right to reinstatement in civil employment, are explored by Michael Stevenson. Peter Neary's topic is the very fruitful and profitable adaptation of Canadian universities to the new demands placed on them by the educational benefits made available through the Veterans Rehabilitation Act of 1945. In their papers, Terry Copp and Mary Tremblay shift the focus to veterans with special medical needs, in one case psychiatric and in the other physical. The contributions of James Struthers and Doug Owram that follow offer insightful and revisionist assessments of the nature of the emerging Canadian welfare state and of postwar Canadian society. The volume concludes with a probing reflection by J.L. Granatstein on the meaning for Canadians of the veteran experience and of their country's participation in World War II. His reproach that historians now downplay the achievements of the generation that helped defeat Hitler will be hard to ignore. Ensuring fairness to the memory of the veterans will, of course, involve more scholarship of the sort exemplified by this collection.

NOTES

1 *Free Press*, London, Ontario, evening edition, 14 December 1917, 2.
2 Walter S. Woods, *Rehabilitation (A Combined Operation)* (Ottawa: Queen's Printer 1953), 13.
3 For the text of this order and amendments, see ibid., 465–76.
4 Woods, *Rehabilitation*, 5.
5 Ibid., 16.
6 Keith W. Olson, *The G.I. Bill, the Veterans, and the Colleges* (Lexington: University Press 1974), 17–18.
7 See appendix 2, 247.
8 Ibid., 249.
9 For the history of women veterans, see Peter Neary and Shaun Brown, "The Veterans Charter and Canadian Women Veterans of World War II," in J.L. Granatstein and Peter Neary, eds., *The Good Fight: Canadians and World War II* (Toronto: Copp Clark 1995), 387–415.
10 Woods, *Rehabilitation*, 64, 69 (with corrections).
11 Ibid., 70–1.

12 Ibid.

13 For the history of Newfoundland veterans of World War II, see Peter Neary, "How Newfoundland Veterans Became Canadian Veterans: A Study in Bureaucracy and Benefit," in James Hiller and Peter Neary, eds., *Twentieth-Century Newfoundland: Explorations* (St John's: Breakwater 1994), 195–237.

14 Charles Ritchie, *The Siren Years: Undiplomatic Diaries 1937–1945* (London: Macmillan 1974), 207.

15 Desmond Morton, *A Peculiar Kind of Politics: Canada's Overseas Ministry in the First World War* (Toronto: University of Toronto Press 1982), 148.

DESMOND MORTON

The Canadian Veterans'
Heritage from the Great War

By 1914, Canada had learned something about veterans. The militia
pension regulations in 1914 had been hurriedly improvised for the
1885 Rebellion and differed only in detail from arrangements made
for the War of 1812.[1] Widows received pensions only if they were in
need, remained unmarried, and "proved worthy of it." Like much else
in Canada, pensions followed the British example. The counterpart of
a host of British military charities was the Patriotic Fund, first established for the War of 1812 and revived, with some changes, for the
Crimean and Boer wars. Private charities, like the Patriotic Fund, were
managed with the whims and wisdom of the powerful and ignored
those they found undeserving.[2] The only public service to veterans was
a distribution of the one commodity Canada had in excess: land. But
even this supply was virtually exhausted in bounty to Boer War veterans.

As ever in Canada, there was an American alternative. In any Canadian short list of American democratic excesses was the "pension evil" –
the notorious and extravagant pay-off of the Grand Army of the Republic (GAR) and its cloud of pension attorneys. When Benjamin Harrison
squeezed into the White House in 1888, the GAR took the credit. "God
save the surplus," cried his pension commissioner, "Corporal" James
Tanner, and pledged to drive a six-mule team through the Treasury. By
the 1890s, spending on veterans, little of it linked to disability or be-
reavement, devoured one-fifth of U.S. national revenue.[3] The British,
in contrast, seemed to pauperize veterans, as any visitor to London discovered when beset by the bemedalled and disabled veterans of the
Empire's wars, selling pencils or begging. The apple-cheeked Chelsea
pensioners were fortunate exceptions.

Between the American Scylla and the British Charybdis, Canadians in 1914–18 synthesized their own solutions. These did not come from the Militia Department. Embroiled in his own chaotic mobilization plans, the minister, Colonel Sam Hughes, had no time to think of his army's veterans, though his expeditionary force had begun to lose men as soon as it started to assemble at Valcartier, Quebec. When pressed, Hughes had nothing better to propose than a tented hospital at Valcartier and St John's Ambulance volunteers to escort convalescents to their homes. A few of the wealthy offered their summer mansions as convalescent homes. In Winnipeg, the Imperial Order of the Daughters of the Empire (IODE) offered a rest home with "a little bit of a motherly touch."[4] The Calgary Brewing & Malting Co. handed over an unprofitable hotel. An MP offered his unmarried daughter.

Sensing an impending scandal, Sir Robert Borden recognized that charity would not do for veterans.[5] In June 1915 he created the Military Hospitals Commission (MHC), directed by prominent businessmen, to meet the needs of sick and wounded soldiers once they returned to Canada. At its head was Sir James Lougheed, a Calgary lawyer, who was government leader in the Senate and a minister without portfolio. Its official guide was the shrewd and perceptive Ernest Scammell, borrowed from the Canadian Peace Centenary Association. The son of an English Baptist minister who had worked hard for war veterans, Scammell set to work on a blueprint for MHC operations that put Canada well ahead of its co-belligerents. Scammell's views dominated a brief and amicable dominion-provincial conference on 18 October 1915.[6]

Scammell's priority was employment – understandable in a country still in the grip of a prewar depression. Patriotic employers would take back their former workers; other veterans must be found work at suitable wages. "With regard to the disabled," warned Scammell, "their care is an obligation which should fall primarily on the state, and this liability cannot be considered as being extinguished by the award of a pension from public funds."[7] A French expert, Dr Maurice Bourillon, had insisted that each disabled soldier could be found suitable work and that many, with training, could even improve their earning capacity. Ina Matthews, sister-in-law of the Montreal multimillionaire J.K.L. Ross, had offered a training scheme to Dr Fred Sexton, principal of the Nova Scotia Technical College. Word of the scheme spread to Ottawa. Even with vocational training in its infancy in Canada, nothing was so powerful as an untested idea.

While the commission met occasionally for garrulous meetings, Lougheed and Scammell got busy. A growing staff acquired scores of buildings and adapted and equipped them as hospitals, TB sanatoria, and lunatic asylums. Samuel Armstrong, who had developed the Guelph Reformatory and the Whitby Hospital for the Ontario government, took over as MHC director. Using the latest "quick-build" methods, the MHC created new institutions across the country, from Halifax's Camp Hill Hospital to the TB sanatorium at Tranquille, British Columbia. After painful and costly experiments with free-enterprise limb makers, the MHC decided to produce prostheses in its own Toronto factory. By 1917, the commission could supply artificial legs, boots, and glass eyes, and face masks for the hideously scarred. Its arms were uncomfortable and ineffective, but no one else's were much better. After struggling with straps, hooks, and pulleys, most frustrated arm amputees tried to get what use they could from their stump. Most Canadian war blind benefited from St Dunstan's, a hostel established in London's Regent's Park. Eager to use blinded soldiers to improve their public image, Canadian charities for the blind protested and persuaded some of the homesick blind to come back to Canada. The MHC responded by creating a special section for the blind under the charge of Captain E.A. Baker, a St Dunstan's graduate who had been blinded as a young Canadian engineer officer in France. The St Dunstan's philosophy and methods, plus Baker's energy, led to the Canadian National Institute for the Blind.[8]

Commission staff soon realized that the disabled defied stereotypes. Out of 138,000 Canadian wounded, fewer than 70 had been blinded and 3,802 had lost limbs.[9] Most of the disabled had been sick, not wounded. Many should never have been enlisted in the first place. Coping with the Militia Department's recruiting mistakes kept the commission busy for a year, treating tuberculosis and heart disease cases, before large numbers of invalids flooded back from England. Even by the war's end, most of the MHC's 7,000 hospital cases had come from training camps in Canada and not from overseas. Tuberculosis, which affected 8,571 of the 590,572 members of the Canadian Expeditionary Force (CEF), required a major commitment of capital and care. By 1917, the MHC had taken over fourteen sanatoria across Canada, transforming them from "glorified summer camps to hospital-like institutions."[10] Euclid Hall in Toronto became home to the commission's "incurables." The mentally ill were consigned to provincial asylums, though "shell shock" cases were hospitalized at Cobourg and subjected, by the MHC's testimony, to "every imaginable treatment," from warm baths to shock therapy. Playing golf allegedly restored one former bank accountant to his stool.[11]

The war brought part of the country's enormous burden of ill health into the army. If postwar Canada was not to stagger under the load and become unattractive to immigrants and foreign capital, Scammell warned, "there must be a minimum of sentiment and a maximum of hard business sense concerning the future of the returned soldier to civil life."[12] In England, Major J.L. Todd, a McGill professor of parasitology, found himself a member of the overseas branch of the Militia Department's Pensions and Claims Board. He took the work seriously: "The biggest thing in Canada at the present time is the whole Pensions question," he reported to his wife. "If it is not removed from politics and put into the hands of a small commission of about three men ... we will have pensions trouble in Canada that, for our size, will make that of the USA look like a beginner."[13] Todd delighted in the hard rationality of French pension practice. French pensions were mean and difficult to get, but no matter how much a veteran earned, his pension was not cut. British pensions were reduced as earnings grew, an obvious disincentive to work.

The disabled, Todd concluded, could work. "Everyone must understand," he proclaimed, "that armless, legless men *can* become self-supporting."[14] From the British, Todd borrowed the basis for assessing disability: since a soldier brought nothing to the army but a healthy body, the market for healthy bodies was "the general market for untrained labour." The French assessed that body by a chart that ruled the loss of both arms, legs, or eyes as 100 per cent disability, a single eye or a lower leg at 40 per cent, and varicose veins at 10 per cent. A burst of Gallic sentiment valued reproductive organs at 60 per cent. Thanks to a well-connected wife and shrewd politics, Todd's ideas led to the creation of the Board of Pension Commissioners for Canada (BPC) in June 1916. Ten-year terms and good salaries were intended to insulate from political pressures the three members: Jack Ross, the Montreal millionaire yachtsman, Colonel R.H. Labatt, a Hamilton offshoot of the brewing family, and Todd himself.

In Todd's system, the key officials were the medical advisers, doctors who would read the files, examine the diagnoses made by local boards, scan the disability table, and make an objective, emotion-free rating of each applicant. Parliament went one step further, giving Canadians the most generous pension rates in the world. After all, Todd's pension system made generosity cheap. Less than 5 per cent of Canada's war disabled got the top rate; the vast majority received 25 per cent or less. One reason was "attributability" – how much of a disability was due to service. A gunshot wound or a battlefield amputation was easy – though one suppurating head wound was attributed to a prewar mastoid operation. Was syphilitic paresis really due to a toilet seat at Camp Hughes? No. Could Lieutenant John Diefenbaker, painfully injured during training in England, seek a pension? Yes, said the pension commissioners, but only if his subsequent discomfort affected his prospects in the market for unskilled labour. Could a soldier knocked down by a bus in the London blackout make a claim?[15] No, said Todd, pensions were not insurance.

This was all made easier to argue by the fact that pensions were not supposed to be an important part of a disabled soldier's earnings. By restoring a soldier's will and ability to work, real wages would soon outpace any pension income. Todd saw eye-to-eye with Scammell. The MHC had already improvised some forms of vocational training – over the objections of doctors, teachers, and the disabled themselves. "Most of the men come back with sluggish mental action," explained an MHC pamphlet. "They have been under military discipline so long, clothed, fed and ordered about that they have lost independence."[16]

Matters improved when the MHC hired Walter Segsworth, a Toronto engineer with a brisk, practical approach. No one ever learned a trade in a hospital, he realized. Invalids should be taught to be busy. Young women hired as "ward aides" at $60 to $75 a month would coax and prod the men into working on crafts. Once ambulatory, they would move into "curative workshops" to practise woodworking, motor mechanics, or shoemaking and to revive factory disciplines and old skills. Serious retraining began at discharge, ideally on the job. Training boards firmly guided a man to his new occupation – preferably something close to his old job. A one-legged carpenter could become a cabinetmaker; a crippled trainman could be a station agent or telegrapher. Teams of ex-salesmen set out to find job opportunities and look after placement and follow-up. When absenteeism became a problem, an inspector was sent to offer a trainee "sound advice as to his future line of conduct" and to emphasize that he was "there for the purpose of applying himself diligently to the learning of his new trade."[17] Social service workers helped families adjust to a disabled breadwinner and his income. Returned Soldiers' Insurance in 1920 provided cheap life insurance coverage that commercial firms refused to provide. Ottawa covered any added cost from workmen's compensation.

Putting the disabled to work was revolutionary, and like most revolutions it ran into trouble. Many courses were too ambitious and too brief for men adjusting to disabilities. Training allowances, calculated to give "decent comfort," paid a couple with three children as much as $110 a month – rather more than an employer would offer a disabled worker. Ontario's Department of Education sabotaged Segsworth's plans when he refused to use only its teachers. The University of Toronto, an important centre for the MHC's rehabilitation programs, backed out after its president, Sir Robert Falconer, felt Queen's Park's displeasure.[18] The University of New Brunswick pledged a fully equipped machine shop and provided some old rusty tools in a basement "unfit for a root cellar." "Most of these [offers] start out with a blare of trumpets," admitted one of Segsworth's assistants, "and end up with very little."[19]

Still, Canada led the way. When the United States entered the war, American officials sought advice from Todd and Scammell. Canadian rehabilitation policy was publicized in pamphlets, posters, and magic-lantern shows. A widely distributed pamphlet was *A Little Chat with Private Pat* or, in the French version, *Poil-aux-Pattes*. "I'll be a real returned soldier," claimed Pat, "when I've got back to work." Providing for his family was a bigger challenge to him than his missing leg. "From the way my old father writes and my wife too, they seem to think there's nothing for me to do but some kid's job like peddling pins or bobbing up and down with an elevator." This was not for Pat. Nor was "scratching paper for my living." Instead, through a back-to-the-land theme that was Sir James Lougheed's main contribution to reconstruction planning, Pat became a farmer: "The country life's the life for me, with a cow and a hen and a honey bee."[20]

Like much propaganda, the Private Pat pamphlet was misleading. The CEF produced few amputees, and if Pat wanted help from the Soldier Settlement Act, adopted in 1917 and greatly extended in 1918, he would be disappointed. Loan committees excluded nursing sisters and the disabled; the Soldier Settlement scheme was intended for serious, physically fit farmers. However, the stereotype showed both the government's determination to instil economic independence in its war veterans and its fear that the veterans would become indigent mendicants with a strong sense of entitlement.

In their prescience, Todd and Scammell had anticipated that what was easy in wartime would be much more difficult when peace returned and the veterans' sacrifices were forgotten. When politicians promised "full re-establishment" in the 1917 election campaign, they really meant that veterans would resume the responsibilities as well as the pleasures of civil life by becoming wholly self-sufficient. A country with a huge war debt would need all the earning power they could muster. Postwar Canada would be poor.

The Military Hospitals Commission accomplished much. It learned how to coax and even bully the bedridden into old work disciplines. "Ward occupations" kept men's fingers and minds busy with handicrafts. "Curative workshops" in hospital basements and sheds moved the disabled closer to their old working skills. Once discharged, ex-soldiers learned new trades, while the commission persuaded employers that the disabled could be valuable workers. D.J. McDougall, blinded during service with the Princess Patricia's Canadian Light Infantry, learned the skills of a masseur at St Dunstan's in London and passed them on at Hart House in the first stage of a teaching career that ended in the university's history department. The Canadian Army Medical Corps' only female amputee, a nurse injured in a hospital bombing, found a job as a social worker among tubercular veterans, while the CEF's sole quadrilateral amputee, Private Curly Christian, was found a job as a billiard marker.

As the war ended, the wisdom of military authorities was given far less credence. "The sooner we in Canada get away from military titles and everything connected with the war," declared Colonel Clarence Starr to waiting Toronto reporters, "the better it will be for the country and the average citizen."[21] To some, "militarization" almost ranked as a disability itself. "When a civilian entered the army," explained Segsworth, "... everything was done to make him a small unit in a large organization. He was taught to obey rather than to think; he was for the most part relieved of the care of his dependents; clothing, food and a place to sleep were provided for him. If he was guilty of a misdemeanour he was punished, but he was not deprived of the necessities of life, whereas in civil life he would have been discharged. Thus the whole system, for the time being, tended to reduce the action of his own will and relieve him of all sense of responsibility."[22]

A robustly civilian Department of Soldiers' Civil Re-establishment (DSCR) under Lougheed, created in 1918 from the MHC, had a cure for militarization. For their own sake, returned men must face cold economic reality, not handouts. Only the disabled would be trained, and the courses for them must be short. Although shell-shock cases might have evaded danger by their mental condition, they must not be encouraged by pensions to evade personal and family responsibilities. "The returned soldier," intoned Lord Atholstan, proprietor of the *Montreal Star*, "must not be allowed to consider himself an unlimited creditor of the State, to be supported in idleness."[23] The government entirely agreed. A repatriation committee, headed by H.J. Daly, manager of the soon-to-be-bankrupt Home Bank, limited its services to providing a cheerful welcome. The new DSCR focused on the disabled, offering medical and hospital care, sometimes in the newly built hospitals at Ste-Anne-de-Bellevue and London, Ontario, but more often in the better adapted of the MHC's system. As for the physically fit, the DSCR offered the returning Ulysses little more than help in finding work. To do more might have crippled the men psychologically. Experts set pensions, selected appropriate retraining programs, and approved Soldier Settlement loans. Like good soldiers, veterans were expected to work hard and be grateful. They had no part in planning their own re-establishment, and except for some selected officers, they had no part in its execution.

The returned men had ideas of their own, however. By the end of 1916, hundreds of wounded survivors of the Second Battle of Ypres had returned, and the flow of convalescents steadily increased. By 1917, most communities had a veterans' association. In Toronto, Mayor Tommy Church worked hard to bring them into his municipal Tory machine. In Montreal, the civic reformer W.D. Lighthall sent for the constitution of the GAR to help local veterans get organized. In Winnipeg, veterans rejected the citizen-run Returned Soldiers' Association and formed their own. Winnipeggers hosted a meeting on 10–13 April when delegates from other provinces gathered to form the Great War Veterans' Association (GWVA). A year later, also in Winnipeg, a prewar club of largely British veterans was reorganized as the Army and Navy Veterans (ANV), with a descendant of Sir Charles Tupper as president. The GWVA was clearly the dominant organization.

Although there were many Canadians who were poor, physically and mentally disabled, and wracked with pain, veterans were different. Their poverty was a conscious result of public policy. Ottawa had set CEF pay scales and had held them steady through the war while other wages and prices had soared. Moreover, the government had decided that disabled veterans and their families would remain poor, for it had based pensions on the wage rates of unskilled labour. The awkwardness of a missing limb, the shame of disfigurement, or the pain of a lung or heart condition was to be joined by the humiliation of poverty. For the first time, a group of mostly poor men approached their government on the basis of a moral entitlement, not charity.

Few of the returned soldiers were socialists; almost everywhere, veterans' organizations veered to the political right. Their members had a special stake in the societies they had helped defend. Nevertheless, the veterans' conservatism had an egalitarian, radical edge. Ex-soldiers remembered their resentment at the barriers of rank and the unearned privileges of the officer class. In Britain, the National Federation of Ex-Servicemen barred officers unless they had risen from the ranks. The American Legion forbade the use of army ranks. In the GWVA, members addressed each other as "comrade." Generous pensions for officers rankled: "That an officer with an arm off should get twice as much pension as a private with an arm off," raged Harris Turner, a blinded Saskatchewan veteran, "is unfair, unjust, unsound, undemocratic, unreasonable, unBritish, unacceptable, outrageous and rotten."[24]

Such tones came easily from the new GWVA. Its officers, notably C. Grant MacNeil, an ex-machine gunner who became secretary-treasurer in early 1919, established themselves as guides and counsel to parliamentary committees and ministers.[25] By insisting on preference for veterans in government hiring, by persuading Parliament to raise pensions for all other ranks to the rate for a lieutenant, and by mobilizing his organization as a voice for widows and the disabled, MacNeil rivalled Scammell and Todd in setting veterans policy. Until the Armistice, the GWVA insisted, it was only the vanguard for a huge returning army. In fact, the association remained primarily an organization of the disabled and was out of touch with most of the 350,000 soldiers who, on 11 November 1918, suddenly felt free to come home if Ottawa could find the means to bring them.

Elaborate demobilization plans, based on British schemes, had proposed releasing "demobilizers" and "pivotal men" to get the economy running soon enough to absorb the rest of the army smoothly. The GWVA itself appealed to Ottawa to keep the troops overseas during the winter, when jobs were always scarce. In fact, it would be hard enough simply to get the Canadians home. Not only was shipping scarce and in high demand, but railway connections with the winter ports of Halifax and Saint John were so worn from wartime traffic that their maximum capacity for troop trains was 20,000–30,000 men a month. Halifax had not yet recovered from the devastating 1917 explosion in its harbour.

The difficulties, delays, and turmoil in repatriating the CEF have been discussed elsewhere. Suffice it to say that the problems were aggravated by policy decisions in Ottawa but that, as in the subsequent war, repatriation was completed far more quickly than anyone had expected. Once in Canada, soldiers travelled by train to the military district in which they had joined or in which they requested a discharge. If they accompanied a unit, a last parade through welcoming crowds and a final "Dismiss" at the city hall or the armouries released them to civilian life. Next day, the men turned in their steel helmets and equipment, collected railway tickets, an allowance for civilian clothes and a modest War Service Gratuity, and were civilians again.

On average, Canadian soldiers who went overseas spent about two years in England and France before they returned. A few spent four years or more away from Canada. Veterans came back to a country far removed from the ideals they had remembered from a distance. Relatives harped on the deprivations they had faced, of "meatless Fridays" or "fuelless Mondays," but to men who had seen wartime France or England, it was obvious those at home had done well out of the war. Inflation had effectively doubled most prices, but wages on the whole had kept pace – though not for soldiers or their families. The Patriotic Fund had stopped raising its allowances in 1917 for fear that community and private generosity would dry up, and the government had increased its $20-a-month separation allowance to $30 only at the end of the war. It seemed easy to identify war profiteers. An automobile cost more than most soldiers had earned during the entire war, yet the number of cars on the road had more than tripled between 1915 and 1919.[26]

For veterans, 1919 was the year of disillusionment. For tens of thousands, the Armistice had restored a prize they might otherwise have lost – their lives. Now, as with all prizes, the problem arose of how to use it. Men came home with wounds to minds and bodies and some with drug and alcohol addictions, to say nothing of the minor afflictions of swearing, gambling, and athlete's foot. They found broken marriages, children who had forgotten them, and families who had already heard more than enough about the war. Scammell and others who had tried to anticipate the veterans' needs had overlooked their restlessness. It was as much part of war as a wooden leg, claimed the veteran and journalist George Pearson: "It is that terrible restlessness which possesses us like an evil spirit; the indefinite expression of a vague discontent, the restlessness of dying men, little children and old soldiers."[27] "There had been a thunderstorm and the atmosphere had failed to clear," wrote Pierre van Paassen. "It was the same petty, monotonous, joyless, suffocating world of three years before, only now I was more intensely aware of it."[28]

There was turmoil everywhere in 1919. French veterans rioted against the back taxes they were expected to pay. British veterans demonstrated for the "homes fit for heroes" which Lloyd George, their prime minister, had promised them. In Canada, restless mobs of veterans attacked labour organizers, Chinese laundries, and price-gouging restaurants. Canada experienced its worst year ever for strikes, of which Winnipeg's general strike in May and June was only the centrepiece. Veterans participated on both sides of the struggle. Some resented the "slackers" and unionists who had benefited from the war. Others contrasted the wealthy wartime profiteers with their own threadbare families.

On a frigid Sunday in January 1919, at Calgary's Allen Theatre, veterans found their issue, calling for a $2,000 bonus for each veteran as compensation for the income soldiers had lost by serving. Applause seekers everywhere, from feminists to the national Liberals, offered them prompt support. So did Toronto's Mayor Tommy Church and Toronto Tories. Fuelled by the bonus issue (which its leaders privately deplored), GWVA membership soared from 20,000 to 200,000 in a year. A bonus crusader, J. Harry Flynn, a flamboyant American who had served in the Canadian Army Medical Corps, seized control of the veterans' organization in Toronto. When GWVA leaders decided that bonus seeking would hurt their efforts for widows and the disabled, Flynn organized a Toronto-based breakaway group, the Grand Army of United Veterans (GAUV).[29]

In Ottawa, the Borden government portrayed the bonus as a $2 billion grab and stood firm. Once the Liberals had chosen William Lyon Mackenzie King as their leader, they forgot the bonus. By November 1919, only Simcoe North's Colonel J.A. Currie backed it. Having built their organizations on the bonus, the veterans' leaders saw their members flow out again when their gratuities were spent. Returned men discovered what Scammell had foreseen in 1915; they would have to make their own way in a world that had little time for their stories and even less for their problems. Flynn's career as a veterans' leader ended with rumours that a young man was his bosom companion.[30] *The Veteran*, organ of the GWVA, with a quarter-million circulation, was almost out of business by 1923.[31]

Medical associations toyed briefly with the notion of public health insurance as a way of finding employment for returning colleagues whose practices had vanished. The urge was frail and soon forgotten, until the 1930s when, once again, too few could afford a doctor's services. Governments ordered married women dismissed from civil service jobs and replaced them with veterans. As any cynic might have predicted, the public soon concluded that veterans were loafers whom only the post office or public works departments would hire. Returned men learned to remove their discharge pins and forget what they had been doing between 1914 and 1918 if they wanted a chance to work.

The separate fates of half a million veterans defy generalization. Some were "Old Originals" from 1914; others were MSA (Military Service Act) men with a few months' service. Half the members of the CEF never got beyond England. Veterans included cooks, orderlies, staff officers, and front-line infantry privates. Most had lived fast and furiously in the present; few had devised a clear idea of how to cope with the future. Some fled to British Columbia or California. Perhaps they had had all the cold they needed for a lifetime. Many who stayed in England, waiving their rights to repatriation, fulfilled the gloomy expectations of the Canadian High Commissioner in London, Sir George Perley, by demanding paid passage back to Canada. Men whose jobs had been held open often resumed them only to quit after a few days or weeks. Employers felt aggrieved; the men themselves wondered why they should still be office boys or apprentices when stay-at-homes had risen in seniority and salary. Only fellow veterans seemed to understand their grievance. Disabled veterans found that their carefully arranged jobs vanished in the 1921 depression. Employing them had turned out to be more patriotic than profitable.

Soldier Settlement, the colonization scheme for veterans, had looked as if it would be a huge benefit; 5 per cent loans and record farm prices promised easy prosperity. Instead, settlers bought farms, livestock, and equipment at equally high prices and then struggled to repay their loans as prices plummeted. By 1930, almost half the 24,709 soldier settlers had abandoned their dreams.[32] The prices of 1919 would not return until another world war a generation later.

Unlike the Canadians, American legionnaires partially won their bonus battle. Canadian leaders such as Grant MacNeil preferred to work for the disabled and dependent. It was a harsh struggle. MacNeil fought for fairer pension legislation and practice. Revenues from a shrinking membership paid for an Adjustment Bureau, whose staff helped widows and veterans present their cases to increasingly hard-faced officials committed to a new policy of "tightening up."[33] In an annual ritual, Pension Act amendments were blessed by the House of Commons, gutted by the Senate, and subverted by the Board of Pension Commissioners for Canada (BPC). Colonel John Thompson, the son of a former prime minister and an arid but ingenious lawyer, used the board's tangle of rules to protect the treasury and sustain Todd's original tight-fisted principles. The 1922 "attributability" argument was typical. Parliament, MacNeil insisted, had promised to give returned men "the benefit of the doubt." Thompson politely agreed, but he added that he never had any doubts.

The new Liberal government, elected at the end of 1921, gave MacNeil a chance to reopen his battle. Choosing deliberately provocative language, the GWVA secretary-treasurer charged the pension board with "a contemptible and cold-blooded conspiracy to deprive ex-Servicemen of rights previously guaranteed by Parliament."[34] Mac-Neil's reward was a royal commission to investigate pensions and civil re-establishment; it was headed by a respected Nova Scotia Liberal, Lieutenant-Colonel J.L. Ralston, the former commanding officer of the 85th Battalion. Within weeks, Ralston decided that MacNeil's specific charge was unfounded: the pension commissioners had merely exploited a minor amendment to the Pension Act with scrupulous rigour. It was irrelevant that Thompson himself had supplied the words.

To his credit, Ralston persisted beyond the narrow point of law. For three years he and his colleagues prodded and probed the state of soldiers' civil re-establishment, from soldier settlement to care for the insane. MacNeil himself was sent to interview witnesses and gather testimony. The result was an inquest into what Canada had really done for her soldiers. It seemed to be sadly little. In all, 40,000 disabled veterans had been retrained and 64 per cent had been placed in skill-related jobs. Then, to save money, training, placement, and follow-up had all been dissolved. By the end of the 1921 depression, one-fifth of all returned men and most of the disabled were jobless, and there were no plans for more help. Employers now openly favoured the able-bodied. Too many veterans had chosen overvalued or unproductive land in the Soldier Settlement plan.[35]

Because settlement and retraining had failed, pension policy mattered more than Scammell and Todd had ever imagined. MacNeil paraded his "human documents" before Ralston as evidence of how arbitrary and unfair BPC rulings had become. Ralston was sufficiently impressed to propose a Federal Appeal Board, complete with "soldier advisers" paid by the government to help veterans prepare their cases. The grounds for a veteran's pension grew. At last, in 1930, any woman unwise enough to marry a man after he was disabled won a guarantee of support. The fear of "pension widows" was overcome.[36] Amendments that year created an even more judicial procedure, with a Pension Tribunal to review BPC decisions and a Pension Appeal Court to review and often reverse the tribunal's rulings. The predictable result by 1933 was a huge backlog. In a few days, R.B. Bennett smashed and rebuilt the system, creating a single Canadian Pension Commission with an Appeals Division that survives, essentially, to this day.

Exhausted and under attack, GWVA leaders tried to keep veterans working together to help those who could not help themselves. Like veterans' leaders elsewhere, they failed. By the 1930s, separate organizations for the disabled had emerged in many countries. In France, the *mutilés de guerre* kept their distance from other veterans; elsewhere, the British Limbless Ex-service Men's Association, in Britain, and the Disabled American Veterans, in the United States, represented the disabled. In Canada, so did the Amputations Association (or "Fragments from France"), the Tuberculous Veterans Association, and the Sir Arthur Pearson Association of War Blinded.

In 1925, after a number of attempts, most rival veterans' organizations came together in Winnipeg, as they had in 1917, but this time under the leadership of senior officers and the inspiration of their wartime British commander, Earl Haig. The result was the Canadian Legion of the British Empire Service League. Except for the Army and Navy Veterans – too conservative to join – and some of the disabled organizations, most Canadian veterans accepted the new organization as their own. The Legion took credit for the 1930 Pension Act reforms and the drastic 1933 reorganization. It won recognition of "burn-out" among aged veterans as the basis for a war veterans' allowance; and it mobilized enough sympathy for veterans that, unlike Franklin Delano Roosevelt with his 1933 Economy Bill, R.B. Bennett's desperate cost-cutting measures left war pensions strictly alone. On the other hand, no one could seriously call Canada's pensions extravagant. In 1932, a quarter of a million men, women, and children shared about $40 million a year. The individual pittance was enough, however, for municipalities to deny relief.

The Great Depression of the 1930s hit veterans especially hard. Farms, professional practices, and businesses nursed into a fragile prosperity through the 1920s collapsed when no one had money and the banks called their loans. Major-General Andrew McNaughton, the wartime gunner and postwar Chief of General Staff, persuaded the government to open relief camps, staff them with veteran officers and NCOs from the CEF, and put unemployed youth to work at a wage of twenty cents a day. The relief campers dubbed themselves "the Royal Twenty Centers," and critics denounced the camps as embodying the type of Prussian militarism they had fought a war to defeat.[37] Some of the young men and even a few of the sergeants went to Spain to start the next war early. Many veterans in the 1930s tried to forget their troubles by commemoration. The decade saw the rise of battalion and battery associations and, in 1934, the creation of the Canadian Corps Association. The Legion turned its energies to organizing a Vimy pilgrimage to unveil the bold Canadian monument on Hill 145, whose capture had cost the 4th Division so many lives. Only months before another war, did King George VI and Queen Elizabeth unveil the national war memorial in Ottawa's Confederation Square. In a decade with few good experiences, the past was a refuge.

All biography has a funereal close. The history of Canada's World War I veterans ends, like most lives, in disappointment, sickness, and death. Still, Canadians have reason for immense pride in the tough, weather-beaten men of the Canadian Corps and all that they accomplished in war and in peace. Like Moses, it was not given to them to pass into the promised land which most of their children and grandchildren would enjoy. It was their children and the children of men who had stayed home and prospered who would be the beneficiaries of an affluent Canada. That is perhaps the rule of human affairs.

The veterans of 1945 would inherit a very different Canada. Unlike the economically ravaged country of 1919, Canada did well out of World War II, and it could afford to do well by all its veterans, not merely the disabled and dependent. It could find the imagination to devise a job-creating credit system, and the resources to offer generous training and education opportunities. Most important, it could absorb all who were willing to work; and in the Canada of 1945, like that of 1919 (or, for that matter, 1998), "high and stable levels of employment" made more difference than legions, charters, the Hon. Ian Mackenzie, or his sturdy deputy and GWVA stalwart, Walter S. Woods.

NOTES

1 Captain John French, who perished heroically at Batoche, left his widow a
   pension of $514 a year; the widow and daughter of Gunner Ryan, who died
   unheroically in his bed, could count on $83. As for Private Neely's widow
   and orphans, they got nothing, for Toronto's police chief claimed that
   Maria Neely was "a loose, profligate woman." See National Archives of Canada (hereafter NA), records of the Department of Militia and Defence,
   RG 9 II A, vol. 185A, file 3744, and Sir Adolphe Caron Papers, MG 27 I D3,
   vol. 98, file 56380, Lt. Col. Grasett to Sir Adolphe Caron, 17 April 1888
   and passim.

2 After the Boer War, for example, it financed an Oxford education for
   Lorne Mulloy, a former Queen's University student who had become
   famous as "the blinded trooper." On Mulloy, see NA, records of the Department of Veterans Affairs (hereafter DVA), RG 38, vol. 69, file 175; NA,
   records of the Governor General's Office, RG 7 G21, vol. 365, file 2425;
   and *Proceedings of the Special Committee Appointed to Consider the Question of
   Continuing the War Bonus to Pensioners, 1920* (Ottawa: King's Printer 1921),
   210. Not everyone approved of the generosity: one man threatened to
   shoot someone if Mulloy got any more money! See 244, no. 52.

3 See Mary R. Dearing, *Veterans in Politics: The Story of the Grand Army of the
   Republic* (Westport, Conn.: Greenwood Press 1974), for a modest view of
   the GAR's alleged depredations. A more detailed and dispassionate account
   of American pension legislation is Gustavus A. Weber and Laurence
   F. Schmeckebier, *The Veterans' Administration: Its History, Activities and Organization* (Washington: Brookings Institution 1934). On U.S. veterans, see
   Katherine Mayo, *Soldiers What Next!* (Boston: Houghton Mifflin 1934);
   Willard Waller, *The Veteran Comes Back* (New York: Dryden Press 1944), esp.
   197–9; Dixon Wecter, *When Johnny Comes Marching Home* (Boston: Houghton Mifflin 1944), esp. 211ff; and Davis Ross, *Preparing for Ulysses: Politics
   and Veterans during World War II* (New York: Columbia University Press
   1969), 6–7. On Tanner, see Waller, *The Veteran Comes Back,* 199.

4 On facilities, see *Report of the Military Hospitals Commission* (Ottawa 1917),
   17–32.

5 The British agreed, but it took two years of aristocratic trench warfare
   before their charities were displaced. See Graham Wooton, *The Politics of
   Influence: British Ex-Servicemen, Cabinet Decisions, and Cultural Change,
   1917–57* (London: Routledge and Kegan Paul 1963), chap. 1.

6 NA, DVA, vol. 225, file 8–62, Minutes of the Interprovincial Conference,
   18–19 October 1915.

7 Ernest Scammell, *The Provision of Employment for Members of the Canadian
   Expeditionary Force on Their Return to Canada and the Re-education of Those Who*

Are Unable to Follow Their Previous Occupations Because of Disability (Ottawa: King's Printer 1916), 5.

8 On Baker, see M.W. Campbell, *No Compromise: The Story of Colonel Baker and the CNIB* (Toronto: McClelland and Stewart 1965). See also Scammell Collection (in possession of the author), Department of Soldiers' Civil Re-establishment, *The Soldier's Return: How the Canadian Soldier Is Being Refitted for Industry* (Ottawa 1919), 24–5.

9 The Royal Commission on Pensions and Re-establishment (Ralston Commission) reported 2,659 leg amputees and 1,143 men with a missing arm. See *Final Report*, Canada, *Sessional Papers* 203a, 1925, 51.

10 Katherine McCuaig, "From Social Reform to Social Service: The Changing Role of Volunteers: The Anti-Tuberculosis Campaign, 1900–1930," *Canadian Historical Review* 61, no. 4 (December 1980): 486.

11 *The Soldier's Return*, 44. See also Tom Brown, "Shell Shock in the Canadian Expeditionary Force, 1914–1918: Canadian Psychiatry in the Great War," in Charles G. Roland, ed., *Health, Disease and Medicine: Essays in Canadian History* (Hamilton: Hannah Institute for the History of Medicine 1984), 308–22.

12 *The Soldier's Return*, 9.

13 Todd to Marjory Todd, 3 October 1915, cited in Bridget Fialkowski, *John L. Todd, 1876–1949: Letters* (Senneville, Que., 1977), 309.

14 Todd diary, 17 March 1916, cited in ibid., 324.

15 Lieutenant Mike Pearson. See John English, *Shadow of Heaven* (Toronto: Lester & Orpen Dennys 1989), 44.

16 Scammell Collection, Invalided Soldiers' Commission, *Some Facts about Occupational Therapy and Curative Workshops* (Toronto 1919). After long months in hospital, complained Colonel Alex Primrose of the CAMC, invalids "have become accustomed to having everything done for them, they lose all ambition and have no desire to help themselves." See Col. A. Primrose, "Presidential Address," *Canadian Medical Association Journal* 9, no. 1 (January 1919): 8–9.

17 Scammell Collection, *Department of Soldiers' Civil Re-establishment*, 22.

18 See Desmond Morton and Glenn Wright, *Winning the Second Battle: Canadian Veterans and the Return to Civilian Life, 1915–1930* (Toronto: University of Toronto Press 1987), 95; NA, DVA, vol. 232, file 2310, Lougheed to Falconer, 4 November 1918.

19 NA, DVA, vol. 225, file 18–02 NB, Norman Parkinson to W.R. Caldwell, n.d. [September 1919].

20 See Scammell Collection, *The Soldier's Return: A Little Chat with Private Pat* and *Le soldat revient: Une causerie avec Poil-aux-Pattes* (Ottawa, 1917).

21 *Daily Star*, Toronto, 3 March 1919.

22 Walter Segsworth, *Retraining Canada's Disabled Soldiers* (Ottawa: King's Printer 1920), 67. See also J.L. Todd, "The Meaning of Rehabilitation,"

Annals of the American Academy of Political and Social Science 70 (November 1918): 6.

23 NA, Andrew Macphail Papers, MG 30 D 150, vol. 11, "Conversation with Lord Atholstan, 17 December 1917."

24 *Harris Turner's Weekly* 2 (January 1919).

25 In 1935, MacNeil was elected as a Co-operative Commonwealth Federation (CCF) member of parliament. Defeated in 1940, he spent much of the rest of his life as a union and CCF organizer. See J.K. Johnson, ed., *The Canadian Directory of Parliament* (Ottawa: Public Archives 1968), 435, and family recollections.

26 In 1915 there were 60,688 passenger cars on Canadian roads; by 1919 there were 196,367. See F.H. Leacy, ed., *Historical Statistics of Canada*, 2nd ed. (Ottawa: Statistics Canada 1983), series T-148.

27 "Fitting in the Returned Men," *Maclean's*, March 1919, 27–8.

28 Pierre van Paassen, *Days of Our Years* (New York: Dial Press 1946), 66.

29 On the bonus campaign, see Desmond Morton and Glenn Wright, "The Bonus Campaign, 1919–21: Veterans and the Campaign for Re-establishment," *Canadian Historical Review* 64, no. 2 (June 1983): 147–67.

30 See Morton and Wright, *Winning the Second Battle*, 183, n32.

31 It vanished so fast that no complete run of the magazine, once the largest-circulation monthly in Canada, exists outside the Library of Congress.

32 Morton and Wright, *Winning the Second Battle*, 208–9.

33 Ibid., 160–4.

34 Cited in Royal Commission on Pensions and Re-establishment, *First Report* (Ottawa 1923), 5. See also *The Veteran*, 24 June and 9 September 1923.

35 By 1939, barely a third of the original soldier settlers remained on the land and half the government's $100 million investment had blown away.

36 One aspect of the American "pension evil" was the practice of marrying young women to aged pensioners to guarantee them an income for the rest of their lives. The last "widow" of the War of 1812 died during the Korean War.

37 See James Eayrs, *In Defence of Canada: From the Great War to the Great Depression* (Toronto: University of Toronto Press 1964), 124–48.

DEAN F. OLIVER

Awaiting Return: Life in the Canadian Army's Overseas Repatriation Depots, 1945–1946

Morale and cohesion in military formations are maintained by a variety of means, some planned and implemented centrally, others unplanned and distributed unevenly. A carefully designed training regimen, whether autocratic or democratic in nature, can foster loyalty to peer group and unit; a charismatic and successful commander can overcome weaknesses in training, doctrine, and equipment to motivate individual performance in the face of extreme distress. Leavened by good training, effective leadership, or other qualities (ideological conviction, for example), fighting formations can face the test of battle reasonably confident of internal stability. Armies and their constituent parts do disintegrate under combat conditions, but the extreme rarity of catastrophic collapse points to the astonishingly widespread success, both temporally and chronologically, of military motivational techniques.

The apparent ease with which military organizations function, however, is deceptive. Whether before, during, or after combat, the challenges of maintaining moral cohesion are intense and pervasive. This, ironically, is as true in the aftermath of war as at any other time. Having survived all lethal perils, the postwar soldier longs for the relative safety of home and family. The same individual who just previously submitted quietly and with conviction to the dictates of military discipline now relaxes, physically and mentally, in anticipation of civilian life. The stress of fighting over, the immediate necessity of subordinating oneself to the larger organization weakens, and the individualism long suppressed by the whole reasserts itself in the constituent parts.

This is a natural and expected reaction to the cessation of combat. In the transition period between war and peace, or even in the aftermath of minor tests of arms, the challenge for the military establishment is to retain the functional efficiency of the organization while simultaneously satisfying, to the greatest possible extent, the personal and emotional needs of the men and women within it. Frequently, it is only by catering to the latter requirement that the former can be assured.

The challenge posed by enforced idleness was not new to the Canadian Army Overseas in the spring of 1945. Since late 1939, tens of thousands of Canadian troops had trained, waited, and grown bored in various camps throughout southern England while their generals and political leaders debated the proper timing and location of their commitment to battle. The troops' resultant eagerness to "have at" Hitler's Germany has been advanced occasionally as a factor contributing to the Dieppe fiasco in 1942 and to the Sicilian deployment the following year. Whether or not Canadian soldiers' longing to die for their country affected strategic policy in such a direct fashion, their behaviour in England during the training period was a serious concern, not only from the perspective of military efficiency and discipline, but also in the light of Canadian-British relations.

At times tensions ran uncomfortably high. During the winters of 1940–41 and 1941–42, there were frequent complaints by British politicians, police officials, and local citizens of public drunkenness, disobedience, vandalism, and other criminal offences by Canadian personnel. "It was common knowledge that the troops were becoming 'browned off' and that morale was suffering," wrote C.P. Stacey and Barbara Wilson in their account of the Canadians in Britain.[1] In the months before Dieppe, it probably reached its lowest ebb. Letters to relatives back home spoke frequently of the troops' distaste for British officers, the bad weather, and the general indifference of many British civilians to the Canadians' presence. The arrival of massive numbers of American soldiers beginning in 1942 did not help matters, for while Canadian-British relations slowly improved, the favourable attention accorded Canadian forces in the British press correspondingly diminished as attention turned to the "Yankee" invasion.

It was not the case that the Canadian Army ignored the extracurricular needs of its troops during the training period. On the contrary, the army appreciated from the beginning the valuable contribution auxiliary services could make to the military effort and the corresponding benefits of a humane approach to personnel management. This was a legacy of World War I. Brigadier F. Logie Armstrong, the Deputy Adjutant General (DAG), argued in November 1939, less than three months after World War II began, that "Canada's enlisted men cannot, as in the last war, suffer through being deprived of the educational advantages which they would have possessed had it not been for enlistment."[2] General A.G.L. McNaughton, the first commander of Canada's overseas forces, understood the problem as well and began personally to lay the foundations for an extensive auxiliary services network while on board the *Aquitania* bound for Britain in mid-December and on the train to Aldershot several days later. Education and social services, he believed, "would tend to keep the minds of the men occupied [and] engaged and prevent them engaging in undesirable activities."[3] Neglect was not the problem. But the Canadians' relative lack of training and experience on their arrival in Britain, early deficiencies in accommodation, poor weather, the Blitz, and other factors all contributed to a lowering of morale during their first years overseas, despite the best intentions of McNaughton and his staff.[4]

Efforts to bolster morale and to ensure amicable relations with the army's British hosts and American allies – "keeping the troops happy," according to Stacey and Wilson[5] – began immediately and increased in intensity over the years. The overseas military establishment and several civilian agencies, including the Salvation Army, the Knights of Columbus, the Young Men's Christian Association, and the Canadian Legion, shared responsibility for this program.[6] Military training still remained the cornerstone of army activity, but in the interests of the soldiers' welfare the authorities supplemented it with a wide range of recreational, educational, and entertainment activities. Auxiliary service organizations and private individuals distributed refreshments, reading material, stationery, and sporting equipment, while stage shows and concert parties produced and staffed by Canadian entertainers soon replaced purely British shows.[7] Civilian and military newspapers, radio broadcasts,[8] and, most important, letters from home helped keep spirits up as well. By the end of hostilities, in fact, all mail for the overseas forces went from Canada by air, even nominally "surface mail" deliveries,[9] in an effort to prevent loneliness and unrest among the troops.[10] This combined offensive against malingering and indiscipline was highly successful, and from the spring of 1942 onwards conditions improved markedly.

In addition to their primary goal of strengthening morale, the auxiliary services had a second function, alluded to by McNaughton at an educational training meeting in March 1941. The army's winter education policy "had been a great help in maintaining morale," the general noted, but it had also been of "undoubted service to the men both in keeping up the habit of education and preparing them for the period of reconstruction after the war."[11] The desire to prepare personnel for civilian life before their release from military service assumed greater significance as the war progressed. Like the army's faith in morale building generally, it flowed from the World War I experience and the widespread belief that not enough had been done to prepare veterans of the Canadian Expeditionary Force for civvy street. The army's actions in this field mirrored those of civilian rehabilitation planners, whose interest in postwar problems dated back to October 1939.[12] The overseas forces, under McNaughton's guidance, were especially progressive in this regard. In the field of military education, for example, the DAG's office in Ottawa long resisted paying the travel expenses of educational officers travelling within and outside Canada and was reluctant to establish a formal Canadian army educational corps.[13] McNaughton, in contrast, expanded on the original cooperative agreement between the Canadian Legion, the Canadian Association for Adult Education, and the Canadian Army to form the Directorate of Educational Services and in 1940–41 placed educational advisers and unit education officers with all overseas formations. Similar appointments were not made to Canada's military district headquarters until June 1943.[14] In addition, McNaughton retained a personal adviser on educational matters in the person of J.B. Bickersteth, warden of Hart House, University of Toronto, who in 1942 became the director of army education for the British War Office.[15] The Directorate of Education survived his departure and remained formally attached to Canadian Military Headquarters, London (CMHQ). So strong was McNaughton's commitment to postwar training that one recent scholar has accused him of paying too much attention to it and not enough to the more martial requirements of his job, such as realistic battle training, manoeuvres, and logistics.[16]

Many of the more serious challenges to the morale of Canadian soldiers overseas had therefore been resolved (or at least addressed) long before the spring of 1945.[17] With Germany defeated, however, the problem assumed entirely new dimensions. There could be no doubt that the majority of military personnel now wanted to go home, the sooner the better. They shared Ottawa's marked lack of enthusiasm for large-scale participation in either the occupation of liberated Europe or the war against Japan, and cared little for continued military service. Even most of those who sought to remain in the army (and there were many who did) demanded as an absolute minimum an extended furlough in Canada and a break from the rigours of overseas soldiering. These individuals believed themselves to be neither short-sighted nor unpatriotic, least of all selfish. They viewed the fall of Hitler's Germany simply, unashamedly, as the end of their mission. VE-day (8 May 1945) provided closure on their military lives. They had succeeded. Now they could go home and, presumably, resume their normal lives. "I just felt that I had done my job," one veteran recalled, "and I was looking forward to just getting back to my wife and child ... That was all I was interested in."[18]

Despite the best efforts of the federal government and the army itself, repatriation was not that simple. Devising an effective, efficient repatriation program was a complicated process, made more so by the existence of thousands of military personnel who had never served overseas and by the division of Canadian recruits into General Service personnel and those who had enrolled under the National Resources Mobilization Act. Still, by September 1944, the Canadian cabinet had agreed on a set of basic demobilization guidelines, which the army published in pamphlet form several days after the German collapse. The plan established repatriation priorities on the basis of an individual's length of military service, with extra points for overseas service and marriage, and promised that after the long-service troops had been combed out and sent home, entire units would begin to move through the repatriation machine. This was a workable plan based on years of military and civilian study, but it could not entirely overcome the loneliness and fatigue of men and women who had been overseas for several years. For them, fairness meant immediate passage across the Atlantic, hasty discharge at the point of arrival, and a one-way ticket to Moose Jaw, Trenton, or Antigonish.

The publication of *After Victory in Europe*, the army's official guide to repatriation, thus helped educate the troops, but it did not appease everyone. Some believed that the priorities were unfair; others, that they were open to too many exemptions. Shipping delays, the result of combined Allied shipping agreements, strikes by British dock workers, and other unforeseen factors were soon severely testing most soldiers' faith in their superiors' repatriation promises. Canadian demobilization planners had anticipated these obstacles, for similar problems had occurred after World War I, but every delay worsened the morale situation and added urgency to efforts to occupy the troops between their withdrawal to the repatriation depots and their movement home. The repatriation system would collapse quickly if the depots became centres of disobedience and unrest. They were vital choke points. Keeping them open and functioning, and keeping their inhabitants reasonably passive were critically important to Canada's war effort in the Pacific, its occupation commitments in Europe, and its rehabilitation program. It was also of political importance to the governing Liberal Party. A string of riots like those that had occurred in Canadian depots in 1918 would affect the Canadian political landscape directly. After all, 1945 was an election year.

As McNaughton had acknowledged years before by the provision of educational services, idle minds could not be occupied by drill and military training alone. The time for that had passed. Instead, morale management would depend on the provision of progressively more generous auxiliary and special services to both the transient and the permanent populations in the camps. Education (especially regarding military and civilian plans for demobilization and rehabilitation programs), recreation, and entertainment were the core elements in this process. The psychological basis for this policy had been proposed in September 1944 by the Civilian Advisory Committee on Psychological Matters in a report to the Director General of Medical Services. The cessation of hostilities in Europe would "involve an immediate emotional dis-orientation" for most personnel, the report noted, necessitating "a plan that will effectively engage the soldiers' interest and enthusiasm."[19] Providing accurate and timely information to the troops would be essential, but more active measures, including rehabilitation seminars, vocational guidance, entertainment, tours, hikes, and field trips to local business and industrial concerns, would also be required. Everything possible had to be done to prepare personnel for their postwar lives and to keep them busy and out of trouble in the meantime. Army planners believed that if soldiers were kept satisfied in this fashion, they would have neither the time nor the inclination to resist military discipline or cause trouble. In a sense, the army planned to reinforce the legitimacy of military authority by making it far less obvious and intrusive. This, in turn, would buttress the bonds of military discipline and ensure the maintenance of order during the transition period. If the specific programs and activities selected helped engender in Canadian soldiers healthy attitudes towards their king and country and for their civic responsibilities, so much the better. Either way, order had to be maintained.

The structure of the repatriation system and the manner in which it processed army personnel determined the timing and nature of appropriate services. Upon the cessation of hostilities in May 1945, Canadian forces in Northwest Europe began concentrating in divisional laagers in the Netherlands to await movement orders for the United Kingdom.[20] Simultaneously, the Canadian Army Pacific Force (CAPF) began moving via Britain to North America, while the Canadian Army Occupation Force (CAOF) was concentrated in Germany. Ottawa and CMHQ granted CAPF personnel priority repatriation status in order to encourage enlistment (it was an all-volunteer formation) and to permit time for retraining in Canada before final deployment to the Pacific. Several other groups also received repatriation priority, including prisoners-of-war, casualties, extreme compassionate cases, and personnel declared essential for civilian or military employment in Canada. These special categories and CAPF personnel began arriving in Britain in late May and early June 1945, several weeks before general repatriation had begun.

For the troops of First Canadian Army still on the Continent, the war was not quite over. Disarming and marshalling surrendered Germans, feeding Dutch civilians, and maintaining public order continued to occupy Canadian troops for weeks after the surrender. Only gradually did the divisional components assemble, turn in their heavy equipment, and prepare to recross the English Channel. Orders for the disbandment of First Canadian Army appeared in early June, by which time the first long-service personnel had begun to move from the Continent. This was phase one of the repatriation plan. These long-service personnel joined the special cases and CAPF troops already in Britain. Those left in Northwest Europe moved in two streams through the main transit camp at Nijmegen to repatriation camps in the United Kingdom. Long-service soldiers, organized in so-called Canada drafts, based on their repatriation point total, continued to leave in small groups. At the same time, First Canadian Army reformed into five divisional groups composed, as much as possible, of units with clear territorial affiliations. Independent headquarters units (including those for the independent armoured brigades and numerous artillery and engineer formations) disbanded, and their personnel were absorbed by the larger divisional groups. In phases two through six of the army plan, the latter formations were to move through Nijmegen to the United Kingdom in the following order:

1st Canadian Infantry Divisional Group
2nd Canadian Infantry Divisional Group
3rd Canadian Infantry Divisional Group
5th Canadian Armoured Divisional Group
4th Canadian Armoured Divisional Group

Phase seven, which was to run concurrently with the other phases, would see the formation of an army "administrative residue" to complete the process.[21]

For the individual soldier, therefore, movement from the Continent depended on several factors, including operational requirements, the point system, divisional grouping, and enlistment in either the CAPF or CAOF. Divisional camps in the Netherlands were temporary facilities, designed to house personnel until they could be reposted rearward, but they were also of necessity large and well equipped, offering a full range of education, recreation, and other auxiliary services. Troops in the lower priority divisional groups spent several months in the Netherlands before even entering the repatriation stream in Britain. However, the key factor in determining one's movement from the Continent was the speed and efficiency with which personnel were moved through the repatriation machine in Britain.

CMHQ fabricated its repatriation infrastructure from the reinforcement and training facilities that were already in existence by 1945. By using existing facilities, CMHQ and First Canadian Army hoped to simplify planning by reversing the reinforcement flow and retaining the logistical, administrative, and command staff already in place. This reorganization of the Canadian reinforcement system began on 12 May with the transformation of several corps, artillery, engineer, and signals reinforcement units and four infantry training regiments into seven Canadian Repatriation Depots (CRDs).[22] CMHQ added another of these in late June and three more in late July, for a total of eleven (see table 1). The total transient capacity by that time was approximately 50,000, more than 60 per cent higher than the original allotment.

From a morale perspective, the place of both the transit camps in the Netherlands (especially Nijmegen) and the repatriation depots in Britain was critical. In both, Canadian personnel would be concentrated for extended periods of time; in both, operational duties would be minimal to nonexistent; and in both, the distractions and dangers of a friendly civilian population were close at hand. The units in the Netherlands were in some respects better positioned to maintain discipline because of the continuing need for prisoner-of-war supervision, humanitarian relief, and other duties, but such nominally military functions were no guarantee of long-term cohesion. As early as December 1944, when finding military tasks for the soldiery was hardly a problem, 2nd Canadian Corps reported a "distinct increase" in desertion and absenteeism. By March 1945, despite several corps orders to unit commanders, increases to the corps' recreational increment, and an accelerated rotational leave program, the situation was no better; Brigadier H.V.D. Laing, the Deputy Adjutant and Quartermaster General (DA&QMG), complained of "an increasing tendency in officers and other ranks to ignore orders issued by this [headquarters] relating to curfew, the unauthorized carriage of civilians in war department transport, the failure to vacate cafes and places of entertainment before 2300 hours, and the order prohibiting the taking of meals in civilian restaurants."[23] To maintain order, he said, careful attention would have to be paid in both sets of camps, those in Britain and those in the Netherlands.

Table 1
Location of Canadian Army Repatriation Depots[1]

1st	Thursley-Bramshott
2nd	Blackdown-Woking
3rd	Cove
4th	Witley
5th	Aldershot
6th	Aldershot
7th	Aldershot (later moved to Horsham)
8th	Farnborough
9th	Haslemere
10th	Leatherhead
11th	Forest Row

Source: National Archives of Canada, DND, vol. 6920, report no. 177, Historical Section, Canadian Military Headquarters, "The Repatriation of the Canadian Military Forces Overseas, 1945–1947"

[1] Each depot had several barracks or administrative "wings" spread around the area indicated.

The CRDs spread throughout southern England were the major potential bottlenecks in the repatriation system. The stability of the Dutch bases depended to a great extent on those across the Channel. Not only would personnel returning immediately from Northwest Europe pass through their barracks, but so would all army personnel currently in the European theatre and any others who arrived as reinforcements, not to mention the roughly 25,000 troops assigned to the CAOF in Germany. While the Canadian camps in Holland would grow progressively smaller as soon as repatriation commenced – because of the return of special cases and high-point personnel and because of reposting to other units – the CRDs in Britain would remain of uniform size and would operate at full capacity until repatriation neared its end. Any delay in clearing people through the depots would mean immediate overcrowding and the relegation of extra guests to the tents. Moreover, the CRDs, as the last stop before embarkation for home, would be particularly susceptible to rumours regarding shipping delays and favouritism.

Combatting the effects of gossip and unforeseen shipping delays on morale in the depots was the joint responsibility of depot staff, auxiliary service organizations, and higher formation commanders, especially Headquarters–Canadian Reinforcement Units (CRU) and CMHQ itself. The latter, advised initially by First Canadian Army and by its own education and auxiliary service officers, formulated overall policy but left its implementation to the units.[24] Despite the existence since 1940 of an extensive auxiliary services network, London's early efforts at central planning were neither innovative nor well received. CMHQ rejected the idea of a khaki college to provide teacher and vocational training to troops still on the Continent (although the Khaki University was later established in Britain), and education officers with First Canadian Army complained that its guidance on educational policy "was not sufficient or definite enough to provide a varied or useful educational curriculum."[25] Not until late January 1945 did CMHQ decide to make instruction in Canadian affairs, civics, and rehabilitation issues mandatory in its education program, a clear reflection of the army's interest not only in maintaining morale but in preparing Canadians for the postwar world as well.[26]

Even before their arrival in the camps, Canadian soldiers had been inundated with rehabilitation information by both civilian and military authorities. Pamphlets with titles such as *The Common Sense of Rehabilitation, Home As You Will Find It,* and *The Organization of Rehabilitation* were circulating freely by the spring of 1945. The Demobilization and Rehabilitation Information Committee (DRIC), a creation of the Wartime Information Board (WIB), coordinated this multimedia public relations effort from its offices in Ottawa.[27] A survey of 7,000 overseas troops in December 1944 indicated that the message was getting through; 52 per cent of those interviewed "had enough" rehabilitation information for their immediate needs, and only 32 per cent wanted more.[28] A civilian poll taken the same month by the WIB found that only 44 per cent of the respondents believed that Ottawa's measures for returned veterans were "about right," while 40 per cent said that they were not enough,[29] numbers that seem to indicate that at this time military personnel were comparatively well informed on postwar planning. Not until late April 1945 did the civilian numbers match the military figures from December, at which time 55 per cent of the respondents were satisfied with Ottawa's plans and only 31 per cent were not.

This is explained in part by the initiative of individual unit and base commanders. First Canadian Repatriation Depot, which handled rotational leave and special cases several months before CMHQ officially revamped the reinforcement system, implemented an extensive education and rehabilitation program in mid-March. Training instructors were at that stage in short supply, but in their absence unit chaplains broke the troops into small groups and did what they could.[30] At 1st Canadian Infantry Training Regiment, later to become the 9th Canadian Repatriation Depot, the postwar education and recreation program also commenced early, with a series of field trips in April to local museums, the Tower of London, and other historical sites.[31]

Such measures were more difficult on the Continent. General H.D.G. Crerar, General Officer Commanding-in-Chief, First Canadian

Army, was opposed to the distribution of postwar information, fearing that it might distract his troops from the task at hand. The army's DRIC representative made this plain at the committee's weekly meeting on 4 April by suggesting that "there should be no talk about rehabilitation overseas until after the victory," despite the claims of the Royal Canadian Navy's representative that rehabilitation programs on naval vessels had caused a marked improvement in morale.[32] On 12 April the army's representative again cited Crerar's view "that no material on the subject of rehabilitation should be distributed to the troops in Europe until he gives the word." The navy's approach, by contrast, was to hold talks and distribute material with a simple reminder that "the war must be won first."[33] First Canadian Army did, however, gradually prepare its recreation and education programs during this period,[34] and although its hesitation in fully publicizing Canada's demobilization and rehabilitation plans was annoying for Ottawa's public relations personnel, it was not entirely crippling. On 5 May, for example, Brigadier Laing, in confirming to all ranks news of the German surrender, reminded them of plans regarding recreation, sports, education, leave, and special courses. These plans had already been made, Laing noted, and would be implemented "forthwith."[35]

Across the English Channel, early May witnessed CMHQ's first moves in establishing a full-fledged repatriation system. On 1 May, 2nd Canadian Repatriation Depot was formed, under Lieutenant-Colonel W.T. Ibbott, with an establishment of 749 personnel, more than 500 of them transferred from reinforcement and training units.[36] The flood of returning troops began almost immediately. Personnel and logistical deficiencies (inadequate staff training, for example) would now have to be remedied on the run. More than 450 transients arrived on 8 May, 600 on 11 May, 1,100 on 12 May, and another 1,322 on 13–14 May. The camp handled the influx "without a hitch," its War Diary recorded, despite a few unspecified "rough spots." What these may have been can be assumed by noting the camp's first significant staff augmentation on 22 May: eighteen additional cooks. The camp also set some precedents on how the transient population could be kept occupied. On 21 May, Ibbott granted extended leave to more than 2,200 transients; three days later, he initiated a program of soldier education and training. If base facilities could not keep the troops occupied, they were better off not being on the base. Leave extensions immediately became a key weapon in the army's efforts to maintain morale.

The potential threat posed by large numbers of dissatisfied military personnel was made evident by the Halifax riot on 7–8 May 1945,[37] but the CRDs had little time to prepare elaborate preventive measures. By early June, First Canadian Army had completed its internal reshuffling for demobilization purposes (made necessary by Crerar's insistence on repatriation by territorial units), and it began shipping to the United Kingdom its first large draft of high-point personnel, more than 9,000 troops in all.[38] London was not entirely prepared to receive them. On 25 May, G.C. Andrews of the WIB complained to the Department of External Affairs that CMHQ's constant requests for guest speakers on rehabilitation matters displayed a regrettable lack of cooperation both between civilian and military authorities and between the three services themselves. Crerar's troops would need attention immediately. External's annual report, Andrews noted, had highlighted the role of Canada House as an information coordinating agency, so he suggested that a committee similar to the DRIC be established in London as soon as possible.[39]

Coordinating information was a critical element in bolstering morale in the repatriation period, but the physical condition and population density of the facilities were, if anything, more important. At the 7th Canadian Repatriation Depot, established at Aldershot in late May, Lieutenant-Colonel J.A. Decker, the Commanding Officer, found the barracks in filthy condition. Cleaning and painting began on 5 June in an effort to "make our guests' stay here as pleasant and convenient as possible," but the first drafts arrived on the thirteenth "and the riot was on."[40] The depot had held a dress rehearsal forty-eight hours before – "It shouldn't be so hard to master," the war diarist recorded prophetically – but this left little time to absorb the lessons of the exercise or to train new staff arrivals in the basics of repatriation paperwork and administrative procedures. The deluge of troops from the Continent was now on the way. On the twelfth, recorded the diarist with an obvious flare for the dramatic, the camp staff waited "like a bunch of expectant fathers. With fingernails chewed down to the elbows and cold sweat on their brows, they waited for their little bundles of joy to be dropped from the murky skies." The "riot" the following day went along "nicely," however.

The camp's monthly operation report, prepared by Lieutenant-Colonel J.A. Calder, who had replaced Decker in June, was not as sanguine as the War Diary's account. Calder noted, without elaboration, that several unspecified problems had arisen which had to be ironed out and that while the morale of both staff and Pacific force volunteers (the majority of the transient population at that time) was "good," the latter's discipline "was a little slack."[41] Two of the camp's three "wings" also made adverse comments about its first month of operations. The exception was A Wing, which noted on 15 June,

"Everything appears to be going very smoothly these days, a great relief even though things are very hectic." By contrast, C Wing described the facilities as "very dirty" when it commenced operations, and B Wing made several complaints about various aspects of the repatriation process. The barracks were in "a filthy, disgraceful condition," it reported, and information on incoming personnel drafts was "very soft and unmilitary"; the transients themselves, Pacific volunteers for the most part, were a noisy, dirty lot. "In most cases," B Wing recorded, "draft officers and NCOs exercise little or no control or supervision. Discipline and soldierly bearing seem to be considered a thing of the past."[42]

This was precisely the problem that CMHQ's education and recreation programs had sought to avoid, but it is difficult to see how, in the immediate aftermath of hostilities, a certain amount of exuberance on the part of the troops, even indiscipline, could have been averted, especially while personnel were on leave. Crerar's resistance to providing postwar information to troops on the Continent before 8 May and his subsequent reshuffling of personnel to ensure unit territorial affiliations did not help matters.[43] To add to the problem, bad weather plagued southern Britain and the Netherlands for part of this period. Another factor was a series of highly optimistic press reports, which appeared first in Canada but were soon relayed overseas, regarding the speed with which Canada's military forces were likely to be repatriated. Canadian authorities were just then involved in detailed and, ultimately, less than successful negotiations with British and American officials regarding their shipping allotment for the coming months, but no agreements had yet emerged to justify wild optimism. Of course, reports of a quick return enjoyed a favourable reception with the troops. Subsequent delays made the generals and politicians look like liars.[44] As the WIB reported on 28 May in reference to civilian opinion in Canada, "Statements that our men will be home before Christmas have been eagerly seized upon, and there is little general appreciation of the magnitude of the transportation problems involved."[45]

This was a volatile situation, to be sure, but it is probably easier to identify now than it was in 1945. Not all the CRDs shared No. 7 Depot's problems, though many reported minor difficulties, especially in the first couple of months. In late June, for example, No. 1 Depot reported a rash of minor criminal offences. "We are favoured by many visits from the police," the War Diary recorded, "who look everywhere and find everything except what they are looking for." The following day, 26 June, it noted: "More and more policemen who do as well as those who were here yesterday."[46] Such problems could not be dismissed, and camp commanders dealt with them in due course, but with few exceptions the repatriation system had been set in motion with relative ease. Problems with the morale of transients and staff were few at first, and the overseas forces' education and recreation facilities soon expanded considerably to meet the added demands of those proceeding through the camps. Even First Canadian Army, possibly the formation most reluctant to prepare in advance, had initiated a vastly accelerated auxiliary service program that began operation on 5 May. By the following month, Royal Canadian Army Medical Corps (RCAMC) facilities in the Netherlands were being converted to rehabilitation training centres.[47] Rehabilitation officials, including the Canadian Legion's president, Alex Walker, toured army formations throughout June; so well briefed were the officers by month's end that the army cancelled plans for an officers' course on rehabilitation legislation.[48] For most of the CRDs and continental transit camps, in fact, the demands of repatriation processing proved surprisingly routine, despite the number of personnel being processed. No. 6 Depot, for example, which began operation on 4 June, received its first drafts six days later but recorded no unusual events or complaints for the rest of the month. Its initial description of administrative procedures can be applied equally to all repatriation depots throughout the 1945–46 period: "The procedure with incoming drafts is to allot them quarters, feed them, then put them through the 'sausage machine,' followed by kit inspection, QM [Quartermaster] parade, and Pay Parade so that they may proceed on leave at the earliest possible moment."[49]

When not on leave, personnel awaiting repatriation participated in the "training" programs. All depots, however, emphasized the need for variety and volunteerism in these activities, and there was virtually no military training. No. 4 CRD's approach to this problem was typical: "Training within the Unit will be mainly Rehabilitation and Educational. As much time as possible will be given to Sports. When time permits, organized tours to such places as Windsor Castle, Winchester Cathedral, etc., will take place. Each Wing will have Rehabilitation Counsellors and Educational advisers. This work will, however, be coordinated by the Chief Instructor at RHQ [Regimental Headquarters]. Motion pictures will form a large part of this training. No military training vehicles or equipment will be on charge to this unit."[50] This program began in earnest on 15 June and included lectures on postwar job opportunities. It was to continue "for the duration of the period that these personnel are in this Unit." After one group of repatriates left (the first departed on 22 June), the next received the same treatment.

The benefits to morale of such extracurricular activities were immediately apparent. No. 1 Depot formed a recreation committee on 18 June "to arouse some interest among the men in sports and recreation," and it reported at month's end that this had "caused a boost in morale which could be felt," especially when the committee established a unit softball team. Movies, shows, and "other diversions" also fell under the new committee's mandate, and a different program ran every night of the week.[51]

Finding the time and personnel to run auxiliary programs was often difficult. From the beginning, the CRDs were understaffed and overworked. Because many of those who were originally on strength had come from the reinforcement units, personnel turnover was extremely high in the early months, owing to the staff's individual point totals and consequent repatriation priority. The army made every effort to freeze depot personnel (especially clerks and cooks) until much later in the repatriation process by declaring them essential; even so, locating and retaining qualified staff was a constant problem. No one wanted a CRD or transit camp posting. For those so assigned, the official estimate of 25.3 days of waiting time before shipping out was a cruel fiction.[52] The job itself was also highly undesirable. No. 1 Depot, for example, the oldest of the group, regularly provided training assistance to the newer camps formed in June and July in addition to its normal duties. Personnel drafts arrived virtually every day during June, several hundred or even a couple of thousand at a time (the War Diary notes the "usual mountain of work" on 10 June), and the administrative task was plagued by the inadequate and frequently inaccurate paperwork that accompanied the soldiers arriving from Europe. This "great paper picnic" affected innumerable personnel, who directed their ire at depot staff. As shipping problems delayed sailings later in the month, the accommodation problem became acute, a further source of complaint. By late June, dozens of transients were sent on extended leave because extra beds were unavailable. And still the flow of arrivals continued. "They are thinking of indenting for sky hooks," the War Diary noted on 29 June.[53]

June–July was a hectic period for most repatriation camps. Troops arrived almost daily, but very few left for Canada. Those who did were usually special cases, Pacific volunteers, or very high point personnel. No. 4 Depot did not ship its first transients "XUK" until 23 June, and there were no more sailings until 17 July when the *Pasteur*, the ship that had left in June, returned for a second load. However, nearly all of the 1,817 who sailed on the seventeenth were bound for the Pacific, as were those from five of the next groups between 17 July and 7 August. Only on 6 August did the camp repatriate a non-CAPF draft, 422 men

and women on the *Britannic*,[54] and these must have been extremely
unusual cases. On 29 June, Ottawa ordered that compassionate and
other urgent cases "be restricted to those of real necessity" in order to
speed redeployment of the CAPF.[55] Facilties were soon filled to over-
flowing, forcing many to move temporarily into tents, where some
remained throughout the summer. Depot staff fought to keep their
heads above water while shipping authorities struggled with the competing needs of the different services and the simultaneous repatriation of civilian dependants.[56] On 25 June, CMHQ, recognizing the
pressures on existing staff and facilities, enlarged the system by agreeing to add several more depots (nos. 8–11). This would provide total
accommodation for over 40,000 transients, with a short-term surge
capacity for up to 10,000 more.[57] The newer camps, with instructors
provided by the original seven, ran much more smoothly when first
established.[58]

Auxiliary programs were crucial to relieving this tension, but CRDs
ran them under extreme pressure. While recreational projects were
especially valuable to help the troops burn off tension, the army never
lost sight of its alternative goal: to prepare them for civilian life in
the postwar period. In late June, Crerar made it mandatory for all personnel under his command to take instruction in citizenship, international affairs, and current news, and to participate in rehabilitation,
reconstruction, and vocational programs.[59] The *First Canadian Army
Handbook of Rehabilitation Training and Welfare in the Post-Hostilities Period*
(prepared in April) was very explicit in emphasizing long-term goals:

"(a) to acquaint every soldier with the changes affecting him, his family, his
community and Canada as a whole, which have occurred during his absence on service."

"(b) to interpret and explain the differences between Canadian 'ways of life'
and corresponding aspects of civilian life in the countries in which he has
served."

"(c) to raise the level of the occupational skill and/or education of the soldier
to enable him to improve his status in civilian life."

"(d) to explain the provisions for post-discharge training and education and
advise regarding them"; and

"(e) in general, to prepare the soldier for his return to civilian life."[60]

This variegated approach "attracted a very high voluntary attendance"[61] and paralleled CMHQ's efforts in the United Kingdom.

The need to handle the entire morale question delicately was
brought dramatically to the fore in early July. As noted previously,
June had been a busy month for the staff of 7th Canadian Repatria-

tion Depot located near Aldershot. July promised more of the same.[62] It rained on Dominion Day, and on the following day, a Sunday, staff worked into the night processing new arrivals. On 3 July several drafts returned from extra leave and others went out for the first time, but all were "still waiting for ships." "These drafts seem to make a bad habit of leaving their barracks in poor condition," the War Diary recorded, but their deportment was explained in part by the rest of the daily entry: "Serials are beginning to get restless – with no definite word on when they may leave and the uncertainty of the future preventing any extra leave. 'We're waiting for ships that never come in' is the theme of [Canada] Serials at the moment." The storm broke on the 4 July: "A usual, normal day ended rather disastrously when Canadian soldiers participated in a riot in Aldershot during the evening." The mob hurled some abuse at camp officers, broke some windows, and destroyed some property, but dispersed after being harangued by the depot commander, Lieutenant-Colonel Calder. On the fifth, Major-General D.C. Spry, Commander, Canadian Reinforcement Units,[63] arrived to speak with the troops, to answer questions, and to explain the shipping problem, but his intervention was ineffective. That night, the troops rioted again, this time showing "signs of organization and malicious intent," the diarist noted. The following day, 6 July, CMHQ emptied No. 7 Depot and sent its occupants to nearby camps; as well, it convened a court of inquiry, while Calder's staff and some former Italian POWs, who had been impressed for the purpose, cleaned up broken glass and repaired local businesses. The rioters, six of whom later received prison sentences, had caused $41,541 in damage. Their "schoolboyish action," noted Spry, threatened to "undermine the good reputation Canadians have built up on the battlefield."[64]

Press reaction in both Britain and Canada was unanimously negative after the 4 July incident; after the second outbreak it became even harsher. But those who had participated in the Aldershot "smash-up" (the "re-invasion" of Aldershot, according to the Montreal *Gazette*)[65] received much sympathy from both the press and their commanding officers. While deploring the violence, CMHQ noted that the troops "were naturally impatient and restless at the delay in getting back to their homes due to the lack of shipping."[66] London's *Daily Telegraph* said the riot's causes were "entirely comprehensible"; the Ottawa *Evening Citizen*, subscribing to the popular view that a few hotheads had twisted a difficult situation to suit themselves, believed the official inquiry would find "nothing sinister"; and the *Maple Leaf*, a Canadian Army newspaper, disowned the behaviour as shameful while pointing out that it had erupted "in the heat of dissatisfaction about the shipping situation."[67] The army's response, to immediately form an ad hoc security battalion to patrol the Aldershot area, was in some ways at odds with this reasoned assessment, but security forces were placed under strict standing orders not to act precipitately against demonstrators, and they were to remain unarmed unless authorized directly by CMHQ in an emergency. Spry, CMHQ, and Ottawa also succeeded in evading the British army's "offer" of a full-strength security brigade; the complications likely to ensue from having armed British troops patrolling Canadian base facilities were not difficult to imagine.[68]

The particular circumstances at Aldershot included factors other than the shipping problem; Spry heard complaints about pay anomalies, poor food, overcrowding, and so on. Nevertheless, the central difficulty was shipping or, more specifically, the effects of shipping delays on the morale of those waiting in the depots. At first glance, this represents a fundamental failure of the army's morale-building campaign. The outbreak of violence, so similar in nature to what had occurred in 1918–19, seemed to indicate that Canada's World War II repatriation planners were no better than their predecessors. Yet the evidence for such unguarded pessimism is weak. CMHQ acted quickly and effectively to forestall further trouble, shutting down No. 7 Depot until the legal proceedings had run their course, and there was no recurrence of the Aldershot problem elsewhere. All CRDs ran at full capacity in this period and all had their share of difficulties, but the events of 4–5 July were more or less unique. There is little indication in the records of other camps that similar outbreaks were brewing. Certainly, Aldershot represented more than simply a few "hotheads" acting irresponsibly, but it should not be interpreted much more broadly than that. On both sides of the Channel, education and recreation programs continued uninterrupted. Rather than signalling the systematic failure of these programs, Aldershot emphasized their necessity ("Keep your men usefully employed" appeared in capital letters, with double underlining, on the contents page of No. 6 Depot's War Diary for 20 July).[69]

But if CMHQ, much to Spry's credit, did not panic and acted effectively both to re-emphasize its training regimen and to eliminate the immediate source of trouble, the reaction of General Crerar was less helpful. Crerar had never been convinced that a repatriation scheme based on individual point totals was a good idea. He believed that the troops wanted to be repatriated by unit on a territorial basis because of their familiarity with friends and comrades. This, he argued, would be easier both logistically and administratively than watering down formations by the constant departure of individuals based on point totals. It would also help maintain unit cohesion while First Canadian Army was still on the Continent. This type of repatriation had been addressed by the army's Demobilization Planning Committee in 1943 and 1944, and a compromise scheme incorporating both point totals and unit priorities had appeared as army policy in May 1945; but Crerar wanted to dispense with individual drafts as quickly as possible and shift the focus entirely to territorial units. Personnel movements to strengthen territorial affiliations had started in May. Aldershot provided Crerar with the opportunity to complete the changeover before leaving his command, because it seemed to indicate that order and discipline had broken down.[70] Throwing personnel together in repatriation camps whose only commonality was a point total on a movement control form was, Crerar believed, a recipe for disaster. Aldershot was proof enough of that.

On 10 July, therefore, just five days after the disturbances, Crerar wrote to all formations in First Canadian Army pronouncing the death sentence on point-based repatriation, or what he called "repatriation by disintegration."[71] Individual priority, he stated, despite its "strong sentimental influence," was not "a rational procedure" and already had reached its "practicable limit." If continued, personnel shortages would soon make it impossible "adequately to maintain and administer the troops yet remaining in this country." Individual priority should therefore now come to an end and unit priority should be "wholeheartedly adopted." "It is quite essential," the army commander continued, "that everyone of you loyally accept the view that the time has come when 'High Point Scores' can no longer be an influencing factor in repatriation, and that the despatch of the balance, and bulk, of the First Canadian Army must now be done in a selected sequence of Divisional Groups, units and sub-units. The 'time factor' of the individual must give way to the 'orderly organization' of the many. The personal longing to 'get home quickly' must be subordinated to the higher duty of each one of us to think, and act, in terms of the greater good for the greater number."[72] This was a tall order, but Crerar promised that "whatever can be done to make the period before repatriation not only bearable, but enjoyable, *will* be done."[73]

Crerar's proposal (his order, in fact) was not without merit. High-point personnel leaving for home had affected administrative efficiency, requiring CMHQ and First Canadian Army to freeze certain occupation categories until replacement personnel could be either trained or found elsewhere. All CRDs had this problem, as did the transit camps and training centres on the Continent. But its merit was outweighed by Crerar's misreading of the situation in Europe and by his underestimation of the troops' most basic desire: to go home. Shipping records clearly reveal that Crerar's impression of the numbers repatriated under the point system was at best erroneous. From 1 January to 30 May 1945, CMHQ's Movement Control Table showed only 17,065 non-casualties repatriated, and only 4,542 of them in May (in other words, since the armistice).[74] Because it took CMHQ and Crerar's head-quarters several weeks after 8 May to calculate the overseas forces' point totals, very few of this number could have been high-point personnel as designated by London, although many were on rotational leave for long service. (The total number of high-point personnel was estimated variously, depending on the cut-off date, at between 30,000 and 50,000 individuals.) Another 15,607 troops went home in June, but because of the explicit, exclusive priority granted CAPF volunteers, very few of these were high-point personnel either. In fact, most of the high-point personnel Crerar alluded to in his 10 July directive had not left Europe; they were sitting in transit camps and repatriation depots playing softball, studying citizenship, and bemoaning the lack of available shipping.

Crerar's change of pace did not go unnoticed. When Minister of Veterans Affairs Ian Mackenzie visited bases in the Netherlands the following week, he found opinion split evenly on the unit versus point system, but he noted that there was "a sense of grievance among the troops here that the government is not carrying out its promise to soldiers that the policy of 'first in, first out' would be followed."[75] Crerar, incensed at the minister's interference (he believed Mackenzie had not read *After Victory in Europe*), sought – and received – strong support from Ottawa. On the Prime Minister's authority, A.G.L. McNaughton, by this time Minister of National Defence, wired Vincent Massey, Canada's High Commissioner in London, to have Mackenzie refrain from further press interviews. "We are all deeply disturbed" by Mackenzie's actions, McNaughton wrote, and suggested a lengthy text which the Veterans Affairs minister might release immediately to "correct" the impression left by his initial comments. The suggested text noted explicitly that Crerar's views were in perfect accord with the repatriation plans of Ottawa and CMHQ, and that no deviation from official policy had occurred.[76]

This was undoubtedly true. Crerar may have acted prematurely, from a statistical standpoint, but he had not acted improperly. The initial policy had foreseen the need to change gears and Crerar had done so, as his position allowed. On the other hand, there is little reason to doubt that Mackenzie's impression of the soldiers' mood was entirely correct. Crerar's decision had sown confusion in the ranks on a massive scale. The system had been under stress at the time of Aldershot, but it had been working, if slowly, subject to the availability of shipping. After Crerar's announcement, despite the proliferation of education, training, and recreation programs, the system faced a loss of legitimacy as a result of the widespread perception (stated explicitly in Crerar's original order) that length of service had been replaced by administrative efficiency as the structure's organizing principle. Consequently, when Lieutenant-General G.G. Simonds, General Officer Commanding (GOC), Canadian Forces Netherlands (CFN, the administrative entity that had replaced First Canadian Army), surveyed the repatriation system in early September, his findings completely validated Mackenzie's earlier fears.[77] The troops, argued Simonds, believed that length of service as the basis for repatriation had been diminished by Crerar's scheme, despite Ottawa's reassurances; morale had suffered as a result, especially among units still in the Netherlands. They complained that promises made in early spring had been broken and that, through the unit system, personnel with much shorter service, including conscripts, were going home first. Simonds acted quickly to bring back greater emphasis on length of service, inserting point categories between each of the divisional groups, but to a certain extent the damage had already been done. For the next several months, the GOC spent much of his time imploring soldiers whose faith in the system had been shaken to remain patient and await their turn. Simonds proved remarkably successful in this endeavour, but in exercising damage control he fired the editor of the *Maple Leaf*, Major J.D. MacFarlane, whose increasingly critical editorials he rightly viewed as a serious threat to morale.[78]

The Aldershot incident, therefore, was not representative of systemic problems in the repatriation system, but it did spur changes that posed a serious threat to army morale. In combatting this danger, Simonds's efforts and those of the military press are especially noteworthy (ironically, Simonds and MacFarlane were on precisely the same side); but in general, the programs that had been working in June continued to operate afterwards, just as others were added to fill particular needs in the CRD and transit camp structure. For example, the army announced a major educational and vocational training program on 7 July that reiterated the main principles of postwar planning: morale, practical training, and "re-orientation" training "to bridge the gap" to civilian life.[79] Popular demand for army courses grew as long as the number of troops remained high; once sailings became more frequent, the press of numbers eased rapidly. But as Crerar prepared to hand his command over to Simonds and the newly created CFN, this development was still somewhat in the future. In July, when 1st Canadian Rehabilitation Training Centre in the Netherlands began its first series of classes, it could accommodate only 351 of the 3,000 applicants.[80]

Throughout July and August and into the fall, the pace of activity at all camps in the repatriation system remained brisk. From late June onwards, westbound sailings helped increase the rate of turnover and slowly reduced the number left on the Continent. Shipping shortages delayed this process more than once (in August and again in November movement totalled less than 15,000), but from June 1945 to January 1946, inclusive, the monthly average was nearly 23,000, and in July, September, December, and January it was more than 31,000.[81]

The Permanent Establishments (PEs), or camp staff, watched the men go with mixed emotions. A speedier process benefited everyone, but as No. 3 Depot reported in early July, "PE this Depot viewing with alarm the situation now existent whereby large numbers of men are being repatriated who have a much lower Repatriation Point Score than they have."[82] Some facilities, especially in the Netherlands, whose role in the repatriation scheme was less crucial than the CRDs, had exactly the opposite problem as essential personnel left regularly for the staging areas in Britain.[83] These facilities were also the first to suffer as westbound traffic dried up the flow of students and trainees, a process in evidence as early as October; by December, most of the major auxiliary service establishments in the Netherlands had closed or were in the process of doing so. The Army Agricultural School at Dordrecht, for example, which sought to train prospective beneficiaries of the Veterans' Land Act, received its first students on 29 July and disbanded on 15 December.[84] The 5th Canadian Rehabilitation Training Centre, established on 17 July, closed on 4 December after most of its staff and students had shipped out for Britain and the repatriation stream.[85]

The CRDs in Britain remained busier far longer, much to the chagrin of their overworked staff. Morale among the transient population there seems to have been better than across the Channel, no doubt because proximity to the ports and the availability of increased shipping made homeward movement increasingly likely. "Their conduct is noteworthy," recorded the 3rd CRD's Protestant chaplain after conducting 150 interviews, "but their language is polluted with profanity."[86] CMHQ did not help the chaplain's problem by providing free beer occasionally at mess dances, but the greater evil for the brass, especially after Aldershot and Crerar's initiatives, was low morale. In an effort to counter this problem, staff and transients painted and cleaned depot facilities throughout the summer and constructed more playing fields, outdoor theatres, and "craft shacks." Personnel awaiting repatriation went on farm leave, regular leave, and extended leave – indeed, any leave that would keep them out of the depots and free from the boredom of camp life. The depots, though operating at capacity, were in fact often nearly empty, for personnel were shipped off as soon as they could be processed. Those returning to the depots at the end of their leave might find another permit awaiting them if shipping had been delayed. Permanent staff had no such luxury, but by late August even some of them had been detailed for home.[87] By late August, as well, the Japanese had surrendered, and consequently morale rose, at least temporarily.

The CRDs were not immune to morale problems after August 1945, but while Simonds was on the Continent he wrestled with the effects of Crerar's hasty switch to unit repatriation. In Britain, fall brought the "thrills of routine" and "the final stages of the paper war," but as a diarist for No. 7 Depot (the unit that had housed the Aldershot rioters) noted, "a glimmer of homeward shores" could be detected in the eyes of the waiting troops. "Mine too," he added.[88] Meanwhile, training selection boards continued to clear personnel for vocational courses, and harried officials from Ottawa continued to deliver speeches to increasingly disinterested audiences; but as fall wore on and the "glimmer" grew stronger, the educational and training system inexorably began to shut down in Britain as it had on the Continent. By Christmas, in a month in which nearly 40,000 personnel shipped for home, many of the programs had run their course and the CRDs themselves were beginning to wind down. In a few months, they would almost all be gone.[89]

The Canadian Army's overseas repatriation camps performed a remarkable logistical feat between the spring of 1945 and that of 1946 (in 1945 there were 395,013 discharges from the armed services, and in 1946 there were 381,031). Built hastily on the foundations of the reinforcement system, repatriation facilities had quickly filled to capacity after Germany's surrender. Not until late June, however, did these troops begin to sail for home in appreciable numbers, a result of shipping shortages and the absolute priority accorded CAPF volunteers. The delays occasioned considerable complaint, but efforts to deflect criticism and to employ the troops' time wisely had been in readiness months before the cessation of hostilities and kicked in smoothly when required. Army planners had several goals – to maintain morale, to provide training, and to reacclimatize military personnel for civilian life[90] – and, by most accounts, they achieved them.

Aldershot was an unfortunate blemish on this otherwise acceptable record, but no one, including the depot staff, General Spry (the CRU commander), and CMHQ, overreacted to the incident. Instead, CMHQ moved quickly to prevent further damage and to restore the morale of those affected. It resisted British calls for further military precautions and redoubled its efforts to utilize auxiliary services and specialized training to combat ill discipline. Aldershot's most significant impact was the effect it had on General H.D.G. Crerar. He used it as an opportunity to accelerate the transformation of the repatriation process into a unit priority system, an evolution foreseen by army planners the previous year but not defined with great precision. Crerar followed the letter of the army's repatriation plan in doing so, but not its spirit. The legitimacy of army repatriation policy, after all, rested on its being perceived as fair by those in the ranks, a consideration affected mainly by the degree to which it rewarded length of service. But when Crerar announced his decision to First Canadian Army on 10 July, almost none of the supposed beneficiaries of the army's length of service preference had actually sailed for home. Shipping delays and the CAPF preference had seen to that. The result, on the eve of Crerar's departure for Canada, was a spreading morale problem that affected to some degree facilities in both Britain and the Netherlands.

Ian Mackenzie appreciated this fact in mid-July, but Mackenzie's public criticism of the general was not the proper route to redress. Minister of National Defence A.G.L. McNaughton, on the Prime Minister's orders, quite properly rebuked his colleague. Crerar's successor, however, confirmed Mackenzie's fears and acted speedily and decisively to counteract them. Whether or not he would have been as successful had shipping delays caused the same problems in the fall as they had in May and early June is an open question; the fact is that they did not, and from June onwards westbound movement averaged nearly 23,000 per month. This, coupled with Japan's surrender, Simonds's efforts, and the extensive auxiliary services infrastructure in Britain and the Netherlands (in part the result of McNaughton's personal interest in army education several years before, a further irony) made for a noticeable improvement in living conditions and morale. The latter remained precarious, especially for the long-suffering and long-serving permanent staff at the army's eleven CRDs, but it did not collapse.

Military efficiency, or at least military cohesion, did not prove incompatible with humanitarianism, social needs, and educational policy. It should be taken as an object lesson in postwar planning, however, that the army's one major attempt to impose military structure and wartime logic in this transition period – Crerar's insistence on the organizational benefits of a unit repatriation policy – might well have proved disastrous had other factors not intervened. Other than this, a notable exception to be sure, the system (and those within it) creaked and groaned a bit, but it (and they) functioned rather well.

NOTES

1 C.P. Stacey and Barbara M. Wilson, *The Half-Million: The Canadians in Britain, 1939–1946* (Toronto: University of Toronto Press 1987), 16, 52.

2 National Archives of Canada (hereafter NA), records of the Department of National Defence (hereafter DND), RG 24, vol. 13271, War Diary, Deputy Adjutant General (DAG), Weekly Progress Report, 21 November 1939, 6.

3 NA, DND, vol. 13721 (microfilm reel T1872), War Diary, General Staff (GS), 1st Canadian Division, 15 December 1939.

4 Stacey and Wilson, *The Half-Million*, passim.

5 Ibid., 93.

6 For a good account of one such effort, see Alan M. Hurst, *The Canadian Y.M.C.A. in World War II* (National War Services Committee of the National Council of the Young Men's Christian Association of Canada, n.d.).

7 Stacey and Wilson, *The Half-Million*, 107–14.

8 In February 1940 the Canadian Broadcasting Corporation agreed to rebroadcast Saturday-night National Hockey League games via short-wave radio to Aldershot, one of the largest Canadian camps, on the following Sunday morning.

9 Stacey and Wilson, *The Half-Million*, 119–20.

10 Auxiliary services in Canada also got off to a very early start, aided immeasurably by the existing network of public and private charities, service organizations, veterans' groups, and civic organizations. The DAG's Weekly Progress Report for 12 January 1940, for example, noted contributions by the Boy Scouts of Canada, private hostels in Victoria, and the "Adopt a Soldier" movement in Montreal (NA, DND, vol. 13271, War Diary, DAG, 12 January 1940, 2).

11 NA, DND, vol. 13681 (microfilm reel T7109), War Diary, G Branch, Headquarters, Canadian Corps, 11 March 1941.

12 Dean F. Oliver, "Canadian Military Demobilization in World War II," in J.L. Granatstein and Peter Neary, eds., *The Good Fight: Canadians in World War II* (Toronto: Copp Clark 1995), 367–86.

13 NA, DND, vol. 13271, War Diary, DAG, 5 August 1941.

14 NA, DND, vol. 13329, War Diary, Directorate of Public Relations (Army), 16 June 1943.

15 C.P. Stacey, *Six Years of War: The Army in Canada, Britain and the Pacific* (Ottawa: Queen's Printer 1955), 420.

16 John A. English, *The Canadian Army and the Normandy Campaign: A Study of Failure in High Command* (New York: Praeger 1991), 79.

17 Despite the difficulties outlined above, there is little indication that army morale ever reached a critical level, even during the winters of 1940 and 1941. Throughout January and February 1941, for example, corps headquarters continued to report "satisfactory" discipline with few courts martial or legal proceedings. See NA, DND, vol. 13681 (microfilm reel T7109), War Diary, G Branch, Headquarters, Canadian Corps, January–February 1941, weekly reports.

18 Letters from William G. Spring, Toronto, 21 November 1992 and 22 January 1993.

19 NA, DND, vol. 2841, file HQS 8350–36, vol. 1, Lieutenant-Colonel G.M. Morrison to members of the Army Demobilization Planning Committee, 8 September 1944.

20 Overseas repatriation arrangements are described in detail in NA, DND, vol. 6920, report no. 177, Historical Section, Canadian Military Headquarters, "The Repatriation of the Canadian Military Forces Overseas, 1945–1947."

21 Ibid., 23.

22 Ibid., 30. In late August, Canadian Reinforcement Training Units were redesignated Canadian Repatriation Units (CRUs).

23 NA, DND, vol. 13719 (microfilm reel T1871), War Diary, Adjutant General and Quartermaster General's Branch, Headquarters, 2nd Canadian Corps, November 1944 to April 1945, entries for 1 December and 6 March, appendix 5.

24 NA, DND, vol. 13610 (microfilm reel T6671), War Diary, A plans – Headquarters, First Canadian Army, 4 December 1944.

25 Ibid., 13 December 1944, appendix 2.

26 Ibid., 24 January 1945, appendix 2, CMHQ Conference on Rehabilitation Training.

27 See NA, DND, vol. 2839, file HQS 8350–21, vol. 2, A. Ross, Deputy Minister (Army), to General Kenneth Stuart, 14 October 1944. See also NA, Records of Boards, Offices and Commissions: Wartime Information Board (hereafter WIB), series 31, vol. 11, file 6–3–1, pt 1, minutes of the Demobilization and Rehabilitation Committee (DRIC), 8 November 1944.

28 NA, DND, vol. 13610 (microfilm reel T6671), War Diary, A plans – Headquarters, First Canadian Army, 13 December 1944, appendix 2.

29 NA, records of the Privy Council Office (hereafter PCO), RG 2, vol. 12, file W–34–10, WIB memo to cabinet, 30 April 1945, 2.

30 NA, DND, vol. 16808, War Diary, 1st Canadian Repatriation Depot (Lorne Scots), 2 Increment, March 1945.

31 NA, DND, vol. 16764, War Diary, 1st Canadian Infantry Training Regiment (9th Canadian Repatriation Depot), April 1945.

32 NA, WIB, vol. 11, file 6–3–1, pt 1, minutes, 4 April 1945.

33 Ibid., minutes, 12 April 1945.

34 See NA, DND, vol. 13610 (microfilm reel T6671), War Diary, A plans – Headquarters, First Canadian Army, April 1945. Throughout this month there were several conferences on these and related matters.

35 NA, DND, vol. 13719 (microfilm reel T1871), War Diary, Adjutant General and Quartermaster General branches – Headquarters, 2nd Canadian Corps, 5 May 1945.

36 NA, DND, vol. 16821, War Diary, 2nd Canadian Repatriation Depot, May 1945.

37 James M. Cameron, *Murray: The Martyred Admiral* (Hantsport, N.S.: Lancelot Press 1980). See also NA, L.W. Murray Papers, MG 30 E 207, vol. 2, "V-E Day Disturbances Enquiry, 1945."

38 NA, H.D.G. Crerar Papers, MG 30 E 157, vol. 5, file 5–5–3, Colonel L.A. Deziel (for DA&QMG) to army, 20 May 1945.

39 NA, WIB, vol. 11, file 6–3–1, pt 2, G.C. Andrews to Undersecretary of State for External Affairs, 25 May 1945.

40 NA, DND, vol. 16825, War Diary, 7th Canadian Repatriation Depot (Infantry), 5 June 1945. The "Infantry" designation arose from CMHQ's initial desire to have the CRDs specialize by branch of service, but this proposal proved unworkable from a logistical standpoint and was quickly dropped.

41 Ibid., report by Lieutenant-Colonel J.A. Calder, CO, 2 July 1945, appended to War Diary for 26 May – 30 June 1945.

42 Ibid. These reports are attached to the War Diary for May–June. B Wing's last-cited comment was recorded 18 June.

43 It should also be remembered that prior to receiving repatriation drafts, the CRDs had first to be cleared of those personnel still in the reinforcement stream at the cessation of hostilities. This represented a forward displacement of more than 30,000 troops, who were then distributed to overseas formations according to need and point total. This occupied much of April and May and added an extra layer of complexity to an already difficult situation.

44 See, for example, NA, PCO, vol. 33, file D–19–R, vol. 2, Canadian Joint Staff Mission, London, to Chiefs of Staff Committee, 28 May 1945, on navy efforts to rewrite a particularly effusive press release.

45 NA, PCO, vol. 12, file W–34–10, WIB memo to cabinet, 28 May 1945, 2.

46 NA, DND, vol. 16808, War Diary, 1st Canadian Repatriation Depot (Lorne Scots), 2 Wing, 25 and 26 June 1945.

47 NA, DND, vol. 16662, War Diary, 1st Canadian Rehabilitation Training Centre (Vught), June 1945.

48 NA, DND, vol. 13610 (microfilm reel T6671), War Diary, A plans – Headquarters, First Canadian Army, 25 June 1945.

49 NA, DND, vol. 16825, War Diary, 6th Canadian Repatriation Depot, 10 June 1945.

50 NA, DND, vol. 16822, War Diary, 4th Canadian Repatriation Depot, 2 June 1945.

51 NA, DND, vol. 16808, War Diary, 1st Canadian Repatriation Depot (Lorne Scots), 3 Wing, 18 and 30 June 1945.

52 NA, DND, vol. 12836, file 391–26, Major-General E.G. Weeks, Major-General in Charge of Administration, CMHQ, to Brigadier J.F.A. Lister, DA&QMG, First Canadian Army, 20 July 1945.

53 NA, DND, vol. 16808, War Diary, 1st Canadian Repatriation Depot (Lorne Scots), Headquarters and A Wing, June 1945 (various dates).

54 NA, DND, vol. 16824, War Diary, 4th Canadian Repatriation Depot, June 1945, appendix 5.

55 NA, DND, vol. 12836, file 391–26, Lieutenant-General J.C. Murchie, Chief of the General Staff, to Lieutenant-General P.J. Montague, Chief of Staff, CMHQ, 29 June 1945. This represented a significant change from early May, when Major-General A.E. Walford, Adjutant General, had advised Montague that the "moral effect of returning substantial number long service [personnel] earlier than Pacific force would be most constructive both overseas and in Canada." See NA, DND, vol. 2841, file HQS 8350–36, vol. 2, Walford to Montague, 4 May 1945.

56 By late June, 8,120 military dependants had sailed from Britain and 2,600 more were ready to go from an estimated pool of some 42,234. See ibid., memorandum, "Return of Dependents," by D.A. Clarke, Director, Canadian Wives' Bureau, 21 June 1945.

57 NA, DND, vol. 12836, file 391–23, "Notes of Meeting ... to Discuss the Expansion of Accommodation for Repatriation Personnel, 25 June 1945."

58 NA, DND, vol. 16826, War Diary, 8th Canadian Repatriation Depot, July 1945, for example.

59 NA, PCO, vol. 99, file R–70–10, vol. 2, minutes of DRIC, 20 June 1945.

60 Cited in C.P. Stacey, *The Victory Campaign: The Operations in North-West Europe, 1944–1945* (Ottawa: Queen's Printer 1966), 616.

61 General Crerar's report to Minister of National Defence, 1 August 1945, cited in ibid., 616.

62 Unless otherwise noted, references to 7th CRD are from NA, DND, vol. 16825, file 2082, War Diary, 7th Canadian Repatriation Depot, July 1945.

63 Spry's functional command was Canadian Repatriation Units, a name in widespread use but not officially sanctioned until late August, despite the renaming of the actual depots from May to July.

64 *Evening Citizen* (Ottawa), 5 July 1945. The best brief account of the circumstances surrounding the riot is Stacey, *Six Years of War*, 431–4. Stacey and Wilson, *The Half-Million*, 170–2, place it in the broader context of Canadian military–British civilian relations. For a comparison with the World War I experience, see Desmond Morton, " 'Kicking and Complaining': Demobilization Riots in the Canadian Expeditionary Force, 1918–19," *Canadian Historical Review* 61, no. 3 (September 1980): 334–60.

65 *Daily Mail* (London), 5 July 1945, and *Gazette* (Montreal), 6 July 1945.

66 Cited in the *Evening Citizen* (Ottawa), 5 July 1945.

67 *Daily Telegraph* (London), 7 July; *Evening Citizen* (Ottawa), 6 July; and *Maple Leaf* (London), 6 July 1945.

68 NA, records of the Department of External Affairs (DEA), RG 25, vol. 2115, file AR414, pt 20, Montague to Crerar, 6 July 1945. Vincent Massey, Canada's High Commissioner to London, thought CMHQ should accept the British proposal.

69 NA, DND, vol. 16825, War Diary, 6th Canadian Repatriation Depot, 20 July 1945.

70 Dean F. Oliver, "Troubled Transition? Morale, Leadership and Canadian Army Demobilization, 1945–46" (paper presented at Wilfrid Laurier University, Centre for Military Strategic and Disarmament Studies, 6th Military History Colloquium, 21–2 April 1995).

71 Directorate of History, DND, document 113.22062, Crerar to all commanders and commanding officers, First Canadian Army, 10 July 1945.

72 Ibid.

73 Ibid. (emphasis in original).

74 NA, DND, vol. 6920, report no. 177, Historical Section, CMHQ, "The Repatriation of the Canadian Military Forces Overseas, 1945–1947," appendix s, 69.

75 Maple Leaf (London), 19 July 1945.

76 NA, Crerar Papers, vol. 4, file 5–5, vol. 2, contains the McNaughton-Massey, Crerar-Montague, and Crerar-McNaughton messages on this incident, all for the 14–18 July 1945 period.

77 NA, DND, vol. 2841, file HQS 8350–36, vol. 3, "Review of Plan for Repatriation" by Lieutenant-General G.G. Simonds, 6 September 1945, and "Report on Repatriation," also by Simonds, 30 September 1945.

78 Globe and Mail (Toronto), 24 September 1945. MacFarlane refused to retract his criticisms, though he did offer Simonds the opportunity of a signed rejoinder. MacFarlane's assessment of the incident, expressed to Simonds at the time the general gave him the news, is a brief but trenchant assessment of both men's conflicting responsibilities: "You did what you had to do and I did what I had to do." This view comes from a letter by MacFarlane written to the editor of the Canadian War Correspondents Association Newsletter, Fall 1993. This and many other documents were provided to the author by Richard N. MacFarlane, Toronto.

79 NA, J.L. Ralston Papers, MG 27 III B 11, vol. 56, file "Rehabilitation, Vol. 1," WIB "Post-War Planning Information," 7 July 1945, 6.

80 NA, DND, vol. 16662, War Diary, 1st Canadian Rehabilitation Training Centre (Vught), 11 July 1945.

81 NA, DND, vol. 6920, report no. 177, 69.

82 NA, DND, vol. 16821, War Diary, 3rd Canadian Repatriation Depot, 5 July 1945.

83 NA, DND, vol. 16126, War Diary, 1 Canadian Demobilization Depot, Royal Canadian Ordnance Corps, 3 and 16 July 1945.

84 NA, DND, vol. 16662, War Diary, 3rd Canadian Rehabilitation Training Centre (Agriculture), 5 July – 15 December 1945.

85 NA, DND, vol. 16663, War Diary, 5th Canadian Rehabilitation Training Centre, 17 July – 4 December 1945. No. 4 CRTC had closed on 5 September, after transferring its few students to other facilities.

86 NA, DND, vol. 16821, War Diary, 3rd Canadian Repatriation Depot, August 1945, appendix 15, Protestant chaplain's report.

87 Ibid., appendix 11, "Intelligence (Morale) Report." No. 3 Depot kept a daily morale summary of both PE and transient personnel, the latter broken down by individual draft.

88 NA, DND, vol. 16825, War Diary, 7th Canadian Repatriation Depot (Infantry), appendix 4, A Wing, 20 August 1945.

89 By that time, only some 24,000 troops were left in Europe, most of them belonging to the CAOF.

90 For an account of this process from an American perspective, see Mark Meigs, "Crash-Course Americanism: The A.E.F. University, 1919," *History Today* 44, no. 8 (August 1994): 36–43.

JEFF KESHEN

Getting It Right
the Second Time Around:
The Reintegration of Canadian
Veterans of World War II

As Canadians devised their benefit programs for the World War II veterans, it might be said that they were guided by the oft-repeated dictum, "Those who cannot remember the past are condemned to repeat it."[1] Of considerable concern to the key mandarins and government ministers, as well as to countless soldiers and civilians, were the years immediately following the Great War – years that, rather than witnessing the arrival of a new and progressive era, as promised during the conflict, saw the emergence of economic and social instability, to which poorly organized and penurious government support programs for veterans contributed. This time around, things would be different. This time, another "lost generation" would not be permitted to develop, nor would there be mutterings about winning a war overseas only to lose the peace at home. Such beliefs were generated not only by the desire to avoid repeating injustices to veterans and to minimize the possibilities of their precipitating postwar social turmoil, but also, as the conflict wore on, by growing support for Keynesian-style interventionism and government social welfare as tools to prevent the return in peacetime of depression conditions.

In November 1918, the fact that veterans were getting at least some support had represented a departure from a pattern in which welfare was distributed on an ad hoc basis and often only to the so-called deserving poor. Even though large-scale state intervention had become necessary to meet the exigencies of the Great War, Ottawa still remained philosophically attached to a *laissez-faire* approach. Consequently, successive dominion governments, no doubt with sincerity, had emphasized the state's unprecedented generosity when dealing with veterans. Meanwhile, most citizens, by focusing on what they too accepted as liberal trends with welfare, and being almost unaware of the many ways in which the Great War had adversely affected its participants, also concluded that ex-soldiers were aptly compensated.

In the newspapers, civilians encountered letters from veterans complaining about government parsimony, as well as reports of their demands for improved benefits. Offsetting such material, however, was extensive propaganda issued by the Military Hospitals Commission and the Department of Soldiers' Civil Re-establishment (DSCR) reassuring citizens that generous pensions, employment opportunities, and first-rate retraining methods were being made available. For instance, the government stressed that more than 80 per cent of physically handicapped veterans who had begun a government-sponsored retraining course eventually finished it; overlooked were the more than 34,000 rejected applicants (78.7 per cent of the total) who, according to the officials, were physically capable of returning to their old jobs. Official communiqués also ignored the substandard quality of numerous retraining centres. In early 1919 The Veteran, the publication of the Great War Veterans' Association (GWVA), complained about the "lack of equipment in the vocational schools" that "forc[ed] students to stand round watching others use whatever ... is available." This, along with the dubious qualifications of many instructors, prompted some trade unions and employers to reject the worth of certificates issued to those who finished these programs.[2]

Meanwhile, to control pension costs, Canadian pension commissioners, acting on orders from their elected masters, commonly denied compensation to veterans unless their injuries were directly related to war service. One soldier, though returning from France with multiple fractures of the arm, was denied benefits because he had broken the same bone before enlisting.[3] Moreover, a sliding pension scale relating to the extent of a soldier's injury, far from extending satisfactory assistance to every applicant, resulted in only some 5 per cent of claimants collecting the highest possible rate, while 80 per cent received less than half of the maximum benefit.[4] With practically every program there were significant discrepancies between the upbeat government claims and the experiences of ex-servicemen. Official reports about the Soldier Settlement scheme, for example, boasted that as of 31 March 1921, 25,433 veterans had harvested more than 2.6 million bushels of wheat. Not mentioned were the many loan applications rejected by the DSCR because its employees, often without ever having seen the land in question, determined that the soldiers had offered the previous owner too much for the property. This forced many veterans to begin farming on remote homesteads purchased by the government, with the result that 80 per cent of the farming veterans went broke within five years – a failure rate assisted by Ottawa's refusal to ease repayment schedules in view of the generally poor harvests in Canada during the first post-war years.[5]

In expressing their dissatisfaction over veterans programs – and perhaps drawing inspiration from the wartime rhetoric about this conflict leading to a new and better age – some veterans, including many who belonged to the GWVA, vented their anger in ways that government authorities considered threatening. Many of the recently repatriated, particularly those of working-class background, looked askance at a land plagued by rising unemployment and inflation, and with disdain at what they saw as the feeble government efforts to ease their reintegration into civilian life. Indeed, perhaps half of the ex-soldiers in Winnipeg, many of whom were unemployed, supported organized labour in the 1919 general strike, which was crushed by the dominion government as a Bolshevist conspiracy but which *The Veteran* portrayed as a justified struggle against employers who, it claimed, "defied and denied working men their common rights."[6]

Disenchantment characterized veterans throughout the 1920s. With the physical and psychological effects of battle persisting for thousands, the government's cautious approach on pensions remained a bitter bone of contention. Not until 1922 did the governing Liberals strike a royal commission under the sympathetic veteran (and, later, Minister of National Defence) J.L. Ralston. Ralston's recommendation of improved benefits eventually led to the War Veterans' Allowance Act of 1930. The act replaced the sliding-scale military pension with monthly payments of $20 to single and $40 to married veterans over the age of sixty who were impoverished. During the Great Depression, this new pension also sustained younger unemployed veterans who had suffered wartime physical or psychological injuries.[7]

With the anger of Great War veterans lingering so long and so profoundly, concern was strong throughout World War II that such a scenario should not be repeated. One poll taken early in the conflict revealed that some two-thirds of Canadians endorsed the proposition that veterans of this war should receive better treatment than their counterparts had a generation earlier.[8] This was deemed essential not only to secure greater social justice but also to prevent the possibility of social turmoil. As a 1941 editorial in *Maclean's* put it, "Our Joes ... [could] become part of an inflammable, disillusioned mass" if after "defeating Hitler," they came home to a country "offering little more" than when they enlisted.[9]

The dominion government appeared to agree with these sentiments. Indeed, the planning process for the postwar reintegration of Canadian soldiers commenced almost immediately the shooting started, and by mid-1945 most of the legislation and administrative framework for the implementation of what became known as the Veterans Charter was complete.

In November 1939 the Minister of Pensions and National Health, Ian Mackenzie (a Great War veteran and former GWVA vice-president), suggested to Prime Minister Mackenzie King that planning start on demobilization and rehabilitation to avoid many of the problems that had followed World War I. This process formally commenced on 8 December 1939 when a special committee consisting of officials from the ministries of Pensions and National Health, Public Works, National Defence, Agriculture, and Labour was created "to give full consideration to and report upon ... the problems which will arise from ... demobilization and discharge."[10] Under its auspices, several subcommittees were established, and by October 1940, to coordinate efforts, the General Advisory Committee on Demobilization and Rehabilitation was struck and put under the direction of Robert England – a twice-wounded veteran of the Great War and winner of the Military Cross, who had served as director of the Canadian Legion Educational Services. It was England's view that government must "learn some of the lessons of [its] former hard experience ... in regard to the thoroughness and sufficiency of rehabilitation plans."[11] Working with England was Walter S. Woods, the Associate Deputy Minister of Pensions and National Health, who had been wounded in the Great War and had later been president of Calgary's GWVA branch and, in 1930, the first chairman of the relatively beneficent War Veterans' Allowance Board.[12] Typical of Woods's principal assistants (first in Pensions and National Health and later in the Department of Veterans Affairs) was Colonel Dougall Carmichael, a twice-wounded Great War veteran (who dealt with pensions), and Major Edward A. Dunlop, a blinded veteran of World War II (who helped administer disability cases).[13] This was a very different set-up from that after the Great War, when civilians and, worse still, patronage appointees, had often made decisions on matters such as military pensions, a policy that had infuriated those returning from overseas.

The new policy direction for veterans took on concrete form when, on 1 October 1941, the Liberal government, acting on recommendations from the General Advisory Committee, announced its Post-Discharge Re-establishment Order. This order paved the way for more generous pensions and post-discharge cash payouts than had been offered in the last war. Its other measures included a guarantee of resuming one's previous employment or obtaining a comparable job with one's former employer following military service;[14] vocational retraining for all veterans up to a period equal to the time they had spent in uniform (not only for the injured, as after the Great War); the provision of free university education; preferences to servicemen for a wide array of civil service posts as well as with the National Employment Service for job placement; the right to claim the newly established unemployment insurance benefits for up to one year; and subsidized loans to start a business. In 1942 the government added the Veterans' Land Act, which provided $4,800 (of which $1,200 was for equipment) financed at 3.5 per cent interest to acquire a full-sized farm or a half-acre hobby operation.[15]

By 1945, several of these benefits had been improved. This development was encouraged by the expanding influence of the new senior mandarins who had been recruited into a number of government departments to help direct the war effort. Many of them were familiar with and supportive of Keynesian strategy to pump-prime the economy (for instance, through enhanced social welfare) in order to offset troughs like that anticipated during the initial peacetime reconversion period.[16] As this centralized state planning effectively mobilized resources for the war, and as it was accompanied by low unemployment and low inflation (the latter secured through controls implemented by the Wartime Prices and Trade Board), public support mounted for continuing government intervention and for better social security legislation to prevent the return of the Great Depression. Indeed, many Canadians concluded that the apparent success of wartime government planning proved the logic of the large-scale state intervention that had been advocated by Canada's left-wing party, the Co-operative Commonwealth Federation (CCF), since its inception in 1932. In 1942 the CCF precipitated the resignation of Conservative leader Arthur Meighen when its candidate, Joseph Noseworthy, defeated him in a Toronto by-election in which the issue of planning for the postwar period (rather than conscription, as Meighen hoped) emerged as central to the campaign. The next year, national public opinion polls showed 47 per cent of Canadians worrying about preparations for peacetime, and in September the Gallup poll reported that fully 29 per cent supported the CCF, compared with 28 per cent each for the Liberal and Tory parties.[17]

Although Prime Minister King fancied himself a social reformer, he was also, when it came to policy decisions, clearly a pragmatist who rarely undertook potentially controversial action unless he deemed it politically necessary. This explains why, from 1943 onwards, King's government showed an increasing willingness to accept social security measures and Keynesian planing for peacetime. That year, a *Report on Social Security for Canada* was delivered to the government by Leonard Marsh, a McGill University professor and research director with the Committee on Reconstruction, out of which came, in 1944, the family allowance program. Also in 1944, a new Department of Reconstruction was created to develop and coordinate policies to expedite the peacetime reconversion process; a new Industrial Development Bank promised to assist businesses with the costs of retooling; and a new National Housing Act pledged millions to end an accommodation crisis. Further reflecting this thrust towards state intervention was the establishment in 1944 of the Department of Veterans Affairs (DVA). Under the guidance of Ian Mackenzie, DVA's task was to coordinate policy with several government ministries and to execute various programs for those soon to be repatriated – programs which ultimately cost some $1.2 billion[18] and which many in the government thought would help achieve postwar social and economic stability by creating a spending stream and a skilled labour market, and consequently offering less chance of the repatriated becoming a force for social disorder.

Throughout the war, the Liberals responded not only to the thrust of civilian opinion but also to a growing recognition that Canada's fighting men would not accept an outcome for veterans similar to that following the Great War. Beginning in 1942, the government received surveys conducted by the Department of National Defence, as well as extracts from letters culled by military censors. These made it clear that considerable distrust existed among soldiers, particularly towards Prime Minister King; it was charged that in order to please Quebec, he had sacrificed the lives of troops in that, by not implementing conscription for overseas service, he had failed to provide adequate reinforcements. Such a government, many soldiers believed, would not hesitate to renege on its promises to reward veterans adequately.[19] When a May 1943 poll asked 900 servicemen whether they believed they would be better off after the war, only 21 per cent expressed optimism, compared with 30 per cent who foresaw hard times (the remainder declined to speculate).[20] It seemed clear, however, that disappointment was not something many servicemen would easily accept. "When you've seen your friends blown to bits around you ... it makes you think," read an excerpt from a letter sent to Canada from Italy in 1943. "It makes you think that the post-war world ... better be good!"[21] By the same token, when 159 Royal Canadian Air Force personnel were polled in mid-1943 about which political party would most likely concern itself with the welfare of veterans, 40 per cent said the CCF, compared with 37 per cent who named the Tories. The

Liberals, disliked for their failure to conscript men for overseas service, trailed with 12 per cent.[22]

During the last two years of the war, the Liberals steadily improved benefits for veterans and, equally important, thoroughly publicized their plans and accomplishments throughout the military. Between 1942 and 1944, minimum monthly payments for those who planned to retrain for a new job or attend university climbed from $44.20 to $60.00.[23] By 1944, government officials were openly talking about offering assistance to some 100,000 prospective farmers – quadruple the number supported under the previous soldier settlement scheme.[24] A life insurance program also was introduced in 1944 under which, without a medical examination and at reduced premiums, veterans could obtain policies in $500 increments up to $10,000.[25]

Operating principally through Ottawa's official propaganda agency, the Wartime Information Board (WIB), DVA distributed millions of booklets, flyers, and posters.[26] King's close adviser J.W. Pickersgill told Davidson Dunton of the WIB in April 1944, "We are going to have a pack of disillusioned and disgruntled hombres," who could become a hostile voting bloc if they did not receive "compelling information" about Ottawa's generous intentions.[27] Also pitching in was the National Film Board with upbeat productions such as *Road to Civvy Street*, while over the Canadian Broadcasting Corporation's armed forces network came programs such as *The Greg Clark Show*, which, each week, provided soldiers with reassuring information about the government benefits that awaited them when peace came.[28] From D-day onwards, military publications such as the *Maple Leaf* and *Khaki* regularly carried columns detailing the broad vistas of opportunity being established for the veterans.[29] As the conflict wound down, the Department of National Defence dispatched personnel overseas to explain DVA policies more fully and also to conduct surveys to gauge the soldiers' postwar career intentions.[30] By the June 1945 federal election, members of the armed forces still showed considerable anger towards Prime Minister King – at least, more than civilians, who gave King approximately 45 per cent support. But more important for the Liberals was the fact that they managed to avoid a political catastrophe among the approximately one million military voters by attracting, according to one survey, 35 per cent support compared with 32 per cent for the CCF and 26 per cent for the Tories.[31]

Although the Liberals had passed a political test at the ballot box, their real challenge still lay ahead, namely, to see that demobilization and rehabilitation programs were effectively applied. The first task was to get Canadian soldiers home. As with the social programs for veterans, the government had started planning early to avoid repeating the mistakes made after the Great War. The Kimnel Park riot in southern England in late 1918, which had left five dead, demonstrated the danger of permitting troops to linger with little to do after the fighting stopped. The riot also revealed the need to create a repatriation process that would at least appear fair, for besides delays caused by a shortage of shipping space in England and the limited capacity of Canada's rail network to transport troops home, anger festered among the soldiers because of plans to demobilize entire battalions rather than individuals based on their length of service. Perhaps such a system was easier to administer, and certainly it facilitated homecoming celebrations (which was a consideration of some top brass), but it precipitated charges of favouritism and, in some communities, flooded local employment markets.[32]

By 1941, even before the United States entered the war, Canada had begun to reserve extra shipping space to transport its men home when peace was achieved.[33] Two years later, as noted above, Robert England's General Advisory Committee on Demobilization and Rehabilitation decided that demobilization should be conducted under a point system that recognized the "first in, first out" principle. In February 1944 each of Canada's three military services was instructed to establish a "demobilization directorate," and in September, as Germany's defeat drew nearer, the Directorate of Reorganization and Demobilization was created to secure as much transatlantic shipping and Canadian railway space as possible, and then to apportion it among the services.[34]

The demobilization scheme called for men to receive two points for each month of service in the Western Hemisphere and three points for each month overseas. However, there were exceptions. Men possessing certain skills critically needed in the postwar economy were sent home more quickly; the military kept behind a number of administrative and service personnel to avoid a breakdown in the demobilization process; a 20 per cent bonus was added to the score of married veterans, widowers, or those with dependent children; preferential treatment was provided to prisoners-of-war; provision was made to excuse men early for family emergencies; and those who volunteered for service in the Far East were given a thirty-day leave to Canada (which became permanent after Japan's surrender). Still, the government assured soldiers that delays over a point system with no loopholes would be minimal and that within one year everyone would be back in Canada.[35]

As described in the previous chapter, the military arranged lectures on topics such as postwar veterans programs in order to keep the troops occupied while awaiting repatriation. In the same spirit, opportunities were provided for personnel to attend special non-credit classes at prestigious universities such as Oxford and Cambridge; correspondence courses were offered; and entertainment was provided on military bases and in nearby towns, where restaurants, nightclubs, and sports facilities were frequently taken over for the exclusive use of soldiers.[36] Nevertheless, a number of letters home expressed bitterness about men jumping the queue, and rumours circulated that in order to please Quebec, Prime Minister King had arranged for the early release of conscripts.[37]

Those in charge realized that it would not take much to trigger problems. This was confirmed at the beginning of July 1945, when anger over delayed repatriation (as the Americans clamoured for extra shipping space), combined with a rumour that three Canadian soldiers were under arrest in the local jail, caused the riots in Aldershot which left nearly 800 shop windows broken and several Canadians under arrest (who ultimately received sentences ranging from twenty-eight days to seven years).[38] With increased vigour, Canada's government lobbied for extra space on vessels heading to North America. Some success was achieved, but more significant was Japan's surrender that August, which freed up American transports. By autumn 1945, Canadian soldiers were being repatriated at a rate of almost 1,000 per day, and by March 1946 fewer than 25,000 troops remained overseas. Thus, further major disturbances were prevented,[39] and the men were delivered into the hands of a government re-establishment program that had been some five years in the making.[40]

Many soldiers believed that they had improved themselves while in uniform; they considered themselves more self-reliant and better able to confront the challenges of life.[41] However, based on experiences following the Great War, military officials and those with DVA realized that many men were unprepared to make the transition to civvy street. As a result, efforts were initiated to minimize the shock by providing "a form of 'basic training' … for civil life."[42]

Soldiers were warned – through WIB publications, lectures prepared for officers, and even a four-day course instituted by the chaplaincy for those awaiting repatriation – that they might find many disturbing changes in their communities and their loved ones.[43] Similarly, those at home recognized that the returning veterans might have changed. Civilian magazines, radio programs, and films recalled how difficult many reunions had been after the last conflict and thus reminded Canadians that those they were preparing to greet might not be the same people they remembered or might not correspond to the deceptively cheery letters they had received from overseas.[44]

Helping to bridge the rifts between soldiers and civilians were the more than 1,200 citizen repatriation committees that had been established in Canada between 1943 and the end of the war. These groups helped ex-servicemen find work or housing, offered direction on how to best utilize government programs, and sometimes provided emergency financial aid.[45] Yet despite the warnings and efforts made on both sides of the Atlantic, veterans often found their transition to civilian life very difficult. For instance, accompanying soaring postwar marriage and birth rates (as people made up for lost time) was a sharp rise in divorce, from 2,068 cases in 1939 to 7,683 by 1946.[46] After years of separation, spouses often found that they were strangers. Many servicemen returning from years of overseas duty and searching for an archetypal tranquil hearth could not deal with women who had grown more independent, having run the home on their own, organized countless volunteer activities, or, in many cases, joined the workforce, often in sectors formerly dominated by men.[47] On the other side of the ledger, no doubt shocking to countless families, was the crudeness of many of the returnees; as a result of the bonding process between soldiers or as a reflection of battlefield conditions, they now drank, gambled, and swore profusely. Then there was the physical disfigurement suffered by some servicemen, which could prove too much for their wives or girlfriends; and the Canadian Medical Association reported that many of those who had succumbed to battle fatigue nurtured a persistent anger that was commonly destructive to marriages.[48] Yet despite these and countless other personal difficulties, the end of World War II, unlike that period following the Great War, did not usher in an era of general bitterness and protest among veterans. This time around, the pains associated with reintegration were not compounded by anger over stingy government support programs and a sense of being unable to get on with one's life.

After proceeding through a (sometimes admittedly too cursory) medical examination on disembarkation in Canada, all those who had served overseas received free train transport to the destination of their choice where, within a month, their formal discharge occurred at the nearest military depot. By VE-day, approximately 250,000 personnel had passed through this system, during which time many of the kinks had been worked out.[49] In October 1944, DVA had established a three-week course for its counsellors so that they could effectively guide veterans through the labyrinth of options open to them.[50] During the critical first year after the war, these DVA counsellors successfully dealt with up to 40,000 veterans a month. Such a record, stressed Ian Mackenzie, was also achieved through the dedication of DVA employees, more than half of whom were veterans. It was common, Mackenzie reported, for DVA offices to stay open beyond normal business hours so eager were department employees to help their former comrades.[51]

During the formal discharge process, personnel had their paper-work completed for a rehabilitation grant (one month's pay), gratuity payments (set at $7.50 per month while in the Western Hemisphere and $15 per month while overseas), and any other special dispensation (such as a $100 cash bonus for winners of gallantry medals).[52] There was also a $100 voucher for clothing.[53] On average, cash payouts were $700, and for veterans who took a re-establishment credit in lieu of job retraining, free education, or the opportunity to start a farm, this figure climbed to approximately $1,200.[54] At a time when the average industrial wage was well under $40 a week, this was a substantial sum. On the basis of this compensation, a veteran could purchase a house, for under the 1944 National Housing Act, one could acquire a prop-erty costing up to $4,000 (quite common at the time) for a 10 per cent down payment (with slightly higher down payment requirements for more expensive homes). With the new Canada Mortgage and Housing Corporation offering mortgages at 5 per cent interest and a twenty-five-year term, monthly payments on a $4,000 home amounted to just over $22. By 1947, as housing stock became available, veterans had committed themselves to the purchase of some $200 million in accom-modation.[55]

Helped by DVA counsellors, veterans assessed their skills and ambi-tions in relation to the available government programs and to the demands of the employment market that were identified by the De-partment of Labour. Most chose to forgo retraining options, nor did they choose to start a farm or business with government assistance; instead, they collected their re-establishment credit and found a job. However, if they were dissatisfied in the resumption of their prewar employment (which was guaranteed to them by law) or if they had not held a job when they enlisted, they received priority placement status with the National Employment Service. Even though some 650,000 veterans entered the job market during the first year after the war, more than 85 per cent of those who used the services offered by the government were successfully placed within two months of their dis-charge, and approximately 95 per cent were placed within fifteen months. Naturally, there were veterans who had difficulty finding suitable employment. In order to avoid repeating the experience of 1919, when many veterans had quickly exhausted their gratuities and became destitute, DVA instructed ex-servicemen to take advantage of new out-of-work benefits which, for up to a year, paid $50 a month to those who were single and up to $128 (or about 75 per cent of the average industrial wage) to a married man with six children.[56]

As promised, the Veterans Charter permitted anyone who had served in the forces to retrain. Ian Mackenzie called the approach an "investment" in Canada's future. "Like ripples from a stone which cover the whole pond," he reasoned, the dissemination of valuable skills would create a more dynamic economy and lead to further job creation.[57] In cooperation with the provinces and municipalities (whose costs Ottawa mostly reimbursed), both DVA and the Department of Labour, in a program called Canadian Vocational Training, prepared veterans for more than one hundred occupations at existing schools (which were kept open during evenings and weekends) and at newly established technical institutes (which acquired equipment from Ottawa's War Assets Board) or by paying employers to train men on the job. By 31 March 1951, 80,110 veterans had passed through this program.[58] Most courses lasted less than a year, during which time the trainee was paid a living allowance which, depending on marital status and number of dependants (to a maximum of six), ranged from $60 to $154 per month. Moreover, this could be supplemented not only by spousal employment but by trainees taking part-time work so long as their pay did not average, on an annual basis, more than a stipulated limit.[59]

Soon, DVA officials were proudly touting the results. By late 1946, the unemployment rate among those who had graduated from a Canadian Vocational Training program was about half that of veterans in general.[60] And in assessing the program after six years, DVA was able to trace the positions of all but 4,741 participants, whom it counted, along with the deceased and unemployed, as comprising "unsatisfactory results," a category encompassing only 10.2 per cent of those who entered vocational training. The rest, 73,141 veterans, were employed in the position for which they had trained (59.4 per cent), were self-employed within their line of training (7.3 per cent), were employed in a different line of work but still indicating satisfaction (15 per cent), were taking more training (1.3 per cent), were still awaiting placement because they had recently finished further courses (2.8 per cent), had rejoined the military (1.8 per cent), or, in the case of some female veterans, had settled into domestic life (2.2 per cent).[61]

Perhaps the most prestigious DVA program (in that it was often trumpeted by officials as proving the government's bold break from the limited initiatives after the Great War) was the provision of free university education for veterans, along with a living allowance identical to that paid under the Canadian Vocational Training scheme. Whereas before World War II a university education had been regarded as something only for the economic and intellectual elite (who in 1939 comprised around 3 per cent of the population), the implementation of this DVA program helped usher in an era in which the ivory tower opened its doors to the masses.[62]

In the fall of 1942, twenty-four veterans enrolled in university; by 15 February 1947 almost 35,000 were in attendance.[63] Said one veteran of this profound change, "A father would never say, 'I want my son to go to university and become a lawyer.' He would say, 'I wonder if I can convince the foreman to take him on in the roundhouse and apprentice as a mechanic' ... My country provided this son of a roundhouse mechanic with a chance [to become a lawyer]."[64] To accommodate this new demand from veterans for advanced education, Canada's small university system expanded tremendously after the war. By 1951, DVA's university program had cost $134,549,468,[65] an expense justified not only as a benefit owed veterans for their sacrifices but also, like the vocational training scheme, as a wise investment in the future. "The country," read a departmental press communiqué, "needs to train, encourage, and retain every scholar she can find, for they constitute the principal group who will keep Canada up with a rapidly changing world."[66]

In 1946, seventeen out of twenty Rhodes Scholarships awarded to Canadians went to veterans, and in universities across the country, twice as many veterans as non-veterans passed with honours.[67] One McGill professor spoke of the attentiveness, keenness, and inquisitive nature of veterans – of "how 20 in a class of 200 could set tone."[68] Significant as well was the fact that veterans often entered university with valuable knowledge gained in uniform; an engineering student might have built bridges with the 5th Canadian Armoured Division overseas; and military life, particularly under intense situations, had likely furnished veterans majoring in philosophy or psychology with insights into human nature beyond those contained in the textbooks.

For veterans who were determined not to work for someone else, the government once again delivered on its pledge to provide adequate assistance. By the end of 1946, 16,489 veterans had received, in addition to their re-establishment credits, special low-interest loans to commence, expand, or improve business enterprises. To encourage banks to invest in ex-soldiers, in 1946 the government passed the Veterans' Business and Professional Loans Act, which covered financial institutions for 25 per cent of losses up to $1 million and 15 per cent thereafter up to $25 million resulting from bad debts owed by veterans.[69]

Meanwhile, the Veterans' Land Act (VLA), between its introduction in 1942 and the end of the war, became more attractive as maximum funding was increased from $4,800 to $6,000 and as recipients were permitted to direct all funds towards the purchase of land (instead of $1,200 being set aside for the acquisition of equipment).[70] Loans remained at a 3.5 per cent interest rate and were amortized over twenty years. Moreover, after making payments for ten years, veterans received clear title to their property. Also helpful was the willingness of many DVA employees to carry out on-site inspections of proposed VLA purchases seven days a week to ensure that veterans obtained fair market value. As well, applicants were carefully screened to ensure that they possessed adequate knowledge of farming; for those who did not, opportunities were offered at government expense to train for a life in agriculture.[71]

Certainly, some applicants under the VLA complained about interfering bureaucrats; but, overall, statistics pointed to a successful program. By October 1946, of the approximately 75,000 veterans who had applied to start a farm, 67 per cent had been approved, the average assistance being $5,126.[72] By November 1947, expenditures by Ottawa under the VLA exceeded $400 million, a figure almost four times as much as the total spent by the Soldier Settlement Board after the Great War.[73] And while good crop prices during the late 1940s and early 1950s helped produce these positive results, so did the generous provisions, careful administration, and extensive training opportunities provided by Ottawa – factors that went a long way in explaining why, by 1955, the value of improvements made to VLA farms exceeded $1 billion.[74]

Every program introduced by DVA was, as far as possible, made available to those who came home reduced in physical capacity. Although compromises often became necessary for disabled veterans (such as opting for a hobby farm rather than a major agricultural enterprise), still, notable improvements were evident compared with the post–Great War period with respect to pension levels, the quality of medical care, and the placement of candidates – and, consequently, to the general degree of satisfaction among Canada's pensionable and disabled World War II veterans.

By no means were pensions lucrative. By 1945, they were set, up to the junior officer level, at a yearly maximum of $900 for a single man, with an extra $300 provided for those who were married, as well as $180 for the first child, $144 for the second, and $120 for each subsequent child up to six.[75] Although veterans criticized these rates, their dissatisfaction was not reinforced by a general aura of bitterness over government repatriation programs. Furthermore, their hostility was eased by the empathetic approach of most pension commissioners, a majority of whom were veterans, and by the quality and success of the DVA medical rehabilitation and job placement services.

The process of applying for pensions started as soon as the wounded arrived in Canada. Hospital ships were met in port by DVA personnel, and usually within a month of their discharge, the injured not only had their basic gratuity and other cash rewards settled, but also their pension. Some applicants were disappointed, for instance, those provided with a low percentage of the maximum allowable reward for what officials deemed relatively minor injuries and also, over time, those who were denied compensation because their ailments became evident too long after the war to be accepted by pension commissioners as war related. Still, the overall record was commendable. By the end of 1945, a favourable response to pension claims had been rendered in 86.3 per cent of cases, the average award being $511.61 per annum, far more generous than the pensions of Great War veterans.[76] Such beneficence received official ministerial sanction. "Wherever a case is in doubt, lean backwards in favour of the man," read a memo in late 1944 from Ian Mackenzie to the DVA pension commissioners. "Canada ... raised $15,000,000,000 for war purposes. The money likewise can be found for peace."[77] Reflecting this spirit, DVA established a Chief Pensions Advocate's office, which offered advice to veterans making claims or appealing their initial rewards. Furthermore, if a veteran returned to work, he still received his pension as long as the injury remained, the justification being that his country still owed him for the sacrifices rendered as well as for his continuing pain and his loss of mobility and enjoyment of life.[78]

At the outset of World War II there had been eight hospitals in Canada, containing 1,501 beds, which were still devoted to the care of Great War veterans. By 1946, DVA was running more than thirty hospitals or wings of existing institutions, with room for 17,000 patients; seven occupational health centres; four facilities to treat paraplegics; and three tuberculosis sanatoria.[79] "An example of the replacement of obsolete facilities," wrote Walter Woods, was the transfer of veterans, including many from the Great War, out of Toronto's Christie Street hospital to the new Sunnybrook facility that opened in 1946 with 1,500 beds at a cost of $15 million.[80] By March 1946, some $55 million had been spent by DVA on hospital construction and the purchase of equipment.[81] Moreover, DVA worked with several university medical faculties to make its hospitals teaching and research institutions as well as treatment centres. For example, cooperation with McGill University meant that veterans in Montreal enjoyed access to Canada's first ultracentrifuge for blood analysis.[82]

When it came to providing access to medical treatment, one might suggest that DVA helped establish the model for what became Canada's 1957 Hospital Insurance Act (whereby Ottawa and the provinces administered insurance for essential hospital services) and Medicare, introduced in 1968 (whereby citizens paid into provincially run insurance plans, also partly funded by Ottawa, to cover services offered by general practitioners and most medical specialists). For any pensionable injury, veterans had the right to use DVA medical facilities, civilian hospitals, or their own doctor for free treatment in perpetuity.[83] Also, free care for all ailments was provided to all veterans during the first year after their military discharge. After that year, veterans earning less than $1,200 per annum continued to receive free hospital care for any ailment; for those earning more than $1,200, DVA facilities provided discounted rates, an important benefit for many veterans when one recalls that approximately one-third of Canadians had no private medical insurance.[84]

While undergoing medical treatment and rehabilitation, veterans received $44.20 per month if single and up to $112.40 per month if married with six children.[85] Starting in January 1945, DVA created a Casualty Rehabilitation Section to coordinate the efforts of government departments that were involved in retraining and reintegrating injured veterans into civilian society. Key to this operation was the District Casualty Rehabilitation Officer (DCRO), who helped the disabled veteran weigh his assets and liabilities in relation to the available training options and the current state of the job market.[86] Also of great assistance was DVA's Publicity Department. For example, soon after the war ended, statistics gathered by the U.S. Federal Security Commission and widely publicized by DVA revealed that, based on a survey of 100 large industries hiring the disabled, 98 employers felt that the accident rate among such veterans was average or below average, while 90 employers considered the productivity from these ex-servicemen to be similar or superior to the norm.[87] Finally, in the case of employers who remained reluctant to hire disabled veterans, DVA often agreed to underwrite a portion of the veterans' salaries until they performed up to average speed, or to cover any extra premiums charged to employers by provincial workmen's compensation boards.[88]

DVA's efforts with handicapped veterans proved fairly successful and no doubt lessened the trauma of men coping with physical disabilities. By mid-1946, of Canada's World War II amputees (who also enjoyed access to improved prosthesis technology),[89] 951 were employed in the private sector, 418 had jobs with the government (including 217 with DVA), and 94 had managed to qualify for a VLA loan; only 325 were unemployed.[90] And as of 30 September 1950, among Canada's 5,093 veterans with a disability rated between 1 and 24 per cent for pension purposes, 89.48 per cent were employed; of the 9,912 with an injury falling within the 25 to 49 per cent bracket, 86.99 per cent had a job; of the 6,312 rated between a 50 and 74 per cent disability, 83.65 per cent were employed; and of the 4,501 classified at a 75 to 100 per cent handicap, 62.5 per cent had managed to rejoin the civilian workforce.[91]

Over the years, grievances continued to emanate from some quarters about the shortcomings of the Veterans Charter. Throughout the 1950s, the Canadian Legion intensified its lobbying to have pensions keep pace with inflation,[92] and merchant seamen fight to this day for complete access to veterans' benefits. But taken as a whole, protests from those who survived the fight against fascism and Japanese militarism paled in comparison to the anger that lingered among so many Great War veterans. This time, the widespread conviction that things had to be different provided for unprecedented action and a generally high level of satisfaction. And even though the careful planning and generous benefits failed to prevent considerable heartache, it is not too much to claim that many marriages were saved and families solidified by DVA through the cash compensation that put many veterans back on their feet. The government's programs offered the more than one million men and women who fought and won Canada's war the prospect of tremendous social mobility.

This pattern derived not only from the desire to do right by veterans compared with their treatment after the 1914–18 war (an attitude particularly strong among many key DVA administrators who had fought in that conflict) and not only from a fear of the hostile political bloc and destabilizing social force that veterans might become if government parsimony once again prevailed; it was also the result of a pervasive desire among Canadians that the end of this conflict should not result in a return to a status quo that had helped create a "lost generation." As World War II progressed, more and more Canadians demanded the continuation in peacetime of a planned economy and the expansion of government social welfare. They displayed a readiness to support the CCF if the King government failed to act. The government had to act. More to the point, it wanted to act. The concrete initiatives developed after 1943 by the mandarins and policy advisers who had been recruited to help run the wartime economy and the process of peacetime reconversion dovetailed Keynesian economic theory with programs for veterans. For besides bolstering the move towards social security, DVA benefits created a spending stream that could help counteract the anticipated postwar slump and, over the long run, promote a more dynamic economy by enhancing the skills of the labour force.

In terms of its extensive planning and generosity, the Veterans Charter can be viewed as part of a campaign by Canadians to search for security and progress out of World War II, which most people believed had been promised but then denied after 11 November 1918. No one wanted to return to the days of the Winnipeg general strike and the Great Depression, and the Veterans Charter was one clear indication of the government's determination that the future would be different from the past. Such attitudes and the programs they generated have contributed to the still-prevailing image of the 1939–45 conflict as a "good war." Not only did World War II result in the defeat of an unquestioned evil, but it helped usher in what most people today consider to be a more humane approach to social and economic affairs. In this development, the Veterans Charter played a major and often pioneering role.

NOTES

1 This quotation comes from the American philosopher and poet George Santayana. See Donald Fraser, comp., *Dictionary of Quotations* (London: Collins 1988), 220.

2 Desmond Morton and Glenn Wright, *Winning the Second Battle: Canadian Veterans and the Return to Civilian Life, 1915–1930* (Toronto: University of Toronto Press 1987), 94, 134; *The Veteran*, February 1919, 20.

3 House of Commons, *Journals* 59, no. 2 (1922): 115.

4 Morton and Wright, *Winning the Second Battle*, 153, 220; Desmond Morton, " 'Noblest and Best': Retraining Canada's War Disabled, 1915–1923," *Journal of Canadian Studies* 16, nos. 3, 4 (Winter 1981): 75–85.

5 Morton and Wright, *Winning the Second Battle*, 148, 204.

6 *The Veteran*, July 1919, 16; David Jay Bercuson, *Fools and Wise Men: The Rise and Fall of the One Big Union* (Toronto: McGraw-Hill Ryerson 1978), 91; D.C. Masters, *The Winnipeg General Strike* (Toronto: University of Toronto Press 1950), 61, 142–4.

7 Robert England, *Discharged: A Commentary on Civil Re-establishment of Veterans in Canada* (Toronto: Macmillan Company of Canada 1943), 29–30.

8 J.L. Granatstein and Peter Neary, eds., *The Good Fight: Canada and the Second World War* (Toronto: Copp Clark 1995), 446.

9 *Maclean's*, 1 September 1941, 9.

10 National Archives of Canada (hereafter NA), Robert England Papers, MG 30 C181, vol. 2, file 1940–4, address by Ian Mackenzie, 6 December 1940.

11 Ibid., vol. 3, file 21, clipping from *Winnipeg Free Press*, 26 March 1943.

12 Walter S. Woods, *Rehabilitation (A Combined Operation)* (Ottawa: Queen's Printer 1953), vi.

13 NA, records of the Department of Veterans Affairs (hereafter DVA), RG 38, vol. 372, news release no. 58, n.d.; NA, Records of Boards, Offices and Commissions: Wartime Information Board (hereafter WIB), RG 36, series 31, vol. 8, file 21–2, news release no. 44, n.d.

14 The exception to this rule applied to veterans who had taken a civilian job first vacated by another serviceman.

15 NA, Ian Mackenzie Papers, MG 27 III B5, vol. 9, file 3–89, undated speech by Mackenzie; NA, records of the Department of National Defence (hereafter DND), RG 24, vol. 12278, file 27–1, Bulletin on Vocational Training, 1944; NA, WIB, vol. 14, file 8–14–C, pt 2, Fieldon to Sutherland, 13 January 1944.

16 See J.L. Granatstein, *The Ottawa Men* (Toronto: Oxford University Press 1982), chap. 6, and Doug Owram, *The Government Generation: Canadian Intellectuals and the State, 1900–1945* (Toronto: University of Toronto Press 1986).

17 Meighen's defeat prompted the Tories at a convention later that year at Port Hope, Ontario, to endorse planks for more state intervention and social welfare. Moreover, in keeping with the spirit of their ideological shift and the former political affiliation of their new leader, John Bracken, the Tories changed their name to the Progressive Conservative Party. See J.L. Granatstein, *Canada's War: The Politics of the Mackenzie King Government* (Toronto: Oxford University Press 1975), chap. 7; and NA, WIB, vol. 16, file 9–2–2, Reconstruction Information, February 1944.

18 Desmond Morton, *1945: When Canada Won the War* (Ottawa: Canadian Historical Association 1995), 6.

19 NA, WIB, vol. 14, file 8–20–2, Brittain to Grierson, 7 October 1943.

20 Directorate of History (hereafter D HIST), DND, 113.3 R4003 V1 (D1), Survey, May 1943.

21 NA, Young Men's Christian Association (hereafter YMCA) Papers, MG 28 I 95, vol. 84, file 1, Report of the Citizenship Committee, 1944.

22 *Canadian Forum*, August 1944, 100. It was not until November 1944 that King implemented conscription for overseas service. See Granatstein, *Canada's War*, chap. 9.

23 NA, DVA, vol. 272, news release no. 54, 28 November 1944.

24 Ibid., news release no. 7, n.d.

25 NA, Mackenzie Papers, vol. 57, file 527–14(b), speech by Mackenzie, 31 December 1945.

26 NA, DND, vol. 12278, file 27–1, various materials.

27 NA, WIB, vol. 8, file 3, Pickersgill to Dunton, 17 April 1944.

28 NA, YMCA Papers, vol. 272, file 8, *Rehabilitation: Learn About It*, 1945.

29 For example, in late 1944, in a series called "Back to Civvies," *Khaki* wrote: "Those ... [policies introduced] at the end of the last war were in no way as far-reaching as those presently in force. Then, the only people who could go to college were students whose courses had been interrupted by the war ... Even at that they had to pay! The government only gave them a repayable loan of $500." See vol. 2, no. 8, 2.

30 D HIST, 113.3 R4003 (D1), "Rehabilitation: A Survey of Opinions," October 1945.

31 *Canadian Forum*, July 1945, 80.

32 See Desmond Morton, "'Kicking and Complaining': Demobilization Riots in the Canadian Expeditionary Force, 1918–1919," *Canadian Historical Review* 61, no. 3 (September 1980): 334–60.

33 NA, DND, vol. 12705, file 272/7, undated memorandum.

34 C.P. Stacey, *Six Years of War: The Canadian Army in Canada, Britain and the Pacific* (Ottawa: Queen's Printer 1955), 432. For more detail on demobilization planning, see Dean F. Oliver, "Canadian Military Demobilization in World War II," in Granatstein and Neary, *The Good Fight*, 367–86.

35 NA, DND, vol. 10508, file 215, A21.009 (D68), *After Victory in Europe*, May 1945; NA, DVA, vol. 272, news release no. 7, n.d.

36 NA, DND, vol. 12279, file 27–2, memo from General H.D.G. Crerar, July 1945.

37 So unyielding did the *Maple Leaf* become in criticizing those in charge of the repatriation process for deviating from the "first in, first out" principle and for supposedly playing favourites that the General Officer Commanding Canadian troops in the Netherlands, Lieutenant-General G.G. Simonds, fired its editor (Oliver, "Canadian Military Demobilization," 379); see 52 above.

38 NA, DND, vol. 12705, file 272/7, Report, July 1945.

39 However, in early 1946, some members of Canada's occupying force in Germany staged a brief sit-down strike, an event that promptly ended when they were threatened with a loss of their gratuity pay. See Christopher Vokes, *Vokes: My Story* (Toronto: Gallery Books 1985), 199.

40 Stacey, *Six Years of War*, 431–2.

41 For example, one veteran recalled that prior to going overseas, he "never knew the proper way to dress, to do anything," but when returning home after five years of service at age twenty-four, he believed himself "a man capable of practically anything" (author's interview with Cliff Humphrey, Edmonton, 22 October 1992).

42 NA, WIB, vol. 17, file 9–6–2–1, "Postwar Planning Information," 7 July 1945.

43 D HIST, 113.3 R4003 (D1), "Trends in Army Thinking," December 1944; NA, DND, vol. 15631, Report of Senior Chaplain (RC), 1st Division, 9 July 1945; Glenbow Institute, Calgary, MU 6222, file 3, *Report Centre*, 11 January 1945.

44 For example, *Chatelaine*, Canada's most widely read women's magazine, wrote that "no man who has faced death and danger ... will return from the war [not] wounded in soul, if not body." The key to eventual happiness, it said, was for wives to "cultivate patience" and to recognize that even in the best of times "probably no marriage ... ever came up to a woman's expectations" (May 1944, 9).

45 NA, Mackenzie Papers, vol. 67, file 527–148, "Budget for Citizen Committees," 27 April 1945.

46 Canada's 1946 marriage rate, compared with the 1941–45 average, rose from 9.7 to 10.9 per 1,000 people, while the birth rate per 1,000 women climbed from 24.0 in 1945 to 28.9 by 1948 (*Canada Yearbook*, 1948–49, 189–91; ibid., 1951, 166).

47 While most women displayed a willingness to step aside from such jobs for veterans and resume "traditional" domestic roles, in some cases resentment was evident. Said one veteran with disdain, "My wife got a war job and became too independent ... After she started earning good money on her own ... she didn't like doing kitchen work anymore." See Diane G. Forestell, "The Victorian Legacy: Historical Perspectives on the Canadian Women's Army Corps" (PH D thesis, York University, 1986), 171.

48 NA, DND, vol. 2093, file 54–27–7–391, "Psychoneurotics Discharged from the Canadian Army," reprinted from the *Canadian Medical Association Journal* 52 (1945).

49 In 1944 the average waiting time between a soldier's discharge and the receipt of his first gratuity cheque was three months. By 1945 this was two months, and by 1946 one month (NA, DVA, vol. 272, news release no. 255, 21 November 1946).

50 Ibid., news release no. 179, n.d. As Woods claimed in the military jargon popular at the time, to effectively implement the numerous programs for veterans required nothing less than a "combined operation." For details, see Peter Neary and Shaun Brown, "The Veterans Charter and Canadian Women Veterans of World War II," in Granatstein and Neary, *The Good Fight*, 392–3.

51 NA, DVA, vol. 272, news release no. 200, n.d.

52 In 1943, not only did the Canadian government take over from Great Britain the payment of rewards to Canada's Victoria Cross winners, but it also added to the list of honours for which cash compensation was provided the Distinguished Conduct Medal, Distinguished Service Order, Conspicuous Gallantry Medal, Distinguished Flying Cross, Military Cross, and Military Medal (NA, DVA, vol. 272, news release no. 152, n.d.).

53 Men often had to wait several months to obtain new clothing because of continuing shortages of cloth, and some ex-soldiers claimed that $100 was not enough to purchase an adequate supply of decent-quality apparel in a rather inflated clothing market. However, such protests failed to gain much steam, considering that Canada's clothing allowance was exceeded in terms of generosity only by South Africa's (*Khaki* 4, no. 24, 10; Woods, *Rehabilitation*, 57).

54 NA, DVA, vol. 372, file "D.V.A. New-Rel," news release entitled "Payments to Veterans," n.d.

55 NA, records of the Department of Labour (hereafter DL), RG 27, vol. 2349, file 22–5–14, "Memorandum on Progress of Veteran Rehabilitation," 1947.

56 NA, DVA, vol. 272, news release no. 162A, n.d.; Woods, *Rehabilitation*, 114.

57 NA, DVA, vol. 272, news release no. 254, n.d.; NA, Mackenzie Papers, vol. 3, file 120, address by Mackenzie, 3 May 1947.

58 Woods, *Rehabilitation*, 107.

59 NA, Mackenzie Papers, vol. 58, file 527–41(3), *Vocational Training on Civvy Street*.

60 This was even true, DVA was happy to report, in parts of the country where unemployment was traditionally high. A press communiqué issued in early 1947 noted that in New Brunswick the jobless rate of those who completed a government retraining course was 5.98 per cent compared with 11.37 per cent among those with partial or no such preparation (NA, DVA, vol. 272, news release no. 261, 16 January 1947).

61 Woods, *Rehabilitation*, 109.

62 See J. Donald Wilson et al., eds., *Canadian Education: A History* (Scarborough: Prentice-Hall 1970), 417, and Paul Axelrod, *Scholars and Dollars: Politics, Economics and the Universities of Ontario, 1945–1980* (Toronto: University of Toronto Press 1982).

63 NA, DVA, vol. 364, file "General Clippings," unidentified and undated newspaper article. See also 121 below.

64 Barry Broadfoot, *The Veterans' Years: Coming Home from the War* (Vancouver/ Toronto: Douglas & McIntyre 1985), 184.

65 See 140 below.

66 Woods, *Rehabilitation*, 107; NA, DVA, vol. 372, file "D.V.A. New-Rel," undated memo entitled "University Training."

67 NA, DVA, vol. 272, *The Carleton*, 20 November 1946.

68 Ibid., unidentified and undated article.

69 Ibid., news release no. 259, 3 January 1947; ibid., news release no. 260, 15 January 1947.

70 NA, Mackenzie Papers, vol. 60, file 527–61(4), Second Report of the Veterans' Land Act for the Fiscal Year Ending 31 March 1944.

71 For those not interested in taking training, it was always easier to qualify to start a 1–2½ acre hobby farm (ibid.).

72 NA, DVA, vol. 272, news release no. 252, n.d.; *Canada Yearbook*, 1947, 1147.

73 NA, DVA, vol. 364, file "General Clippings," *Winnipeg Tribune*, 13 November 1947.

74 Ibid., *Red Deer Advocate*, 17 November 1954.

75 NA, DVA, vol. 183, file 31–8–44, memo to the Governor in Council, 17 March 1944.

76 NA, Mackenzie Papers, vol. 11, file 3–125, undated speech by Mackenzie.

77 NA, DVA, vol. 272, news release no. 52, 15 November 1944.

78 Also helping to build a measure of satisfaction among pensioners was the fact that the government showed increasing flexibility in some areas. Just weeks after VJ-day, it raised the pension rate for total deafness from 50 to 80 per cent of the maximum allowable reward. Furthermore, DVA

began adding together instead of averaging rewards for multiple injuries, a change that resulted in more cases of 100 per cent pension coverage (ibid., news release no. 153, 22 November 1945).

79 NA, Mackenzie Papers, vol. 11, file 3–125, speech by Mackenzie, 11 December 1945.

80 Woods, *Rehabilitation*, 324. New DVA hospitals also appeared in Montreal, Ste Foy, Victoria, Halifax, and Saint John, while new wings were added to the Ottawa Civic Hospital and to University Hospital in Edmonton. See NA, DVA, vol. 364, file "General Clippings," *Province* (Vancouver), 17 May 1954, and *Colonist* (Victoria), 19 June 1955.

81 NA, DVA, vol. 272, news release no. 193, 23 March 1946.

82 Ibid., news release no. 139, n.d.; NA, DVA, vol. 364, file "General Clippings," *Daily News* (St John's), 18 April 1955.

83 However, unless one lived in an outlying area and did not have easy access to a DVA facility, the government imposed strict guidelines on the costs it would accept from private practitioners (NA, DVA, vol. 272, news releases nos. 205, n.d., and 215, n.d.).

84 NA, DVA, vol. 364, file "General Clippings," *Blyth Standard*, 20 October 1954; Roger Graham, *Old Man Ontario: Leslie M. Frost* (Toronto: University of Toronto Press 1990), 234.

85 NA, DND, vol. 12278, file 26–37, Department of Pensions and National Health memo, 1 January 1944.

86 NA, DVA, vol. 272, news release no. 179, n.d.

87 NA, England Papers, vol. 2, file 1940–44, "Employment of Canada's Disabled," pt 1.

88 NA, WIB, vol. 17, file 9–6–2–1, "Postwar Planning Information," 7 July 1945.

89 Although men could choose cosmetic arms with spring-loaded fingers, more significant advances were made with hooks manipulated by a tug from the opposite shoulder. Progress was also evident with artificial legs. Soon after the war, the Toronto *Globe and Mail* reported on the adoption of a German invention that helped wearers develop "a natural gait" by allowing them to "receive a sensation through slight and varying pressure on the abdominal muscles when the leg moves" (NA, DVA, vol. 362, file 1946–62, *Globe and Mail*, 15 November 1945).

90 NA, DVA, vol. 272, news release no. 228, n.d.

91 Woods, *Rehabilitation*, 370.

92 In 1955, after federal parliamentarians provided themselves with a hefty pay raise, the Canadian Legion demanded a 67 per cent increase in military pensions. They received 20 per cent. See NA, DVA, vol. 364, file "General Clippings," *Press* (Timmins), 25 March 1955; *Examiner* (Prince Rupert), 11 March 1955.

The Veterans Charter: The Compensation Principle and the Principle of Recognition for Service

"The Veterans Charter" was the term devised by the Government of Canada to characterize the compendium of legislation designed for the veterans of World War II. While aimed at different social and economic effects, Charter legislation embodied two allied but distinct principles: "the compensation principle" and "the principle of recognition for service." This chapter focuses on the second principle, particularly as it affected the entitlement and disentitlement to benefits in the past and as it continues to influence the Department of Veterans Affairs (DVA) today and into the future.

The legislation contained in the Veterans Charter can be grouped into the following categories:

1 legislation whose principal aim was veteran reintegration into civil life: the Veterans Rehabilitation Act (1945), the War Service Grants Act, 1944 (especially the component dealing with re-establishment credits), the Veterans' Business and Professional Loans Act (1946), the Veterans' Land Act, 1942, the Reinstatement in Civil Employment Acts (1942 and 1946), and the provisions for "veterans' preference" in the Civil Service Act;
2 legislation providing for "compensation": the Pension Act and the War Veterans' Allowance Act;
3 legislation providing for life insurance: the Veterans Insurance Act (1944);
4 legislation providing for physical rehabilitation: the Treatment Regulations of 1946;

5 legislation relating to contingencies where rehabilitation had proved impossible: the War Veterans' Allowance Act, 1946, and the Civilian War Pensions and Allowances Act (1946);

6 legislation whose sole purpose was to establish level of entitlement with respect to other Charter legislation: the Allied Veterans Benefits Act (1946), the Special Operators War Service Benefits Act (1946), the Women's Royal Naval Services and the South African Military Nursing Service (Benefits) Act (1946), the Supervisors War Service Benefits Act (1946), the Fire Fighters War Service Benefits Act (1946), and the various entitlement provisions of the Civilian War Pensions and Allowances Act (1946).

Ian A. Mackenzie, the Minister of Veterans Affairs from 1944 to 1948, declared that the Veterans Charter was created "in the same high spirit of service which inspired Canadians to fulfil their obligation in the crucible of war."[1] Even so, the Veterans Charter should not be considered as part of the moral legacy of World War II. Whatever good the Charter may have done, and it was obviously substantial, it was not morally necessary. Instead, the Charter and the focus of the department charged with its administration represented the approach which the Canadian government chose for the postwar treatment of veterans.

If chronological order can be taken to reveal government priority, "civil re-establishment" was uppermost in the minds of Ottawa's planners. Other than certain necessary amendments to the Pension Act, which amounted to an extension of its application to World War II, the first measure put in place on behalf of veterans was the "Post-Discharge Re-establishment Order," PC 7633, of 1 October 1941. This order, its subsequent amendments, and its repeal and reissue as PC 5210, finally matured into the Veterans Rehabilitation Act (1945). This act was directed at the education of the veteran. Other re-establishment legislation such as the Veterans' Land Act stood for settlement in primary industry, while the Veterans' Business and Professional Loans Act was geared towards establishment in the professions, business, or trade and (with the re-establishment credit provisions of the War Service Grants Act) was directed more towards those whose career requirements seemed assured. The Reinstatement in Civil Employment Acts and the "veterans preference" with respect to civil service jobs were also aimed at re-establishment; however, they conveyed special employment rights rather than benefit entitlements as such.

Benefit entitlement legislation, though anticipating a diversity of occupational paths, attempted to ensure that there would be no duplication of expenditures. In other words, each act was deemed to embody distinct but equal opportunities for those who took advantage of its provisions. A veteran could have a change of mind, of course. One might, for example, decide that one wished to return to school rather than being a farmer; however, to do so one would have to agree to repay the Veterans Land Administration before accepting a rehabilitation grant.

One of the key governing principles was that veterans should enjoy these equal benefits only to the degree entitled by their service. This created many difficult questions, as Frederick Lyon Barrow detailed in his 1964 study.[2] Non-duplication meant that although veterans could have as broad a choice in the matter of re-establishment as their abilities indicated, completion of one program of re-establishment, whether satisfactory or not, precluded any other attempt. This principle failed to take into account that it was impossible to equalize satisfaction or even the monetary value of the benefit. In practice, there were some who could gain substantially from a small business subsidy, whereas others required additional funds (for example, the extension of tuition or a $2,320 "conditional" or long settlement grant under the Veterans' Land Act) in order to secure the investment. It was thus also a question of whether, given two individuals with equal service but different talents, equity should be defined in terms of absolute dollars invested in their re-establishment in civil life or in satisfactorily establishing them in a career. There were other anomalous difficulties, as Barrow also noted:

Where service was in the Western Hemisphere only, there was an inconsistency in World War II legislation that should not be repeated. Eligibility under the Veterans' Land Act required at least twelve months' service (unless pensions were being paid for disability); under the Veterans Rehabilitation Act, there was no such minimum requirement. As a result, a non-pensioner with three or four months' service in Canada could be started on a university course ... and it can be argued that he had not earned this type of rehabilitation.[3]

Barrow was a lawyer and a former pension advocate, and the secretary of DVA. Accordingly, he was very familiar with the terms that determined veterans' equity. The quoted passage contains the essential criteria: length of service, injury or non-injury, and service overseas or in Canada. These criteria, in turn, stood for different levels of recognition of the degree to which service was valued. The evidence from the postwar era, for example, that to be injured and in receipt of a pension should equal the entitlement warranted by having served overseas appears in both the Veterans' Land Act and the War Veterans' Allowance Act. In the Pension Act and the pension provisions of the Civilian War Pensions and Allowances Act, on the other hand, earned entitlement was replaced by what was called a "matter of right." In other words, a disability pension was always additional to whatever one's service entitled one to receive. Moreover, the fact of pension meant, automatically, full recognition with respect to the Veterans' Land Act and the War Veterans' Allowance Act, and carried special weight in terms of subscription to a contract of insurance under the Veterans Insurance Act. Indeed, if the pensionable injury prevented the exercise of the re-establishment benefit, the legislation, which was normally time-limited from the date of discharge, was held open.

Understanding veterans' benefits as levels of recognition helps to explain many incongruities that would not have existed if the programs had focused solely on general re-establishment or had been less complicated and perhaps less subjective in their criteria for entitlement. One area of concern for many veterans who volunteered for general service concerned the NRMAs (departmental parlance for National Resources Mobilization Act troops, who were conscripted). General Service veterans in 1944 likely would have believed strongly that NRMAs should be ineligible for benefits under the War Service Grants Act. Such an attitude, however, overlooked the fact that after the National Resources Mobilization Act was amended in 1942, NRMAs were required to serve wherever ordered.

In contrast to the attitude towards NRMAs, there is no evidence that there was ever an active effort to exclude members of any of the civilian groups from benefits. There was, however, a hierarchy of esteem, which corresponded in many ways to the criteria determining levels of recognition in the armed forces. In these terms, the Merchant Navy fared relatively well, while the Voluntary Aid Detachment, a group of medical volunteers who enrolled to serve anywhere but who remained in Canada, "failed to establish the claim for veterans' benefits."[4] In strict terms of the need for re-establishment, there may have been an equal need to re-educate or resettle such individuals after the war, but need was secondary to perception.

Except for those who were injured, it may safely be inferred from the legislation that the highest value in terms of earned entitlement went to those whose service required them to engage the enemy. Without ever denigrating the contribution of the veterans who had never been ordered overseas, Parliament deemed their earned entitlement to be less (as, for example, in the re-establishment provisions of the War Service Grants Act) or as taking longer to earn (as in the Veterans' Land Act). Given that those who served in Canada were no freer to attend to their personal development and were always subject to transfer or overseas posting, the only explanation for the difference in treatment must be that they were never ordered into battle.

Level of recognition was less important in the insurance act, which was a benefits-only plan in the sense that operating costs were excluded from premium assessment. However, in the case of treatment, recognition was very important for veterans receiving class 1 treatment (full hospitalization and full pension entitlement during the period of treatment). Again, if the sole criterion had been physical rehabilitation and fitting the veteran for employment, the level of recognition would not have been a factor; the only aim would have been to make the veteran healthy.

Finally, level of recognition was absolutely critical in the War Veterans' Allowance Act and in the allowance provisions of the Civilian War Pensions and Allowances Act. These allowances, as originally conceived, were for those who had been unable to make a successful transition to civil re-establishment because of difficulties arising from engagement with (or the apprehension of engagement with) the enemy. These allowances were created amid the certainty that the experience of war might create a condition called pre-ageing or might cause mental disability or insufficiency. This "burnt-out pension" provided for early retirement at age sixty (or fifty-five for women); it applied as well to any pensioned individual who, because of pensionable disability, was unemployable, essentially as a top-up to pension benefits. It also provided for early retirement for any person who, though not pensioned, appeared to be unemployable, provided that person had served in a theatre of war. (As chair of the War Veterans' Allowance Board, Walter S. Woods, advised a parliamentary committee in 1941 that this last provision, contained in a 1938 amendment to the War Veterans' Allowance Act, had extended entitlement to some 8,324 Great War veterans.[5] What proportion of that number had actually experienced pre-ageing as a result of the stresses of war and how many had succumbed to substance abuse, Alzheimer's disease, post-traumatic stress syndrome, or other problems remains a subject for further research.)

The range of legislation in the Veterans Charter suggests the operation of very broad assumptions concerning type and area of service and the meaning of physical injury. Nevertheless, the system went very far towards reconciling such disparate aims as compensation for injury, veteran satisfaction with reintegration into civilian life, the needs of family and community, and the needs of the national economy in ways that all could accept as fair.

There is no evidence of any representations being made to government on behalf of industrial workers, who might have considered that they too had experienced unusual hazards occasioned by war or who might have found that their skills were not suited to peacetime. Those who made representations to the General Advisory Committee on Demobilization and Rehabilitation (GACDR), which was formed in 1940, did so in the context of their military or near-military contribution in the war. Nevertheless, questions of general re-establishment were apparently raised within the advisory committee itself. Robert England, secretary of the GACDR, wrote of his conflict with those who envisioned a program of rehabilitation that would serve more than veterans. In his book *Discharged: A Commentary on Civil Re-establishment of Veterans in Canada* (1943), which, though not an official publication, was partly a report on the work of the GACDR, England wrote – both for the assurance of those who might have had misgivings over the prospect of a total system of social assistance and against those who had caused those misgivings – of his success in keeping the advisory committee on track. In the winter of 1941–42, a group with an eye on broader social reform had obviously frustrated him in his task of ensuring a program of benefits for the young men and women returning from the war. Rather than attempting to bring this faction into line, England succeeded in having them redirected to the Committee on Post-War Reconstruction, which was detached from the system of benefits being created for veterans. Implicitly, England had successfully kept veterans' benefits separate from questions of postwar reconstruction.[6]

England's is good evidence that the GACDR did not view returning soldiers with any kind of calculating detachment as "economic units." That detached view would have held that the Canadian state, with the task of re-establishing a civil economy but with limited resources, would have determined to limit its "seed money" to the 10 per cent of the population who could clearly and exclusively be viewed as a category (and for whom there was some plausible basis for extending such benefits). Viewed in this way, Canadian veterans would no longer have appeared as a wronged class, as implied in the normal legal sense applied to "compensation."

Discharged is filled with England's anxiety about instituting any form of social benefit. His book consistently argues against a permanent national program of welfare and against the continuance of veterans' benefits in the long term. To the extent that the book is an insight into the mind of the GACDR, there is no sense that it looked to an omniscient government to achieve a permanently entrenched social and economic reconstruction. Instead, *Discharged* saw Canada on the brink of a practical social experiment, though one with potentially long-term consequences. England never promised that proposed solutions and improvements, even if based on expert opinion and testimony, would be the best, fairest, most economical, or most rational. Instead, he saw that immediate action was necessary to meet the veteran discontent he anticipated based on his Great War experience.

While the CBC's *Johnny Home Show* instructed the country that the returning veterans could expect to be rewarded for their service, veteran expectation may not have been the sole source of the concept of level of recognition in the Veterans Charter. Considering the prominence of serving and former officers on the GACDR,[7] the importance of recognizing the level of service was probably linked to the level of esteem and gratitude which the officer ranks felt towards those who had borne the brunt of the battle. Whether gratitude had a role is perhaps less important than the evidence in the legislation that the "debt owed" would be calculated in accordance with a system that rewarded volunteer service, overseas service, service in a theatre of war, and injury or death.

In the Department of Veterans Affairs Act (1944), especially the section on regulation-making authority, it could be argued that Parliament anticipated that the DVA might operate in some respects as a province – notably, through its building, maintaining, and staffing a complex network of hospitals and other medical and rehabilitation institutions. In other areas, however, DVA chose to fulfil its mandate through endowment, buying rather than creating services and ensuring, for example, that universities were prepared to receive the influx of veteran beneficiaries of the Veterans Rehabilitation Act. There is some discernment implied here, for if DVA had been a runaway bureaucracy, there would have been no holding back from the impulse to build its own schools. However, the department was (and continues to be) remarkably self-limiting, choosing to build relationships with the Red Cross and various other benevolent institutions and volunteer agencies wherever possible.

In the years bridging the immediate postwar period and the commencement of a movement into special care for an ageing clientele, DVA oversaw the devolution of hospitals to the provinces; it relinquished provisions for medical treatment to provincial health care; it aligned veterans' benefits with the Old Age Security program, the guaranteed income supplement, and the Canada Pension Plan; and it began to redefine client relations in small but significant ways. For example, welfare officers became "area counsellors." Thus, while the department is in many ways tied to the past in preserving and accommodating sentiments that have been largely forgotten elsewhere, there is good evidence that it has responsibly kept to the principle of reintegrating the veteran in civil life. These changes have gone forward with the guarantee that any additional entitlements to veterans will also be preserved.

More than one million men and women were affected by the Veterans Charter. Of these, a substantial number remain attached to, or have come back to, the department. Exact numbers are difficult to determine, for monthly statistics focus on program use rather than total client numbers. There is accelerating mortality and, in some areas, accelerating intake; there is an extension of full benefit payments to veteran survivors for a period following the death of the veteran and continuation of special survivor benefits thereafter. Pension payments may also be made to former members of the regular forces. In aggregate, it appears that roughly a quarter of a million individuals, veterans, the dependants of veterans, or retired members of the regular forces receive some share of the $1.8 billion annually that is paid with respect to military service. Deducting some 20,000 regular forces pensioners and 73,000 or so survivors, we are left with about 157,000 of the surviving half million veterans, most from World War II, who continue to maintain a relationship with DVA. The fact that one-third of surviving veterans remain clients holds great potential interest. Arguments could be made about the fostering of dependency or about the enduring cost of war; or, since veteran clients appear at first glance to defy ordinary mortality by dying at a rate that is less than that projected for non-clients,[8] this might even be a redeeming argument for social welfare. However, these questions remain largely unexamined.

The military ethos, which it was suggested might account for the concept of recognition of service, is less prominent now in the DVA. Nevertheless, this cultural link with the armed forces, the segment in society that has perhaps most often taken care of its own, can be seen in the pride evident within the department that veteran social maintenance legislation continues to ensure benefits that exceed benefits afforded to non-veteran seniors.

The "compensation principle," which in the immediate postwar years embodied and promoted a public sentiment favouring benefits conferred as an earned entitlement, still survives. Initially, this principle seemed necessary, since economic and social objectives were never sufficient in themselves to warrant the payment of veterans' benefits. These objectives existed, to be sure, but they were wrapped in the sentiment of recognition and level of sacrifice. Now, when the veteran population has declined both absolutely and relative to the entire population and, because of age and retirement, has ceased to be much of a factor in terms of economic and social objectives, this sentiment remains. The public, especially the veteran public, needs to be assured that the government continues to acknowledge the debt owed.

As the number of clients decreases, the department in some areas has begun to buy services, developing a special advocacy relationship with the provinces and others and representing veteran interests in such matters as ensuring nationally equitable health, disability pension, and nursing-home care. Benefit issues remain; indeed, in the explosion of needs that comes as people age, it is very difficult to keep pace. From World War II to the 1990s, the essential issue has always been the need for recognition.

In veterans legislation, where initial entitlement, though not necessarily the payment of a benefit, is earned through service, entitlement in law becomes a testimony to the value of one's service. Better pensions and improvements in elder care, the speed of decisions, and the delivery of services are the concrete objectives of the department, as well as of the veterans' lobby. Without denying an authentic concern for the well-being of veterans, efforts in this direction may also proceed from the need to ensure that the grateful nation remains grateful.

The Veterans Charter is no longer a standard reference at DVA. Employees of the department consider their relationship to clients in terms of an act or subset of acts and regulations relating to special needs or entitlements. In fact, some of the employees who even know of the Veterans Charter imagine that it was a list of general principles. Nevertheless, the unifying principle of recognition for service continues to guide the department's work, both in the determination of benefit entitlement and in the realm of commemoration. Recognition also remains fundamental to veterans' organizations, which continue to pursue benefit reform.

The best characterization of where veterans find themselves a half-century after the end of the war can be found in Robert England's book, *Twenty Million War Veterans*. He wrote in 1950 of the veterans of World War I, but there is no significant difference in the application of his words to the generation of World War II:

Almost inevitably a veterans organization turns back to the past. Its link is memory ... a startling necrolatry and a new emphasis on anonymity – the burial and the cult of the *Unknown Soldier,* the keeping of the eternal flame, the Cenotaph, the Last Post, the two minute silence (11th hour, 11th day, 11th month), the blood red poppy symbol of sleep and stilling of pain. The shadow world of the veterans' loneliness and disorientation [is] peopled with those "who grow not old as we who are left grow old." The esoteric symbols [do] not suggest Christian triumph so much as poignant, irreparable human loss, a dignified and disconsolate grief for the fallen, and some irrational and vague intimations of an immortality to outweigh the sacrifice. So accustomed have we become to this ... ritual of absent comrades that we hardly realize how abnormal and inexplicable has been its growth.[9]

It is important for veterans to continue to believe in the justice of the cause for which they risked their lives, a cause in which sacrifice created a better world. Whatever their motives for joining up, these veterans fought for our freedom from fascism in the people's war for democracy, for the liberation of Europe, and for all the good we continue to commemorate. For them, it must be so. They want to believe that their sacrifice has endowed a lasting moral legacy. As they move towards the end of their lives, this recognition becomes more and more crucial. Entitlement is recognition, and recognition is key.

The department does much in the way of recognition. In financing pilgrimages, conducting ceremonies, pursuing the creation of medals and other decorations, maintaining the books of remembrance, and, in 1994 and 1995, facilitating the many activities of the Canada Remembers program, the department has done much more than similar ministries in other countries. Unfortunately, for all that, DVA will never be able to ease the veterans' anxiety over what the future will make of their history.

NOTES

1 Ian Mackenzie, "Foreword," *The Veterans Charter: Acts of the Canadian Parliament to Assist Canadian Veterans* (Ottawa: King's Printer 1946), 7.

2 Frederick Lyon Barrow, *A Post-War Era: A Study of the Veterans Legislation of Canada, 1950–1963* (Ottawa: Queen's Printer 1964), 3–86.

3 Ibid., 92–3.

4 Walter S. Woods, *Rehabilitation (A Combined Operation)* (Ottawa: Queen's Printer 1953), 244.

5 Robert England, *Discharged: A Commentary on Civil Re-establishment of Veterans in Canada* (Toronto: Macmillan Company of Canada 1943), 106.

6 Ibid., 88–9.

7 Ibid., 73–81.

8 Veteran mortality is calculated based on mortality projections contemporary to the 1971 decennial census; accordingly, the application of these rather pessimistic projections to the total estimated veteran population and contrasted with the average age of those in receipt of benefits can give the appearance that veteran clients enjoy longer life.

9 Robert England, *Twenty Million World War Veterans* (Toronto and New York: Oxford University Press 1950), 56.

MICHAEL D. STEVENSON

National Selective Service and Employment and Seniority Rights for Veterans, 1943–1946

On 21 June 1945, the Ford Motor Company placed a full-page advertisement in the *Windsor Star.* This outlined proposals to grant seniority, based on the time they had spent in the armed forces, to veterans who had not previously worked for the company. By definition, this policy would lead to the displacement of many union men who had joined the workforce between 1939 and 1945, but Ford officials defended the fairness of their plan:

Today and everyday, more and more veterans of this war are coming home. They want – and are entitled to – more than just three cheers and a brass band to welcome them home. They want to know where they stand on jobs now, and job security for the future. Every Canadian who realizes what our boys did in this war wants to do everything that is fair to help them when they take up the tasks of peace. Seniority rules are designed to provide the employee with an equitable and just measure of security in his job. Can anyone possibly have a greater claim to this seniority than the veteran – the man who through these war years not only gave up his job and the comforts of an easy life at home, but in hundreds of thousands of instances risked his very life? The Company's seniority proposal for veterans is absolutely fair. Right now is not one minute too soon to assure the veteran that we want to do the fair, square thing for him – knowing and appreciating his tough, hard years of sacrifice.[1]

Ford's scheme was vociferously opposed by the United Auto Workers (UAW), the union that represented the company's workers. In the tense months leading up to the long and bitter strike that the UAW launched against Ford in September 1945, union officials complained that the issue of integrating veterans into the workforce was being used by the company as a labour-splitting device.[2]

In truth, the Ford-UAW dispute was a microcosm of a larger debate that occurred between 1943 and 1946 concerning the issues of seniority and hiring preferences for Canadian veterans. Three main groups were involved in this debate. The Canadian Legion and government officials from the Department of Pensions and National Health (DPNH) and the Department of Veterans Affairs (DVA) waged a vigorous campaign to secure hiring preferences for discharged military personnel and special seniority rights for veterans who did not return to their old jobs or who entered the workforce for the first time upon their discharge. By contrast, leaders of the Canadian Congress of Labour (CCL) and the Trades and Labor Congress of Canada (TLC) steadfastly opposed any government proposal to give veterans an advantage by overriding seniority provisions in existing collective bargaining agreements. Caught in the middle were the higher-ups of the National Selective Service (NSS) – the agency created within the Department of Labour in 1942 to regulate and mobilize the labour force during World War II. In the event, NSS failed to find a satisfactory compromise between the positions of the unions and the veterans' organizations. This failure illustrates the practical limitations of government interference in the labour market in Canada at the time.

For most Canadian servicemen and servicewomen, the transition to civilian life proceeded with few difficulties; generous government assistance guaranteed a smooth passage back to civilian life. By 31 January 1947, more than 135,000 discharged men and women had received unemployment benefits, more than 112,000 persons had completed or were enrolled in vocational training programs, more than 640,000 men and women had taken advantage of a re-establishment credit scheme, and more than 50,000 veterans had received benefits under the Veterans' Land Act.[3] In their search for work, many veterans had benefited from the provisions of the Reinstatement in Civil Employment Act, 1942 (RCEA). Under the terms of the RCEA, discharged veterans were legally entitled to return to the jobs they had held prior to their enlistment in the armed forces. Reinstated employees were also able to count their time in the military when calculating seniority.

Nevertheless, there were thousands of Canadian veterans for whom the return to civilian life meant either unemployment or uncertain work. Fewer than 200,000 men and women qualified for protection under the RCEA to return to civilian jobs,[4] despite the fact that more than one million veterans had been discharged from the armed forces by the end of 1946. Veterans without reinstatement privileges who obtained work after they were discharged found themselves at the bottom of the seniority ladder, behind men and women who had entered the workforce during the war. In addition, many veterans experienced grave difficulties securing employment. In April 1946, for example, more than 70,000 male veterans were unemployed. More than 25,000 of these men had been employed at some time since discharge but could not find permanent jobs.[5] Moreover, some of these men had lost their jobs in unionized workplaces because of their low seniority status. This situation, which tended to pit workers who had benefited from the wartime employment boom against those who had gone into uniform, had an explosive potential. What follows is an account of the efforts to secure hiring and seniority privileges for veterans not covered by RCEA legislation.

DPNH and NSS officials first debated the issues involved in seniority rights and hiring preferences for veterans in 1943. This debate was fed by the findings of two subcommittees of the General Advisory Committee on Demobilization and Rehabilitation (GACDR), the advisory body formed by the government in 1940.[6] The subcommittees in question were those dealing with demobilization and employment, the first dominated by DPNH officials and the second by representatives of NSS. After months of difficult and at times acrimonious discussion, these two groups agreed on four proposals to be put forward to the GACDR with respect to the employment of veterans: (1) that due weight be given to a veteran's record of service training in establishing qualifications for civilian employment; (2) that the existing preference for veterans in government employment be expanded and extended into the postwar period; (3) that employment preference for veterans be administered through local employment committees in order to create a "favourable atmosphere" and allow employers "to accord willingly a preference for qualified ex-servicemen"; and (4) that the Employment Service of Canada grant priority in employment referral to qualified veteran-applicants.[7]

At the insistence of the subcommittee on demobilization, a fifth proposal – clause (e) – was also put forward. This called on the dominion government and the provinces to enact legislation after wartime controls on employment had expired that would require employers to list all employment vacancies with the Employment Service of Canada (after 1945, the National Employment Service). This would allow the Employment Service to be the final arbiter in the selection of candidates to fill these positions and would thereby empower the agency to give hiring priority to veterans. Clause (e) was included in a list of resolutions adopted by the GACDR in June 1943, but some NSS officials immediately opposed its implementation. NSS Chief Enforcement Officer T.R. Walsh expressed "grave doubts" about the legality of extending restrictive controls into the postwar period once the application of the War Measures Act had been rescinded. There was also little chance that provincial authorities would allow Ottawa to keep control of labour regulation after the wartime emergency had passed.[8] Other NSS leaders called for the implementation of a quota hiring system for veterans to allow the government to escape a potentially thorny problem; this expedient would represent a "forthright and effective" policy and would remove the necessity of endorsing the "quite impractical" GACDR recommendations.[9]

The most interesting response to clause (e) came from the National Employment Committee (NEC) of the Unemployment Insurance Commission. I.R. Lewis of the T. Eaton Company, one of Canada's largest retail outlets, insisted that veterans could be looked after without resorting to the "drastic compulsion" envisioned in clause (e).[10] Representatives of the Canadian Retail Federation echoed Lewis's assertion and took the position that clause (e) would be "a little more mandatory in its implication" than retail employers could support.[11] Other NEC representatives argued that NSS could not administer such a sweeping requirement. United Farmers Co-operative Company President R.J. Scott wanted a quick end to "cumbersome and quite unsatisfactory" employment controls in the postwar period, arguing that the entire "listless and annoying" NSS operation should be "dispensed with as soon after the war as possible."[12] Union representatives on the NEC likewise refused to endorse clause (e). Their objection, which would be heard over and over again in the next few years, was that to favour veterans in this fashion would undermine collective bargaining agreements.[13]

The developing controversy over clause (e) manifested itself in jurisdictional wrangling between NSS and DPNH officials. Specifically, the DPNH refused to endorse an NSS proposal for giving employment interviews at military discharge depots.[14] In January 1944, Walter S. Woods, while still Associate Deputy Minister of Pensions and National Health, told NSS Director Arthur MacNamara that all discharge functions fell under DPNH jurisdiction and that the only NSS "excuse" for interviewing veterans should be to identify any men who needed to be directed to essential positions in war industry.[15] This friction eased, however, with the formation of the Inter-departmental Co-ordinating Committee on Rehabilitation (ICCR) in February 1944. Thereafter, attempts were made to forge a consensus between the two agencies.[16]

In April 1944, after the ICCR and the GACDR had agreed to drop the contentious clause (e) of the previous year, MacNamara lobbied the War Cabinet to legislate seniority rights and hiring preferences for veterans who had served overseas. This request was referred to the War Manpower Committee of cabinet in May 1944 and a heated discussion followed. While many officials on the committee supported MacNamara's proposal in principle, some prominent cabinet ministers were aghast at the idea of extending more government control to the private sector. C.D. Howe, minister of the powerful Department of Munitions and Supply, informed Labour Minister Humphrey Mitchell that MacNamara's scheme would have the effect of forcing civilians to wait until all overseas veterans had been placed in jobs before they could apply for employment. This prospect would touch off an immediate rush from war industries to civilian industries to beat the stream of discharges from the armed forces once the war was over. Howe also noted that the proposal assumed that the direction of labour by NSS would continue into the postwar period. This should be resisted, he said, for it "would certainly be a shock to industry to be told at this time that a free market for labour cannot exist in the future."[17]

On 21 June 1944 the War Manpower Committee endorsed a priority system for overseas veterans, but this required only that the Employment Service send a qualified veteran to a job ahead of a civilian worker. Cabinet approved this recommendation on 27 June 1944, with Humphrey Mitchell noting that the directive, which was not publicized and had no statutory basis, imposed no legal obligation on the employer to accept any veteran into his employ.[18] Thereafter, on 5 August 1944, MacNamara established the Committee on Priority and Seniority Rights of Veterans (CPSRV) under the chairmanship of M.M. Maclean.[19] Its job was to continue to study the issues of employment preference and seniority rights for Canadian veterans.

Given the weak response of cabinet, the focus of the debate shifted to union organizations and the Legion. The Legion's position called for legislative hiring preferences and seniority rights that would apply to all veterans, regardless of their status under the RCEA. At the June 1944 Legion convention, which was held in Vancouver, a report was received from the rehabilitation committee demanding that the "intolerable situation" with respect to job protection for veterans be addressed by the dominion government. Claiming that a "fundamental principle" of justice for veterans was at stake, the rehabilitation committee called for action to give every veteran priority in hiring and full recognition on seniority rolls of time spent in the armed forces.[20] In the autumn of 1944, the Legion reiterated its position in a document entitled "October Memorandum on the Employment of Veterans in Unionized Industry." This document made the case for government intervention to ensure that veterans would not find themselves "legally debarred from employment in the industry or occupation of their choice" as a result of the enormous sacrifices they had made through military service. Specifically, the October Memorandum, which remained the Legion's definitive statement on the issues in question for the duration of the war, called for three measures: (1) that a veteran who had served overseas, regardless of RCEA standing, should have preference in employment over any civilian employee hired after his enlistment; (2) that after completing a probationary period of employment, a veteran should have seniority protection beginning from the date of his enlistment; and (3) that these privileges should be extended into the postwar period to a date that would be decided by negotiation.[21]

This Legion's demand for legislated hiring and seniority rights for veterans was condemned by union leaders across the country. C.H. Millard, National Director of the United Steelworkers of America, regarded the claims being made on behalf of veterans as a "subtle and sinister effort" to smash union power throughout Canada.[22] Nevertheless, the leaders of the CCL, the national labour body to which the steelworkers belonged, attempted to adopt a conciliatory approach to the many issues arising from the reintegration of veterans into Canadian society. The basic position of the CCL was that all levels of government should cooperate to avoid having "idle money, idle machines, or idle men" in the country.[23] At the 1944 annual convention of the CCL, which was held in Quebec City from 16 to 20 October 1944, Legion General Secretary J.C.G. Herwig exhorted delegates to adopt a flexible policy towards the hiring of veterans. Claiming that "no solution [could] be found which [did] not involve sacrifice on someone's part," Herwig called on Canadian unions to accept that the time spent by an individual in the armed forces should count towards seniority in employment.[24] Inevitably, this would mean that some civilians who had entered industry for the first time during the war would find themselves moved lower on the seniority ladder, but that would only be fair. According to Herwig, wartime hiring should be seen as having been temporary, and veterans possessing the necessary qualifications should be given preference in employment in the postwar economy. While the CCL delegates passed a non-binding motion calling for cooperation with the Legion, the executive council of the organization passed a resolution in December 1944 which left the negotiation of the relationship between war service and seniority to local unions. This resolution also affirmed the view that only through a public policy of full employment could "a competitive struggle between veterans and displaced civilians for an inadequate number of jobs" be avoided.[25]

While Legion and CCL officials were sparring over principle through the summer and autumn of 1944, companies across Canada were grappling with individual cases. In Toronto, for example, twenty-three veterans were laid off in August 1944 by Research Enterprises Limited (REL).[26] ICCR officials immediately investigated the layoff and reported that a union seniority clause had operated against the veterans. A few days later, Walter S. Woods, who was now deputy minister of the newly created Department of Veterans Affairs, told his minister, Ian Mackenzie, that REL had only a few employees who had returned to it under the terms of the RCEA. The position of the management of the company, moreover, was that the seniority provisions of the collective agreement took priority over any obligation to ex-service personnel.[27] In this regard, REL President W.E. Phillips informed DVA that the union had refused to endorse any revision of the seniority arrangements.[28] At a meeting of the ICCR in October 1944, the officials present resigned themselves to accepting the sanctity of union seniority clauses, but they agreed that any company operating without a union should be forced to retain a veteran in preference to a nonveteran.[29]

In January 1945 the CCL and TLC representatives on the CPSRV called for a national convention of all parties involved in the dispute over the employment of veterans. Preliminary meetings were subsequently held at the local or industry level, but many government officials saw the labour proposal as a sham, the more so when a meeting in March 1945 with eighteen unions involved in the railway trades failed to make any headway.[30] In April 1945, Pat Conroy, secretary-treasurer of the CCL, told CPSRV chairman, M.M. Maclean, that his organization still wished to participate in a national meeting of government, business, and labour groups, but Maclean did not pursue this offer in view of the failure of the CCL to persuade union locals to relax seniority rules.[31] In April also, the CCL submitted its annual memorandum to the dominion government. In keeping with previous policy, this promised cooperation on the seniority and preference issues, but insisted that Ottawa still "bore the full brunt of the responsibility for ensuring post-war full employment."[32] A Legion-sponsored meeting held at the Seigniory Club in Montebello, Quebec, and attended by representatives of business and government (but not labour) also failed to achieve any breakthrough.[33]

In May 1945, MacNamara told Woods that he had "seriously considered" seeking a legislated solution to the issues that had arisen, but that he had been deterred from doing so because of the litigation that would inevitably ensue. MacNamara ventured – and this typified the outlook of NSS – that it would be better to seek to cooperate with the unions than to coerce them. Coercive legislation would be unfortunate, he said, for it would "raise a barrier between veterans and other civilian workers."[34] Other government officials, however, continued to favour a quota system in relation to the hiring of veterans. One of these, Lieutenant A.M. Shoults, Assistant Director of Demobilization (Navy), claimed that only 35 per cent of male veterans qualified for civilian reinstatement in employment under the RCEA and that further government intervention was therefore imperative.[35]

Needless to say, this prospect was anathema to the unions. Only when there was no collective bargaining agreement, A.R. Mosher reiterated, could a quota for veterans be contemplated.[36] In the same spirit, Percy Bengough, the president of the TLC, pointed out that his organization was honouring the provisions of the RCEA to the letter and that many union men had been deemed more important to the industrial war effort than many of those who had enlisted. In a direct reference to Herwig and other Legion officials, Bengough charged that the wartime record of union men was being misrepresented by "rabid individuals in their efforts to enhance the waning prestige of their own organizations." These individuals, he asserted, should lobby the government for full employment rather than trying "to put the boy who has served overseas in his father's job."[37] For their part, the CCL leaders continued to insist that "hard and fast statements of policy regarding seniority" should be avoided until a national conference of all the parties involved had met to debate the issue.[38] Of course, the calling of such a conference had already been categorically rejected by NSS.

In April 1945 the Royal Commission on Veterans' Qualifications was appointed. This commission was chaired by Colonel Wilfrid Bovey, and its purpose was to study the complex issue of veteran reintegration into Canadian society. One of the members of the commission was J.C.G. Herwig of the Legion. CCL officials encouraged local unions to submit policy statements to the commission, and Bovey and his colleagues became increasingly aware of union opposition to any attempt to legislate seniority protection and employment preference for veterans. The submission of the Winnipeg Trades and Labour Council, for example, ridiculed the fact that "vast quantities of printer's ink" were being used up by the government to inform Canadians of the needs of veterans without there being any plan of action to give them work. Deriding the attempts to "saddle industry and the trade unions with a responsibility that rightly belongs to the government," union leaders in Winnipeg called on Ottawa to abandon its "negative policy" and start acting constructively. There should be a retirement age of sixty years, a pension plan guaranteeing a minimum of fifty dollars per month, and a thirty-hour work week with no reduction in wages.[39]

Although the Bovey Commission did not initially address the issue of veteran seniority and employment preference rights, the simmering labour dispute between Ford and the UAW in Windsor soon brought these matters forcefully to its attention. Bovey assessed the UAW position as being "very satisfactory," but Ford officials, supported by J.C.G. Herwig, offered evidence "concerning union action prejudicial to ex-servicemen."[40] Not surprisingly, UAW officials refused to consider their position prejudicial to any veteran. Both sides in the dispute had developed their positions before the onset of the strike in September 1945. On 28–29 October 1944, the UAW District Council had adopted a "Model Clause on Veterans' Seniority."[41] This was divided into two main sections. Section 1 stipulated that any UAW member who had left the employment of Ford subsequent to September 1939 to perform military service would accumulate seniority based on that service and would be rehired if he applied for reinstatement within ninety days of his discharge. Also, any man disabled within ninety days of discharge could apply within ninety days of the end of his disability. A man who had been a probationary employee at the time of his enlistment would be allowed to count his time in the armed forces first towards the completion of his probationary period and then towards the accumulation of seniority. All this the UAW was legally obligated to do under the RCEA. The second section of the model contract, however, went beyond the RCEA and covered veterans who had not been in the employ of the company at the time of their enlistment. A man in this category would receive full seniority credit for his time in the armed forces if he satisfied four requirements: (1) that he applied for and obtained employment within twelve months of discharge; (2) that he had not exercised his reinstatement privilege in any other plant or with any other company; (3) that he would not be employed for the purpose of displacing another worker; and (4) that he would submit his discharge papers to the company after his probationary period, whereupon company and union officials would certify his claim for seniority. Although the model clause was generous, it specifically sought to safeguard the seniority status of established UAW members.

The Ford proposal was very different. Entitled "Ford Motor Company Proposals for Seniority for Returning Veterans," it identified four categories of veterans and specified the arrangements that would apply to each.[42] The fourth clause was the most contentious; it covered men who had no experience with the company whatsoever. Anyone in this category who had volunteered or been conscripted and sent overseas and had resided in Essex County for a year before enlistment would be entitled to full seniority for military service if hired within ninety days of discharge. The effect of this provision would be to allow Ford to hire large numbers of local veterans to replace union men who had less seniority. Not surprisingly, the introduction of such a scheme was bitterly opposed by the UAW. As George Burt, the regional director of the UAW, wrote, Ford was "not interested in the veterans but only interested in destroying the union."[43]

In August 1945 the CPSRV, which had been dormant for four months after being merged with the ICCR, was reconvened to consider recent developments relating to the employment of veterans. Three items of business were discussed: (1) the Ford and UAW proposals; (2) Shoults's quota suggestion; and (3) CCL attempts to get locals to adopt a conciliatory approach to the seniority issue. The committee members concluded that there was little hope of a negotiated settlement before the massive influx of discharged men commenced in late 1945. Accordingly, they called for legislative action to resolve the difficulties that had arisen. They felt that the "urgency of the problem" was such that "no useful purpose" would be served by trying to obtain the cooperation of unions and employers "on the matter of priority or equality of employment of returned men with no seniority in employment."[44] This matter could be dealt with only "by a defined government policy," something that had been missing to date. For his part, Lieutenant Shoults continued to press for a quota system to be legislated. Companies that felt they were being unfairly treated would have the right to appeal. A quota system would not be perfect, but it would be "fairer to the serviceman than obliging him to skulk around war plants."[45]

Thus goaded into action, Arthur MacNamara drafted an order-in-council for consideration by the Cabinet Committee on Demobilization and Re-establishment (CCDR), which was formed in October 1945 to screen proposals dealing with veterans' issues before they were sent to cabinet.[46] The draft order, entitled the Overseas Veterans' Employment Order, duly received CCDR approval in November. Its remarkably limited scope revealed MacNamara's scepticism about the chances of any comprehensive and coercive measure being endorsed by cabinet. The draft order provided that a range of employers would be prohibited from hiring any person who was not an overseas veteran unless the vacancy had been filed with the National Employment Service and it had been shown that no such veteran was available to fill the post. This preference would last until 1 January 1947, and part-time, seasonal, agricultural, and most rural industries would be exempt from its provisions.[47] In effect, MacNamara's proposal resurrected clause (e) of 1943 but reduced its scope and specified a termination date for its application. Even this diluted proposal, however, did not pass scrutiny by cabinet, which decided to postpone action on the proposed order indefinitely.[48]

The employment issues arising out of the reintegration of veterans were also considered within the dominion government in this period by the Advisory Committee on Rehabilitation and Re-establishment (ACRR), which was formed in June 1945. Acting through the Department of Labour, the ACCR arranged consultations with the unions and the Legion. Two meetings were held; the first, on 31 October, brought together representatives of the railway unions with Canadian Pacific and Canadian National; the second, on 6 December, mixed representatives of the TLC, CCL, and Canadian and Catholic Confederation of Labour with Legion officials. The railway unions took the position that the Legion framework was useless, since few employment opportunities existed in the railway industry. The railway managers expressed sympathy for the veterans but insisted that they were bound by the terms of their collective agreements. The proposals of the Legion "would be most difficult to reconcile with practical railway operations," they said. At the December gathering, Percy Bengough and A.R. Mosher again firmly opposed any action that would weaken or abrogate existing collective bargaining agreements, but they now encouraged the government to introduce legislation requiring that new job opportunities be offered to ex-servicemen.[49]

As a result of these meetings, MacNamara prepared a report that argued against adopting the proposals of the Legion. This report also recommended that the seniority issue be dropped "for the time being" within the government and be considered instead by the Parliamentary Committee on Veterans Affairs.[50] Earlier, on 17 December 1945, CCL leaders had circulated a letter to all members of parliament and senators condemning the repeated attempts of the Legion to convince the government to breach the seniority clauses of collective agreements. In the CCL's view, the Legion's call for an "open door for veterans" was neither valid nor reasonable.[51] Although the responsibility for finding work for veterans lay "directly at the door of government," this responsibility must not be honoured at the expense of trade unionists.

In April 1946 the Legion reiterated to the government its position that work in war industry should have been classified as temporary employment and that the calculation of seniority in all workplaces should take full account of the time an individual had spent in uniform. The April brief called for the establishment of procedures to (1) enable veterans to compete on an equal footing with civilian workers who had acquired seniority rights during the war; (2) enable veterans to gain sufficient back-dated seniority to guarantee that they would not be placed at the bottom of the seniority ladder as a result of their absence from the workforce during the war; (3) guarantee that any probationary period required of a veteran prior to the establishment of seniority rights would not exceed six months; (4) guarantee that any preference for veterans would not lead to the displacement of other employees; (5) allow veterans to take advantage of the preference option only once; and (6) ensure that the administration of preference rules would be carried out in the same manner as the RCEA. The brief also asked that local committees be authorized to act as arbiters of any dispute that might arise.[52]

But the impetus for a legislative solution to the hiring and seniority problems had been lost by this date. In April 1946, CCL officials placed the issue of veteran seniority at the bottom of a list of demands they submitted to the dominion government; no "enduring benefit" would result if civilian workers were "displaced from employment by veterans."[53] Department of Labour officials also began to wash their hands of the affair. M.M. Maclean, the former chairman of the disbanded CPSRV, bluntly asserted that departmental officials should leave the matter alone "until such time as the government or Parliament has made a decision on policy."[54] Cabinet next considered the issue on 27 June 1946 when it debated a resolution, put forward by DVA and the Department of Labour and supported by the Legion, to give veterans who had served overseas preference in hiring for public service positions of a temporary and seasonal nature. But even this tepid measure failed to win approval. Since there had been no downturn in the economy since the end of the war, cabinet concluded that remedial measures to ensure the employment of veterans were not necessary.[55] With this decision, a three-year quest on behalf of veterans officially ended.

This examination of the failed initiatives to secure hiring and seniority privileges for veterans highlights the non-compulsory nature of government policy affecting discharged military personnel. The Veterans Charter is a testament to the commitment of the Canadian government to avoid the mistakes of the post–World War I era and the shabby treatment of Great War veterans. The Charter succeeded because it was based on the principle that special provisions for veterans would not impinge on the economic security of any other citizen. Indeed, few Canadians could possibly have objected to the significant government expenditures designed to educate, house, and train men and women who had served their country in uniform. But the seniority and hiring question was a zero-sum game in which a civilian worker would be displaced from his or her employment in favour of a veteran. In the face of increasingly powerful opposition from organized labour, the government refused to impose a legislative solution that would guarantee the employment status of veterans.

NOTES

The research for this chapter was funded by a Social Sciences and Humanities Research Council of Canada doctoral fellowship.

1 *Windsor Star,* 21 June 1945.
2 National Archives of Canada (hereafter NA), records of the Department of Labour (hereafter DL), RG 27, vol. 2345, file 22–5–5, Maclean to Mac-Namara, 24 July 1945.
3 NA, records of the Privy Council Office (hereafter PCO), RG 2, series 18, vol. 98, file R–70, vol. 2, "Statistics Pertaining to Ex-service Personnel, January 1947."
4 Walter S. Woods, *Rehabilitation (A Combined Operation)* (Ottawa: Queen's Printer 1953), 209.
5 NA, PCO, series 18, vol. 98, file R–70, vol. 2, various monthly statistical reports; NA, DL, vol. 984, file 3, "Minutes of the Rehabilitation Information Committee, 19 November 1946."
6 The GACDR was formed through the passage of PC 5421 on 8 October 1940. Fourteen subcommittees eventually reported to this interdepartmental committee. Brigadier-General H.F. McDonald chaired the GACDR until his death in September 1943. Walter S. Woods succeeded McDonald as GACDR chairman. For an excellent flow chart of the GACDR structure, see NA, PCO, series 18, vol. 30, file R–70–12, "Structure of the GACDR."
7 NA, DL, vol. 2345, file 22–5–5, Needham to MacNamara, 10 June 1943.
8 Ibid., Walsh to MacNamara, 18 June 1943.
9 Ibid., Phelan to MacNamara, 5 July 1943.
10 Ibid., Lewis to Tallon, 16 July 1943.
11 Ibid., Hougham to Tallon, 2 July 1943.
12 Ibid., Scott to Tallon, 5 July 1943.
13 The NEC formally rejected clause (e) on 16 August 1943. See NA, DL, vol. 880, file 8–9–2–2, pt 1, "Minutes of the 12th Meeting of the NEC, 16 August 1943."
14 NA, DL, vol. 2345, file 22–5–5–1, vol. 1, MacNamara to Foster, 8 October 1943.
15 Ibid., Woods to MacNamara, 10 January 1944.
16 The first meeting of the ICCR was held on 29 March 1944, with Woods and MacNamara leading delegations from their respective departments. See NA, records of the Department of Veterans Affairs (hereafter DVA), RG 38, vol. 191, file Rehabilitation-ICCR, vol. 1, Crawford to Woods, 23 February 1944, and minutes of the first ICCR meeting, 29 March 1944.
17 NA, DL, vol. 885, file 8–9–17, pt 3, "Minutes of the War Manpower Committee of Cabinet, 21 June 1944." Howe and Minister of Transport J.E. Michaud were the only two members of the War Manpower Committee to oppose the preference measure; Minister of Defence J.L. Ralston, Minister

of Agriculture James G. Gardiner, Minister of National War Services L.R. Laflèche, and the Canadian Legion representative endorsed the plan.

18 NA, PCO, series A 5a, vol. 2636, file Cabinet Conclusions, "Cabinet Conclusions, 27 June 1944."

19 NA, DL, vol. 2345, file 22–5–5, Maclean to MacNamara, 2 October 1944.

20 NA, records of the Canadian Labour Congress (hereafter CLC), MG 28 I 103, vol. 207, file 207–8, "Report of the 10th Dominion Convention, June 1944."

21 Ibid., "October Memorandum on the Employment of Veterans in Unionized Industry."

22 *Evening Telegram* (Toronto), 12 September 1944.

23 *Canadian Unionist* 18, no. 4 (October 1944): 78.

24 Ibid., 18, no. 6 (December 1944): 141.

25 Ibid., 19, no. 1 (January 1945): 9.

26 NA, DVA, vol. 191, file Rehabilitation-ICCR, vol. 2, Crawford to McRae, 1 September 1944.

27 Ibid., Woods to Mackenzie, 7 September 1944.

28 Ibid., Phillips to Crawford, 5 September 1944.

29 Ibid., "Minutes of the 9th ICCR Meeting, 5 October 1944."

30 NSS officials clearly viewed the CCL proposals for a national conference with suspicion. The meeting on 20 March 1945 with the railway unions was a complete failure. At the 6 April 1945 meeting of the ICCR, CPSRV member T.R. Walsh claimed that he "could see no real value in proceeding further on a conference basis," and a resolution calling for the discontinuance of all negotiations with the unions was adopted. See NA, DVA, vol. 191, file Rehabilitation-ICCR, vol. 2, "Minutes of the 11th ICCR Meeting, 6 April 1945."

31 NA, DL, vol. 2345, file 22–5–5, Conroy to Maclean, 19 April 1945.

32 *Canadian Unionist* 19, no. 5 (May 1945): 180.

33 NA, CLC, vol. 191, file 191–7, Dowd to Herwig, 9 March 1945; Herwig to Dowd, 19 March 1945; Conroy to Maclean, 19 April 1945; and Maclean to Conroy, 26 April 1945.

34 NA, DL, vol. 2345, file 22–5–5, MacNamara to Woods, 10 May 1945.

35 Ibid., Shoults to MacNamara, 9 April 1945.

36 NA, CLC, vol. 237, file 237–3, Shoults to Conroy, 7 July 1945, and Mosher to Conroy, 12 July 1945.

37 NA, DL, vol. 2345, file 22–5–5, Bengough to MacNamara, 26 July 1945.

38 NA, CLC, vol. 237, file 237–3, Dowd to England, 29 May 1945.

39 NA, DL, vol. 2346, file 22–5–11–5, vol. 1A, Winnipeg Trades and Labour Council submission to the Bovey Commission, 19 July 1945.

40 NA, DL, vol. 2345, file 22–5–5, Bovey to MacNamara, 6 July 1945.

41 Ibid., "UAW Clause on Veterans' Seniority."

42 Ibid., "Ford Motor Company of Canada Proposals for Seniority for Return-ing Veterans."

43 Ibid., Burt to Dowd, 29 June 1945.

44 Ibid., "Minutes of the CPSRV Meeting, 1 August 1945."

45 Ibid., "Memorandum to the ACRR."

46 The CCDR was formed at the 3 October 1945 cabinet meeting, and it carried on the duties of the disbanded GACDR. See NA, PCO, series A 5a, vol. 2636, file Cabinet Conclusions, "Cabinet Conclusions, 3 October 1945."

47 NA, PCO, series 18, vol. 98, file R–70–3, "Draft of Overseas Veterans' Employment Order."

48 NA, PCO, series A 5a, vol. 2636, file Cabinet Conclusions, "Cabinet Conclu-sions, 22 November 1945."

49 NA, DL, vol. 2345, file 22–5–5, MacNamara to Mackenzie, 23 January 1946.

50 Ibid., MacNamara to Mackenzie, 23 January 1946.

51 NA, CLC, vol. 171, file 171–29, Conroy to all locals, MPs, and senators, 17 December 1945.

52 NA, DL, vol. 2345, file 22–5–5, "Canadian Legion Memorandum to the Dominion Government, April 1946."

53 Canadian Unionist 20, no. 4 (April 1946): 87.

54 NA, DL, vol. 2345, file 22–5–5, Maclean to MacNamara, 2 May 1946; Maclean to McCullogh, 4 June 1946.

55 Ibid., Heeney to MacNamara, 28 June 1946.

PETER NEARY

Canadian Universities and Canadian Veterans of World War II

It was during World War II that universities in Canada met big government. This encounter had several dimensions. Governments looked to universities to carry out essential war-related scientific and technical research, and this led to a mutually advantageous flow of research funds between Ottawa and the country's postsecondary institutions. Once started, this stream continued to run. Universities and the national government also worked closely together on arrangements for bringing students into military service. The goal here was to ensure fairness and to meet the requirements of the armed forces while respecting the needs of industry and society for educated workers and skilled professionals. Finally, universities cooperated with Ottawa in fashioning a program to meet the postwar needs of veterans who qualified for support to pursue higher education. It is this latter aspect of the growing interaction and interdependence of government and universities after 1939 that will be explored here.

Like much else connected with the future of those who had served in World War II, the starting point of the universities' interest in veterans affairs was PC 7633 of 1 October 1941, "The Post-Discharge Reestablishment Order."[1] Its promise of financial support for veterans whose rehabilitation would involve higher education had clear implications for enrolment in Canadian universities. When the victory was won, fuelled by the commitment of the government to give rehabilitation benefits of one kind or another to everyone who had served in the armed forces during the war, demand for the services of Canada's postsecondary institutions could be expected to grow dramatically.

Universities would have to be ready for this, and in order to prepare themselves, they would have to start planning forthwith.

The first step was taken in the autumn of 1942 when the executive committee of the National Conference of Canadian Universities (NCCU), the principal lobby for the country's postsecondary institutions, appointed a committee to study the postwar problems that Canadian universities were likely to face.[2] In January 1942 this committee presented an interim report, and thereafter it held three meetings: in Ottawa, 31 August 1943; in Kingston, 3–5 January 1944; and in Hamilton, 12–13 July 1944.[3] The committee was chaired by President N.A.M. MacKenzie of the University of New Brunswick. Its other members were President Robert Newton, University of Alberta; Dean Daniel Buchanan, University of British Columbia; L'Abbé Arthur Maheux, Laval University (Quebec City); Chancellor G.P. Gilmour, McMaster University (Hamilton, Ontario); Registrar Thomas H. Matthews, McGill University (Montreal); President Sidney Smith, University of Manitoba; President D.J. Macdonald of St Francis Xavier University (Antigonish, Nova Scotia), representing the Maritime institutions; the Very Revd Philippe Cornellier, Rector, University of Ottawa; H.A. Innis, University of Toronto; and Vice-Principal W.E. McNeill of Queen's University (Kingston, Ontario). The secretary of the committee was A.B. Fennell, the secretary-treasurer of the NCCU and registrar of the University of Toronto.[4] At the meeting in Kingston in January 1944, Matthews undertook to draw up the report of the committee with the assistance of MacKenzie and Fennell.[5] This document, which was eventually printed by University of Toronto Press and translated into French, was presented by MacKenzie on 12 June 1944 to a meeting of the full NCCU held at McMaster University.[6] It was adopted the next day[7] and thereafter guided the approach of the universities towards the veterans. At the invitation of Fennell, H.W. Jamieson, Superintendent of Educational Training, Department of Pensions and National Health, was present at the key 12–13 June 1944 meetings.[8]

Following a one-page introduction, the *Report of the National Conference of Canadian Universities on Post-War Problems* had sections dealing with "Problems Arising from P.C. 7633" and "Other Post-War Problems." Next came thirteen recommendations and nine appendices. In effect, the appendices were a set of research reports by some of the leading scholars and university administrators in the country. They covered a wide range of subject matter and were thoughtful and elegantly composed, as indeed was the whole report. In order, by author and title, the appendices were as follows: (1) W.E. McNeill, "The National Government and Education in Great Britain, Canada, and the United States"; (2) G.P. Gilmour, "The Problem of Additional Staff at the End of the War"; (3) (by a special subcommittee), "Special Matriculation for Ex-Service Men and Women"; (4) L'Abbé Maheux, "Etudiants Démobilisés"; (5) R.C. Wallace, "The Arts Faculty and Humane Studies"; (6) H.A. Innis, "The Problem of Graduate Work in Canada"; (7) (brief of the Manitoba Educational Association Committee on Articulation of High School and University), "Articulation of High School and University in Manitoba"; (8) Sidney Smith, "Succession Duty Acts and Charitable Bequests"; and (9) W.H. Brittain, "Role of the University in Adult Education."

In the opening lines of the introduction, the authors of the report spelled out in no uncertain terms the challenge that now faced the member institutions of the NCCU:

Canadian universities will have heavy burdens laid upon them during the coming months and years. At the same time they will have an unprecedented opportunity to render an essential service to the nation and especially to the men and women who are themselves rendering to us all such service in the war. To meet their manifold obligations adequately and to play their full part in the post-war world the universities must find appropriate solutions to a large number of problems, and in an age of reconstruction they must, to some extent, reconstruct themselves.[9]

The problems identified in the report arising out of PC 7633 were organized under four headings. The first concerned the number and distribution of ex-service students, that is to say, how many student veterans there would be and which institutions they would attend. For guidance on these matters, the authors of the report relied on various polls and surveys that had been undertaken among members of the armed forces by the Department of Pensions and National Health, which was soon to be abolished in favour of a Department of National Health and Welfare and a Department of Veterans Affairs (DVA).[10] The second problem discussed in relation to PC 7633 was finance. Currently, it was noted, fees covered less than half the cost of educating a student, but with surging enrolment the net cost of running the universities would increase significantly. This was because the institutions would need new staff and new buildings and equipment. How to provide these constituted the third problem posed by PC 7633. The fourth section was headed "Problems of Organization." This category subsumed a variety of issues: the need for summer courses and acceleration; the likely demand for refresher courses; admission requirements; the separate needs of French-speaking students; whether there should be academic allowance for active service; what the curriculum should be for returned students; and the veterans' need for advisory services.

In a passage that captures the flavour of the whole document, the following analysis was advanced with respect to curriculum:

Whether returned men should be taught in separate classes is a matter of dispute. The proponents of segregation believe that the technique of instructing more mature students should differ from that which is most appropriate to younger boys straight from school. They argue further that the initial rustiness of the returned man will put him at a disadvantage which may be unduly discouraging. This is the point of view adopted by Yale University which plans to put its returned men into classes entirely by themselves.

Those who advocate the melting-pot, on the other hand, stress the importance of restoring to the returned man as soon as possible the feeling that he "fits in" and that he is regarded as a normal citizen in the post-war world. They see a danger in a separate class of "returned men" who might, to some extent, feel that they were a race apart and that their interests were special ones conflicting in some measure with those of other undergraduates.

In certain subjects such as Economics, Sociology, and Political Theory, where the war experiences of the veterans will be germane to the matters discussed, and where the group-discussion method with which many of them will be familiar is particularly applicable, some degree of segregation may prove effective, but this would not, in general, apply to the exact sciences. Possibly a mixture of the two methods will be found most efficacious with complete separation in the refresher courses and in most of the elementary classes and a thorough intermingling in advanced work.

It is generally thought that returned men will be particularly interested in the social significance of their studies and will want to be convinced of the real value to themselves of the work they undertake. This should be taken into account in planning their courses. One interesting suggestion that has been made is that we should offer for their benefit a course on "Canadian Affairs since 1939" so that they may be mentally acclimatized and not feel out of touch with Canadian life.[11]

In the section of the report headed "Other Post-War Problems," the topics covered were the future of the liberal arts course, postgraduate courses, international studies, scholarships and bursaries, the need for a "more uniform and simple" standard of matriculation,[12] adult education, taxation, and the future of the NCCU itself.

Inter alia, the recommendations in the report called for (1) more surveys of the armed forces by the Department of Pensions and National Health; (2) the introduction of a procedure, to be administered by the Wartime Bureau of Technical Personnel, whereby universities could obtain the early release "from industry, government services, or the Armed Forces" of persons needed for teaching duties;[13] (3) the granting of academic allowance for active service "only in exceptional cases, such as the wiping out of old conditions, or the granting of standing for examinations missed because of enlistment, and the giving of credit for such courses taken on active service as might be considered equivalent to undergraduate courses";[14] (4) the establishment of a joint consultative committee by the universities, the armed services, the Canadian Legion Educational Services, the Department of Pensions and National Health, and the Department of Labour; (5) continuation and extension of the existing program of dominion-provincial bursaries to ensure "that no able students, in any field of learning, be prevented by economic disability from equipping themselves for national service";[15] (6) the improvement and expansion of graduate (including medical) education; (7) the revision of curricula so as to "afford a better understanding of other countries, for example, China, Russia, and the South American Republics";[16] (8) the introduction by Ottawa of scholarships and fellowships to facilitate study abroad by Canadian students and to bring overseas students to Canadian institutions; (9) the establishment of a university course in physical and health education; (10) the extension, with government support, of what was already being done in adult education; and (11) the inclusion by the dominion, provincial, and municipal governments "of university buildings of a public or semi-private nature ... as a part of any programme of publicly-financed construction adopted to augment the available employment opportunities and prevent the onset of economic depression."[17] With respect to the issue of a uniform matriculation for Canadians, the recommendations noted that the NCCU had now established a committee "to consider and report upon the possibility of simplifying and unifying the entrance requirements of various universities, so that boys and girls in any province may without undue hardship prepare for admission into universities in other provinces."[18]

Not surprisingly, the key recommendation, number six in the list, concerned money:

The Conference of Canadian Universities warmly welcomes and commends the admirable provisions made under P.C. 7633 for returned men and women and is most anxious that the full intent of these shall become a reality. The Order will, however, greatly increase beyond the normal the total number of university students, and since the fees of students at the present do not meet more than one-half of the cost of their college education it is probable that the total cost of each university's operation will increase by an amount greater than the fees received from demobilized students.

The Conference therefore represent to the Dominion and to the Provincial Governments that financial help through the appropriate channels be granted to the universities to cover this net increase beyond the fees, so that the universities may be able to give to our returned men and women the full benefits intended by the generous policy of the Dominion Government.

This call for financial help was backed up by McNeill's detailed and well-researched comparative study of the support given to education by the national governments of Great Britain, Canada, and the United States. Under Canada's federal constitution, except for the protections for denominational school rights specified in section 93 of the British North America Act, education was a matter of provincial legislative responsibility. However, McNeill cited example after example to prove that "the close relation of Education to national welfare [had] from time to time brought some forms of it under the care, stimulation, and bounty of the central government." His examples were grouped under seven headings: (1) "Education of Wards of the Government"; (2) "Education for National Defence and Its Corollary"; (3) "Education in Civilian Fields of National Importance"; (4) "Educational Aspects of Relief Projects"; (5) "Educational Services of the Canadian Broadcasting Corporation"; (6) "Educational Services of the National Research Council"; and (7) "The Education Branch of the Dominion Bureau of Statistics." Over the years, Ottawa had educated aboriginal Canadians, run military and naval colleges, offered military training in universities and schools, granted educational charters (to Queen's University and Frontier College), provided for technical and vocational education, trained pilots for civil aviation, maintained schools of navigation, given grants-in-aid to individual students, and financed youth training plans and much else. The message in all this, though not directly stated, was perfectly clear: Ottawa had a national responsibility in relation to veterans and there was no constitutional barrier to national public spending in the field of education to meet that obligation. Indeed, the dominion government could keep its promises to the veterans only by investing in universities on a countrywide basis. Simply put, a national duty required a national response. Nothing else would do.

The government's response to the universities' request for special funding to educate the veterans came in a letter which the first Minister of Veterans Affairs, Ian Mackenzie, wrote to President James S. Thomson of the University of Saskatchewan, the sitting president of the NCCU, on 19 March 1945.[19] Since Canadian universities were diverse, wrote Mackenzie, it would be necessary to devise a formula for the payment of grants that would "ensure uniformity regarding the services to be rendered by the universities" in return for such payments.

Before a submission could be made to Treasury Board, therefore, the universities would have to confirm their willingness to accommodate student veterans as follows:

(1) So arrange admission dates that fully qualified veterans can enter a university within three months of their acceptance for a course and without disadvantage to themselves.
(2) Provide a counselling and advisory service for veterans which will cooperate with the Department of Veterans Affairs regarding the suitability of veterans for university education, as well as advise veterans on courses of study and aid their adjustment to their studies.
(3) Provide summer sessions in order to accommodate veterans.
(4) Avoid excessively large classes which would impair the effectiveness of instruction.
(5) Insure adequate residence accommodation, and provide a housing service to aid veterans in procuring accommodation.
(6) Engage additional, qualified instructors for veterans' classes when necessary.
(7) Establish loan funds or other assistance for veterans to finance their courses beyond the period of eligibility for benefits under the Post-Discharge Re-establishment Order.
(8) Control incoming numbers of civilian students so that veterans may have the fullest opportunity to make use of university facilities.
(9) Re-adapt courses to the special needs of adult veterans seeking to enter professions.

Mackenzie added that DVA regarded university education "as an exceedingly important part of the rehabilitation programme," not only because of the advantages it would give to individual veterans but because of its "broad implications" for the future development of Canada. The government was anxious to assist the universities, he said, but it could not "recommend that veterans be charged higher fees than those which prevail for non-veteran students"; hence the need for a formula that would "indicate the additional services to be provided for veterans." In conclusion, Mackenzie asked Thomson whether he would consider it advisable to appoint a commission to supervise the payment of grants if they were made available.

Thomson's reply, dated 2 April 1945, assured the minister that the universities were not out "to 'cash in' on any scheme of education for demobilised men and women."[20] At the same time, they would be "gravely handicapped" unless assisted. He suggested that in order to ensure that money was spent for the purpose intended by the government, either a commission could be set up to supervise expenditure or the universities could submit signed statements, with requisite accounting, specifying that the funds received had been used to educate veterans. After meeting with DVA Deputy Minister Walter S. Woods in Ottawa, Thomson reported to the executive committee of the NCCU in Toronto on 30 April 1945 on the proposed establishment by DVA of an advisory committee on university education.[21] This idea was endorsed by the executive, and the Advisory Committee on University Training for Veterans (hereafter the Advisory Committee) was then established by PC 3206 of 3 May 1945.[22] The purpose of the committee was to advise the Minister of Veterans Affairs "on matters relating to the university training provided under The Post Discharge Re-Establishment Order, being Order in Council P.C. 5210 of July 13th, 1944"[23] (one of the periodic embellishments of PC 7633).

Those named to the Advisory Committee, which thenceforth played a pivotal role in relations between the universities and the government, were Sperrin N.F. Chant, Director General of Rehabilitation, DVA; the Very Revd Philippe Cornellier; Mgr Cyrille Gagnon, Rector, Laval University; Milton F. Gregg, President, University of New Brunswick; F. Cyril James, Principal, McGill University; H.W. Jamieson, now Superintendent of Educational Training, DVA; Norman A.M. MacKenzie, now President of the University of British Columbia; W.A. Mackintosh, Director General of Economic Research, Department of Reconstruction; Mgr J.L. Olivier Maurault, Rector, University of Montreal; John E. Robbins, Department of Trade and Commerce; Sidney Smith, President-elect, University of Toronto; James S. Thomson; H.M. Tory, President, Carleton College (Ottawa); R.C. Wallace, Principal, Queen's University; and Walter S. Woods.[24] Woods was named chairman of the committee and Jamieson was named secretary. Members of the committee were to "be paid their actual and necessary expenses when absent from their places of residence in connection with the work of ... [the] Committee."[25] The terms of reference subsequently spelled out for the committee were to advise on "(a) Policy with respect to contributing to the additional counselling, instructional and administrative costs incurred by Canadian Universities in their service to discharged personnel. (b) Policy with respect to undergraduate and post-graduate training outside of Canada. (c) Policy with respect to ensuring that suitable Canadian University facilities are used to the fullest extent. (d) Other problems which may arise as demobilization proceeds."[26] The first meeting of the committee was held on 28 May 1945 at the Chateau Laurier in Ottawa.[27] Thereafter, the committee met ten more times, the last meeting being held at the Daly Building Annex, Ottawa, on 9 February 1951.[28] At the first meeting, President Thomson noted that the policy of the government with respect to university education for veterans was "more enlightened" than that of any other country he knew about.[29]

Following the formation of the Advisory Committee, Woods recommended favourably to the Deputy Minister of Finance the request of the executive committee of the NCCU for a payment by the government of $150 per year above and beyond tuition fees on behalf of each student veteran.[30] The request for this payment was endorsed in a resolution passed unanimously by the Advisory Committee at its first meeting.[31] By the terms of this resolution, the subsidy program would begin on 1 January 1945, and there would be a cap of $500 on the tuition fees, student fees, athletic fees, and subsidy the government could pay on behalf of a discharged person. In the preamble of the resolution, it was noted that the Dominion Bureau of Statistics had found that the proportion of income derived from tuition fees in all Canadian colleges and universities in 1943–44 had been 33 per cent. This proportion varied significantly, however, from institution to institution. Thus, while the percentage of yearly income from tuition fees was only 20 per cent at Laval, it was 25 per cent at the University of Saskatchewan, 33 per cent at McGill and the University of Toronto, and 40 per cent at the University of British Columbia, University of New Brunswick, and Queen's.[32] At all Canadian universities, the cost of paying instructors was said to constitute about 60 per cent of the annual budget. The subsidy called for by the NCCU and the Advisory Committee was eventually granted by PC 215/4940 of 13 July 1945, which was issued under the authority of the War Measures Act.[33] The amount of the payment, or "supplementary grant" as it was officially called, was set at the requested maximum of $150 per student; it covered individuals on behalf of whom fees were being paid under the Post-Discharge Re-Establishment Order, and it applied to the period 1 July 1945 to 30 June 1946. The $500 cap also was specified, as was the requirement that if fees were paid for only part of an academic year, the supplementary grant would be prorated accordingly.

On 18 December 1945 the Veterans Rehabilitation Act received assent. This consolidated in statutory form the rehabilitation benefits introduced by PC 7633 and then refined by PC 5210 of 13 July 1944.[34] Under the terms of the act, the Minister of Veterans Affairs could, on a discretionary basis, pay the fees of a veteran to attend university and give the veteran a living allowance while he or she was there. The fees and allowances payable on behalf of an individual veteran corresponded to his or her length of service. In order to qualify, a veteran was required to "commence or resume university training within fifteen months after discharge, except for good reason shown to the satisfaction of the Minister."[35] Initially, a married veteran was paid $80 per month and a single veteran $60 per month.[36] The allowance for the wife of a married male veteran was thus $20 per month; that for a fully dependent parent was $15.[37] Allowances were also given for dependent children at the rate of $12 each for the first two children, $10 for the third, and $8 each for the fourth, fifth, and sixth.[38] Veterans could earn up to $75 in other income without having their allowances reduced.[39] But in the case of wages paid in connection with training (e.g., to students in chartered accountancy, law, pharmacy, nursing, and in postgraduate medical training in hospitals) the limit was $40 per month.[40] From 1 November 1945, the wife of a male veteran receiving an allowance could herself earn up to $75 per month without affecting her husband's payment.[41] If she exceeded the $75 limit, her husband would then be paid as a single man plus allowances for children.

On 1 January 1948 there were increases in all dependants' allowances and, effective 1 June of that year, the restrictions on the other earnings of a male veteran and the earnings of wives were removed.[42] A limit of $75 per month was, however, kept on the additional earnings of part-time demonstrators, interns, and suchlike on the grounds that the earning of income in excess of that amount would involve the sacrifice of time "which should be devoted to ... [the] full-time training programme."[43] Under section 11 (4) of the act (as amended on 31 August 1946), the minister was authorized to make the supplementary grant first provided for in PC 215/4940 to any university where veterans being supported were studying.[44] Section 11 (5) of the act (as amended separately on 31 August 1946) authorized the minister to provide money to any university in Canada to make emergency loans to veterans who were receiving allowances under the act.[45]

In the autumn of 1945, as expected, veterans, both male and female, began flooding into the classrooms of Canadian universities by the thousand, with the object of improving their lives and finding a secure future for themselves and their families. Principal F. Cyril James, an economist by training, caught the flavour of the times when he wrote to Jamieson on 12 October 1945: "My own class has grown from about 52 last year to 295 and will be over the 300 mark next week, which gives you an idea of what has happened at McGill."[46] Although principal of the university, James was now teaching three days a week. As table 2 shows, the high point of enrolment by veterans in Canadian universities (though not in all universities) came in 1946, when there were some 35,000 registrations. By comparison, the entire full-time undergraduate enrolment in Canadian universities and colleges in 1939 had been only 35,164.[47] Such was the measure of the demand for which the universities had been preparing themselves for so long.[48] By academic year, the distribution of student veterans as of 15 February 1947 was as follows: first year, 15,000;

Table 2
Number of Student Veterans Assisted by the Government of Canada,
31 December 1943 – 31 December 1952

Year	1st year	2nd year	3rd year	4th year	Postgraduate	Total[1]
31 Dec. 1943	42	12	11	3	5	73
31 Dec. 1944	315	117	64	21	37	554
31 Dec. 1945	14,000	3,600	1,400	1,000	500	20,500
31 Dec. 1946	16,000	12,000	4,000	2,000	1,000	35,000
31 Dec. 1947	7,400	10,700	8,600	2,900	900	30,500
31 Dec. 1948	2,100	5,200	8,000	6,500	1,300	23,100
31 Dec. 1949	878	1,375	3,692	7,104	1,090	14,139
31 Dec. 1950	247	597	1,112	4,170	843	6,969
31 Dec. 1951 (estimate)	66	246	488	2,025	700	3,525
31 Dec. 1952 (estimate)	19	45	161	899	451	1,575

Source: Veterans Affairs Canada (VAC), DVA 66–38–2–1, Minutes of Advisory Committee on
University Training for Veterans, 9 February 1951, Superintendent's Report, 2
[1] M.C. Urquhart, ed., and K.A.H. Buckley, asst. ed., *Historical Statistics of Canada* (Toronto:
Macmillan Company of Canada 1965), 601, gives the following figures for full-time enrolment in
universities and colleges in Canada for these years: 35,692 in 1943; 35,132 in 1944; 38,376 in 1945;
61,861 in 1946; 76,237 in 1947; 79,346 in 1948; 75,807 in 1949; 69,111 in 1950; 64,036 in 1951;
59,849 in 1952.

Table 3
Number of Students Enrolled in Pre-matriculation Classes, by District,
31 January – 31 March 1946

District	31 Jan. 1946	28 Feb. 1946	31 March 1946
Halifax	138	147	162
Charlottetown	42	53	74
Saint John	87	118	186
Quebec	35	54	75
Montreal	366	674	674
Ottawa	295	325	315
Kingston	234	332	344
Toronto	1,672	1,840	2,453
Hamilton	205	316	407
London	629	854	1,104
Winnipeg	862	860	1,145
Regina	330	420	579
Saskatoon	427	491	497
Calgary	501	609	682
Edmonton	316	365	485
Vancouver	550	754	860
Victoria	8		
Total	6,689	8,212	10,042

Source: VAC, DVA, file 66–38–2–1, Minutes of Advisory Committee on University Training for
Veterans, 25 February 1946

Table 4
Distribution of Trainees by Faculty, 15 February 1947

Courses	1st year	2nd year	3rd year	4th year	5th year	Postgrad.	Total
Arts (including pre-professional)	5,422	4,663	1,976	691	61	444	13,257
Engineering	4,027	2,963	751	290	1	61	8,093
Commerce and finance	1,149	1,406	588	185	1	9	3,338
Agriculture	553	650	173	69	3	29	1,477
Medicine	486	185	46	9	2	584	1,312
Law	629	416	111	13	–	17	1,186
Education	401	323	90	25	–	36	875
Forestry	385	263	40	12	–	3	703
Pharmacy	271	269	37	2	–	4	583
Art	178	135	34	18	–	3	368
Dentistry	221	61	5	7	–	13	307
Nursing	188	–	–	–	14	77	279
Veterinary	124	93	12	7	–	–	236
Health and physical education	111	103	11	2	–	–	227
Architecture	154	52	6	2	2	1	217
Optometry	108	74	4	–	–	–	186
Social work	106	40	2	–	–	31	179
Theology	69	63	27	5	–	14	178
Journalism	74	66	19	1	–	–	160
Music and dramatics	49	64	24	3	–	4	144
Physiotherapy	36	10	–	–	–	–	46
Occupational therapy	39	16	–	–	–	–	55
Home economics	42	27	5	8	–	1	83
Industrial relations	43	7	–	–	–	–	50
Library	26	2	–	–	–	–	43
Other	178	68	–	–	–	–	246
Total in Canada	15,069	12,019	3,961	1,349	84	1,346	33,828
In United States	210	109	65	39	1	448	872
In United Kingdom and Europe	–	–	–	–	–	–	218
Total training in universities	–	–	–	–	–	–	34,918
In pre-matriculation classes, 31 Jan. 1947	–	–	–	–	–	–	5,225
Total	–	–	–	–	–	–	40,143

Source: VAC, DVA, file 66–38–2–1, Minutes of Advisory Committee on University Training for Veterans, 17 March 1947, appendix A

Table 5
The University of Saskatchewan, 1946–1947

College	% of veterans in each college	% of students in each college who were veterans
Agriculture	12.3	73.5
Arts and science	24.2	41.8
Commerce	15.4	83.2
Education	7.8	66.5
Engineering	28.5	63.0
Graduate	0.9	32.8
Home economics	0.8	15.7
Law	3.2	78.9
Medicine	0.7	32.0
Music	0.2	26.9
Nursing	0.1	4.9
Pharmacy	5.9	66.2

Source: W.P. Thompson, *The University of Saskatchewan: A Personal History* (Toronto: University of Toronto Press 1970), 136

second year, 12,000; third year, 4,000; fourth year, 1,400; and graduate study, 1,400.[49] The Veterans Rehabilitation Act also provided support for pre-matriculation training. As table 3 shows, many veterans availed themselves of this opportunity.

The seven universities in Canada most favoured by the veterans – 75.5 per cent of all such registrations in November 1946 – were, in order, the University of Toronto, McGill, University of British Columbia, University of Saskatchewan, University of Alberta, University of Manitoba, and Queen's.[50] In 1947–48 veterans accounted for 49 per cent of the student body of the University of Toronto, and in 1948–49 they accounted for 42 per cent.[51] As late as 1949–50, veterans still accounted for 21 per cent of all university students in Canada.[52] Table 4 shows the programs in which the veterans were registered as of 15 February 1947. How all this affected the University of Saskatchewan in the academic year 1946–47 is highlighted in table 5. In 1945–46, this university had made thirty-three new appointments, and at the height of the veteran boom "total attendance was more than double that of pre-war years."[53]

In November 1945, in order to assist the universities with their teaching requirements, DVA made it possible for a postgraduate student being supported under the Veterans Rehabilitation Act to take a half-time university teaching post without loss of benefits. For a veteran who did this, "two months of half-time combined training and teaching" would "be regarded as the equivalent of one month in full-time training."[54] Study abroad was yet another option available to some veterans; the country most favoured was the United States (U.S.

Table 6
Distribution by Faculty of Trainees in the United States, 15 February 1947

Courses	1st year	2nd year	3rd year	4th year	5th year	Postgrad.	Total
Arts (including pre-medical, pre-dental and pre-engineering)	38	24	11	16		129	218
Engineering	56	37	23	10	1	34	161
Commerce and finance	19	9	9	4		38	79
Agriculture	4		1			18	23
Law	5	2				3	10
Medicine	9	2	3			129	143
Dentistry	21	2	3			5	31
Pharmacy			1				1
Optometry	4					1	5
Veterinary	1					1	2
Education	2	1	1			31	35
Theology	20	10	2			11	43
Public health nursing	3		1			6	10
Social science	1	1		2		11	15
Architecture	3	5	3	2			13
Forestry	2	1	1	1		4	9
Health and physical education	3	2		1		2	8
Journalism	5	4	2	1			12
Art	2		1			2	5
Library						2	2
Music	1	5	1			2	9
Physiotherapy	1						1
Industrial relations						1	1
Household science and economics		1	1	1		6	9
Political science	3	1	1			8	13
Horticulture	1					2	3
Language (Chinese)		1				1	2
Osteopathy	6	1		1		1	9
Total	221	109	65	39	1	448	883

Source: VAC, DVA, file 66–38–2–1, Minutes of Advisory Committee on University Training for Veterans, 17 March 1947, appendix B

beneficiaries of the G.I. Bill of Rights also studied in Canada),[55] but veterans also attended institutions in the United Kingdom and other European countries. Table 6 summarizes the situation *vis-à-vis* the United States as of 15 February 1947. Where Canadian students were studying in the United States as of 15 February 1947 and 31 December 1949 is shown in table 7. As of 31 December 1949, there were also 73 Canadian veterans pursuing vocational training in the United States.[56] This made a total of 703 Canadian veterans studying there. By the same date, 1,713 of 1,892 Canadian veterans had completed

Table 7
Distribution of Canadian Veterans in Training in United States Universities

	15 Feb. 1947	31 Dec. 1949
University of California (Berkeley)	29 ⎱	20
University of Southern California (Los Angeles)	9 ⎰	
University of Chicago	28	35
Columbia University	64	42
Cornell University	35	22
Gordon College of Technology		6
Harvard University	59	55
University of Illinois		8
Iowa State College		6
Massachusetts Institute of Technology	18	10
Mayo Foundation	11	
University of Michigan	17	20
University of Minnesota	32	29
New York State College of Forestry		7
New York University		6
Northwestern University		8
Ohio State University		7
Oregon State College		10
University of Oregon	21	27
University of Pennsylvania	10	7
Philadelphia Textile Institute		7
University of Pittsburgh	7	
Princeton University		6
Stanford University	12	8
University of Washington	32	24
Wayne State University		10
University of Wisconsin	13	21
Yale University	16	17
Other university training institutions	460	222
Total	883	630

Source: VAC, DVA, file 66–38–2–1, Minutes of Advisory Committee on University Training for Veterans, 17 March 1947, appendix C, and 6 February 1950, Superintendent's Report, 3

their courses of study in the United States.[57] Of these, 179 had not yet acted on their undertaking to return to Canada but were "being reminded regularly of the conditions under which assistance was granted."[58] As of 15 February 1947, 33,828 veterans were studying in Canada, 872 in the United States, and 218 in the United Kingdom and continental Europe. When the 5,225 who were in pre-matriculation classes on 31 January were added to these, the grand total came to 40,143.[59]

By 15 January 1951, as shown in table 8, 1,710 student loans to the amount of $406,572.90 had been made to veterans. The average individual loan had been $238 and the average total amount per veteran had been $287.[60] To 21 December 1950, 377 recipients of these loans had commenced repayment and $56,572.67 had been received back in principal and interest (payable at 5 per cent).[61] An analysis of 9,119 student veterans in receipt of allowances at 30 November 1945 showed that 2,308 (25.3 per cent) were married and 6,811 (74.7 per cent) were single.[62] As time passed and the baby boom got under way, the percentages tipped dramatically in favour of the married category. At its ninth meeting, on 20 November 1948, the Advisory Committee heard that the ratio of married to single veterans was continually increasing. Some 1,200 individuals had changed from single to married status between the final examinations in the spring and the beginning of the fall term, and 50 per cent of the supported veterans in university were now married.[63] By definition, the number of dependants the government was supporting was also increasing. At the University of Saskatchewan, the veterans were older than their civilian counterparts and in 1946–47 had an average age of 25.4 years.[64] According to W.P. Thompson, writing in 1970, approximately 40 per cent of the veterans who attended the University of Saskatchewan were married and "25 per cent had one or more children."[65] On 25 February 1946, James S. Thomson of that institution had told the Advisory Committee that the male veterans had developed in the services qualities that were not evident in the general undergraduate body: "This has come about by the discipline of having to live together. The Services have done a remarkable job in developing a maturity of social outlook and a sense of responsibility which should be conserved and developed on the university campus."[66] This typified the situation across the country. Canadian universities had not only grown but had taken in students of very different outlook and expectations.

As the educational program of DVA moved into high gear, the Advisory Committee monitored events closely. At its third meeting, on 13 November 1945, it considered recommendation 41 of the Royal Commission on Veterans' Qualifications, which was being chaired by Wilfrid Bovey and had issued its second interim report in September 1945. Recommendation 41 called for the establishment of an independent committee to deal with the postwar problems of universities.[67] It was decided that it would not be "advisable to set up a separate organization independent of the Department of Veterans Affairs and unrelated to the Advisory Committee on University Training."[68] Instead, it was recommended that the Minister of Veterans Affairs establish a board within DVA "to review and/or recommend financial or other assistance from the Dominion Government to colleges or universities for the training of veterans and, generally, to take

Table 8
University Loan Funds for Student Veterans, 1946–1951

University	1946–47		1947–48		1948–49		1949–50		1950–51		Total, 15 Jan. 1951	
	No. of loans	Amount	No. of loans	Amount	No. of loans	Amount	No. of loans	Amount	No. of loans	Amount	No. of loans	Amount
Nova Scotia Technical College	–	–	1	$250.00	–	–	–	–	–	–	1	$250.00
St Francis Xavier	3	$950.00	4	800.00	–	–	–	–	–	–	7	1,750.00
Dalhousie University	7	2,200.00	18	5,150.00	–	–	–	–	–	–	25	7,350.00
Acadia University	–	–	7	1,795.00	–	–	–	–	–	–	7	1,795.00
University of New Brunswick	1	200.00	1	400.00	1	$300.00	11	$2,725.00	–	–	14	3,625.00
Mount Allison University	–	–	1	300.00	–	–	–	–	–	–	1	300.00
Laval University	7	2,900.00	6	1,700.00	8	2,430.00	8	2,285.00	5	$1,510.00	34	10,825.00
McGill University	45	11,935.00	69	17,354.00	59	13,968.00	44	11,076.00	30	7,494.00	247	61,827.00
Sir George Williams College	8	2,250.00	12	3,486.00	4	975.00	3	610.00	–	–	27	7,321.00
Carleton College	1	200.00	–	–	1	275.00	1	160.00	–	–	3	635.00
Queen's University	9	2,144.00	16	4,077.00	29	6,275.50	47	9,603.75	22	6,203.00	123	28,303.25
University of Toronto	45	14,020.00	119	29,289.00	114	26,432.00	113	27,040.00	45	10,562.00	436	107,343.00
Osgoode Hall	6	2,425.00	5	600.00	6	1,275.00	6	2,550.00	–	–	23	6,850.00
McMaster University	–	–	2	356.00	–	–	1	325.00	–	–	3	681.00
Ontario Agricultural College	1	200.00	5	1,500.00	3	1,125.00	2	500.00	–	–	11	3,325.00
Ontario Veterinary College	3	1,350.00	24	6,670.00	20	5,400.00	8	1,150.00	–	–	55	14,570.00
University of Manitoba	15	2,570.00	23	5,370.70	15	2,604.00	8	1,145.70	6	1,164.00	67	12,854.40
University of Saskatchewan	20	5,385.00	38	7,475.00	57	12,220.00	23	6,465.00	8	1,960.00	146	33,505.00
University of Alberta	29	6,295.00	45	9,025.00	56	11,900.50	27	6,061.75	28	5,783.00	185	39,065.25
University of British Columbia	44	12,135.00	79	18,293.00	77	15,127.00	70	13,425.00	22	4,818.00	292	63,798.00
Victoria College	–	–	2	250.00	–	–	–	–	1	350.00	3	600.00
	244	$67,159.00	477	$114,140.70	450	$100,307.00	372	$85,122.20	167	$39,844.00	1,710	$406,572.90

Source: VAC, DVA, file 66–38–2–1, Minutes of Advisory Committee on University Training for Veterans, 9 February 1951, Superintendent's Report, 7

appropriate action in respect to the needs of any or all of the colleges or universities referred to it by the Advisory Committee on University Training for Veterans or brought to its attention by the head of any college or university."[69] The recommendation was duly accepted, and on 4 December 1945 the Committee on University Requirements was authorized by PC 7129.[70]

The chair appointed to the new committee (for a ten-month term) was Robert England of Sidney, British Columbia. England was the author of the influential *Discharged: A Commentary on Civil Re-establishment of Veterans in Canada* (1943) and one of the architects of the Veterans Charter, the larger program of benefits for Canadian veterans of which the Veterans Rehabilitation Act was part. The other members appointed to the committee were the Very Revd Philippe Cornellier, Principal R.C. Wallace, R.B.Bryce of the Department of Finance, and L.J. Mills of DVA.[71] The energetic England met with the Advisory Committee on 25 February 1946 and soon afterwards submitted an interim report to the Minister of Veterans Affairs. This document ranged widely over the issues that had arisen in relation to the education of veterans and put forward a number of recommendations for the consideration of DVA and the Advisory Committee. The report noted that most universities had "abandoned the academic year and arranged to accept veterans twice or three times a year, concentrating courses within a shorter period."[72] By the same token, arrangements had been made at the larger institutions "for all-year operation."[73] Universities were giving priority to veterans (as indeed they were required to do under the terms of the supplementary grant scheme), and it had been necessary for many of them to exclude some non-veterans. In the view of most of the universities, however, it was "not practicable to exclude completely all non-veteran freshman entrants."[74] The report concluded that the matter would "require tactful and firm handling by the universities" if veterans were to receive "priority in the very limited accommodation available."[75]

An appendix to the report gave a university-by-university survey of the situation with respect to the facilities available to meet the influx of veterans. At the University of Toronto, first-year science and engineering students were being taught in a surplus defence industry plant at Ajax, twenty-five miles from the city, where assembly-line huts had been made over into classrooms and laboratories.[76] At the University of British Columbia, where 3,200 veterans were already enrolled, 112 huts had been moved to campus at a cost of $300,000, "half of them for general university purposes and half as residences for students."[77] At the same time, the university had a $5 million construction program in progress to provide a new physics building and new accommodation for pharmacy, home economics, and applied science as well as an addition to the library. At McGill, where 3,076 were now enrolled, Sir William Dawson College had been established in the former Royal Canadian Air Force No. 9 Observer Training School at St Johns, Quebec, and in February 1946 there were 400 single and married veterans being housed and fed there.[78] McGill had plans for "an enlargement of [the] Redpath Library, new wings at Royal Victoria College and Douglas Hall, enlargement of Engineering building and Physics Building, with additional construction of Engineering, Physics and Chemistry group."[79] Like Canada itself, universities were having to adapt in myriad ways, and they were not only coping but prospering. A big short-term demand was allowing them to reinvent themselves and build for a brighter tomorrow. This was very much in keeping with the spirit of the times.

Not surprisingly, a continuing concern of the Advisory Committee was the academic performance of the veterans. On 4 December 1945, PC 7224 had laid down that a grant could not "be continued to a discharged person who, having failed in one or more classes or subjects in any academic year, fails in more than one of the supplementary examinations next offered by the university in any such classes or subjects."[80] Thus, for the veteran, examination results were even more important than was normally the case. In practice, the veterans met a high level of achievement, though there were many casualties; in 1946–47, for example, 77 per cent passed unconditionally, 10 per cent were able to continue with one condition, and 13 per cent failed to qualify for continued assistance.[81] At its 19 November 1947 meeting, the Advisory Committee heard that of 16,000 student veterans no longer in training, 4,000 had finished their programs, 3,000 had used up their entitlement, 4,000 had voluntarily withdrawn, and 5,000 had failed.[82] The number of withdrawals was said to be a reflection of the "good employment situation" in the country.[83] Of those who had not succeeded, 1,200 were repeating the failed year and paying for it themselves. In 1948, 81 per cent of the veterans passed without condition, 8 per cent passed with one condition, and 11 per cent failed.[84] In the view of Jamieson, the last-mentioned figure indicated "weaknesses in the universities' assessment of capacities during and at the end of the First Year."[85] Evidence of this was also to be found in "the large number who on repeating First Year did extremely well."[86] For "veterans of mature years and long service," failure was indeed "a serious problem."[87]

In November 1946 the Advisory Committee acted to assist deserving veterans who fell from grace and lost unexpired entitlement. The resolution in this regard recommended as follows: "A student-veteran whose assistance in university training has been discontinued because of failure to make the required academic standing, and who thereafter continues at university for one year at his own expense during which time he fulfils the academic requirements, and who is recommended by his faculty, may be reinstated not more than once during his university career."[88] This recommendation was given effect by a letter that Jamieson sent to all district administrators on 21 March 1947.[89] Table 9 shows that, to 1951, there were 2,604 reinstatements and that 358 (13.7 per cent) of these students had failed again. Of the 1,660 who had failed in 1948–49, 817 repeated at their own expense. This was said to exemplify a small dropout rate and the "continued determination" of the veterans "to complete the course."[90] In November 1948 it was reported that DVA had a policy of following up dropouts and failures, which were said to constitute some 40 per cent of registrations.[91] On 6 February 1950 the Advisory Committee heard that 20 per cent of the ex-service students in the Toronto district were not receiving allowances and that of this group 20 per cent were repeating work.[92]

Under the terms of PC 4059, veterans who did well in their studies could have their benefits extended beyond their service entitlement.[93] The conditions here were that the veteran had to complete at least one year of study, pass all subjects, either achieve second-class honours standing or be in the top 25 per cent of his or her year, and be recommended for further support by the scholarship committee of the university attended. In February 1951, Jamieson reported that 9,000 veterans had started university work without enough service credit to see them through to graduation. Fully 6,068 (67.4 per cent) of these had received extensions of benefits "on a 'scholarship' basis."[94] Indeed, second and third extensions had not been uncommon, and a few of the current recipients were on their fifth and sixth extensions. During the academic year 1950–51, 28 per cent of the undergraduates and 40 per cent of the postgraduates receiving assistance were on extended benefits.[95]

To assist the veterans with their studies and fulfil one of the commitments made when the supplementary grant was given, the Advisory Committee promoted counselling services at the universities.[96] In August 1946 the Conference of University Veterans' Advisers was held at the University of British Columbia and a committee was established to coordinate activities across the country.[97] The chairman of this committee was S.N.F. Chant, now head of the Department of Philosophy and Psychology at the University of British Columbia, and the vice-chairman was William Line of the University of Toronto. The other members were Captain L. Clermont of the University of Montreal and A.J. Cook of the University of Alberta. In connection with the establishment of the committee, it was agreed that the Veterans' Advisory

Table 9
Repeaters and Reinstatements, by District, 1950–1951

District	Repeating 1950–51	Reinstated	Again failing	Percentage again failing
Montreal	86	241	17	7.1
Toronto	44	813	131	16.1
Vancouver	43	550	97	17.6
Winnipeg	40	240	29	12.1
Halifax	19	134	14	10.4
Edmonton	15	110	10	9.1
Kingston	14	197	17	8.6
London	10	98	14	14.3
Saint John	9	70	6	8.6
Saskatoon	9	117	18	15.4
Hamilton	3	22	5	22.7
Quebec	1	12	–	–
	293	2,604	358	13.7

Source: VAC, DVA, file 66–38–2–1, Minutes of Advisory Committee on University Training for Veterans, 9 February 1951, Superintendent's Report, 4

Service at the University of Toronto would act as a "central agency."[98] In March 1947 and again in January 1948, the Advisory Committee supported plans by the University Veterans' Advisory Service, of which Margery King was secretary, to hold national conferences.[99]

In November 1946 the Advisory Committee commissioned Chant to explore the possibility of making "a comprehensive objective study of the university training programme for veterans."[100] This was needed because the experience of the veterans could be expected to influence the work of universities generally. Chant's preliminary report, given in March 1947, recommended that the study to be undertaken "should be basically factual rather than a cumulation of opinion and impression; that it should be broad in scope; should extend over a period of years; and that interim reports on certain phases should be released from time to time."[101] On the strength of this advice, a subcommittee was appointed, consisting of Chant, Wallace, Smith, and James, to define the scope of the study and seek funds to support it.[102] Research was subsequently begun with the objective of investigating "the unusual success of veterans in spite of the unfavourable educational arrangements that prevail at present."[103] In November 1948, when Chant reported to the Advisory Committee on the progress of the study, it was noted that grant support from the Carnegie Corporation would be contingent on "an appropriate person" being named to lead the project and an outline being produced of the work to be done.[104] MacKenzie was assigned to review matters and to determine if Robert

England "might be persuaded to undertake the assignment."[105] When money was not forthcoming from either Carnegie or the Rockefeller Foundation, the hope was expressed that England would be able to complete the proposed study with the aid of a Guggenheim Foundation Fellowship, but there is no evidence in the documentary record that this ever happened.[106]

Two groups of students of special concern to the Advisory Committee in 1946 and 1947 were those seeking admission to medical and dental faculties. In 1946, to facilitate applications from veterans, most medical and dental faculties deferred acceptances until September, some even holding off until the fall term was almost ready to start.[107] By the spring of 1947, however, it was clear that there were more veterans who wanted to study medicine and dentistry than there were places available for them. In the circumstances, the Advisory Committee was asked to consider establishing "a reasonable quota" for veterans in faculties of medicine and dentistry and to ensure that qualified veterans would be notified of acceptance at an early date.[108] This would "permit candidates to proceed with the formulation of their housing and summer employment plans and would minimize the excessive 'shopping around' and hasty decisions with respect to second choices of occupation."[109] On the advice of MacKenzie, these delicate issues were referred to the executive of the NCCU for consideration.[110] On 19 November 1947 the Advisory Committee heard that while most faculties of medicine and dentistry were giving "priority to qualified veterans," there was "also a large backlog of highly qualified civilians applying for this limited accommodation."[111] To ease the situation, sixty Canadian veterans were currently being assisted to study medicine and dentistry in the United States.[112] In February 1950, Jamieson reported to the Advisory Committee that there was "a backlog of 62 veterans academically qualified for admission to Medicine" and that 127 others were in pre-medical courses.[113] Many other veterans who had wanted to study medicine and were qualified to do so had moved on to faculties such as engineering and commerce, where admissions had been increased to meet the demand. In total, 1,672 veterans had been admitted to first-year medicine (see table 10); of these, 22 were being assisted to study in the United States and the United Kingdom.[114] The backlog for dentistry was 12 with another 33 in predental courses.[115] Some 759 veterans had been admitted to dental faculties (see table 11), of whom 44 were being assisted to study in the United States.[116]

An issue of a different sort arose in relation to law students studying at Osgoode Hall in Toronto. This matter was pressed on the Advisory Committee by the Canadian Legion and arose from the fact that of 224 veterans registered in first year in 1947–48 (50 of whom were university

Table 10
Veterans Studying Medicine, 1 February 1950

	Edmonton	Saskatoon	Winnipeg	London	Toronto	Kingston	Ottawa	Montreal	Quebec	Halifax	Outside Canada	Total
Number admitted	139	72	198	151	433	142	50	288	25	152	22	1,672
Number graduated	18	–	12	9	36	4	–	61	3	5	–	148
Number on allowances	108	27	112	120	243	99	28	184	19	117	18	1,075
Number continuing at own expense	11	1	57	17	62	16	5	9	2	25	2	207
Percentage of veterans in total enrolment	54%	48%	46%	48%	35%	35%	13%	33%	35%	50%	–	–

Source: NA, DVA, file 66–38–2–1, Minutes of Advisory Committee on University Training for Veterans, 6 February 1950, Superintendent's Report, 11

Table 11
Veterans Studying Dentistry, 1 February 1950

	Edmonton	Toronto	Montreal	Halifax	Outside Canada	Total
Number admitted	117	427	138	33	44	759
Number graduated	11	43	14	1	7	76
Number on allowances	97	264	99	32	31	523
Number continuing at own expense	–	45	6	1	2	54
Percentage of veterans in total enrolment	71%	59%	62%	67%	–	–

Source: VAC, DVA, file 66–38–2–1, Minutes of Advisory Committee on University Training for Veterans, 6 February 1950, Superintendent's Report, 11

graduates), only 126, or 56.3 per cent, had passed.[117] Among non-veterans, the passing rate was 54.0 per cent. By contrast, in 1946–47, 72.1 per cent percentage of the veterans in the first-year class had been successful. Of those who had failed in 1947–48, moreover, 39 were repeating at their own expense. The response of the Advisory Committee to this unfortunate situation was to recommend that the Canadian Legion, "with due deference to the autonomy in academic matters of the Osgoode Hall Law School," take the problem up with the Canadian Bar Association.[118] The committee also approved a resolution requesting Jamieson to ask the Dean of Osgoode Hall to provide "the facts relating to this matter if he cares to do so."[119]

Looking to the future, the Advisory Committee also concerned itself with the employment opportunities that would be available to veterans on graduation. On 12 November 1946 the committee heard a report from J.R. Dymond of the Wartime Bureau of Technical Personnel on the work of the Inter-departmental Advisory Committee on Professionally Trained Persons. The latter committee had been established at the urging of DVA and NCCU and was "surveying professional opportunities for young people in Canada."[120] The Advisory Committee endorsed the group's work as "a major contribution to education in Canada."[121]

By March 1947, information had been submitted to DVA concerning medicine, dentistry, nursing, social service, veterinary science, forestry, osteopathy, petroleum engineering, and aeronautical engineering.[122] Simultaneously, a general report was being prepared for the Inter-departmental Advisory Committee by F.E. Whitworth of the Dominion Bureau of Statistics. The aim of DVA in all this was to ensure that the research now in progress "should be perpetuated in such a way that continuous inventories might be established for each of the important professions in Canada for the particular use of universities, secondary school systems, and individual young Canadians making choice for their careers."[123] In November 1947 the Advisory Committee heard from Dr Orville Ault, Director of Personnel Selection, Civil Service Commission, that the civil service, the country's "largest single employer," was "making every effort to secure a good proportion of outstanding university graduates" and would shortly be hiring 125 agricultural students for summer jobs.[124] In the same spirit, the National Employment Service was making officers available on campuses in the last month of each academic year. In 1951 the career goals of 1,362 veterans studying in Canada, the United States, and Europe (897, 339, 126, respectively), were tabulated as indicated in table 12.

The veterans sought to promote their own interest and welfare through local campus organizations (McGill was the hot spot in this

Table 12
Occupational Goals in 1951 of Veterans Pursuing Postgraduate Training under the
Veterans Rehabilitation Act

| Occupation | Year of completion | | | |
	1951	1952	1953 and after	Total students[1]
Biology[2]	147	79	19	245
Business administration	44	11	1	56
Chemistry[3]	55	40	11	106
Dentistry	4	4	–	8
Dietetics	1	1	–	2
Economics & political science	50	31	5	86
Education[4]	26	9	–	35
Engineering	65	24	11	100
Geology	50	19	7	76
Humanities[5]	99	83	26	208
Law	12	–	–	12
Medicine[6]	58	23	11	92
Pharmacy	5	–	1	6
Physics and mathematics	64	35	9	108
Psychology	36	10	16	62
Public health nursing	13	1	–	14
Social welfare	64	4	–	68
Theology	10	8	1	19
Not elsewhere classified	30	22	7	59
Total	833	404	125	1,362

Source: VAC, DVA, file 66–38–2–1, Minutes of Advisory Committee on University Training for
Veterans, 9 February 1951, Superintendent's Report, 8
[1] Distribution: in Canada, 897; in the United States, 339; in Europe, 126
[2] Including agriculture, horticulture, forestry, and entomology
[3] Including agricultural chemistry
[4] Including guidance
[5] Including dramatics, English, geography, history, languages, philosophy, etc.
[6] To certification by Royal College of Physicians and Surgeons of Canada

regard) and through the National Conference of Student Veterans,
which met for the first time in Montreal on 27 and 28 December
1945. In her letter inviting Ian Mackenzie to attend, Barbara E. Jackson, secretary of the McGill Student Veterans' Society, wrote that
while Canada's rehabilitation legislation was "probably the most generous in the world," there were improvements that could be made.[125]
Four specific issues were identified by the New Brunswick Veterans'
Club for consideration by the conference. These related to housing
conditions, the need for a larger differential between the grants paid
to married and single students, the need for "progressive increases" in

allowances after the first year of the program, and inclusion of the cost of books in fee payments.[126] Mackenzie did not attend the conference, but General E.L.M. Burns (who on 13 September 1945 had succeeded Chant as Director-General of Rehabilitation at DVA) addressed the opening session.[127] The conference was also attended by Brigadier Milton Gregg, a future Minister of Veterans Affairs, and by J.C.G. Herwig of the Canadian Legion. About 175 people attended the opening session.

In his speech, Burns stressed that while DVA "wanted to see that veterans had every reasonable facility to complete their education without undue hardship or worry," those present should remember three things before making "any recommendation for increased allowances."[128] These were that the allowances were not "intended to cover the whole cost of subsistence and education"; that they could not be raised for university students without being raised for those on vocational training and those receiving out-of-work assistance (which in turn had to take account of wage rates); and that "university student veterans were already getting very much more in the way of benefits than those who took the Re-establishment Credit or vocational training." Subsequently, Burns reported to Woods that his speech had been "well received" and that the delegates had been "in the great majority, sound and reasonable."[129] "They appreciate," he stated, "the danger to their own cause of being singled out for more favourable treatment than they are already receiving. Toronto and Queen's Universities in particular seemed inclined to feel that the plan was essentially fair at the present time and that there was no great justification for asking for more."

Perhaps the most important outcome of the gathering in Montreal was the formation of the National Council of Student Veterans, which was headed by Len Starkey, the chair of the conference and the leader of the McGill society.[130] A brief submitted to the government following the conference incorporated all the resolutions that had been passed.[131] Its first section called on the federal government "to recognize full employment for all citizens as the cornerstone of its rehabilitation program." Specifically, the government was urged to "carry through a public works program, subsidize industries, and undertake any other measures ... necessary to maintain full employment." The rest of the brief was organized under three headings: housing, financial matters, and educational issues. Despite Burns's cautionary words, the section on finance included a resolution in favour of increasing the married allowance by $40 per month and the single allowance by $20 per month. The brief also made the point that twenty-nine educational institutions (twenty-six of them universities) had been represented at the conference by sixty-three delegates and that the gathering had therefore been "representative of the fifteen thousand veterans attending universities throughout Canada" and also, because their problems were similar, "of the seventeen thousand veterans taking vocational training of all types."

In November 1946 a delegation from the McGill Student Veterans' Society (of which Frank B. Common was now president) went to Ottawa to press various claims, including the need for a commuters' allowance, but it did not have much success.[132] A second national conference was held at McGill on 27–29 December 1946. This time Jamieson attended and spoke on behalf of DVA. In his report on the proceedings, he observed that his "firm statement" to the opening session had been well received, especially by the representatives of the larger universities.[133] "It is evident," he continued, "that the great majority of student-veterans realize that their interests are not well served by continuous requests for unlimited assistance on the part of a minority which, for the past year, controlled the organization ... I am firmly convinced that existing provisions are meeting the essential needs of the persons for whom the legislation was designed and that a very small minority has dominated the representations made to this Department. The great majority appreciate the measure of assistance to those who are willing and able to help themselves." Jamieson also noted that the major universities outside Montreal "were not adequately represented" at the conference.

The big news at the 1946 gathering was Starkey's ouster as president. This happened in the second session, which was held in camera, and occurred after four members of the executive offered their resignation because of lack of confidence in the president. The issue at stake was his "political affiliation" and his "making use of his position as president, to further the ends of his own political party."[134] (Earlier in December, John Wallace and Jack Ord, two student veterans at the University of Toronto, had publicly charged that "ex-service students across Canada were protesting the 'Communist domination'" of their national organization.)[135] Following a stormy debate, a non-confidence vote was carried by 43 votes to 14, whereupon Starkey resigned and John Schierbeck of Macdonald College, a thirty-three-year-old naval veteran of Danish extraction and a postgraduate student in horticulture, was elected chairman of the conference and then president of the council.[136] After the uproar, the conference moved on to familiar business, but one report of the proceedings ended on this sobering note:

It was felt that the Conference as a whole accomplished little that is likely to have very practical results. It was largely dominated by a "demanding" attitude on the part of certain delegates who seemed to feel that the function of such a Conference was to see "how much more could be obtained from the government." There was, however, very definite appreciation of what is already being done by D.V.A. and a growing feeling by many that it is time for the veterans to see what they can do for themselves rather than expecting the government to do more. One delegate who had attended both conferences summed up this growing sense of self-responsibility as being indicative of the fact that the veteran students are one year nearer to being civilians and one step further from being servicemen.[137]

Under Schierbeck's leadership, the National Council of Student Veterans kept up its lobbying campaign, though not with the previous intensity.[138] With Starkey's downfall, DVA sailed into smoother waters in its relations with the organized veterans. In effect, its control over events, always firm, became even stronger. In the spring of 1947, veterans at the University of Toronto presented President Sidney Smith with an "Ex-Service Committee Brief."[139] This advanced four claims to "alleviate hardship conditions existing and affecting the student veteran on the Campus." The students wanted "tutorial assistance for all student veterans requiring it"; a cost of living bonus "to compensate for a general cost of living increase of $8.00 a month since August 1944"; a "Broadening of Veterans Life Insurance to permit insuring of Veterans' dependents"; and a "health insurance measure for a student veteran's dependents, similar to his own benefits ... to safeguard [the] health of the family and the financial stability of the veteran." Smith duly brought this forward to the Advisory Committee but without significant effect.[140] Tutorial assistance was left to the discretion of individual universities, and the proposed cost-of-living increase was refused because it would in effect be an increase in the living allowance, about which policy had already been established. Group medical insurance, the Advisory Committee heard, was already being studied by the Veterans' Advisory Service at a number of institutions.

Above all, the university presidents on the Advisory Committee were concerned about the continuation of the supplementary grant scheme. Since the initial allocation had been only for the period 1 July 1945 to 30 June 1946 this created obvious uncertainty. In 1946 the report of the Committee on University Requirements recommended that in future, while maintaining the limit of $150 per student, the supplementary grant should not be an across-the-board payment but should be "based upon the actual expenditures by universities in meeting the instructional needs of veterans."[141] This was because of "the wide variation in costs and fee scales, the difference in sources of other income and the wide variety of needs." The fixed grant system tended "to accentuate wide differentials in cost." When, by PC 4060, the government renewed the program on 1 October for another year (1 July 1946 to 30 June 1947), it did so on the basis advocated by England and his colleagues.[142] On 12 November 1946 the Advisory Committee considered the grant issue again and unanimously agreed on a resolution calling on the government to guarantee the payment of the supplementary grant for as long as veterans were attending universities under the terms of the Veterans Rehabilitation Act.[143] In fact, by PC 3799 of 23 September 1947, the existing arrangement was extended for another year (1 July 1947 to 30 June 1948). In response to this, the Advisory Committee passed a lengthy resolution on 16 January 1948 requesting that the grants next be extended for the period 1 July 1947 to 30 June 1951.[144] On 20 January 1948 a delegation from the Advisory Committee met with Finance Minister Douglas Abbott, and on 6 March 1948, PC 943 granted their request.[145] To 30 June 1950, $16,568,685.63 was paid in supplementary grants. By definition, as table 13 shows, the largest payments went to the seven universities that had attracted the bulk of the students.

On 1 June 1950, with the end of the training program for veterans (and therefore of the supplementary grant scheme) in sight, F. Cyril James gave a timely title to his presidential address to the annual conference of the NCCU, which was held that year at Royal Military College, Kingston. This was "Education: A National Problem." Reflecting on the passing of the veteran generation, he had this to say:

Every Canadian university, this spring, is granting degrees to larger numbers of students than at any previous graduation ceremony in its history. The veterans who came to us after discharge from the armed forces of Canada and her allies have now, in the great majority of cases, completed their academic courses, and the country is richer by tens of thousands of trained men and women who have equipped themselves at our universities to play a more significant part in our national life.

That fact is familiar to all of you. Representatives of Canadian universities worked with representatives of the Dominion Government during the darkest days of the recent war to formulate the plans that would give each qualified veteran the chance to obtain a university education. This Conference has on many occasions discussed the problems arising out of the veteran influx, and it has formally recorded its warm praise of the magnificent policy of the Government, administered through the Department of Veterans Affairs.

All of this I recall to your minds for a special reason. It underlines the fact that *education – and particularly University education – is of fundamental importance to the welfare, and indeed to the existence of Canada as a nation. Doctors, dentists and nurses* are essential for the maintenance of our national health; *teachers* are needed for our schools; *engineers* and *scientists* are necessary if we are to utilise

Table 13
Supplementary Payments to Canadian Universities to 30 June 1950[1]

University	Total	% of payments to all institutions
Toronto	$3,863,951.27	23.32
British Columbia	2,515,529.48	15.18
McGill	1,916,141.00	11.56
Saskatchewan	1,195,640.00	7.22
Alberta	1,195,292.92	7.21
Manitoba	990,621.06	5.98
Queen's	818,000.17	4.94
Western Ontario	530,185.90	3.20
New Brunswick	439,348.17	2.65
Dalhousie	421,501.80	2.54
Forty-eight other institutions	2,682,473.86	16.19
All institutions	$16,568,685.63	

Source: VAC, DVA 66–38–2–1, Minutes of Advisory Committee on University Training for Veterans, 9 February 1951, Superintendent's Report, 5

[1] The "current income" of Canadian universities and colleges, 1945–50, was as follows: $19,153,149 in 1945; $25,533,820 in 1946; $32,820,978 in 1947; $36,841,640 in 1948; $39,589,920 in 1949; and $40,458,592 in 1950. "Current income" included income from endowment, government grants, student fees, and miscellaneous payments. See Dominion Bureau of Statistics, *Higher Education in Canada, 1944–46* (Ottawa: King's Printer 1949), 92; *Survey of Higher Education 1946–48* (Ottawa: King's Printer 1950), 66; and *Survey of Higher Education 1948–50* (Ottawa: Queen's Printer 1952), 80–1.

efficiently the resources of our farms, forests and mines; *specialists of many kinds are required for the research appropriate to national defence;* while intelligent men with trained minds are needed in every branch of governmental and business administration.

If the Universities of Canada should cease to function or should fall far below the standard of their present work, the people of Canada would be confronted with a sad alternative. Either they would depend ignominiously on the University graduates of other countries to fill the thousands of important posts in Canada for which higher education is a necessary qualification, or Canada would sink to the level of a third-class power dependent on richer and wiser neighbours for the crumbs of its livelihood.[146]

When Canada had come into existence in 1867, continued James, it had made sense to make education a provincial responsibility. Now, however, in greatly altered circumstances, education was "the nation's business."[147] It was still appropriate to have primary and secondary education run exclusively by the provinces, but the universities of Canada had become "national institutions" with a national clientele

Table 14
Expenditures for Training of Veterans

	To 1950–51 ($)	1951–52 ($)	1952–53 ($)	1953–54 ($)	1954–55 ($)	Total ($)
VOCATIONAL						
Allowances	46,456,033	181,405	79,072	46,630	97,033	46,860,173
Tuition and fees	5,767,352	143,821	102,990	92,589	123,178	6,229,930
Total	52,223,385	325,226	182,062	139,219	220,211	53,090,103
UNIVERSITY						
Allowances	85,410,013	2,790,283	1,230,368	531,621	275,319	90,237,604
Tuition and fees	31,329,364	929,975	354,941	153,866	82,127	32,850,273
Supplementary grants	17,810,091	30,457	–	–	–	17,840,548
Total	134,549,468	3,750,715	1,585,309	685,487	357,446	140,928,425
Grand total	186,772,853	4,075,941	1,767,371	824,706	577,657	194,018,528

Source: Department of Veterans Affairs, Annual Report, 1955

and national responsibilities.[148] The logic of this was national funding, and James looked forward to the day when there would be a Canadian university grants committee. In the light of all that had happened since 1945, James's point of view was understandable; dominion government money had radically altered the Canadian university scene for the better. Through their involvement in veterans' affairs, Canada's university presidents had feasted at the well-provisioned table of the state and were anxious not to lose their dining privileges. They had seen the future and knew that it worked. To 1955, the total expenditure of the Government of Canada on the vocational and university training of veterans, including allowances, tuition fees, and supplementary grants, was $194,018,528 (see table 14). This funding had fuelled sweeping change.

The Veterans Rehabilitation Act had transformed not only the careers and lives of tens of thousands of individual Canadians but the institutions through which its benefits were delivered. In the case of the universities, the act stimulated action by the federal government to give the universities the means to acquire new faculty and provide urgently needed new facilities. These benefited postsecondary education in the country long after the great wave of veterans had been educated and re-established. A big short-term demand left behind it important long-term resources. Of necessity, the universities had to learn quickly after 1945 how to deliver new services in new ways to a larger and more diverse student body than ever before. In the public interest, they were able to work together through the NCCU and the Advisory Committee, and this enabled them to innovate to an unprecedented extent. The legacy of the period was a fresh generation of Canadian professionals and a university system that was more complex and capable than it had previously been. The compact body of university leaders, all of them men, who responded to the needs of the times, participated in stirring national events and acquired a distinctly pan-Canadian outlook. They had forcefully impressed upon them the beneficent possibilities inherent in collective action organized by the federal state. This was something a later generation of Canadians, faced with mounting public debt and influenced by anti-tax and anti-statist ideas, was inclined to forget. That the royal commission which recommended the creation of the Canada Council should have had as one of its members Norman MacKenzie, who had played such an important role in the successful administration of the Veterans Rehabilitation Act, was no surprise. This new body was designed to perpetuate the many good things the dominion government had done through the war and the immediate postwar period.

The Canadians who built the cultural institutions and social safety network of the 1950s knew what the state could accomplish because they had first-hand experience of its achievements. All over Canada, the successes of the 1945–50 period were remembered fondly by the men and women who had fought and won the war and secured the peace. But for the historian, some questions inevitably remain. Rich as the DVA documentary record is, it is hard to pinpoint the characteristics of the elite group among the hundreds of thousands of Canadian ex-service men and women who got the cream of the benefits provided for in the Veterans Rehabilitation Act. Did officers, for example, fare better than enlisted men? And did the DVA counsellors, the gatekeepers of the training system, have an agenda of their own? No doubt, the preferences of individual veterans within the general framework of the Veterans Charter were also important. After all, the benefits of the Veterans Rehabilitation Act had to compete with the re-establishment credit scheme and the benefits of the Veterans' Land Act, which had their own attractions. Who among the veterans preferred which benefit must remain an open matter, at least for the time being.

Further research will likewise be required to understand the impact of the Veterans Rehabilitation Act on opinion in Quebec. As table 13 suggests, the French-language universities did very poorly indeed in the distribution of supplementary grants, despite the participation of prominent French-Canadian academic administrators in the work of the NCCU and the Advisory Committee. Laval University ranked twenty-third in the list of universities receiving the grants and the University of Montreal twenty-fifth. The Maritime universities likewise lagged, though not as badly. What explains this outcome? Historically, there had been a low rate of participation in university education in Quebec, and this may have been a factor. There is also good anecdotal evidence to support the view that although the benefits of the Veterans Rehabilitation Act were legally available to volunteers and conscripts alike, the DVA system ensured that in practice they were reserved overwhelmingly for volunteers. Because of lingering doubts in Quebec about the conduct of the war, the province's mix of volunteers and conscripts may have worked against it in the distribution of training benefits. But again this is something that, for the moment, can only be speculated upon.

It can scarcely be doubted, however, that the relative positions of French- and English-language institutions under the Veterans Rehabilitation Act had a negative impact on ever-vigilant nationalist opinion in Quebec. The contrast between what happened at McGill and what happened at the University of Montreal, two scholarly solitudes in one city, was plain to be seen. This was perhaps the inevitable result of the way the war had been fought, but it carried a price just the same. Thus, in the 1950s, when Maurice Duplessis fought federal government intrusion into postsecondary education of the sort favoured by F. Cyril James, it was against the backdrop of a big federal program that had almost bypassed Quebec's French-language universities. The *épanouissement* of the latter institutions, albeit under quite different auspices and for quite different purposes, came in the 1960s. In that decade also, the country's English-language institutions themselves experienced another great wave of change. This built upon the stunning achievements of the glory days of the late 1940s, when so much in Canada had been started and so much had seemed possible.

NOTES

I am grateful to Jock Bates and R.A. Young for advice and comment and to Don Ives and Ken Hawkes of Veterans Affairs Canada for research assistance.

1 For PC 7633 and the amendments thereto, see Walter S. Woods, *Rehabilitation (A Combined Operation)* (Ottawa, Queen's Printer 1953), 465–76.
2 Veterans Affairs Canada (hereafter VAC), records of the Department of Veterans Affairs (hereafter DVA), file 66–27–3, *Report of the National Conference of Canadian Universities on Post-War Problems* (hereafter *Report*) (Toronto 1944), 5.
3 Ibid.
4 Ibid.
5 VAC, DVA, file 66–27–3, NCCU, Committee on Post-War Problems, minutes of meeting of 3–5 January 1944.
6 Ibid., Fennell to Jamieson, 24 May 1944.
7 *Report*, 1.
8 VAC, DVA, file 66–27–3, Fennell to Jamieson, 24 May 1944, and Thomson to Jamieson, 8 June 1945.
9 *Report*, 7.
10 The act creating the Department of Veterans Affairs received assent on 30 June 1944. See Woods, *Rehabilitation*, 37.
11 *Report*, 22–3.
12 Ibid., 26.
13 Ibid., 29.
14 Ibid., 29.
15 Ibid., 30.
16 Ibid., 31.
17 Ibid., 32.
18 Ibid., 29.

19 VAC, DVA, file 66–38–2, vol. 1.

20 Ibid.

21 Ibid.

22 There is a copy of PC 3206 in VAC, DVA, file 66–38–2, vol. 1.

23 VAC, DVA, file 66–38–2, vol. 1.

24 Ibid.

25 Ibid.

26 Ibid., Jamieson to James, 10 May 1945.

27 Ibid.

28 VAC, DVA, file 66–38–2–1, Minutes of the Advisory Committee on University Training for Veterans (hereafter Minutes), 9 February 1951.

29 Minutes, 28 May 1945, 1.

30 VAC, DVA, file 66–38–2, vol. 1, Woods to Clark, 23 May 1945.

31 See attachment to Minutes, 28 May 1945.

32 In discussion, Sidney Smith reported on a study at the University of Toronto concerning the relationship, by faculty, of fees to actual costs. This study yielded the following information:

	Actual Cost	Tuition Fees
Arts	$411	$150
Medicine	675	250
Applied science	518	250
Household science	440	175

33 There is a copy of this order attached to Minutes, 25 February 1946.

34 Woods, *Rehabilitation*, 89.

35 Minutes, 17 March 1947, 7.

36 Ibid., 8.

37 Minutes, 20 November 1948, appendix A, Superintendent's Report, 1.

38 Ibid., 2.

39 Minutes, 25 February 1946, Confidential Letter no. 185.

40 Ibid.

41 Ibid.

42 Minutes, 20 November 1948, appendix A, Superintendent's Report, 2.

43 Ibid.

44 *Statutes of Canada*, 1946, 485.

45 Ibid.

46 VAC, DVA, file 66–38–2–2, vol. 1.

47 M.C. Urquhart, ed., and K.A.H. Buckley, asst. ed., *Historical Statistics of Canada* (Toronto: Macmillan Company of Canada 1965), 601.

48 On 31 March 1949, when Newfoundland became a province, Ottawa also assumed responsibility for about sixty veterans who were attending Canadian universities with the support of the government in St John's. See Minutes, 20 November 1948, 7.

49 Minutes, 17 March 1947, 2.

50 Minutes, 12 November 1946, 4, "Summary of Enrolments of Veterans in receipt of allowances, as furnished by D.V.A. District Offices as of November, 1946."

51 Minutes, 20 November 1948, appendix A, Superintendent's Report, 2.

52 Minutes, 6 February 1950, Superintendent's Report, 1. According to this same source, the equivalent United States figure was 40 per cent.

53 W.P. Thompson, *The University of Saskatchewan: A Personal History* (Toronto: University of Toronto Press 1970), 133.

54 Minutes, 25 February 1946, Confidential Letter no. 154.

55 Minutes, 13 November 1945, 9.

56 Minutes, 6 February 1950, Superintendent's Report, 3.

57 Ibid.

58 Ibid.

59 Minutes, 17 March 1947, appendix A, "Distribution by Faculties of Trainees as at February 15th, 1947."

60 Minutes, 9 February 1951, Superintendent's Report, 7.

61 Ibid., and Minutes, 6 February 1950, Superintendent's Report, 9.

62 Minutes, 25 February 1946, appendix 1, "Data re Veterans in Receipt of University Training Allowances."

63 Minutes, 20 November 1948, Superintendent's Report, 2. See also Minutes, 6 February 1950, Superintendent's Report, 1.

64 Thompson, *The University of Saskatchewan*, 133.

65 Ibid., 133–4.

66 Minutes, 25 February 1946, 5.

67 In addition to Bovey, the original members of the royal commission were F.W. Smelts, D.G. Lyons, Hector Dupuis, J.C.G. Herwig, and F.S. Rutherford. The executive secretary was A.E. Fortington. On 8 May 1945, Stewart R. Ross was appointed to replace Rutherford, who had resigned.

68 Minutes, 13 November 1945, 6.

69 Ibid.

70 There is a copy of PC 7129 in VAC, DVA, file 66–38–2, vol. 1.

71 VAC, DVA, file 66–38–2, vol. 1, "Interim Report of Committee on University Requirements," 1.

72 Ibid., 2.

73 Ibid.

74 Ibid.

75 Ibid.

76 VAC, DVA, file 66–38–2, vol. 1, "Interim Report of Committee on University Requirements," appendix 2, "Notes on University Accommodation for Veterans," 1.

77 Ibid.

78 Ibid., 2. This college should not be confused with the later College d'enseignement général et professionnel of the same name. See Stanley

Brice Frost, *McGill University for the Advancement of Learning*, vol. 2, 1895–1971 (Kingston and Montreal: McGill-Queen's University Press 1984), 240.

79 VAC, DVA, file 66–38–2, vol. 1, "Interim Report of Committee on University Requirements," appendix 2, "Notes on University Accommodation for Veterans," 2.

80 There is a copy of PC 7224 attached to Minutes, 25 February 1946.

81 Minutes, 19 November 1947, 3.

82 Ibid.

83 Ibid.

84 Minutes, 20 November 1948, appendix A, Superintendent's Report, 5.

85 Ibid.

86 Ibid.

87 Ibid.

88 Minutes, 12 November 1946, 6.

89 Minutes, 17 March 1947, appendix H.

90 Minutes, 6 February 1950, appendix, Superintendent's Report, 5.

91 Minutes, 20 November 1948, appendix A, Superintendent's Report, 5.

92 Minutes, 6 February 1950, appendix, Superintendent's Report, 5.

93 For the relevant section of PC 4059, see Minutes, 17 March 1947, 2.

94 Minutes, 9 February 1951, Superintendent's Report, 1.

95 Ibid.

96 Minutes, 13 November 1945, 9.

97 Minutes, 12 November 1946, 3.

98 Ibid.

99 Minutes, 17 March 1947, 5–6, and 16 January 1948, 2.

100 Minutes, 12 November 1946, 3.

101 Minutes, 17 March 1947, 4.

102 Ibid., 5.

103 Minutes, 19 November 1947, 6.

104 Minutes, 20 November 1948, 2.

105 Ibid.

106 Minutes, 6 February 1950, 3. England had been a Guggenheim Foundation Fellow in 1945.

107 Minutes, 17 March 1947, 3.

108 Ibid., 3.

109 Ibid., 4.

110 Ibid.

111 Minutes, 19 November 1947, 2.

112 Ibid.

113 Minutes, 6 February 1950, 2.

114 Ibid., 3.

115 Ibid.

116 Ibid.
117 Minutes, 20 November 1948, 6.
118 Ibid., 7.
119 Ibid.
120 Minutes, 12 November 1946, 3. See also appendix C, "Survey of Professionally Trained Persons."
121 Ibid.
122 Minutes, 17 March 1947, 30.
123 Ibid.
124 Minutes, 19 November 1947, 4.
125 VAC, DVA, file 66–27–4, vol. 1, Jackson to Mackenzie, 9 December 1945.
126 Ibid., memorandum attached to Plommer to Woods, 7 December 1945. A.G. Plommer was president of the University of New Brunswick Veterans' Club.
127 Ibid., memorandum by Burns to Woods, 29 December 1945.
128 Ibid.
129 Ibid.
130 VAC, DVA, file 66–27–4, vol. 1, "Report of the National Conference of Student Veterans, Montreal, Quebec, December 27–29th 1945." The others named to the council were G.P. Lagenière, University of Montreal; J. Testart, University of Western Ontario; G.E. King, Ontario Training and Rehabilitation Institute, Toronto; N.E. Wright, University of Manitoba; W. Rorkem, University of Alberta; and A.E. Hart, Dalhousie University.
131 Ibid., "Brief to the Dominion Government Submitted by the National Conference of Student Veterans."
132 Ibid., memorandum by Riches to Rutherford, 30 November 1946.
133 Ibid., memorandum by Jamieson to Rutherford, 2 January 1947.
134 Ibid., "Report of National Conference of Student Veterans, McGill University, Montreal, December 27–29th, 1946," 1.
135 S. Roger G. Beaufoy, ed., *A Report on the 2nd National Conference of Student Veterans*, 17. Beaufoy, of the Canadian Vocational Training Centre No. 8, Red Deer, Alberta, attended the 1946 conference. The report was printed at the School of Printing Trades, Red Deer. There is a copy in VAC, DVA, file 66–27–4, vol. 1. See also "Communist Pressure on Campus Charged," *Globe and Mail* (Toronto), 13 December 1946. This article includes the following: "Communists are trying every ruse to dominate veteran and student organizations in Canadian universities, but their attempts are being successfully broken up, John Wallace, University of Toronto student, declared here yesterday ... Another University of Toronto student-veteran, Jack Ord, reported that ex-service students across Canada have risen in protest of Communist domination of their official organization, the National Conference of Student Veterans, which claims to represent over 40,000 students. He said that a Red 'pressure group' had attempted

to use the movement to further its own interests. The University of British Columbia has withdrawn entirely on this account; Dalhousie University has refused to consider entrance, and McGill has ousted a Communist from leadership of its own Veterans' Society on the same grounds, Ord claimed." In the event, the University of British Columbia was represented at the 1946 conference in Montreal by G. Livingstone and J. Boyd.

136 The other members elected to the council were L. McIntyre, Dalhousie University; C. Dean, Sir George Williams College; J. Testart, University of Western Ontario; E. Barnard, Laval University; G. Livingstone, University of British Columbia; and G. Swinton, Montreal Art Association, who represented students in vocational training. See VAC, DVA, file 66–27–4, vol. 1, "Report of National Conference of Student Veterans, McGill University, Montreal, December 27–29th, 1946," 7.

137 Ibid., 7.

138 In an introductory letter to "the final brief covering the sessions held in Montreal December 27th to 29th, 1946," Schierbeck wrote as follows: "An alien philosophy knocks at our door. During the past quarter century it has had a hearing from the Canadian people and they want nothing of it; now it grows insistent and uses those cherished privileges which we believe to be the right of every law abiding Canadian to exercise, to attack us from within. The next twenty years will show whether we can unite in determination to exclude this insidious venom and at the same time offer every Canadian those same material advantages which it holds out to attract the unwary. We can do this only if [we] unremittingly undertake to expose the disastrous consequences of dictatorship in the community where we work and live. That, we believe, is one way in which Student Veterans can in some measure repay Canada the debt they owe for what they have received" (enclosure in VAC, DVA, file 66–27–4, vol. 1, Schierbeck to Jamieson, 17 March 1947).

139 VAC, DVA, file 66–27–4, vol. 1, copy attached to memorandum by Jamieson, 10 March 1947.

140 Minutes, 17 March 1947, 6.

141 Minutes, 25 February 1946, 4.

142 For PC 4060, see Minutes, 12 November 1946, appendix E.

143 Minutes, 12 November 1946, 3.

144 Minutes, 16 January 1948, 1–2.

145 Ibid., 3; Minutes, 20 November 1948, appendix A, Superintendent's Report, 1.

146 VAC, DVA, file 66–27–3, "Education: A National Problem," 1 (emphasis in the original).

147 Ibid., 3.

148 Ibid., 4.

TERRY COPP

From Neurasthenia to Post-Traumatic Stress Disorder: Canadian Veterans and the Problem of Persistent Emotional Disabilities

As long as there have been wars, individuals have suffered from the after-effects of traumatic experiences. Stories of nightmares, involuntary trembling, and dramatic reactions to sudden noises are part of the lore of every combat veteran's family. Folk memory and literature, if not formal history, are full of examples of the returned soldier who became a burnt-out case, the promising young man who was never the same again, the chronic alcoholic who couldn't get over the war. The universal character of this phenomenon is easy enough to establish. What requires investigation are the intellectual and ultimately social constructs developed to explain the persistence of pain and the reality of chronic neurosis.

By the end of World War I, psychiatrists had generally abandoned their belief that "shell shock" was the product of enormous forces of compression and decompression, what the French called *vent du projectile*,[1] and had agreed to interpret mental breakdown in war as a form of neurosis. Few of the physicians who ran the military hospitals or organized psychiatric care for veterans had read Sigmund Freud systematically, but they used his insights freely. As Ernest Jones, who popularized Freudian views to English-speaking audiences, put it, "The facts of the war itself accord with Freud's view of the human mind as containing beneath the surface a body of imperfectly controlled and explosive forces which in their nature conflict with the standards of civilization."[2]

War neuroses and their treatment became a new focus for psychiatry and the infant academic discipline of psychology. The practitioners of both professions quickly developed ways of explaining the problems of chronic neurosis in veterans which fitted their professional interests. Some were directly influenced by psychodynamic theory and saw their patients as involved in a "flight into illness," which might be countered with painful electrical treatments to encourage a "flight into health." More often, simple psychotherapy, which stressed the need to exercise will-power to overcome nervous symptoms, was the preferred method. As Desmond Morton and Glenn Wright have argued, in Canada even this modest treatment process was supposed to end with "a flat and final pension payment of five hundred dollars."[3] Instead, the Royal Commission on Pensions and Re-establishment chaired by J.L. Ralston recommended, much against medical advice, that pension entitlement for the "neurasthenic" veteran who had failed to overcome his condition be authorized.[4]

The neuropsychiatrists and front-line medical officers who had argued against pensions believed that this type of state support simply reinforced a neurosis as part of what Freudians called "secondary gain." The primary gain from a symptom is freedom from anxiety or conflict; the secondary gain consists of the practical advantages that can be achieved by using the symptom to manipulate others.[5] War neuroses were the product of trauma and were expected to disappear when the trauma ended. Pensions might prevent the soldier from working through his problem and might encourage the formation of a chronic neurosis that was unlikely to disappear. Freudians believed that true traumatic neuroses had no unconscious meaning and consequently that patients' dreams were not amenable to interpretation. Experience suggested, however, that some veterans transformed a traumatic neurosis into a psychoneurosis – in the context of pensions or other forms of secondary gain.

Following up on the report of the Ralston Commission, large numbers of Canadian veterans sought assistance for neuropsychiatric problems. By 1927, some 9,000 veterans were in receipt of pensions for "shell shock and neurosis,"[6] and thousands more had had their claims rejected. Caution must be exercised in analysing these or other numbers, however, for the wide variance in psychiatric diagnoses makes any attempt to quantify the incidence of post-traumatic neurosis impossible.

One study of World War I veterans examined men who had enlisted in Waterloo County's 34th Battalion. Information was obtained on forty-six volunteers who served in France, and the author, Michael Wert, was able to link the personnel records of the survivors with their Veterans Affairs files, as well as with local funeral home records. Thirty-six survived the war, but thirty-one were wounded or invalided through sickness. Five of these suffered from "shell shock," two from "neurasthenia." In the postwar period, sixteen of these men obtained pensions for varying periods, and almost all the others sought pensions for physical ailments with accompanying psychosomatic symptoms. One veteran who received a 15 per cent disability award for deafness sought to increase his rate on neuropsychiatric grounds, claiming that bouts of depression and other symptoms were war related. His application, which reveals a textbook case of what would now be called post-traumatic stress disorder, was rejected, as were others whose case histories included similar problems.[7]

Dr J.B.S. Cathcart, the chief neuropsychiatrist in the Department of Pensions and National Health, as well as the psychiatrists who worked with veterans at the Toronto and Winnipeg neuropsychiatric centres for out-patients, became firm opponents of pensions for psychiatric problems. They were convinced that men elaborated symptoms and sought to avoid recovery. At the outbreak of the war in 1939, Cathcart argued for policies designed to avoid post-traumatic neurosis by early treatment of shell shock and an insistence on return to duty.[8] The physician who actually established the neuropsychiatric service of the Canadian army in World War II, Dr Colin Russell, shared this view, advocating the use of electric shock as part of the cure of the "psychoneuropath." Treatment was a mental contest which must result in "the victory of the physician."[9]

Psychologists took a different approach to the pension question, one that advanced their professional agenda. The development of IQ and personality tests during World War I had given psychologists a methodological tool that could be portrayed as scientific and promised to transform their discipline. The newly formed Canadian Psychological Association developed its own instrument, the M-test, and sought to use it to screen individuals unfitted for the duties a soldier was required to perform in a modern army. Under the leadership of Brock Chisholm, the Canadian Army established the Directorate of Personnel Selection, and screening for personalities predisposed to neurosis was added to its mandate.

The development of Canadian Army psychiatry is described in Copp and McAndrew's book *Battle Exhaustion*[10] and need not be repeated here. It is sufficient to note that both psychiatrists and psychologists presented arguments about mental casualties of war which were rooted in the desire to prevent the emergence of a postwar neuropsychiatric pension problem. Both groups were confident that the incidence of shell shock and subsequent neurosis could be dramatically reduced if their recommendations were followed.

By 1945, psychiatrists with front-line experience were far less certain that either personnel selection or a treatment regime, based on the principles of proximity, immediacy, and expectancy, made much difference. Battle exhaustion, their preferred term for shell shock or what we today call combat stress reaction, seemed to occur in relation to the intensity of the combat experience as perceived by the soldier. It was clear that many individuals who could be labelled neurotic continued to function in combat, while others who appeared to be some of the finest specimens of young manhood broke down under varying degrees of pressure. Early treatment close to the front lines, with pressure to return to one's unit, also turned out to be of dubious value; only a small percentage of battle exhaustion casualties were sent back to face combat in 1945, because the evidence of recurrence of symptoms was too strong.[11]

With the end of the war, the army's psychiatric service was quickly disbanded, and the problem of veterans who exhibited continuing symptoms of neurosis was handed to the newly formed Department of Veterans Affairs (DVA). The Division of Treatment Services appointed Dr Travis E. Dancey as adviser in psychiatry, and thus Dancey became one of the key figures in policy development. An MD with a one-year diploma in mental hospital psychiatry, Dancey had begun his career at McGill University and the Verdun Protestant Hospital for the Insane. His background and interest in various physical therapies, such as insulin subcoma, fitted well with the resolutely anti-Freudian approach of the McGill medical faculty and the prestigious Montreal Neurological Institute. Dancey joined the army and, after service as a psychiatrist in the Montreal military district, worked overseas at No. 1 Neurological Hospital in Basingstoke.[12] When the 2nd Canadian Corps appointed Dr Burdett McNeel as corps psychiatrist in the fall of 1944, Dancey took over No. 1 Canadian Exhaustion Unit, where he was exposed to front-line psychiatry. In the battle of the Rhineland in February and March, 1945, Dancey dealt with hundreds of battle exhaustion cases, using various physical therapies and experimenting with hypnosis.[13]

Dancey's experience in Northwest Europe challenged his view that early treatment would cure battle exhaustion and raised doubts about the value of personnel selection, but he remained convinced that delayed, or recurring, chronic neuroses could be avoided or minimized by removing all prospects of "secondary gain." He described the Canadian approach to war-related neuroses in a paper presented to the American Psychiatric Association in May 1950. Titled "Treatment in the Absence of Pensioning for Psychoneurotic Veterans," the paper described the policy of the Canadian Pension Commission to claimants who exhibited neurotic symptoms:

A neurosis is a disorder that has its roots in childhood and may increase in severity throughout the years and is utilized by the subject, through unconscious mechanism, to avoid painful experiences and to escape certain responsibilities. Because of repetitive patterns of thinking and behaviour the subject is prone to take advantage of situations that may arise and will further protect him. Any encouragement toward the acceptance of his illness as a means of escaping his responsibilities is therefore dangerous and may well develop from compensation in the form of the payment of money. The subject, under such conditions, is apt to feel more and more disabled and to demand repeated increases in his income from a state that has already assumed a certain responsibility for his illness.[14]

Dancey went on to note that the initial policy of providing treatment only for conditions that arose in the first year following demobilization had been reversed, and veterans with chronic neuroses were able to obtain therapeutic assistance at veterans' hospitals. In 1948, the first year of the program, 420 veterans were admitted to programs of analytically oriented psychotherapy, modified insulin treatment, or group psychotherapy.[15]

The pension commission's insistence on refusing pensions was endorsed by the Director of Treatment Services, Dr J.N.B. Crawford, a veteran of the Hong Kong expedition and Japanese prisoner-of-war camps, who was convinced that if he ever allowed himself to "gratify his dependency needs," he would lose his grip and avoid all stressful situations and work. When Crawford moved to the Department of National Health and Welfare, however, the stone wall began to crumble. Constant pressure from veterans who had not responded to treatment led to an increasing number of awards for neuropsychiatric disabilities.[16]

Nonetheless, Dancey continued to oppose this trend. He had been instrumental in developing a research project designed to follow up the post-discharge adjustment of soldiers treated for battle exhaustion at No. 1 Canadian Exhaustion Unit from October 1944 to May 1945, and his research team interviewed 346 of the 1,271 men admitted. The report[17] is a deeply flawed document, which will be the subject of a separate paper; it is sufficient to note here that Dancey and others who read the report in 1950 accepted the conclusion that all but a small minority of the men who had broken down in battle had made a satisfactory adjustment to civilian life. Those who were having difficulty were said to have been "poorly adjusted before enlistment." Further, the report suggested that the group that had experienced most combat stress had made the best adjustment to civilian life.[18]

Dancey and other DVA psychiatrists continued to advocate treatment in place of monetary compensation. They contrasted the Canadian system with what was happening in such countries as the United Kingdom and New Zealand, where thousands of veterans were pensioned for neurosis and where psychiatrists reported a "vicious spiral" that was creating "widespread hypochondria and dependence on pharmaceutical aids."[19]

In Canada, the mechanism through which pensions for neurosis were granted was the Assessment and Rehabilitation Unit of DVA. This "backdoor route" for veterans who had been denied awards by the Canadian Pension Commission was sharply criticized by Dancey in a 1960 article,[20] but by then the unit was making decisions on the merits of each case and was recognizing the existence of post-traumatic stress disorder. Dancey believed that all that prevented a flood of applications was the lack of publicity and the complexity of the appeal process.

The uneasy compromise between psychodynamic doctrine and the empirical evidence of veterans suffering from war-related chronic neurosis persisted until the 1980s. The challenge to the status quo developed in the United States when an alliance of Vietnam veterans and radicalized psychiatrists mounted a well-organized campaign to force the American Psychiatric Association (APA) to include "post-Vietnam syndrome" as a recognized disorder in the association's *Diagnostic and Statistical Manual*.[21] The APA had developed this manual as a physicians' desk reference for psychiatrists. Recognized mental illnesses were described, providing a basis for categorizing a bewildering variety of symptoms and providing patients with illness labels that would be accepted by employers, insurance companies, and the Veterans Administration (since 1988 the Department of Veterans Affairs).

The first manual, known as DSMI, published in 1952, included a category called gross stress reaction, usually a combat stress reaction, which was described as a temporary condition. The authors specifically rejected the concept of delayed or chronic stress reactions insisting, as Canadian and American officials did, that chronic neurosis developed among predisposed individuals. In DSMI, the symptoms of delayed stress reaction were categorized under forms of behaviour such as alcoholism, drug abuse, and depression. The second edition, DSMII, was developed between 1965 and 1968, before American attitudes to the Vietnam war had changed.[22] The apparent success of battlefield psychiatry in Vietnam, where the rate of breakdown was 5 to 7 per cent instead of the 20 per cent level reached in World War II, persuaded the authors to drop gross stress reaction from the manual, and no other reference was made to war-related disorders.[23] Psychiatrists working with veterans of Vietnam and earlier wars were stunned by this decision. They had encountered numerous examples of delayed stress reactions and were looking for help from the leaders of their profession. Between 1968 and 1980, when DSMIII appeared, groups such as Vietnam Veterans against the War joined with other antiwar activists in pressing for change. Robert J. Lifton, a popular writer and psychiatrist, worked with psychiatrist Chaim Shatan and a young social worker, Sarah Haley, to force the profession to recognize delayed stress reaction as a diagnosis for thousands of troubled Vietnam vets.[24]

Shatan, a Canadian, had studied at McGill during World War II and had been exposed to veterans labelled chronic neurotics. Convinced that many veterans suffered from delayed traumas caused by their "inability to grieve in the combat zone," he developed the case for post-Vietnam syndrome in a series of articles and public presentations.[25] In 1973, Lifton published *Home from the War*,[26] which criticized the U.S. government, the military, and the psychiatric profession. The stage was set for forcing changes in DSMIII. In 1980 the APA capitulated, agreeing that a diagnosis of post-traumatic stress disorder (PTSD) could be applied to veterans and other survivors of traumatic events. The characteristic symptoms were described as "re-experiencing the traumatic event; numbing of responsiveness to, or reduced involvement with the external world; and a variety of autonomic, dysphoric, or cognitive symptoms."[27]

These events initially had little impact in Canada. Young Canadians who had volunteered to serve in Vietnam were all but invisible, and the PTSD diagnosis seemed to be specific to that war.[28] It is not yet possible to trace the pattern of acceptance of the diagnosis by Veterans Affairs Canada (as DVA is now alternatively known),[29] but it is evident that by the mid-1980s, veterans' advocates were employing the concept in presentations to the Canadian Pension Commission.[30]

In 1990, Dr Lynne Beal, a psychologist serving as a consultant to the Dieppe Veterans and Prisoners of War Association, appeared before the Senate Subcommittee on Veterans Affairs to review a "Report to the Minister of Veterans Affairs on a Study on Canadians Who Were Prisoners of War in Europe During World War II." Dr Beal told the subcommittee that a large number of Dieppe veterans were suffering from PTSD, thus alerting Senator Jack Marshall and his colleagues to the problem.[31]

Dr Beal developed a questionnaire designed to identify those veterans, especially former prisoners-of-war, who reported symptoms. She concluded: "Forty-eight percent of [Dieppe] POWs had PTSD in 1946 and forty-two percent of POWs ... Only 5% receive pensions for psychological disabilities. There appears to be no relationship between having PTSD and getting a psychological disability pension ... There appears to have been no significant initiative to diagnose PTSD in these POWs after this disorder was identified."[32] Dr Beal reported that the incidence of PTSD was also high among veterans of the Dieppe Raid who were not taken prisoner. Her questionnaire produced rates of 27 per cent in 1946 and 30 per cent in 1992. While there are serious methodological problems with an investigation employing a questionnaire without a clinical interview or corroborating evidence, it is clear that any form of inquiry into the presence of PTSD symptoms among World War II and Korean veterans would identify a large number exhibiting symptoms that might be attributed to post-traumatic stress.

We now live in a world in which PTSD is a well-established mental health diagnosis. In the United States, very large resources have been directed towards the treatment of the illness, and academic research on the topic is a growth industry. In Canada, journalists have begun to write about PTSD in the context of the transformation of the Canadian Armed Forces' peacekeeping role to the far more stressful peacemaking role in such trouble spots as Bosnia. As a result, Veterans Affairs Canada is under pressure to re-examine its approach to PTSD, particularly with regard to psychological disability pensions. All of this activity suggests the importance of developing a clear policy and assigning adequate resources to deal with a problem that will grow in importance over the next several decades.

The following points need to be considered in the formulation of such a policy:

1 Steps should be taken to ensure that the commissioned and non-commissioned officers of the Canadian Armed Forces clearly understand what is known about the causes and prevention of stress reactions. National Defence has prepared an excellent training film for this purpose, but this is only a first step in promoting systematic approaches to the management of stress.
2 We must develop methods of debriefing soldiers and celebrating their return from combatlike assignments so that the value of their contribution is formally recognized by the Canadian public. Evidence from the Vietnam War suggests that the lack of public recognition was a significant factor in the development of cases of PTSD.
3 The most sophisticated prophylactic system will not eliminate delayed stress reaction in the form of PTSD.[33]

Even if the armed forces develop outstanding programs in each of these areas, it is likely that Veterans Affairs Canada will have to cope with a growing number of stress reactions, some of which will be serious enough to be labelled PTSD. Veterans Affairs Canada should look to the American experience in this area and establish a program similar to the PTSD clinical teams created by the United States Veterans Administration (VA) in 1989 and the outreach programs devoted to the treatment of war zone veterans suffering from PTSD. The teams were able to deal with referrals from VA centres and with self-referrals. Obviously, the number of Canadian veterans likely to suffer from PTSD would be very much smaller than in the United States. It is possible that a single clinical team could address a large part of the problem.

The first report of the PTSD Clinical Teams Program concluded with words that speak directly to us all and serve as a conclusion to this chapter:

When young men and women go off to serve their country in time of war, many of them give little thought to what will happen when they come home. No deal is struck and no covenant is signed between those who risk all to serve, and those whose lifestyles and liberties are protected by that service. What binds the soldier to the nation is faith and trust. And it is, in the end, out of a sense of fairness, justice and decency, that a nation honours the faith and trust its young men placed in it when they went off to war. The PTSD Clinical Teams Program has taken its place as an important part of the immense enterprise of rewarding the faith and redeeming the trust of those who served their country when they were called.[34]

NOTES

1 Tom Brown, "Shell Shock in the Canadian Expeditionary Force 1914–1918: Canadian Psychiatry in the Great War," in Charles Roland, ed., *Health Disease and Medicine: Essays in Canadian History* (Hamilton: Hannah Institute for the History of Medicine 1984), 308–22.

2 Quoted in Louise E. Hoffman, "War, Revolution, and Psychoanalysis: Freudian Thought Begins to Grapple with Social Reality," *Journal of the History of the Behavioural Sciences* 17, no. 2 (1981): 251–69.

3 Desmond Morton and Glenn Wright, *Winning the Second Battle: Canadian Veterans and the Return to Civilian Life, 1915–1930* (Toronto: University of Toronto Press 1987), 133.

4 Ibid., 176. Clause 28 of the Pension Act reads in part:

28. (2) When in the opinion of a medical neurological expert an applicant for pension or a pensioner has a disability which is purely functional or hysterical no pension shall be paid, but such member of the forces shall immediately be referred to a Neurological Centre for treatment.

(3) In cases in which the functional or hysterical disability disappears as the result of treatment the Commission may, in its discretion, award a gratuity in final payment not exceeding five hundred dollars but no pension shall be paid.

(4) When as a result of treatment the functional or hysterical disability has not disappeared a pension shall be awarded in accordance with the extent of the disability: Provided the applicant or pensioner has not unreasonably refused to accept or continue treatment.

Quoted in Robert England, *Discharged: A Commentary on Civil Re-establishment of Veterans in Canada* (Toronto: Macmillan Company of Canada 1943), 301.

5 Charles Rycroft, *A Critical Dictionary of Psychoanalysis* (London: Nelson 1968).

6 J.P. Cathcart, "The Neuro-Psychiatric Branch of the Department of Soldiers' Civil Re-establishment," *Ontario Journal of Neuro-Psychiatry*, May 1928, 44–59.

7 Michael Wert, "From Enlistment to the Grave: A Case Study of the 34th Battalion's Experience with the Great War" (honours BA thesis, Wilfrid Laurier University 1990).

8 National Archives of Canada (hereafter NA), records of the Department of National Defence (hereafter DND), RG 24, vol. 19466, memo, J.S. Cathcart to Deputy Minister, Department of Pensions and National Health, 4 October 1939.

9 Colin Russell, "The Nature of War Neuroses," *Canadian Medical Association Journal* 41 (1939): 550.

10 Terry Copp and Bill McAndrew, *Battle Exhaustion: Soldiers and Psychiatrists in the Canadian Army, 1939–1945* (Montreal & Kingston: McGill-Queen's University Press 1990), chap. 6.

11 Ibid., chap. 7.

12 Travis E. Dancey, "The Awarding of Pensions on Psychiatric Grounds," *Treatment Services Bulletin*, February 1948, 25. The following discussion is based on interviews and correspondence with Travis Dancey as well as on his published articles.

13 NA, DND, vol. 15951, War Diary, No. 1 Canadian Exhaustion Unit (February/March 1945), and interviews.

14 Travis E. Dancey, "Treatment in the Absence of Pensioning for Psycho-neurotic Veterans," *American Journal of Psychiatry* 107 (November 1950): 347.

15 Ibid., 348.

16 Letter, Travis Dancey to Terry Copp, 10 October 1992.

17 R. Notman, "A Survey of 1271 Neuropsychiatric Casualties Passing through No. 1 Canadian Exhaustion Unit in North-West Europe between October 1944 and May 1945. Follow-up Studies of the Post-discharge Adjustment (up to January 1950) of 346 Members of the Above Series," Ottawa, DVA, Project no. 44, 1950.

18 Ibid., 81–92.

19 Harold Palmer, "The Problem of Neurosis in Ex-Soldiers," *New Zealand Medical Journal* (1949), 129.

20 Travis E. Dancey, "The Neurosis Problem Case and the Assessment and Rehabilitation Unit," *Medical Services Journal* 16, no. 10 (November 1960): 866.

21 Wilbur J. Scott, "PTSD in DSMIII: A Case Study in the Politics of Diagnosis and Disease," *Social Problems* 37, no. 3 (1990): 294–310.

22 Ibid., 297.

23 Ibid., 297.

24 Ibid., 299.

25 Chaim F. Shatan, "The Post-Vietnam Syndrome," *New York Times*, 6 May 1972.

26 Robert J. Lifton, *Home from the War – Vietnam Veterans: Neither Victims Nor Executioners* (New York: Simon and Schuster 1973).

27 Scott, "PTSD in DSMIII," 294.

28 For a review of the Canadian dimension of the problem, see Major Robert H. Streich, PH D, "Post-Traumatic Stress Disorder and the Canadian Vietnam Veteran" (unpublished paper, n.d., Defence and Civil Institute of Environmental Medicine, Downsview, Ontario).

29 Veterans Affairs Canada is the "applied title" for the department, formulated in accordance with the Federal Identity Program. This program was established by Treasury Board and requires that the word "Canada" be used. Statutes, however, still refer to DVA.

30 Personal communication.

31 Lynne Beal, "Post-Traumatic Stress Disorder in Prisoner of War and Combat Veterans of the Dieppe Raid," submission to the Senate Subcommittee on Veterans Affairs, 16 August 1994 (Senate of Canada, *Proceedings of the Subcommittee on Veterans Affairs*, Tuesday, 16 August 1994, issue no. 3:30).

32 Ibid., 31.

33 This argument is developed in my brief to the Senate Subcommittee on Veterans Affairs (ibid., issue no. 6, 28 September 1994).

34 Alan Fontana, *The Long Journey Home: The First Progress Report on the Development of Veterans Affairs PTSD Clinical Teams Program* (West Haven, Conn.: DVA Medical Centre 1990), 54.

MARY TREMBLAY

Going Back to Main Street: The Development and Impact of Casualty Rehabilitation for Veterans with Disabilities, 1945–1948

After World War I, Canada was one of the first countries to develop specialized programs for medical rehabilitation, vocational training, pension assessment, and the provision of prosthetic services for veterans with disabilities.[1] The Canadian programs focused on early "retraining for those who were handicapped for their pre-enlistment occupation,"[2] and as a result, disabled veterans provided some of the first significant examples that such individuals could live and work in the community.[3] However, despite their example, programs for medical rehabilitation and vocational training for disabled civilians did not develop during the 1920s and 1930s, and most disabled Canadians lived in poor socio-economic circumstances, isolated from community life.[4] During this period, only provincial workmen's compensation boards offered funding for medical treatment, pensions for disability, and limited opportunities for vocational retraining.

During World War II, the Canadian government developed a comprehensive framework of programs, services, pensions, and allowances to support the re-establishment of veterans into civilian life. The legislation providing these benefits, the Veterans Charter, was administered by the Department of Veterans Affairs (DVA), which was established in 1944 to coordinate all aspects of veterans' benefits and services. Throughout the development of the Veterans Charter, the needs of the disabled attracted considerable discussion. Government policy supported their full economic and social rehabilitation, and a Casualty Rehabilitation Section was established to provide them with specialized services. Walter S. Woods, Deputy Minister of Veterans Affairs,

sought to staff this section with World War II veterans who had successfully adapted to their disabilities.

Between 1945 and 1948, more than 29,000 seriously disabled veterans returned to Canada and participated in programs administered
by DVA. By 1948, more than 65 per cent of them were employed and
another quarter were enrolled in training programs or were receiving
treatment.[5] Among this group were many whose disabilities would
have resulted in unemployment and exclusion from society had they
been civilians. But as a result of the comprehensive policies and programs included in the Veterans Charter, most disabled veterans returned fully to civilian life, ready to take up their roles on Main Street.
The success of the programs for World War II veterans provided an
impetus for a re-examination of Canadian policy for civilians with disabilities, which began in the late 1940s.

This chapter describes the development of the Casualty Rehabilitation Section under Major Edward A. Dunlop from 1945 to 1948. It dis-
cusses his philosophy of rehabilitation, the use of the individual case
work method, and the strategies developed to find employment and
to support the disabled veteran's return to community life. It also
describes how the District Casualty Rehabilitation Officers (DCROs)
liaised with staff in the newly established Treatment Services Branch
and with members of the National Council of Veterans Associations
and of citizen rehabilitation committees to implement a program of
full economic and social rehabilitation. Finally, it outlines the impact
of DVA policies between 1945 and 1950 on the development of civilian
disability policy.

On 8 December 1939 the Canadian government, through order-in-
council PC 4068½, established a Special Cabinet Committee on Demobilization and Re-establishment with the Minister of Pensions and
National Health, Ian Mackenzie, as chairman.[6] This committee created the interdepartmental General Advisory Committee on Demobilization and Rehabilitation (GACDR) chaired by Brigadier-General H.F.
McDonald, chairman of the Canadian Pension Commission, with
Walter S. Woods of the War Veterans' Allowance Board as vice-chairman. The GACDR in turn established fourteen sub-committees to address all aspects of the question "What does the country owe to those
who, forsaking everything, offered their lives in its defence – to try and
compensate for the time that was lost and the opportunities that were
missed?"[7]

Between 1940 and 1944, the needs of veterans with disabilities were
addressed by the Sub-Committee on the Retraining of Special Casualties. Planning for re-establishment of disabled veterans focused on the

expansion of existing Department of Pensions and National Health (DPNH) hospitals and the short-term use of civilian hospitals.[8] During the war, DPNH hospitals were usually staffed by older physicians and nurses who had previously cared for World War I pensioners. Finding new staff who were equipped to deal with the medical care of young disabled veterans was difficult. Many of the senior medical leaders from Canadian universities had enlisted in the Royal Canadian Army Medical Corps (RCAMC) at the outbreak of the war. They were based in Canadian military hospitals in England or in field hospitals on the battlefields. During this period, most medical graduates enlisted directly in the RCAMC following graduation, and this limited the number of newly trained physicians available to staff DPNH hospitals. Moreover, the central thrust of medical practice during the war years was on acute medical treatment on the battlefield.[9]

Soldiers returning to Canada often complained of poor conditions in the DPNH hospitals. Jack Higman had become paraplegic following a motorcycle accident in England in 1942. After returning to Canada the following year, he recalled his early treatment at Christie Street Military Hospital in Toronto: "They fed us, they changed the bed, they gave us enemas. That was about our life. Outside of reading papers and books and ... listening to the little radios we had, that was our life. There was nothing else ... We had the old wooden [wheelchairs] which you couldn't fold up. There was only one."[10] Complaints about the poor quality of care and overcrowding in the hospitals were common between 1943 and 1945 as the growing number of returning casualties overtaxed the system (figure 1).[11] J.L. Ralston, the Minister of National Defence, joined the criticism in 1944: "I fear that D.P.&.N.H. [Department of Pensions and National Health] do not realize the magnitude and the urgency of the problem and are depending on hospitals which will not be constructed for many months."[12]

Initially, Ian Mackenzie, the responsible minister, defended his department and argued that a hospital such as Christie Street was "an institution in which have been assembled all the finest and latest of surgical equipment and appliances ... attended by the cream of the medical profession of this great city."[13] By 1944, however, Mackenzie had become frustrated with his senior bureaucrats, who appeared more concerned with fending off encroachment from the Department of National Defence than with improving their hospitals. In response to a memo from his deputy minister about planning, Mackenzie testily noted, "The important question is – Have we enough beds? It does not matter whether it is a Defence responsibility or D.P.& N.H. but it is vital that enough beds are ready or in sight."[14]

Early planning by the Sub-committee on the Retraining of Special Casualties called for re-establishment to be handled by personal welfare

Figure 1
Source: Globe and Mail, 8 August 1944
(Courtesy of The Globe and Mail, Toronto)

services officers located in DPNH.[15] Assistance with employment would be provided through the National Employment Service of the Unemployment Insurance Commission. In addition, welfare officers were to work with national associations such as the Canadian National Institute for the Blind, the War Amputations of Canada, and service clubs such as the Kiwanis. As a result, assistance varied across the country, with no uniform standards. Soldiers were often discharged before treatment was completed or before their pensions, retraining, or employment plans were established. For example, John Gartshore, wounded in the Dieppe landing in 1942, returned to Canada and to Christie Street Military Hospital: "It was a factory. There were twenty-five of us on the ward ... I was in there from January to April 1943 ... I was in there with a bunch of old World War I guys, who had been there since 1918. It was pretty awful! ... I was on my way into this operation and he [an official] wanted me to sign my discharge. I said, 'To hell with you.' My feeling was that you have to fix me up before you bounce me out. This is what they were doing in that early stage."[16]

Gartshore's friend John Counsell, who had become a paraplegic following a gunshot wound in the same raid, had a similar experience.

Defence Minister Ralston wrote to Robert England, secretary of the GACDR, to complain about Counsell's situation:

There is one point I wish to bring to your attention and which I have mentioned to your Minister. It is the lack ... of first hand personal contact with the soldier who is being discharged ... Lieutenant Counsell of Montreal, a Dieppe hero ... received the Military Cross at the hands of the Governor-General in a hospital ward a short time ago. Lieutenant Counsell's pay was withheld under some regulation which probably is a pay and allowance regulation (I'm going to look this up) but the point is that he had no information as to what his rights were, what his pension would be etc., so that he could make his plans. It seems to me there should be somebody from the Department of Pensions and National Health to make personal contact with the man.[17]

Counsell's later experience with DPNH further highlighted the slowness of officials in responding to demands for improved services for disabled veterans. In 1943, after rehabilitating himself at home, Counsell secured a new Everest & Jennings self-propelled wheelchair and learned how to transfer independently in and out of the wheelchair and into an automobile. He quickly recognized that the combination of a folding self-propelled wheelchair and an automobile modified to be driven with hand-controls could provide a new means of independent transportation for many disabled veterans who were confined to bed because of the DVA's standard issue of wooden and wicker wheelchairs. Lewis Wood, chairman of the Toronto Rehabilitation Committee of the Citizens' Committee for Troops in Training, described Counsell's idea: "The rehabilitation of paraplegic, double amputation, and other cases requiring chairs [is] as a practical problem in need of intensive study and the application of a new point-of-view ... He [Counsell] regards *mobility as the initial road to Rehabilitation.*"[18]

Counsell was unsuccessful in his attempts to persuade officials at Christie Street to purchase these chairs, despite the intervention of John Catto, a veterans' welfare officer, who wrote: "We might say that it is only since obtaining this chair that Mr. Counsell has been able to be around to any great extent. The way in which he handles himself, getting in and out of motor cars, and in and out of ordinary chairs, on to this wheel chair, is really amazing, and certainly I as a layman can see a great improvement in his physical well-being, since this chair has been obtained."[19] Robert Wilson, the superintendent of the Toronto Orthopaedic Division of the DPNH, agreed that this new type of folding wheelchair would be convenient for veterans who travelled by car. But he argued, "The price of $162.50 is quite high, and the intrinsic value of the chair certainly would not warrant payment of such a figure."[20] These wheelchairs were not purchased until February 1945, when DVA finally agreed to provide them to all veterans with spinal cord injury.[21]

One early development in DVA had a significant effect on the subsequent rehabilitation of disabled veterans. In January 1945, Mackenzie requested the secondment of Brigadier Wilfred P. Warner, Deputy Director-General of Medical Services (Army), to study the medical care offered in all the department's hospitals.[22] Dr Warner's report criticized the quality of care and outlined a comprehensive plan to improve matters. Despite intense criticism of his report by bureaucrats in DVA, Warner was appointed the first Director-General of Treatment Services in March 1945.[23]

By the end of 1945, Warner's policies had resulted in the development of highly specialized programs led by physicians who held joint university appointments. (Many of these physicians were themselves veterans). His concept of joint university appointments for physicians meant that veterans would be able to receive the highest quality medical care available in Canada. Ian Mackenzie described this new approach: "Our attitude is that the men and women who have contributed so much to the winning of the war must have the very best of medical treatment – and this new scheme will provide it."[24] Many innovations in treatment were undertaken following the war, and veterans with disabilities were often the first group of Canadians to have access to coordinated medical rehabilitation treatment programs.[25]

One dramatic example of medical innovation was the treatment of veterans with spinal cord injury. As a result of new approaches to medical care initiated at No. 1 Canadian Neurological Hospital at Basingstoke, England, mortality rates had decreased from over 80 per cent in World War I to below 10 per cent.[26] Four specialized treatment centres for spinal cord rehabilitation were established across Canada; the first of these, Toronto's Lyndhurst Lodge, opened in January 1945. The other programs were at Ste-Anne-de-Bellevue, Quebec; Deer Lodge Hospital, Winnipeg; and Shaughnessy Hospital, Vancouver. These programs revolutionized the life experiences of veterans with spinal cord injury, with more than 70 per cent returning to live and work in the community.[27]

The Treatment Services programs were designed to provide medical treatment and rehabilitation. However, Warner and the other members of Treatment Services recognized that the return to civilian life involved more than this, and they developed a close partnership with the department's Casualty Rehabilitation Section, which was established in January 1945.

The goal of the Casualty Rehabilitation Section was the economic and social rehabilitation of disabled veterans.[28] Its first supervisor was Major Edward A. Dunlop, a veteran who had lost his eyesight during the war. Dunlop's appointment reflected Woods's philosophy that "a man who has been seriously disabled and who has regained control, as it were, and mastered the ordinary functions of life despite his disability can, by his mental attitude and his physical mastery of handicaps be a tremendous inspiration to others."[29] In an early speech, Dunlop argued that "almost every disabled veteran can be so successfully re-established that he can be on a job in which he is 100 per cent efficient, which is temperamentally suitable to him, and which offers him the same opportunity for a career as he would otherwise [have had]."[30] This philosophy was to underline the activities of Casualty Rehabilitation throughout his tenure as supervisor.

Dunlop developed a new approach to employment for disabled veterans. He argued as follows:

The pressure of two wars, both by increasing the number of disabled persons, and by increasing the call on the nation's manpower resources, has led us to a widened and expanded horizon. Many thousands of persons have been employed who would otherwise have been labelled "unemployable." This has led us to the realization that not only have the disabled the right to work, but that they have the right to – and the ability to perform – the *right* job ... We must reject any of the obsolescent approaches to the employment problem ...

First – One which seeks to schedule or reserve certain jobs for disabled persons. Jobs such as, say, elevator operator, or night-watchman ... This approach has no regard for the ability of the man concerned and would result, in fact, in condemning many thousands of persons to jobs away below their proper level of attainment.

The second approach is to seek to list jobs suitable for persons with a specific disability ... This approach suffers from the same flaw as the former one, and in addition, makes no reference to the oft-proven ability of a man to do a job, which on the face of it would seem impossible.[31]

Dunlop's approach built on the work of Walter Segsworth and Thomas Kidner, who had established a system of classification of occupations by type of disability as the cornerstone of Canadian World War I policy.[32] Dunlop argued against large-scale placement programs: "The disabled cannot be rehabilitated in groups. There is no one scientific method for handling any one group of disabled persons. It is too essentially a human matter. There are so many variations of capacity, aptitude, determination, to put it on an impersonal and machine footing."[33] His programs were based on four requirements for successful rehabilitation: selective job placement according to the veteran's abilities; determination on the part of the veteran; training; and the education of employers and the public.[34] To implement this program, the Casualty Rehabilitation Section developed the new position of District Casualty

Rehabilitation Officer. During 1945, DCROs were recruited across Canada and were given training courses taught by Dunlop and by medical staff from Treatment Services, staff from workmen's compensation programs, and faculty from Canadian universities.[35] DCROs were then placed in hospitals run by Treatment Services, sometimes specializing in specific fields of disability, and in the district offices of DVA.

In order to place veterans in appropriate employment, Dunlop proposed the development of an individualized case work approach. DCROs would liaise with Treatment Services and coordinate a veteran's economic and social rehabilitation (see figure 2).[36] The DCRO would meet the veteran in hospital for a bedside interview and would follow him through the various stages of rehabilitation until he returned to employment and community life. This approach enabled the DCROs to understand each veteran's needs. Counselling was provided by the DCROs to support veterans as they began to explore career options. In addition, the DCROs, with their specialized knowledge of the range of benefits and services available, could advise each veteran on his full range of entitlements, including education, vocational training, and on-the-job training. During World War I, only education and training to the level of pre-enlistment occupation had been offered to disabled ex-servicemen.[37] World War II veterans, however, could qualify for education and training programs at universities and technical institutes across Canada. Indeed, Dunlop argued that "if a disabled person is going to be able to perform a particular job efficiently, then with but a little added care, he can be trained for it through normal facilities."[38] As a result, many disabled World War II veterans were among the first groups of disabled students to attend institutions of higher education in the country.[39] In setting out his plans, Dunlop stressed that his primary objective was to assist the disabled to return to ordinary occupations in competitive industry: "Sheltered workshops, home industries or colonies do not form a part of the programme."[40]

Many seriously disabled veterans found Dunlop's emphasis on employment a novel concept. Dr Al Jousse, first medical director of Lyndhurst Lodge, remembered the ironic response of some veterans: "That struck some of them as being amusing. They couldn't get a job during the thirties when they were able-bodied ... Having been in the army, having become a paraplegic, they were now expected to go to work. Nobody wanted them before. Now they were encouraged to do what they were never able to do of their own volition."[41]

The DCROs quickly developed links with business and industry in their districts, visiting personnel officers to identify possible positions for individual veterans. When these officers were not supportive, DCROs were encouraged to approach senior management directly. Initially, the

The responsibilities of the case worker would be:
(1) to survey the man's case – over a long period to become thoroughly familiar with the man and his background.
(2) to raise the man's morale, if need be.
(3) to sow in his mind as seeds, the possibilities that lie before him, and help the man to analyze his assets and liabilities of physical and mental capacity, experience and personality, and inclination.
(4) to get the man to set for himself a job objective, and when set, to make sure that that objective is practicable and to make sure that such a job can be made available.
(5) to insure that everything is done to assist that man in attaining that objective, be it training or anything else.
(6) to make the maximum use of existing facilities to bring in "consultants" on the case – e.g. Occupational Counsellors, Kiwanis, or other service clubs, c.v.t., etc., as necessary.
(7) to pair the man and the job on the spot, under the eyes of the foreman.

Figure 2
Edward A. Dunlop's definition of the responsibilities of a District Casualty Rehabilitation Officer, 1945
Source: VAC, DVA, box 557, vol. 3, file 5401–01, Edward A. Dunlop's speech on casualty rehabilitation, 24 January 1945, 3

DCROs took a very active role in helping veterans seek employment and accompanying them to job interviews. By 1948, after three years' experience in job placement, Dunlop wrote that "the most satisfactory rehabilitation follows when the disabled veteran obtains his own job through his own efforts," with the DCRO's main role being to "help a man plan an effective job finding campaign."[42]

During the 1940s, citizens' rehabilitation committees had been formed across Canada to help re-establish veterans back into the community.[43] The DCROs developed links with the committees and, in larger cities, encouraged the establishment of disabled veterans' advisory subcommittees to address the specialized needs of these veterans. The members of the subcommittees were drawn from workmen's compensation boards, plant superintendents, personnel managers, industrial panels of provincial medical societies, organized labour, and foremen's clubs. These subcommittees provided another avenue for identification of employment opportunities.

Dunlop's case work approach to rehabilitation was wholly new, for there were no civilian models. Indeed, most civilians had no access to physical rehabilitation and vocational training unless they were injured in the workplace. The concept of a committee of concerned business and community leaders working to support the return of disabled veterans to the community was also new. Provincial workmen's compensation programs had generally focused on pensions rather than on an extensive and coordinated physical, economic, and social rehabilitation model like the one Dunlop developed.[44]

The fourth requirement of the casualty rehabilitation program was public and employer education. Educational programs were developed to emphasize successful examples of disabled veterans in employment. "Back to Work" exhibitions, featuring disabled veterans demonstrating their skills, were held across the country, often sponsored by citizens' rehabilitation committees and local industries.[45] Various forms of print media were also used. Magazine articles focused on skills. An early 1945 article by Dunlop entitled "Disability vs 'Can-Do'" described the wide variety of jobs that could be filled by disabled veterans.[46] A *Speakers Handbook*, outlining the general philosophy of Casualty Rehabilitation and describing successful case histories, was developed for use by DCROs in presentations to service clubs.[47] This manual was used in conjunction with an illustrated handbook, which had photographs of disabled veterans in a wide variety of occupations. The book was said to have value both to employers and to "persons who have not adjusted well or who have suffered recent disability."[48] Between 1946 and 1948, DVA also published monographs on the employment of disabled Canadians, including those with tuberculosis.[49] These were among the first such books published in Canada since W.E. Segsworth's *Retraining Canada's Disabled Soldiers* had appeared in 1920.

Not surprisingly, the civil service became a major source of employment for disabled veterans. Veterans preference was provided for those "who had been disabled in the Armed Forces to such an extent that they are unable to pursue their pre-war avocation."[50] There were the usual difficulties, however. Captain Lorenzo Robichaud remembered the response of one government department to his application for employment following graduation from the University of Montreal's law school:

After I graduated, I wrote [DVA] looking for a job. They sent an employment officer to see me and we went to Ottawa together. We went to the Justice Department where I had an interview with one of the lawyers, who happened to be an amputee himself. We discussed things. All he had to tell me was, "You are in a wheelchair. People have to work hard here." We left it at that and I went back to Montreal. A few weeks after, I was called to report to the Montreal office of the Department of Veterans Affairs [to the Veterans' Bureau]. They had no opening for a lawyer, but they took me in as a Principal Clerk.[51]

While the civil service was an important initial source of employment, many disabled veterans received only temporary or term appointments.[52] When they sought to move to permanent positions, many found their way blocked by regulations that called for physical fitness. By 1948, Dunlop had begun to argue for changes to civil service regulations to ensure that disability was no longer a barrier to permanent employment.[53]

The Casualty Rehabilitation Section was also responsible for social rehabilitation. The DCROs helped veterans gain access to benefits such as preference in the purchase of scarce automobiles, building materials for housing, funding for equipment, and home modifications.[54] They helped clarify the complex and somewhat confusing sets of government rules and regulations, and worked to ensure that the benefits for disabled veterans were both available and uniform across the country.[55] This was an important role, for in the immediate post-war years, disabled veterans faced a myriad of regulations inconsistently applied.

One of the most difficult issues for the DCROs was pensions and the role of pension medical examiners and the Canadian Pension Commission.[56] In 1943, Robert England had argued:

Compensation for disability meets the economic inadequacy occasioned by physical inability in the ordinary labour market, but it does more. It corrects partially the frustration resulting from lack of locomotor, manual, or other capacity, or skill; covers that portion of extra expense which any physical handicap occasions; and checks the sense of grievance or psychoneurosis that might feed on the consciousness of the physical defect, which would (if there were no pension) be a constant irritant in its reminder of the ingratitude of one's fellows. But compensation or pension does not cover the whole area of privilege, benefit and service, given the pensioner. Treatment, training, preferences in employment, specialised placement and a life-long contact with the Department are his. The easement given by his pension is thus the *gate of opportunity* through which he can become a competent citizen.[57]

Despite England's concept of a "gate of opportunity," DCROs encountered considerable difficulty with the Canadian Pension Commission's practices. Pensions were not the responsibility of the DCROs, but because of their close involvement with veterans, they were often all too aware of injustices.[58] The activities of the Canadian Pension Commission are beyond the scope of this chapter, but the relationship between Casualty Rehabilitation and the commission deserves future research.

Some employers, arguing that they needed only to top up wages to meet the salary level, reportedly lowered salaries to veterans with pensions. This was against government policy, and the DCROs were responsible for ensuring that employers understood the guidelines. Gordon Hunter, a welfare officer, remembered that "sometimes the DVA welfare officer might go around and talk to the employer, and most often he would explain the facts of life. But again you had to be very careful because he could let the fellow go."[59]

Following World War I, three principal associations for disabled veterans had been established: the War Amputations of Canada, the Sir Arthur Pearson Association of War Blinded, and the National Society of the Deaf and Hard of Hearing. Throughout World War II, these organizations provided the new casualties with a variety of services, some of which were funded by DPNH and, later, by DVA. In addition, the associations acted as lobby groups to ensure the development of programs, services, and pensions. In 1945 the Canadian Paraplegic Association (CPA) was formed under the leadership of Lieutenant John Counsell to lobby the government to develop rehabilitation programs for veterans and civilians with spinal cord injury.[60] The CPA was the first organization in the world founded and administered by individuals with spinal cord injury. These four organizations were included in the National Council of Veterans Associations, which regularly lobbied government. Influential CPA board members in the late 1940s included Walter Gordon, Group Captain H. de M. Molson, Major-General E. de B. Panet, Major Conn Smythe, and Brigadier W. Warner, Director-General of Treatment Services.

There were approximately 30,000 seriously disabled Canadian veterans registered with Casualty Rehabilitation. The seriously disabled were defined as those "whose disabilities are of so serious a nature as to involve extensive re-adjustment in the veteran's occupational life."[61] A 1948 analysis showed that disabilities relating to the musculo-skeletal systems and to tuberculosis and other respiratory disorders were the most common (table 15).[62] The same survey found that 65 per cent of seriously disabled veterans were employed part-time or full-time, 25 per cent were in training or receiving treatment, 5 per cent were unemployed, 1 per cent could not be rehabilitated, and 4 per cent were of unknown status (table 16). Rates of employment, analysed by severity of disability, ranged from approximately 75 per cent for those with disability assessed below 75 per cent, to 55 per cent for those assessed as completely disabled. Employment rates varied by type of disability, with amputees having rates as high as 80 per cent, while veterans with tuberculosis had employment rates of under 50 per cent. The employment rates were dramatically better for veterans than for the civilian disabled, although proper statistics on employment for disabled civilians had never been compiled in Canada. Indeed, physical rehabilitation programs were rarely available in civilian hospitals, and funding for equipment such as wheelchairs was only provided through personal financing or charities.[63]

Table 15
World War II Disability Classification, 31 January 1948

Disability	Number of cases
Amputation	2,043
Other serious disabilities of the muscular and skeletal systems	10,021
Partial and total losses of hearing and sight	1,769
Injuries to the central nervous system involving one, two, or more limbs or organs, epilepsy, and other conditions	981
Diseases of the heart and vascular system	2,292
Tuberculosis and other respiratory disabilities	8,317
Mental and emotional disabilities	731
Others	3,378
Total	29,534

Source: Edward A. Dunlop, "Report on the Vocational Rehabilitation of Disabled Veterans as at January 31, 1948," *Treatment Services Bulletin*, May 1948, 40

Table 16
Rehabilitation Status, 31 January 1948

	31 May[1] 1947	31 Jan. 1948
Employed	12,701	19,607
Unemployed	1,987	1,694
Receiving treatment or other services	10,680	7,080
Rehabilitation not feasible	180	690
Status unknown	2,914	463
Total	28,462	29,534

Source: Edward A. Dunlop, "Report on the Vocational Rehabilitation of Disabled Veterans as at January 31, 1948," *Treatment Services Bulletin*, May 1948, 41
[1] First month for which comparable figures were available

The example of the successful return to employment and participation in community life of World War II veterans with disabilities led many of those who participated in Treatment Services and Casualty Rehabilitation to consider the application of these new principles to civilians. With the support of Brigadier Warner, some programs in DVA hospitals and rehabilitation centres were opened on a small scale for civilians. One of the most striking examples was the provision of rehabilitation for civilians with spinal cord injury, which began in the late 1940s at the four spinal cord rehabilitation centres. This brought dramatic results, especially for the many who had previously been bedridden. James Burke had been a patient in a chronic care hospital for more than seven years following an accident that had left him a paraplegic. Forced to declare himself a pauper to get hospitalization, he recalled, "When I got my wheelchair from the Canadian Paraplegic Association, it might have been a d.v.a. acquisition, who knows. Anyway they gave it to me and that changed my life. I could get out, go around the neighbourhood, use it for physical tone up. I was curious to see the world after all this time."[64]

During the late 1940s, Dunlop, Warner, and other DVA officials began to work to address the needs of civilians with disabilities.[65] In 1951 the first National Conference on the Rehabilitation of the Physically Handicapped in Canada was sponsored by DVA and the Departments of Labour and National Health and Welfare. This led to the formation (by PC 6806 of 29 December 1951) of the National Advisory Committee on the Rehabilitation of Disabled Persons. This, in turn, laid the foundation for a Canadian rehabilitation program for civilians with disabilities. Many of the people involved (including Dunlop, who participated in the development of this program in the 1950s and 1960s) had started at DVA.

The impact of the veterans on the lives of individuals with disabilities in Canada has been summarized as follows:

The veterans set the pace, they ventured out in wheelchairs in all kinds of weather. They drove hand-controlled cars and travelled by plane and train. They attended school and university, social events, the theatre and later played wheelchair sports.

In fact they pioneered successful living and working in the community. By their example they taught the public that there was life energy and purpose in human beings even when seriously physically impaired.

They demonstrated that once educated appropriately they could compete successfully in professions, business, specialized trades and live in their own homes.

Thus, they demonstrated that as taxpayers they more than returned to government coffers the costs of outlay for rehabilitation.[66]

Between 1945 and 1948, DVA undertook the development of the most comprehensive medical treatment and rehabilitation programs for disabled veterans in the world. These programs demonstrated that it was possible for seriously disabled Canadians to live and work in the community. Medical treatment and rehabilitation were provided through Treatment Services under the leadership of Brigadier W. Warner, and economic and social rehabilitation was provided by the Casualty Rehabilitation Section led by Edward A. Dunlop. These two men developed a coordinated team approach that supported the disabled veteran from the bedside to full participation on Main Street.

While other sections of the Veterans Charter supported the economic and social rehabilitation of disabled veterans, it was the pioneering work of Warner and Dunlop that shaped the broad overall approach to rehabilitation for disabled World War II veterans. Edward A. Dunlop left DVA in 1948 to become executive director of the newly formed Canadian Arthritis and Rheumatism Society, an organization that pioneered the development of rehabilitation for civilians with arthritis in Canada. Warner remained at Treatment Services until his death in 1955. He was acclaimed by his medical colleagues not only at DVA but across Canada.

NOTES

I gratefully acknowledge the assistance of the many veterans who shared their experiences with me. I am also indebted to the Canadian Paraplegic Association, the Sir Arthur Pearson Association of War Blinded, Ken Hawkes (Veterans Affairs Canada, Charlottetown), and Robert McIntosh (National Archives of Canada, Ottawa). The research for this chapter was funded by a grant from the Hannah Institute for the History of Medicine and by a fellowship in gerontology from the Royal Canadian Legion. All tape recordings and transcripts of interviews cited here will be deposited in the Archives of Chedoke-McMaster Hospitals and the Faculty of Health Sciences, McMaster University.

1 W.E. Segsworth, *Retraining Canada's Disabled Soldiers* (Ottawa: King's Printer 1920). See also T.B. Kidner, "Vocational Work of the Invalided Soldiers' Commission of Canada," *Annals* 80 (November 1918): 141–9.

2 Robert England, *Discharged: A Commentary on Civil Re-establishment of Veterans in Canada* (Toronto: Macmillan Company of Canada 1943), 161.

3 Desmond Morton and Glenn Wright, *Winning the Second Battle: Canadian Veterans and the Return to Civilian Life, 1915–1930* (Toronto: University of Toronto Press 1987).

4 Dennis Guest, *The Emergence of Social Security in Canada*, 2nd ed. (Vancouver: University of British Columbia Press 1991).

5 Edward A. Dunlop, "Report on the Vocational Rehabilitation of Disabled Veterans as at January 31, 1948," *Treatment Services Bulletin*, May 1948, 39–42.

6 Walter S. Woods, *Rehabilitation (A Combined Operation)* (Ottawa: Queen's Printer 1953), 5–6.

7 Ibid., 9. Brigadier McDonald, a distinguished World War I veteran, was also an arm amputee and a member of the War Amputations of Canada. Despite his disability, he had continued to serve during World War I and was Chief of Staff to General Turner. At the time of his appointment as

chairman of the General Advisory Committee, he was an honorary president of the War Amputations of Canada (England, *Discharged*, 89–90).

8 England, *Discharged*, 161–78. See also National Archives of Canada (hereafter NA), records of the Department of Veterans Affairs (hereafter DVA), RG 38, vol. 187, file 7297, Minutes of the Sub-Committee on the Retraining of Special Casualties.

9 W.R. Feasby, *Official History of the Canadian Medical Services, 1939–1945, Organization and Campaigns*, vols. 1 and 2 (Ottawa: Queen's Printer 1953). Dr E.H. Botterell recalled his experience on returning from England to take charge of neurosurgery at Christie Street Military Hospital in January 1945: "Christie Street hadn't adequately converted from being a quiet pension hospital to an active veterans' general hospital ... There were 100 paraplegics there, 100! They were just ... receiving routine nursing, no positive medical treatment ... They were just being left alone and given basic nursing. This was a very traumatic experience for me because we had been very active about this in our hospital in England ... These people were just being left alone because ... the nurses anticipated that they would all perish within six or eight months, or 90% of them, because that is what happened in World War I" (University of Toronto Archives, interview of E.H. Botterell by V. Schatzer, Kingston, Ontario, 26 April 1979, 28–9).

10 Author interview with Jack Higman, Mississauga, Ontario, 3 March 1992.

11 *Globe and Mail* (Toronto), "Amply Inadequate," editorial, 8 August 1944. See also ibid., "Canada's Florence Nightingale," editorial cartoon, 8 August 1944; NA, William Lyon Mackenzie King Papers, MG 26 J, file C 7409, Counsell to Mackenzie King, 10 October 1944; NA, Ian Mackenzie Papers, MG 27 III B5, vol. 53, file 519–39(3), *Gazette* (Montreal), "Who is Falling Down?" 20 March 1945; and *Telegram* (Toronto), "Women Carry Signs Asking New Hospitals," 9 September 1944.

12 NA, Mackenzie Papers, vol. 53, file 519–39(3), Ralston to Mackenzie, 17 July 1944.

13 NA, Mackenzie Papers, vol. 7, file 3–66, Mackenzie speech to the Toronto Business Men's Branch of the Canadian Legion, 28 April 1943, 5.

14 NA, Mackenzie Papers, vol. 53, file 519–39(3), Mackenzie to Wodehouse, 26 July 1944.

15 England, *Discharged*, 173–6. See also NA, DVA, vol. 187, file 7297, Minutes of the Sub-Committee on the Retraining of Special Casualties 1940–43.

16 Author interview with John Gartshore, Ancaster, Ontario, 11 March 1994. See also Veterans Affairs Canada (hereafter VAC), DVA, box 557, vol. 1, file 5401–01, for letters of complaint and departmental reaction between 1940 and 1943.

17 NA, Robert England Papers, vol. 3, Ralston to England, 11 March 1943.

18 VAC, DVA, box 163, vol. 6, file 31–15, Wood to Bell, 16 December 1943. (emphasis added).

19 Ibid., Catto to Wright, Director of Rehabilitation, Department of Pensions and National Health (hereafter DPNH), "Re: Paraplegia, Serious Orthopaedic and Double Amputation Cases," 20 December 1943.

20 Ibid., Wilson to Bell, 11 December 1943.

21 Mary Tremblay, "Going Back to Civvy Street: A Historical Account of the Impact of the Everest & Jennings Wheelchairs for Canadian World War II Veterans with Spinal Cord Injury," *Disability & Society* 11 (1996): 149–69.

22 NA, Mackenzie Papers, vol. 53, file 519–39(3), Mackenzie to McNaughton, 30 January 1945.

23 In one last attempt to maintain control over the hospitals, DPNH bureaucrats tried to have Treatment Services transferred into the new Department of National Health and Welfare. The transfer of Treatment Services was resisted and the medical care of veterans remained under the control of the DVA. See NA, Mackenzie Papers, vol. 53, file 519–36(4), Mellon to Mackenzie King, 28 March 1945.

24 Ibid., DVA news release no. 139, 18 October 1945.

25 A. Neufeld, "Good Medicine and Dr. W.P. Warner," *Treatment Services Bulletin* 10, no. 2 (1956): 127–30. See also Woods, *Rehabilitation*, 321–49.

26 E.H. Botterell et al., "Paraplegia Following War," *Canadian Medical Association Journal* 55 (September 1946): 249–59.

27 Mary Tremblay, "The Canadian Revolution in the Management of Spinal Cord Injuries," *Canadian Bulletin of Medical History* 12 (1995): 101–32.

28 Woods, *Rehabilitation*, 350.

29 NA, DVA, vol. 187, file 7297, Woods to Park, 19 May 1944.

30 VAC, DVA, box 557, vol. 3, file 5401–01, script for address by Major Edward A. Dunlop, 24 February 1945, 2.

31 Ibid.

32 Segsworth, *Retraining Canada's Disabled Soldiers*; Kidner, "Vocational Work of the Invalided Soldiers' Commission of Canada," 141–9.

33 VAC, DVA, box 557, vol. 3, file 5401–01, script for address by Major Edward A. Dunlop, 24 February 1945, 5.

34 Ibid., 3.

35 VAC, DVA, box 285, vol. 1, file 69–4, Edward A. Dunlop, "Tentative Syllabus for CRO Training Course no. 2, 15–27 October 1945."

36 VAC, DVA, box 557, vol. 3, file 5401–01, Edward A. Dunlop, speech on casualty rehabilitation, 24 January 1945, 3.

37 Morton and Wright, *Winning the Second Battle*, 94.

38 VAC, DVA, box 179, file 32–4, Edward A. Dunlop, "Canada's Programme for the Rehabilitation of Disabled Veterans, 1948," 3.

39 D.G. Petrie, "Paraplegics at University," *Caliper* 3, no. 1 (1948): 16–17.

40 Dunlop, "Canada's Programme for the Rehabilitation of Disabled Veterans, 1948," 1. Dunlop echoed the beliefs of Botterell and Jousse, who had argued in 1946 that the "primary purpose of treatment at every stage

from bed to brace-walking is to return the patient to independent life beyond the confines of hospitals or paraplegic colonies" (Botterell et al., "Paraplegia Following War," 258).

41 Author interview with Dr A. Jousse, Toronto, Ontario, 17 January 1991.

42 Dunlop, "Canada's Programme for the Rehabilitation of Disabled Veterans, 1948," 8. See also author interview with John Gartshore, 1994. Gartshore joined the DVA in 1945 and became the first DCRO in Hamilton, Ontario.

43 Woods, *Rehabilitation*, 217–18, 294–300.

44 Guest, *The Emergence of Social Security in Canada*, 39–47. See also M.E. Whitridge, "Some Observations on the Evolution of Rehabilitation in Canada," *Medical Services Journal Canada* 23 (1967): 869–94.

45 VAC, DVA, box 180, file 32–4–4, "Back to Work Exhibitions," 1945–48. See various memos and reports outlining exhibition planning.

46 Edward A. Dunlop, "Disability versus 'Can-Do,'" *Manufacturing and Industrial Engineering* 9 (1945): 30–40, copy in NA, Mackenzie Papers, vol. 36, file B 91B. See also G. Hewelcke, "They Walk ... Though Paralyzed," *Maclean's*, 1 February 1946.

47 VAC, DVA, box 180, vol. 1, file 32–4–1, *Speaker's Handbook*, Casualty Rehabilitation, 1946.

48 VAC, DVA, box 180, file 32–4–5, Tubb to Smith, 2 July 1947.

49 DVA, *Employment of Canada's Disabled: Veterans and Others* (Ottawa 1948); DVA, *Employment of the Tuberculous* (Ottawa 1948).

50 Woods, *Rehabilitation*, 211–14.

51 Author interview with Lorenzo Robichaud, Buctouche, New Brunswick, 24 September 1994. Robichaud later moved with the department to Ottawa and rose to the position of Deputy Chief Pensions Advocate in the late 1960s. During his time in the department, he was the only individual using a wheelchair.

52 Woods, *Rehabilitation*, 211–15. Between 1939 and 1951, 100,621 appointments to the civil service were temporary and 19,099 were permanent. No record has been found of how many of these appointments were for veterans with disabilities in either category.

53 VAC, DVA, box 283, vol. 2, file 69–1–1, Dunlop to Woods, 18 October 1948. The Reinstatement in Civil Employment Act, 1942, was available to disabled veterans, but reinstatement was not required if "the employee was physically or mentally incapable of performing any available work." See Woods, *Rehabilitation*, 201.

54 VAC, DVA, box 282, file 69, Boulanger to Dunlop, 2 August 1945.

55 VAC, DVA, box 282, vol. 1, file 69–1, G.G. Mahon, "Casualty Section Staff Directive no. 7," 11 January 1946.

56 Interview, John Gartshore, 1994, 20.

57 England, *Discharged*, 146 (emphasis added).

58 Interview, John Gartshore, 1994, 42–6.

59 Author interview with Gordon Hunter, Hamilton, Ontario, 22 August 1994, 16.

60 Tremblay, "The Canadian Revolution," 141–3.

61 Dunlop, "Report on the Vocational Rehabilitation," 39–42.

62 Ibid., 40–2.

63 Edward A. Dunlop, "Rehabilitation Needs of the Disabled in Canada," *Treatment Services Bulletin* 5, no. 6 (1950): 304–11. See also Whitridge, "Some Observations on the Evolution of Rehabilitation in Canada," 869–94.

64 Author interview with James Burke, West Hill, Ontario, 20 December 1992. Burke moved from hospital to live at the YMCA in Toronto, which was accessible to wheelchairs. He began to write for newspapers and magazines and had a successful career as a writer and author in Toronto until his retirement in the 1970s.

65 Edward A. Dunlop, "Our Disabled Citizens – What of Them?" *Canadian Welfare* 22, no. 8 (1947): 15–20; W. Warner, "Notes on Medical Rehabilitation in Canada," *Treatment Services Bulletin* 5, no. 6 (1950): 299–303; D. Graham, "Rehabilitation of the Arthritic," ibid., 5, no. 11 (1950): 488–93; and A. Temple, "Rehabilitation as It Concerns the Physician," ibid., 5, no. 11 (1950): 475–7.

66 E.H. Botterell and A.T. Jousse, "The Evolution of Spinal Cord Rehabilitation" (Hannah Institute for the History of Medicine, videotape, 1988).

Family Allowances, Old Age Security, and the Construction of Entitlement in the Canadian Welfare State, 1943–1951

On a hot midsummer day in 1944, in the midst of the parliamentary debate over family allowances, Prime Minister William Lyon Mackenzie King captured precisely the symbolic change in thinking about wartime social policy which underpinned Canada's emerging welfare state. "Charity has become a nauseating thing," King told the House of Commons. "The new order is not going to have things done as charity. What is to be done will be done as a matter of right."[1] This shift in emphasis from charity to entitlement has long been viewed as a central metaphorical turn in the construction of the welfare state. The idea of universality is perhaps its strongest building block. Services or income transfers delivered comprehensively to all citizens on the basis of defined social rights or entitlements, rather than selectively to the few on the basis of poverty or abject need, have proved to be potent tools for eliminating stigma, dissolving distinctions between the deserving and undeserving poor, and building social solidarity through a sense of common citizenship across classes, ethnicities, and regions within nation-states. As Nancy Fraser and Linda Gordon have recently argued, "people who enjoy 'social citizenship' get 'social rights,' not 'handouts.' They receive aid while maintaining their status as full members of society entitled to 'equal respect.' And they share a common set of institutions and services designed for all citizens." According to Gosta Esping-Andersen, " 'Middle-class' universalism has protected the welfare state against backlash sentiments."[2]

Between 1943 and 1951, two programs – family allowances and old age security (OAS) – emerged as the most critical platforms for building new social rights of citizenship into the heart of the Canadian welfare state. By 1952, Ottawa's spending on both initiatives had surpassed the entire pre–World War II budget and amounted to almost twice what its total contribution to unemployment relief had been during the 1930s.

As universal entitlements that emerged during the reconstruction era and expressed a heightened valuation of the rights of children and the elderly, family allowances and old age security seemingly had much in common. Yet in subsequent decades the history of each program diverged markedly. While old age security received periodic adjustments to reflect changes in the cost of living, family allowances, until 1973, remained frozen at the levels originally established in 1945. In 1992, after a series of income tax clawbacks on benefits for average and upper-income earners, family allowances were abolished altogether in favour of a return to "means testing" through child tax benefits paid only to families with children below a specified income threshold. Old age security, in contrast, has survived as the flat-rate floor of Canada's complex three-tiered public pension system. However, since 1989 the "universality" of the scheme has been compromised by increasing levels of benefit clawbacks on the individual income of wealthier retirees. In a key change announced in the 1996 federal budget, OAS will disappear entirely for those retiring after 2001, to be replaced by a new family income-tested seniors' benefit.[3] For both children and the elderly, in other words, Canadian social policy has moved dramatically away from the universalist discourse of the 1940s and towards an emphasis, as Michael Prince argues, on "market-based equity over citizenship-based entitlements."[4]

The end of universality in family allowances and its pending demise in old age security call attention to why these programs emerged on such a basis in the first place and to the differences in their original bases of support. Was Canada's commitment to universality the product only of a unique historical moment within the political culture of the 1940s? If so, what specific purposes did it serve in the wartime and immediate postwar reconstruction era? Were the arguments for universality similar in both programs? Why were the elderly subsequently able to mount a much stronger defence of their entitlement than Canadian mothers were? Finally, what does the collapse of universality in family allowances and its retreat in old age security portend for the future direction of Canada's welfare state?

"Family policy," Susan Pedersen argues in her comparative study of family allowances in Britain and France, "is often wage policy in another guise."[5] Her insight applies directly to the genesis of Canada's family allowance program in 1944. Without the unusual dilemmas of wage regulation faced by the Canadian government in World War II, it is doubtful that a universal family allowance scheme would ever have come into existence. In no other industrial nation, perhaps, was such a major social program so exclusively the product of state-centred imperatives or so critically dependent on the exigencies of political timing and transient economic circumstances.

A brief comparison with three other nations that also put into place comprehensive family allowance schemes by the 1940s will illustrate this point. In France, the movement for children's allowances developed out of a strong societal base. Financed primarily by employers, family allowances were created during the interwar decades through a coalition of businessmen (who were anxious to forestall unionization and high wages) and conservative pro-natalists (who sought to boost France's population and shore up the family). In England, the children's allowance movement was led by social feminists such as Eleanor Rathbone, whose Family Endowment Society conducted a vigorous campaign for the idea throughout the 1920s and 1930s as a means of securing societal recognition for the work of mothering. Australian support for children's allowances, although weaker than in France and England in the years before World War II, surfaced continually in government reports and royal commissions from 1907 onwards as a logical complement to the nation's complex system of national wage arbitration.[6]

In Canada, by contrast, almost no significant societal discourse or public pressure for family allowances – except in Quebec – can be found in the years before 1943. The subject was briefly discussed and dropped by a 1929 parliamentary inquiry into social insurance. Testifying before this committee, social-work and union leaders strongly opposed the idea on the grounds that it would erode the responsibility of business to pay a living family wage. Between 1930 and 1943 family allowances were mentioned only once in Parliament, and then only in reference to the birth of the Dionne quintuplets. The allowances did not arise at all as an issue in either the 1935 or the 1940 national election. Nor did Canadian social feminists – who campaigned actively for the creation of provincial mothers' allowance programs for worthy widows during World War I – move on from this success to take up the wider cause of family allowances during the interwar years. In Canada, as in the United States, the voice of social feminism became increasingly quiescent in the 1930s. Organized labour reiterated its opposition to family allowances in 1940, during the first year of the war, and business remained totally silent on the matter. In short, before its emergence in Leonard Marsh's 1943 advisory committee report to Parliament on *Social Security for Canada*, the family allowance was an idea disconnected from any significant societal sources of organizational, institutional, or political support.[7]

Why, then, did it suddenly explode into public debate between 1943 and 1945 to become Canada's first universal social program, on a scale rivalling or surpassing similar children's endowment schemes in Britain and Australia? The answer must be found in the specific convergence of policy problems impinging on the wartime Liberal government of Mackenzie King, none of which were necessarily linked to family allowances, but for all of which family allowances provided an opportune solution.

Most pressing was the delicate wartime politics of wage stabilization. In Canada, as in Australia, France, and Britain, a core attraction of family allowances was their utility as a "social wage." As a means of coming to the economic rescue of workers with large families, without touching off inflationary increases to basic wage rates, family allowances emerged as an attractive policy option for the state managers of Canada's highly controlled wartime economy. This explains why two of the key bureaucratic advocates of the scheme in the wartime Canadian state were the Governor of the Bank of Canada and the Deputy Minister of Finance, men not otherwise known as champions of social reform. Family allowances would meet the "legitimate needs" of labour by placing more money in the hands of workers while allowing government to keep the rate of inflation under control, Bank of Canada Governor Graham Towers told Mackenzie King in June 1943 in arguing for the scheme. Also, paying children's allowances directly to low-income workers seemed a fair trade-off for the wartime tax credits that were already being granted to higher-income earners with dependent children, and for the downward extension of the wartime income tax into the ranks of the working class in 1942.[8]

The doubling of Canada's labour movement under the tight labour market conditions of World War II, and a series of crippling strikes against wartime wage policies between 1941 and 1943, added a sense of urgency to this endeavour. Unlike American unions, Canadian labour had no equivalent to the Wagner Act to protect collective bargaining rights during the early years of the war. Consequently, labour leaders refused to agree to a "no-strike" pledge. In order to quell a wave of strikes within war-controlled industries, where wages had been frozen at 1929 levels, state officials searched for policy tools to dampen the fires of working class unrest, which had reached a peak unseen since 1919. Family allowances offered one such option, senior civil servants and representatives of the National War Labour Board suggested during the summer of 1943. However, in order to make the scheme palatable to organized labour, it was important that it not be connected too directly in the public mind with Ottawa's wage stabilization policy. Herein lay one powerful argument for universality. By paying children's allowances to all families, not simply to those with low income, Ottawa could legitimately claim that the scheme was an instalment on promises of postwar social security rather than a device for enhancing unpopular wartime wage controls.[9]

A related problem for King's Liberal administration was the rapid growth of support for the Co-operative Commonwealth Federation (CCF), Canada's democratic socialist party, which eclipsed the Liberals in public opinion polls during 1943, the same year in which King's government committed itself to family allowances. By promising a "cradle to grave" welfare state and the continuation of high levels of state economic planning after the war, the CCF tapped into a strong public demand for social security and for protection against a return to prewar Depression conditions. The presence of this pressure from the left gave King a strong hand to play in overcoming internal opposition from powerful conservative ministers in his own government, who were aghast at the anticipated $250 million annual cost of the scheme. Family allowances, King argued vehemently in support of the legislation in cabinet discussions, "might be the one thing necessary to save liberal democracies such as Canada."[10]

Unlike large-scale programs for public works or nationalization of key sectors of the economy, which were advocated by the CCF to fend off the anticipated postwar depression, family allowances offered a simpler and far less bureaucratic method for maintaining the high levels of spending needed to support demand and full employment after the war ended. For this reason it had great appeal to the liberal Keynesian economists in the Bank of Canada and the Department of Finance, who opposed direct job creation through massive public works as a countercyclical strategy and who wanted rapid postwar decontrol of Canada's state-managed wartime economy.[11] As Health and Welfare Minister Brooke Claxton argued when defending the scheme in Parliament, "Family allowances increase the buying power of those groups who not only need the money but who are most certain to use it immediately ... [They] *are better than public investment expenditure*. In the first place they are continuous and non-seasonal. They go all year round. In the second place they spread consuming power over a larger range of occupations and in the third place, they stimulate private enterprise by providing steady markets for output."[12] In other words, family allowances offered a far less interventionist Keynesian alternative to the socialism of the CCF, and they were supportive of rather than antagonistic towards the needs of private capital.

Family allowances were attractive to government for other reasons as well. The universality of the scheme made it a "great Canadian measure," Claxton argued, "because it treats all Canadians from end to end of the country absolutely alike."[13] In a literal sense, this was untrue. Family allowances represented a massive horizontal transfer of income from the childless to those with children. However, it did so by reaffirming the importance of the family, an institution that crosscut the powerful linguistic, regional, and class divisions that normally fissured Canadian society. By reaffirming the economic value of a common Canadian citizenship, family allowances helped to build loyalty to the federal state itself.[14]

Unlike other measures of social security, such as unemployment insurance, which was principally paid to wage-labourers concentrated in the cities of central Canada, family allowances represented, as one rural member of parliament put it, "one of the first measures in which the farmer has been permitted to share and share alike with urban folk." In a nation with more than 40 per cent of its labour force still engaged in rural or seasonal resource industries such as farming, fishing, and logging, family allowances constituted a major expansion of the welfare state into rural life. Since the largest families and lowest per capita incomes existed in the resource-gathering periphery rather than in the core industrial heartland of southern Ontario and Quebec, family allowances effected a major regional transfer of income under the guise of lifting children out of poverty.[15]

Placing the family allowance on a universal basis underpinned its status as a "right," not charity – a critical factor at a time when memories of the humiliating means tests for unemployment relief during the 1930s were still fresh in people's minds and when anger over Canada's means-tested old age pension scheme, launched in the 1920s, was building. Conservative Party proposals that aid to poor families should be provided through in-kind services rather than in cash meant "going back ... to some such set-up as was adopted ... during the worst period of the depression," Claxton argued. Means-testing family allowances "would lead to a kind of policing ... an interference with individual freedom, and a degree of regimentation which the people of Canada would not stand for." It would also mean, other Liberals argued, sending "thousands of ladies with spectacles and long noses to inquire into the private family affairs of the people of this dominion."[16]

The universality of family allowances resolved some constitutional problems that might otherwise have arisen. Because family allowances went automatically to every child, they did not violate the provinces' primary constitutional jurisdiction over charity and social welfare. Instead, as Ottawa argued, they fell within the federal government's prerogative to make payments directly to its citizens. It was precisely the means-tested, conditional nature of old age pensions that had placed that scheme within provincial responsibility for social welfare. Family allowances, on the other hand, were "not charity, because the payments [were] of right," government spokesmen argued: "One is not 'entitled' to charity ... [This] is simply a gift by this parliament to some section of its taxpayers."[17] The legal argument that family allowances were a gift from the government to its citizens, however, stood in some tension to the prevailing Liberal claim that the payments were a fundamental social right. Gifts, after all, are discretionary and can be stopped at any time – as many Canadian mothers would discover when family allowances were suddenly abolished in the 1992 federal budget. The scheme's $250 million annual price tag also gave Ottawa a potent argument for hanging on to the lucrative provincial taxing powers it had usurped for the duration of the war. Keynesian arguments linking taxation and fiscal policy to the management of overall levels of investment and demand in the national economy made federal finance department officials extraordinarily reluctant to give up centralized control of income taxation revenue in postwar Canada. Wealthy provinces such as Ontario, on the other hand, were just as anxious to regain the fiscal autonomy they had lost to Ottawa during the 1940s.

In the difficult postwar bargaining over the division of taxation revenue, the continuing large expense of family allowances became a strategic lever for winning new tax agreements with the provinces which would extend Ottawa's wartime dominance of personal and corporate income tax into peacetime. By being first off the mark with family allowances in the postwar politics of social security, the federal government quickly gained the upper hand in its fiscal dealings with the provinces.[18]

Since the universality of family allowances both underpinned and was premised on the idea of a new social "right" of citizenship, what precisely was the nature of the right being recognized and to whom did it belong? Although a wide range of arguments, many of which have already been summarized, were made on behalf of the scheme in Parliament, at bottom the defence of family allowances came down to one core claim – that they would provide equality of opportunity for children in large families to get a fair start, as Mackenzie King put it, in "the battle of life."[19] "The fundamental justification for children's allowances," he told Parliament, "is that the wage system takes no account of the family status of the wage earner, and that, in a considerable sector of Canadian industry, the wages being paid are not sufficient to give the worker a family income sufficient to keep his family in health and decency and up to a reasonably current standard. Family income must somehow be supplemented or, alternatively, a substantial proportion of the population must be doomed to extreme poverty."[20]

At bottom, then, family allowances were not so much a right earned by individuals as they were compensation paid by the liberal state for the indifference of capitalism to family size or need. "It is a new concept," stated Justice Minister Louis St Laurent, "that because the state controls the general economy of the nation, it may have some moral obligation to relieve particular hardships which the system it maintains may impose upon some individuals." It was not practicable, he argued, "to have a scale of wages measured by the needs ... of those who receive the wages." Consequently, government had a "moral obligation" to bridge the difference through family allowances.[21]

In deriving a new social right of citizenship from the recognition of a systemic injustice of capitalism, government arguments for family allowances had much in common with the justifications for unemployment insurance, legislated four years previously, but with one key difference. Although unemployment insurance was premised on the acknowledgment that individuals could be rendered jobless "through no fault of their own," their right to insurance benefits depended on the regular payment of premiums while they were working. Through their contributions, workers earned a "stake" in the scheme. No similar principle informed family allowances. As a result, no strong basis existed for defending the extent of income supplementation that it would provide in years to come. As a "gift" from the state, family allowances more than most other social programs would remain hostage to the political whims and shifting economic priorities of the liberal state.

Had family allowances been justified primarily in recognition of the work of mothering rather than because of deficiencies in the male breadwinner wage, this might not have been the case. Women so entitled could have developed an effective political constituency in defence of the economic value of their labour within the home. In marked contrast to maternalist arguments for widows' pensions during World War I, which explicitly recognized motherhood as a "service to the state," the 1940s debate over family allowances almost omitted women. Instead, the discussion in Parliament focused on guaranteeing equal opportunity for children, compensating fathers for low income, and winning the support of men for defending their country.[22] To the extent that women figured at all in these discussions, it was only in the context of being trusted to use the money wisely in the interests of their children or in being encouraged, through family allowances, to leave the workforce quickly at the end of the war in order to pro-

duce babies and free up jobs for returning veterans.[23] Only Dorise
Nielsen, a Communist member of parliament, explicitly argued that
payments made to wives, "who had the care and responsibility as well
as all the trouble that is connected with the upbringing of children,"
would enhance their "independence" and help them "attain that
stature of full citizenship which they should have."[24]

The immediate political and economic impact of family allowances
in Canada was substantial. For a tired Liberal administration that
had been almost ten years in office, the implementation of family allowances, just before the 1945 federal election, became the single
most important factor in staving off the CCF threat from the left
and winning another majority government. With the collapse of the
1945–46 Dominion-Provincial Conference on Reconstruction, government promises of national health insurance, housing legislation, and
contributory old age pensions were put on hold. As a result, family
allowances became not only Canada's first universal social program
but also the only tangible fulfilment of the Liberals' wartime pledges
to ensure an adequate national minimum of health and decency in
postwar Canada.[25] As a partial replacement for massive levels of
wartime spending, the scheme did its part in helping to maintain high
levels of consumer demand and employment during the early years of
postwar demobilization. It also helped to consolidate Ottawa's dominance of the hugely lucrative new sources of income tax that had been
uncovered during the war.

For many if not most of the 1,400,000 Canadian families who began
receiving monthly cheques from Ottawa in 1945, the financial significance of family allowances, especially in the scheme's first five years,
cannot be understated. Providing an average monthly payment of six
to eight dollars for each child, according to their age, family allowances approximated 15 to 20 per cent of family income for households with three to five children in rural Saskatchewan, the Maritimes,
and parts of working-class Montreal, according to studies done in the
later 1940s. Since the payments were added to rather than deducted
from existing welfare benefits, a typical mother with three children in
Ontario's mothers' allowance program saw her income jump by almost
40 per cent once the scheme was up and running in 1945. For poor
families with a large number of children, the financial impact of the
scheme was even greater. Families depending on intermittent earnings
from fishing or logging, and families where the father was sick or simply absent, often looked to the program for their only regular source
of monthly cash income.[26]

But the scheme's early and substantial impact on poverty soon began to fade once it had fulfilled its immediate political objectives for

the government. Within a decontrolled postwar economy that was experiencing a phenomenal and mostly unexpected economic boom, family allowances quickly lost their relevance either as a strategy for moderating union wage demands or as a means of preventing another depression. Children's benefits had not been a key union objective before the war; consequently, protecting their value after 1945 was a low priority for trade unionists. Under the shelter of new collective bargaining legislation and full employment, Canada's burgeoning postwar labour movement was interested in winning a higher standard of living on the picket line rather than through bargaining with the state for a social wage. Given the rapid collapse in public support for the socialist CCF, which dropped below 10 per cent in public opinion polls after 1948, family allowances also lost their political rationale as a means of staving off a serious threat from the left. The scheme did continue to transfer significant amounts of income from core to peripheral regions of Canada, but in the context of rapid rural depopulation after World War II, the importance of even this regional exchange was soon lessened. Nor did the 1950s see the rise of a strong women's movement capable of articulating the connection between family allowances and the economic value of women's work in the home.[27]

Instead, the principal argument for family allowances remained compensation for the inadequate wages of the working poor. As soon became apparent, however, the needs of the poor quickly fell off the political agenda after 1945. The six to eight dollar monthly scale for family allowances remained frozen, despite a 25 per cent jump in the cost of living between 1945 and 1948 as price controls came off Canada's wartime economy. By 1955, the consumer price index was 55 per cent above the levels of a decade earlier, when family allowances first took effect, and the cost of clothing and food had jumped by 74 and 80 per cent, respectively, yet the monthly benefits per child remained unchanged. As a result, within ten years the value of the family allowances, measured in 1951 constant dollars, had plunged by 40 per cent, and by the mid 1960s by more than 100 per cent. Benefit scales, which even in 1945 had been pegged at less than half the real monthly cost of raising a child, in order to avoid eroding the work ethic, were rapidly allowed to decay even further. Family allowances became the only federal program in which overall spending fell below the growth in personal income in the first two decades after World War II.[28] Indeed, the allowances paid per child were to remain unchanged until 1973, by which point any contribution the scheme made to attacking child poverty had atrophied to insignificance.

Why did the rights of poor children, first acknowledged through family allowances, exert such a weak claim on the state? Apart from the reasons cited above, the scheme's narrow focus on family size as the principal cause of poverty must be singled out as a critical drawback. "The greatest single factor in creating differences between one family ... and another," Brooke Claxton had argued in defence of the scheme, "is neither their wages, nor their health; it is the number of their children." Family allowances would "correct that disparity by attempting ... to bridge the gap between wages and the number of children."[29] Although obviously significant, family size was in fact only one of many causes of child poverty in postwar Canada, and its salience weakened over time as the number of large families diminished and the proportion of single mothers grew. The scheme's more important breakthrough lay simply in providing the precedent for an income supplement to the working poor. The significance of this innovation, however, was masked by the continued focus on big families as the primary cause of poverty. Only in the late 1960s did government officials begin to acknowledge the multifaceted sources of poverty among the working poor and turn to income supplementation as a possible answer.[30]

Because of Canada's postwar population boom, it was easy to overlook the erosion of family allowances. Federal spending on the scheme leaped by 125 per cent between 1946 and 1964 even as benefit levels remained constant and as their economic value shrank rapidly.[31] In other words, the ballooning cost of family allowances, which simply reflected rising fertility and large-scale immigration, helped to disguise the program's quickly diminishing impact in fighting poverty.

The claims of poor children were also eclipsed by those of the elderly in the postwar politics of Canada's welfare state. Ironically, the creation of old age security – Canada's second universal social program, launched in 1951 – by adding another $300 million annually to federal spending, rapidly undermined federal support for keeping family allowances in alignment with the rising cost of living.[32] While both programs shared a surface resemblance as universal transfer payments paid to Canadians within a specific age range, in practice the political basis for their support differed dramatically. The family allowance scheme was a wartime social policy initiative shaped and defined primarily by the state. By contrast, the movement for universal old age pensions developed from a broad societal base. As a result, the politics of aging quickly trumped concern over child poverty in the two decades following World War II.

Unlike family allowances, which developed without linkages to any previous government program or any organized political constituency, the creation of old age security was a direct response to the mounting sense of injustice over the contradictions of Canada's non-contributory, means-tested old age pensions, which had been established in 1927. Widespread dissatisfaction with this plan – by the elderly, their children, industry, labour, and government – provided a more complex pattern of interests behind the meaning of entitlement constructed through universal old age pensions in 1951.

By the late 1940s, Canada's first pension scheme had a rapidly growing caseload and evaporating public support. Reaching more than 40 per cent of the Canadian population aged 70 and over, or 293,000 Canadians compared with only 42,000 at the beginning of the Great Depression,[33] means-tested old age pensions were something of a social policy anomaly, becoming less popular as more people depended on them. Ottawa, which paid 75 per cent of their cost, intensely disliked transferring money to be spent by provincial regimes which it viewed as patronage ridden, bureaucratically incompetent, and fiscally unreliable. Moreover, as Canada's population aged, federal finance officials grew increasingly alarmed during the deficit-ridden 1930s at the projected mounting expense of non-contributory old age pensions.[34] Provincial governments, for their part, resented administering a scheme which, because of its low $20 monthly ceiling and rigid eligibility requirements defined by Ottawa, was politically unpopular. But the principal source of anger generated by old age pensions was from the elderly and their children. Virtually all of it was directed against the means test.[35]

The means test, which stipulated that a pensioner's total income, including the pension, could not exceed $365 annually and which continued to hold children financially responsible for part of their parents' support, stood in fundamental contradiction to the idea that pensions were somehow a "social right." Moreover, because the first decade of pension administration in Canada occurred during the Great Depression, the means test was enforced with increasing bureaucratic vigour and sophistication during the late 1930s by cash-strapped provincial governments.[36]

As a consequence, it became a target of growing protest from the elderly themselves, who developed a rising sense of entitlement out of their experience as clients of the system. For example, the stated purpose of British Columbia's Old Age Pensioners' Organization, launched in 1932, was "to preserve [pensioners'] status as citizens, entitled to pensions as [a] legal and social right, and not by way of relief or charity; and to enable them to maintain their dignity and self-respect as pioneer citizens of Canada." In this sense, pensioners' organizations were formed in order to demand that governments live up to their original vision of pensions as a right, not charity, as articulated when the scheme was created in the late 1920s.[37]

Once World War II began, the contrast between pensions as an entitlement and the actual treatment of the elderly under means-tested provincial schemes grew even greater. "We have got to realize that ... the rights of a man and woman do not dissolve and vanish when they are no longer able to work," the *Vancouver Sun* argued in a powerful 1940 editorial entitled "Our Gestapo for the Aged." "Once that is understood, we shall as a nation go ahead to remove the shame and stigma from our treatment of the aged. We shall call off the gestapo from their enforced and ignominious spying and probing into the lives of old men and women."[38] Labelling the means test an "abasement of the aged," the Toronto *Globe and Mail* agreed: "It burrows into the most intimate affairs of its victims, trying to sniff out any actual or potential revenue they might have ... Aging parents have actually been encouraged by officials to sue their children, forcing them into courts to prove that they could not afford to give support. By such degrading methods does bureaucracy satisfy itself."[39]

In comparison with the new stigma-free social entitlements, such as unemployment insurance and family allowances, which were put in place between 1940 and 1944, means-tested old age pensions appeared increasingly anachronistic. They were "a throwback to the poor laws of the last century," to which the "vast majority of Canadians were unalterably opposed," Liberal members of parliament warned the cabinet during the late 1940s. In a national newspaper advertisement campaign demanding an end to the means test, the Canadian Congress of Labour concisely summarized the mounting sources of public anger:

The Means Test denies thousands of Canadians the right to receive an Old Age Pension. The Means Test states that any amount received from children or any source must be calculated and held against the applicant for pension. Owning a house is a further stumbling block to a pension. A small allowance for military service, or for long years with a firm, all count against the old age pensioner. We don't apply the Means Test when we pay Children's Allowances. There is no need to apply the Means Test to Old Age Pensions.[40]

Paradoxically, public opposition against the means test grew steadily, even though the benefits it paid out and the amount of income it allowed pensioners to earn doubled between 1942 and 1949.[41] As the means test drew an ever-wider circle of the elderly into its scope with each successive policy liberalization, it increased the number of families whose income and assets were subjected to financial scrutiny by the state. It also fuelled the anger of those who still remained left out of its terms. "The idea of saying to people who have saved a little, who have got their own homes together, who have paid taxes and helped contribute to the wealth of the country, that, whereas others in destitute circumstances can qualify, those people cannot qualify for the old age pension – that just does not make sense at all," one member of parliament argued. The means-tested pensions scheme was "inherently discriminatory," an Ontario newspaper pointed out, "for though it aids those most in need, it doesn't benefit those who are perhaps in a lesser degree of need but who get no pensions even though they have helped pay the pensions of others."[42]

This growing sense of injustice at the "unequal citizenship" inscribed in old age pensions was summed up in a single phrase that was heard increasingly in the late 1940s: the means test was "vicious in principle," vicious not only because it stigmatized the poor but, more importantly, because it "penalized thrift" among those elderly who just failed to qualify under its terms. "Regardless of its merits or demerits," government officials acknowledged by 1949, "even if generously conceived, the means test has fallen into such disrepute that public opinion will not be satisfied with anything short of its complete abolition."[43] Rather than enhancing benefits or lowering the age of eligibility, getting rid of the means test and thus establishing old age pensions unequivocally as a universal social right was the number-one objective of almost everyone speaking about old age pensions in Canada during the late 1940s.

The idea of pensions as a "right" emerged not only in reaction to the debate over means testing but as a core bargaining demand of organized labour. In 1949, almost three-quarters of Canada's 3,500 industrial pension plans were the product of wartime negotiations.[44] During the late 1940s, Canadian affiliates of American industrial unions in mining, steel, and automobiles, following the lead of their parent unions south of the border, had targeted the creation or enhancement of company pension plans as their key bargaining objective. But whereas the benefits of private U.S. pension plans could be integrated within the contributory insurance framework of the 1935 Social Security Act, Canadian unions discovered that "a parallel scheme cannot be set up in Canada under our present old age pension law. The unpopular means test stands in the way." Income derived from industrial schemes was simply deducted from rather than added to benefits available through Canada's old age pension plan. Thus, the means test represented a strong disincentive to the creation of private pension coverage. "Hence the anxiety of labor organizations to have that means test abolished," newspapers pointed out.[45]

By 1950, unions such as the United Auto Workers were seeking a $100 monthly old age pension for their members, half of which they wanted to see derived from a universal government old age security scheme. The movement "for industrial pensions ... [has] infiltrated from the United States and looks now as though it might be outpacing the government's own thinking on old age security," the Toronto *Globe and Mail* observed at the beginning of 1950. "Both industry and labor have begun to press for the contributory pension as the only answer. Both realize that the scope of industrial pensions ... [is] limited and that they should have a good national basis to build on if they are going to pad out the government plan."[46]

If the means test had to go, what should take its place? This became the key social policy issue debated within government during the late 1940s. Should Canadian pension policy follow the precedent of American Social Security by building a sense of entitlement along social insurance lines, through the contributory principle? Or should the idea of pensions as a social right, rather than as charity, follow the model of family allowances by paying an identical sum to every elderly citizen?

At first, the answer seemed unequivocal. Old age pensions must be placed firmly on the "contributory principle," Canada's Finance Minister argued in 1943, when benefit ceilings under the means-tested scheme were boosted for the first time in over sixteen years.[47] But as soon became apparent, Ottawa's understanding of the term "contributory" was murky. The Green Book proposals on postwar social security, prepared for the 1945 Dominion-Provincial Conference on Reconstruction, recommended a two-tiered pension system. Ottawa would provide a $30 monthly pension for everyone age seventy or over. In a second tier, provincial governments would administer means-tested pensions, cost-shared equally with Ottawa, for those between the ages of sixty-five and sixty-nine. The new universal old age pension scheme would "not ... be completely contributory, nor completely non-contributory," federal officials argued ambiguously, because its $200 million annual price tag would "be financed by a National Welfare Tax of 5 per cent payable on all incomes," a fund that could also be used to underwrite federal proposals for national health insurance. Government officials were clearly uneasy with the vagueness of this contributory linkage but argued that it was the best they could do "without the necessity of amendment to the British North America Act," an option that had little chance of success given the complex range of issues already facing the reconstruction conference.[48]

When the conference broke up in failure because of disagreements over tax sharing, both old age pensions and health insurance fell off the federal government's policy agenda. In no circumstances would Ottawa assume the massive cost of a universal pension scheme in the absence of provincial agreement on the division of income and corporate tax revenue. Four years later, facing a national election with a new leader, Louis St Laurent, the Liberal Party could no longer remain silent on pension reform. Like Canada's other political parties, the Liberals promised to abolish the means test if they were returned to office. St Laurent remained convinced, however, that "the only practical way in which an old age pension scheme without a means test could be provided is through a direct contributory system." Paying pensions out of income tax revenue was politically unacceptable. "Why should I ... get a pension of $40 per month and hand back only something of the order of 45 or 50 per cent of it to the treasury?" he asked Parliament. "The only way in which a pension, as of right, can be paid to Canadians who reach the age is on a direct contributory system. Then ... we will get what we pay for, and we will pay for what we get."[49]

Old age pensions along these lines sounded a lot like American Social Security, which was also the model favoured by the Progressive Conservative Party, which controlled the government of Ontario, Canada's wealthiest province, and enjoyed the support of most of the nation's newspapers on the issue. Contributory pensions would "entitle a person to payments as a matter of right," but the value of this right, business commentators pointed out, would be limited by the insurance principle that could "put a brake on demands for higher benefits which may increase costs far beyond original estimates." Paying pensions "on the basis of need ... leaves too much room for political determination of the right to an allowance and its amount," Canada's former Deputy Minister of Labour argued. A contributory scheme, on the other hand, would remain true "to the basic principle of rewarding the producer."[50]

Such comments echoed thinking within the federal Department of Finance, which also wanted to see a contributory pension scheme constructed along lines similar to U.S. Social Security. Finance officials recognized that Ottawa could not back away, politically, from its 1945 Green Book pledge of a minimum universal pension of $30 a month, particularly once provincial consent to a new tax-sharing formula had been reached. Any further growth in public pensions beyond this base could come through a second-tier scheme, beginning at age sixty-five, based on compulsory employer and employee participation, in which benefits would be related to contributions. This plan would, however, require a constitutional amendment, and its administration, finance officials acknowledged, would be "difficult and costly," for it would involve "the keeping of records on every employed person in the country." Nevertheless, it "would act as a buffer against demands" and was the only way of developing "(when combined with a universal free pension) … reasonably adequate pensions for at least all employees."[51]

Given this strong support for a U.S. – style social security scheme, why was one not created in 1950–51 when Canada's pension system was reformed? Three arguments developed cogently by officials in the Department of National Health and Welfare doomed the application of the American pension model to Canada. First, it would not get rid of the means test, the principal political objective behind pension reform. "While public opinion *seems* to favour *contributory* insurance," the department argued in 1950, "the *probable* fact is that the public is chiefly concerned about the abolition of the means test. Contributory old age insurance is favoured as a means to this end." Yet the public was wrong. Given the rural and resource-based nature of much of Canada's economy, in which "40 per cent of its people earn … [their] living through non-wage earning employment," a huge segment of the population would be left without any right to protection in old age if pensions were based on a payroll-financed scheme, as the American experience demonstrated. Furthermore, wage earners would need more than a decade of contributions before even minimal pensions could be paid: "Consequently, for years to come, hundreds of thousands of insured persons will receive inadequate old age insurance benefits and will still have to apply for a supplementary means test pension paid from general tax funds."[52] Hundreds of thousands more would be stranded outside the scheme altogether, adding their "pressures for increased pensions to the uninsured." In other words, the value of the contributory principle as a buffer against the politicization of pension benefits was overstated.[53]

A true contributory scheme also promised to be enormously complex and costly to operate. A brief 1950 visit to the massive bureaucracy that housed America's Social Security Administration in Baltimore convinced federal officials of just how "cumbersome and unnecessarily complicated [the] administrative machinery" for such a task would be. To maintain an equivalent record base in Canada would require an additional 5,000 civil servants. Finally, a public pension scheme based on compulsory employer and employee contributions would discourage the growing movement for private pensions. "It would be a great mistake for Government even to appear to monopolize the field by undertaking a complex and ambitious insurance scheme which would be expected to provide adequate pensions on retirement for everybody," Health and Welfare officials advised the Liberal cabinet: "The

Government should seek instead, through the provision of a *minimum security pension*, to bring the *extra* cost of an adequate retirement provision within the reach of the largest possible number. As much leeway as possible should be left for individuals alone, or individuals together with their employers, to build on top of the Government pension a supplementary scheme ... which will be regarded ... as being adequate." Since private schemes would be developed through direct payments from individuals or their employers, it was important that the government plan "should not be financed on a directly contributory basis."[54] The proper role for the state in the pension field was to remain clearly residual to private interests.

Within this context, the Department of National Health and Welfare put forward its own recommendation for a non-contributory, universal old age pension of $40 a month to be paid to all those aged seventy or over. This proposal would "abolish the means test" and would be "simple and inexpensive" to administer, for it could easily be "integrated with the present family allowance administration ... [using] the same machines, equipment, and staff." It would avoid the creation of a "dual system of old age pensions – one for those who are covered by insurance and another for those who ... cannot be included," with all the political dangers this might entail. Most importantly, a minimum basic universal pension would "not conflict with industrial pension schemes" in two crucial ways. First, by providing low benefits and a high age threshold for eligibility, the scheme would encourage individuals, along with their employers, "to build on top of the admittedly inadequate government provision," establishing the "more wholesome approach ... that government is *not wholly* responsible for providing for the retirement needs of its aged people."[55] Second, because it did not necessitate the creation of huge reserve funds, a non-contributory state scheme would avoid "what could be a very dangerous and unwholesome influence in the field of private enterprise ... [and a] serious interference with the operations of private investment houses."[56] In short, universality provided the best defence for asserting a residual and limited responsibility of the state for both the well-being of the elderly and the investment of capital.[57]

Faced with competing visions from within the bureaucracy and cabinet on the future directions for pension policy, Prime Minister St Laurent turned the issue over to an all-party committee of Parliament in order to find a consensus. After conducting extensive hearings lasting over five months, and after wide-ranging research into pension schemes in Europe, Australia, and the United States, the committee recommended unanimously in June 1950 in favour of the

Health and Welfare plan for a universal scheme of old age security, set at $40 a month, for all Canadians of seventy years and over. Like Health and Welfare officials (who played a key behind-the-scenes role in shaping its report), the parliamentary committee remained impressed by the administrative simplicity of a universal flat-rate scheme, by the far wider coverage it would provide to all Canadians, not simply wage earners, and by the greater ease with which it would "support and stimulate supplementary plans under private auspices," as well as increasing "the incentive of the individual to provide through personal saving for his old age." The committee's residual approach to pensions was highlighted by its recommendation that benefits be kept "substantially below minimum subsistence levels" so that the elderly would not find themselves "in more favourable economic circumstances than those not yet retired who are still actually engaged in productive employment."[58] Unlike the Department of National Health and Welfare, however, the committee argued that some form of contributory principle was vital because of its "psychological value." Rejecting the more orthodox social insurance model embodied in U.S. Social Security, the committee argued for a modified "pay-as-you-go" pension scheme, financed through some form of new taxation on employers, employees, and the general public.[59]

The Old Age Security Act, passed in 1951, simply incorporated the committee's recommendations. The importance of the contributory principle was embodied within a special "2–2–2" formula for financing the pension scheme. Its $300 million annual cost would be paid for by 2 per cent increases in the rate of personal income tax, the rate of corporate income tax, and the federal sales tax, all of which would be deposited into a specially earmarked old age security account. Through this mechanism, the scheme would be "based soundly and solidly on the contributory principle," argued Health and Welfare Minister Paul Martin. However, by this time the political meaning of the term had been subtly transformed. Rather than legitimizing individual rights to pensions, it powerfully underscored their cost. As Martin told Parliament, through the "establishment of a special fund ... it becomes abundantly clear to everybody that the government has no income of its own but can only pay out with one hand such money as it takes in with the other hand by taxation. It is made very obvious that the contributory principle is being followed."[60] Within a decade, however, any semblance that old age security was a "contributory" pension had faded to insignificance, for it became impossible to make meaningful political distinctions between the share of income or sales tax increases targeted to the needs of the elderly as opposed to those of other members of society. The abolition of the means test through universality rather than the contributory principle endured as the key legacy of the 1951 pension reforms.

Within the last few years, argues Ken Battle, universality has been "killed off in child and elderly benefits without any public discussion to speak of, let alone any mandate from the voters."[61] A close look at the origins of universality in family allowances and old age pensions during the critical years 1943–1951 sheds light on why the defence of common citizenship and shared entitlement has been wound down in old age security and eliminated in family allowances. Universality in social provision for children and the elderly was the product of transitory political and economic policy dilemmas of the 1940s, not a broadly based social democratic vision. Family allowances, a primarily state-centred initiative, represented a specific response to the politics of wartime wage regulation, the immediate threat of a postwar depression, and the short-lived electoral challenge of the socialist CCF. Although the needs it addressed for supplementing the incomes of the working poor and the cost of raising children were long term, the political commitment to sustaining these obligations proved weak. As the scheme's economic value was allowed to decay rapidly in the first two postwar decades, the significance of the social rights it embodied waned as well. Lacking a strong political constituency from their inception, family allowances became an early target for the "politics of stealth" which, through tax clawbacks and inflation, have characterized Liberal and Conservative government assaults on universality during the deficit-conscious budgets of the past decade.[62]

The social entitlement represented by old age security has been more difficult to challenge. Unlike family allowances, old age pensions as a universal right emerged – as Liberal government representatives acknowledged at the time – "as the result of an overwhelmingly public clamour."[63] The sense of indignity and unequal citizenship built up through two decades of means-tested old age pensions, juxtaposed against the social entitlements granted to others during the war, created a powerful movement for universality as the simplest, quickest, and most comprehensive way of creating an unchallenged right to pensions free of stigma.[64] Eliminating the means test was also an essential demand of both labour and business in order to clear the way for bargaining over industrial pensions. Possessing a strong societal base of support from its inception, OAS, unlike family allowances, has been increased periodically to track changes in the cost of living. Indeed, Ottawa's one attempt to de-index the pension, in 1984, produced the single most effective organized protest by the elderly in Canada's history.[65]

However, despite possessing stronger political support, entitlement through OAS faced sharply defined limits. From its beginning, the scheme incorporated a residualist logic. Pensions were kept below adequacy and financed on a pay-as-you-go basis in order to guarantee political and economic space for private pension coverage as the principal means of providing Canadians with security in old age. This minimalist approach to pension policy, embodied within OAS, was carried over into the creation of the Canada Pension Plan in the 1960s as the contributory tier of public pension policy. As a consequence, Canada today spends a smaller share of its gross domestic product on public pensions "than every other OECD [Organization for Economic Cooperation and Development] country except Australia ... and Japan."[66] With pension policy as with child benefits, Canada's initial 1940s commitment to universality was deceptive. Beneath the rhetoric of entitlement lay the enduring power of residualist principles, which have increasingly re-emerged to dominate social policy debates surrounding children and the elderly in the 1990s.

NOTES

An earlier version of this paper was published under the title "Universality Revisited: Family Allowances, Old Age Security and the Construction of Entitlement within the Canadian Welfare State, 1944–1991," in Hans Bak, Frits van Holthoon, and Hans Krabbendam, eds., *Social and Secure? Politics and Culture of the Welfare State: A Comparative Inquiry* (Amsterdam: VU University Press 1996).

1 Canada, House of Commons, *Debates*, 17 July 1944, 5335.

2 Nancy Fraser and Linda Gordon, "Contract versus Charity: Why Is There No Social Citizenship in the United States?" *Socialist Review* 22, no. 3 (1992): 45–6; Gosta Esping-Andersen, *The Three Worlds of Welfare Capitalism* (Princeton: Princeton University Press 1990), 69; T.H. Marshall, "Citizenship and Social Class," in his *Class, Citizenship, and Social Development* (Chicago: University of Chicago Press 1977), 113.

3 Michael Prince, "From Meech Lake to Golden Pond: The Elderly, Pension Reform and Federalism in the 1990s," in Frances Abele, ed., *How Ottawa Spends, 1991–92: The Politics of Fragmentation* (Ottawa: Carleton University Press 1991), 308, 321; Ken Battle, "The Politics of Stealth: Child Benefits under the Tories," in Susan D. Phillips, ed., *How Ottawa Spends, 1993–94: A More Democratic Canada?* (Ottawa: Carleton University Press 1993),

417–48; and "Ottawa Backs Off Immediate Cuts for Seniors," *Globe and Mail* (Toronto), 7 March 1996. Under the recently announced changes, single retirees with an income of over \$52,000 a year and couples with a combined income of over \$78,000, beginning in 2001, will no longer receive OAS benefits. At present levels of clawback, singles are cut off at \$85,000 and couples at \$170,000.

4 Prince, "From Meech Lake to Golden Pond," 347.

5 Susan Pedersen, *Family, Dependence, and the Origins of the Welfare State: Britain and France, 1914–1945* (Cambridge: Cambridge University Press 1993), 413.

6 Pedersen, *Family, Dependence, and the Origins of the Welfare State*, passim; on children's allowances in Australia, see Rob Watts, *The Foundations of the National Welfare State* (Sydney: Allen & Unwin 1987), 45–60.

7 Brigitte Kitchen, "The Introduction of Family Allowances," in Jim Albert and Allan Moscovitch, eds., *The Benevolent State: The Growth of Welfare in Canada* (Toronto: Garamond Press 1987), 224–34. In Alison Prentice et al., *Canadian Women: A History* (Toronto: Harcourt Brace Jovanovich 1988), the introduction of family allowances receives only a brief one-paragraph reference (262). There is no equivalent within Canadian feminism to Britain's Family Endowment Society led by Eleanor Rathbone. On the silencing of social feminism in the United States during the 1930s, see Linda Gordon, *Pitied but Not Entitled: Single Mothers and the History of Welfare* (New York: Free Press 1994), 209–52; and Leonard Marsh, *Report on Social Security for Canada, 1943* (Toronto: University of Toronto Press 1975), 196–208.

8 Raymond B. Blake, "The Genesis of Family Allowances in Canada," in Raymond B. Blake and Jeff Keshen, eds., *Social Welfare Policy in Canada: Historical Readings* (Toronto: Copp Clark 1995), 249–50; Bob Russell, "The Politics of Labour Force Reproduction: Funding Canada's Social Wage, 1917–1946," *Studies in Political Economy* 14 (Summer 1984): 65; Doug Owram, *The Government Generation: Canadian Intellectuals and the State* (Toronto: University of Toronto Press 1986), 311–14.

9 Laurel Sefton Macdowell, "The Formation of the Canadian Industrial Relations System during World War II," *Labour/Le travail* 3 (1978): 175–96; Blake, "The Genesis of Family Allowances," 249; Kitchen, "The Introduction of Family Allowances," 236. In Parliament, Prime Minister Mackenzie King denied any linkage between family allowances and wartime wage stabilization policy: "Family allowances have never been intended as a substitute for higher wages nor will they serve as such" (Canada, House of Commons, *Debates*, 25 July 1944, 5336).

10 Blake, "The Genesis of Family Allowances in Canada," 252.

11 Owram, *The Government Generation*, 303–10; see also Robert Malcolm Campbell, *Grand Illusions: The Politics of the Keynesian Experience in Canada, 1945–1975* (Peterborough: Broadview Press 1987).

12 Canada, House of Commons, *Debates,* 26 July 1944, 5394–5 (emphasis added).

13 Ibid., 26 July 1944, 5393.

14 Annalee Gorz, "Family Matters: The Canadian Family and the State in the Postwar Period," *Left History* 1, no. 2 (Fall 1993): 10, 18–19; Dominique Jean, "Family Allowances and Family Autonomy: Quebec Families Encounter the Welfare State, 1945–1955," in Bettina Bradbury, ed., *Canadian Family History: Selected Readings* (Toronto: Copp Clark Pitman 1992), 428.

15 Canada, House of Commons, *Debates,* 27 July 1944, 5499, 5482, 5490; 26 July 1944, 5397.

16 Ibid., 1 August 1944, 5726; 27 July 1944, 5469; 28 July 1944, 5533.

17 Ibid., 27 July 1944, 5466–7. On the "gift" defence for the constitutionality of family allowances through the federal spending power, see the speech by federal Justice Minister Louis St Laurent, 25 July 1944, 5350–2.

18 Keith G. Banting, *The Welfare State and Canadian Federalism* (Kingston and Montreal: McGill-Queen's University Press 1982), 68, 117; David R. Cameron, "The Growth of Government Spending: The Canadian Experience in Comparative Perspective," in Keith Banting, Research Coordinator, *State and Society: Canada in Comparative Perspective,* Background Study no. 31, Royal Commission on the Economic Union and Development Prospects for Canada (Toronto: University of Toronto Press 1986), 40.

19 Canada, House of Commons, *Debates,* 25 July 1944, 5330–1.

20 Ibid., 28 July 1944, 5533.

21 Ibid., 25 July 1944, 5352–3.

22 The flavour of the paternalist discourse surrounding family allowances is captured in the speech of future Health and Welfare Minister Paul Martin when endorsing the scheme: "*A father* needs the most help when his income is generally low, at a time when his family is at the top level in so far as numbers are concerned. Generally, *the father* is making less when the needs of his family are greatest" (ibid., 26 July 1944, 5404; emphasis added).

23 Ibid., 27 July 1944, 5494, speech by M.E. McGarry; ibid., 26 July 1944, 5432, speech by R.T. Graham.

24 Ibid., 26 July 1944, 5401, speech by Dorise Nielsen.

25 Jean, "Family Allowances and Family Autonomy," 428.

26 Ibid., 412, table 1; James Struthers, *The Limits of Affluence: Welfare in Ontario, 1920–1970* (Toronto: University of Toronto Press 1994), 123.

27 Veronica Strong-Boag, "Home Dreams: Women and the Suburban Experiment in Canada, 1945–1960," *Canadian Historical Review* 72, no. 4 (December 1991): 471–504.

28 Jean, "Family Allowances and Family Autonomy," 407, 423; National Archives of Canada (hereafter NA), records of the Department of National Health and Welfare (hereafter DNHW), RG 29, vol. 2111, file 21–1–3, vol. 4, "Income Maintenance Measures in Canada," November 1965.

29 Canada, House of Commons, *Debates*, 1 August 1944, 5726.

30 Struthers, *The Limits of Affluence*, 231–60.

31 NA, DNHW, vol. 2111, "Income Maintenance Measures in Canada."

32 Jean, "Family Allowances and Family Autonomy," 429.

33 Canada, House of Commons, *Debates*, 10 March 1950, 636, speech by Paul Martin.

34 NA, DNHW, vol. 2376, file 275–4–2 (1), "Memorandum Regarding Old Age Security," n.d but circa December 1949.

35 For an excellent recent study of the impact of Canada's first old age pension scheme on family relationships, state attitudes towards the elderly, and the creation of a "culture of entitlement," see James G. Snell, *The Citizen's Wage: The State and the Elderly in Canada, 1900–1951* (Toronto: University of Toronto Press 1996).

36 James Struthers, "Regulating the Elderly: Old Age Pensions and the Formation of a Pension Bureaucracy in Ontario, 1929–1945," *Journal of the Canadian Historical Association*, new series, 3 (1992): 235–55.

37 James G. Snell, "The First Grey Lobby: The Old Age Pensioners' Organization of British Columbia, 1932–1951," *B.C. Studies* 102 (Summer 1994): 5. See, for example, Ontario Premier Howard Ferguson's March 1929 statement to the legislature that pensions were "in no sense a charity or gratuity" but were being paid "as a matter of right" and in "recognition of the obligation of the state to give a comfortable, decent, old age to the needy elderly citizen who had put his best efforts into making his contribution to the upbuilding of the country" (Struthers, *The Limits of Affluence*, 65–6).

38 "Our Gestapo for the Aged," *Vancouver Sun*, 3 December 1940, cited in Snell, "The First Grey Lobby," 18.

39 "Abasement of the Aged," *Globe and Mail* (Toronto), 17 June 1949.

40 "It's Up to Ottawa to End the MEANS TEST," half-page advertisement by the Canadian Congress of Labour, reproduced in the *Galt Reporter*, 4 February 1950. The advertisement was placed in newspapers across Canada and incorporated a coupon to be clipped by readers and mailed directly to their member of parliament, demanding that "the means test should be removed immediately from the Old Age Pension law." One MP noted, "I have had more requests about this means test than I have ever had about anything else" (Canada, House of Commons, *Debates*, speech by William Bryce, 6 March 1950, 489).

41 Maximum ceilings on pension benefits increased from $20 monthly in 1942 to $40 by 1949, and allowable annual income jumped from $365 to $600 for individuals (Canada, House of Commons, *Debates*, 10 March 1950, 636).

42 Ibid., speech by Stanley Knowles, 10 March 1950, 657; "Contributory Pensions," editorial, *Windsor Daily Star*, 29 April 1949.

43 NA, DNHW, vol. 2376, file 275-4-2 (1), "Memorandum regarding Old Age Security," n.d. but circa December 1949. The phrase "unequal citizenship" is taken from Sheila Shaver, "'Considerations of Mere Logic': The Australian Age Pension and the Politics of Means Testing," in John Myles and Jill Quadagno, eds., *States, Labor Markets and the Future of Old Age Policy* (Philadelphia: Temple University Press 1986), 112.

44 NA, DNHW, vol. 2376, "Memorandum Regarding Old Age Security."

45 "Old Age Security," *Oshawa Times-Gazette*, 24 February 1950.

46 "Ray of Light Foreseen for Age Pension Plan," *Globe and Mail*, 13 March, 1950; "Government Sees Demands for Social Security Talks," *Citizen* (Ottawa), 23 January 1950.

47 Struthers, *The Limits of Affluence*, 75.

48 NA, DNHW, vol. 23, file 21-2-6, Working Committee on Old Age Pensions, "Report on Dominion Proposals," 16 July 1945; ibid., memo on "Old Age Pensions," July 1945.

49 Canada, House of Commons, *Debates*, 20 February 1950, 62.

50 "20 Years of Old Age Pensions," *Galt Reporter*, 4 November 1949; Bryce Stewart, "What Should Canada Do About Pensions?" *Financial Post*, 7 January 1950.

51 NA, DNHW, vol. 2376, file 275-4-2 (1), Mitchell Sharp, "An Approach to Old Age Security," 5 December 1949; ibid., "Report on the Meeting of the Working Committee on Old Age Security," 19 April 1950. Identical arguments informed the creation of the Canada Pension Plan between 1963 and 1965.

52 NA, DNHW, vol. 2376, file 275-4-2(1), "Memorandum Regarding Old Age Security," n.d. but circa December 1949, 8-10 (emphasis in original). Health and Welfare officials noted, "In 1949 – 14 years after the U.S. old age insurance law was passed – there are still more people in receipt of old age assistance on a means test than there are in receipt of old age insurance."

53 Ibid., 10-12.

54 Ibid., 17-20, (emphasis in original).

55 Ibid., 20-5 (emphasis in original).

56 Ibid., 14. Health and Welfare officials also argued that their plan was "just as much a 'contributory' system as the so-called insurance scheme ... All consumers in Canada contribute ... to the total revenues of the country from which non-contributory pensions would be paid. Hence a tax-supported system is just as truly a 'contributory' system as a so-called social insurance plan" (20).

57 On the residualist nature of Canada's current pension system, see John Myles, "The Politics of Dualism: Pension Policy in Canada," in Myles and Quadagno, eds., *State, Labor Markets and the Future of Old Age Policy*, 97.

58 NA, DNHW, vol. 2376, file 275–4–1 (1), "Findings: Joint Committee of Senate and the House of Commons on Old Age Security," June 1950, 8–10, 17.

59 Ibid., 25–6.

60 Archives of Ontario, Records of the Ministry of Treasury and Economics, RG 6, series III–6, box 1, "Statement on Old Age Security by Paul Martin to Federal-Provincial Conference," December 1950; Canada, House of Commons, *Debates*, 25 October 1951, 387, speech by Paul Martin.

61 Battle, "The Politics of Stealth," 440.

62 Ibid. See also Gratton Gray, "Social Policy by Stealth," *Policy Options* 11, no. 2 (March 1990): 17–29.

63 Canada, House of Commons, *Debates*, 23 June 1951, 4568, speech by David Croll.

64 On this point, see also Snell, *The Citizen's Wage*, especially 156–217.

65 Prince, "From Meech Lake to Golden Pond," 332–6.

66 Myles, "The Politics of Dualism," 86.

DOUG OWRAM

Canadian Domesticity in the Postwar Era

Since the 1960s, or even earlier, historians in the United States have emphasized the impact of the Cold War on the psyche of the average American. The Cold War has become an explanation for the insecurities and anxieties of the postwar age. As David Halberstam wrote, America has been obsessed with it.[1] Everything from movies to the emphasis on the family has been seen through a Cold War filter.[2] Recently and elaborately, Elaine Tyler May has argued for a social construction of "containment" that derived from the Cold War and applied to family relationships, propriety, and, most especially, the role of women. Her book *Homeward Bound* opens, symbolically, with a couple being married in a fallout shelter, a wedding covered by *Life* magazine. The act, she said, was a metaphor for the postwar years.[3] May, it must be emphasized, is simply a modern example of a strong theme in American historiography – namely, that the Cold War had created a period of exceptionalism. Americans became timid and conformist, even paranoid, in the face of the Soviet threat and the possibility of nuclear war.

On the surface it would seem that, for several reasons, what was true in the United States was also true in Canada. As C.P. Stacey noted many years ago, World War II marked the beginning of a North American defence system. First in the Ogdensburg arrangement and subsequently in the Hyde Park Agreement, Canada became part of such a defence system. This was confirmed and extended after the war, with the North Atlantic Treaty Organization (NATO) and the North American Air Defence Agreement (NORAD). Culturally, the arrival of television, as well as the tremendous economic power of postwar America, accelerated a trend that had been under way for decades, moving towards the integration of Canadian and American cultures. In the years after the war, leading Canadian intellectuals worried about American influence. Canada, concluded Harold Innis, had gone from colony to nation and back to colony, all within his own lifetime.[4] Every economic statistic backed up the thesis of North American integration. By 1950, when the Korean conflict took the Cold War to new levels, some 75 per cent of foreign investment and two-thirds of all Canadian exports and imports were directly dependent on the United States.[5]

This combination of integration in defence, culture, and economics has led many, myself included, to see the 1950s as perhaps the most continental of all decades in Canadian history. As well, general patterns of domesticity, suburbanization, and conformity seemed closely parallel north and south of the border. Even at the most basic level of all, fertility, Canada and the United States replicated each other more than any other two nations in the world. The baby boom was, in demographic terms, a North American phenomenon, unaffected by the border. Indeed, there was a greater difference between English and French Canada than between English Canada and the United States.[6]

For this reason, when I began research on a comprehensive postwar study,[7] I started with the assumption, drawn from American research, that the Cold War would be a powerful force shaping Canadian attitudes towards family and home life after the war. A slightly simplified version of the hypothesis went something like this: Canadians returned from the rigours of warfare to seek out a home life. They were initially apprehensive, but once the economy held its course, they became increasingly optimistic about the future. Buttressed by unprecedented levels of veterans' benefits and by new social programs, they built houses in unprecedented numbers, initiated the baby boom, and acquired considerable new levels of prosperity. Yet something was wrong. The same adults who had fought in the war and shown so much courage turned timid and domestic. They became, in William Whyte's famous 1956 term, the "organization men" (and women). Afraid to transgress social norms, this was the quintessential other-directed generation. Their quest for conformity would, within a few years, cause a reaction – partly generational – that contributed to the entirely different decade of the sixties. Under it all, according to the hypothesis, was a paranoid society, in which world war and nuclear destruction, internal enemies, and international conspiracies stifled dissent and bred insecurity. In such a world, domesticity was encouraged, gender rules accentuated, and freethinking reduced. Speech, dress, sexuality (or fear of the abnormal in all cases) conformed to a relatively narrow pattern when contrasted with both the lively 1930s and the turbulent 1960s.

As the poet said, beware of Greeks bearing gifts – or, in this case, of American historians bearing conclusions. I could not say for sure whether the American studies would hold up to close examination, but the more work I did on the postwar years, the more I concluded that the Cold War in Canada had had nothing like the effect that American historical writing had led me to expect. For Canadians, the postwar values – which were indeed very much like those south of the border – seemed to have been derived from domestic experience rather than international politics.

Most directly, Canadians returning from the war had experienced some fifteen years of disruptive forces. Their hopes and fears were the product of the terrible war that had so recently ended in victory. The seeds of domesticity for the late 1940s and 1950s were sown during the war. If you had asked a Canadian soldier or war worker what they were fighting for (not against) in World War II, the odds are that they would have answered "home." The idea of home, really a short form for a million personal recollections of friends, family, and normal daily activities, seemed much more immediate and pressing than abstract concepts such as democracy or faraway places like Poland. Government agencies and the popular press both sensed this. In fiction, magazine articles, poems, and newspapers, the vision of "home" was recreated in hundreds of variations. Coca-Cola advertisements showed returning soldiers and sailors coming back into the embrace of the family. Automobiles were portrayed as being built "by home-loving, home-owning craftsmen."[8] The fictional short stories that abounded in magazines and newspapers built their themes around the maintenance or renewal of home.

Part of the reason for the prevalence of the idea of home was its flexibility. To the soldiers overseas, home meant "over there," the return to family, friends, and civilian life, a sense captured in a short story of the time: "Dick Bannerman closed his eyes. It was over for him – at last –, the waiting. He was leaving for home in two days. Home! he held the word within him until it began to expand and blossom with a ripe rich fullness he could hardly contain."[9] For those who remained in Canada, "home" was shorthand for the notion of reunion with loved ones, with the idea that relationships put on hold could soon be resumed. It was depicted in advice to young women on how to handle that "long dreamed of moment when that man's here again, when you cease to carry the torch alone."[10] It also took on material meanings, as the consumption of household items became associated with intimacy, romance, and the fulfilment of dreams. People selling everything from stoves to mouthwash tried to associate their products with an idealized image of home. Community Silverware, aiming squarely at concepts of romance, marriage, and the establishment of all the trappings of home, was especially blatant, running a series of advertisements that unabashedly made silverware a necessary adjunct to homelife: "Joy ... Joy ... Joy! The sun and the moon and the stars. The big shining world with a white fence around it. There's a great day coming. When HE'S BACK HOME FOR KEEPS."[11]

Much of this rhetoric was, of course, the stuff of propaganda. Government had good reason to encourage a romantic, idealized view of home life. It had to remind the soldiers of the reasons for their sacrifice and encourage those back in Canada to work harder, contribute to war bonds, and accept higher taxation and the absence of consumer goods. Yet behind the rhetoric was a reality that made the idea of home an especially powerful appeal. The generation that came of age in the late 1930s and early 1940s – more than a quarter of the Canadian population – could scarcely remember a time in which home life had not been threatened. First there had been the Great Depression, which had affected the ability of their parents to provide comfort as well as affecting their own future possibilities. Throughout the 1930s, politicians and economists scouted the skies for signs of improvement. The reality, however, was that the decade saw a lower standard of living overall than the 1920s. For many families, it brought unrelieved disaster. Lifelong jobs were lost. Farms were buried under dust storms. People migrated from region to region in search of work. Others doubled up, as grandchildren grew up in their grandparents' house and newly married couples lived at home because they could not afford a place of their own. For tens of thousands in the 1930s, home was a makeshift thing, subject to the vicissitudes of the economy and seldom close to what their parents had hoped for.

This disruption was all the worse because North Americans were used to economic progress. The filling of the frontier lands and continuing immigration had created more or less continual economic growth. There might be bad years or individual setbacks, but Canadians and Americans had been accustomed to the idea that each succeeding generation would live a better material life than its predecessor. This was the promise both of the new land and of the technological revolution that had dominated the economic landscape since the Industrial Revolution. Yet for those born in the teens or twenties, this promise had been elusive.

World War II ended the depression, but it caused a further disruption of people's lives. More than a million individuals, mainly those who came of age in the depression, joined the military. As many as 350,000 of them were stationed overseas at the height of the war.[12] In rough terms, this meant that more than one-half of the male population of military age was in uniform at some point during the war and nearly one third of them served overseas at one time or another. Military age was also marrying and child-rearing age. Thus, these people who in other times could have expected to be forming families were bivouacked in England or patrolling the North Atlantic, or, later in the war, fighting their way through Italy and France.

Some were already married when the war began. Others married in haste because it had begun. The marriage rate increased by one-third between 1938 and 1940.[13] For these people, the war meant separation for up to six years. Couples who had barely had time to adjust to married life had to live apart and put their lives on hold, and wonder whether their relationship would survive the distance. In some instances, periods of leave or a home posting might allow at least intermittent contact. But in many cases, especially for the troops posted to England from 1939 on, there were six long years in which husbands and wives or sweethearts waited anxiously for the end to come. The separation also carried the constant fear that there would never be reunion. For the approximately 42,000 who died in the war and for those who loved them, the dream of home was shattered.[14]

The war also disrupted the lives of those on the home front. World War II, even more than the Great War, was a total war, embracing the entire industrial and resource capacity of Canada. Life changed in thousands of small and not so small ways as the economy and society adjusted to a war footing. The face of the workforce altered dramatically as thousands of women moved into office and factory positions previously held by men. There had always been women who worked outside the home, of course, but the numbers in World War II were unprecedented. Up to 1.2 million women were working at any one time, a participation rate of nearly 33 per cent. This increase had many effects: on women, on social attitudes, and on children. Along the way, it further disrupted the traditional concept of home and family; for the war, which had already taken husbands and fathers overseas in large numbers, brought into the factories and bureaucracies large numbers of women who would normally have remained at home – the middle-class housewife and mother.[15] Traditional family patterns were thus disrupted. With many fathers overseas, large numbers of women were faced with raising children alone. These same women often had to make arrangements with relatives, friends, or, as the war went on, government-supported day-care systems, so that they could leave their children and go off to work. Throughout the war, social workers and

psychologists fretted about a generation of children raised in a hap-
hazard manner.

Even the money that Canadians were earning was of limited use.
After years of making do because of lack of money, Canadians now
had to make do because of lack of goods. This was a total war, and
the industrial capacity of Canada was increasingly directed to military
necessities. By 1941, production of a wide range of appliances was
being restricted in order to reserve metals for the war effort. Refrigerators, vacuum cleaners, washing machines, and a host of other goods
virtually disappeared from the market. Automobile production ground
to a halt as factories turned to producing military vehicles. Even if a
used car could be found, its use was severely restricted by a shortage of
tires and by gasoline rationing. The average Canadian was allowed
only 120 gallons of gasoline per year by 1943. Nor were the alterna-
tives without their problems. Taxis were restricted to operations within
fifteen miles of their home base, and even travel by bus was restricted
to a round trip of no more than fifty miles.[16]

It was not only the big expensive goods that were restricted;
the small ones were too. Indeed, for somebody trying to raise a family,
the small things probably brought the war home more strongly than
the lack of cars or refrigerators. Rationing of sugar, butter, coffee, tea,
and meat all severely limited the family diet. Prohibitions on import-
ing canned fruit made tomato juice the vitamin-c source of necessity
for most. Shopping became a matter not of what could be afforded, as
it had been in the depression, but of what could be found. "Shopping
is becoming more and more like a treasure hunt," wrote one woman
in 1943. "Someone tells someone else that there is kleenex on sale at
a drug store and the rush is on. Within a couple of hours stocks are
cleaned out. Women with babies are finding shopping particularly
difficult. Wool for knitting them clothes can only be got occasionally
and it is difficult, sometimes impossible, to buy flannelette. Stores
have to be gone over with a fine tooth comb in order to scratch up a
few diapers."[17]

Worst of all was the housing. The fierce attachment of Canadians
of this generation to their homes and gardens became a subject of
derision by the 1960s. Given their experiences, the derision was
hardly reasonable. To put it simply, they grew up and came to adult-
hood at a time when Canadian housing was in an abysmal state. The
construction industry has always been extremely sensitive to economic
downturn, and it is hardly surprising, therefore, that it collapsed in
1929–30. Even after halting recovery began in other areas of the
economy towards the end of the 1930s, construction remained slug-

gish. Throughout the decade there were fewer houses being built than families being formed. In other words, the availability (and given the absence of repairs, the quality) of Canadian housing was in decline. A good many children and adolescents who grew up in the 1930s lived in crowded, run-down conditions. Hundreds of thousands of families could not afford to own or rent their own place and had to share with others. Newly married couples found themselves forced either to live apart or to share quarters with parents. By the beginning of World War II, it was estimated, more than a million Canadians lived in residences with less than one room per person.

The war made things worse. Building materials were diverted to the war effort, and thus the new prosperity did not rekindle housing starts. It was mid-war before the value of permits reached that of the late 1920s. Much more than this was needed, for the war created tremendous new pressures. Thousands of Canadians moved to take advantage of desirable jobs in war industries or government. Urban centres gained at the expense of rural areas and smaller towns. Nor were all urban centres equal. The bulk of the jobs were created in a few large cities. Montreal, Ontario's "Golden Horseshoe" (from Oshawa to Hamilton), Vancouver, Halifax, and Ottawa became magnets that drew thousands. Those who went to these centres found jobs more readily than they found accommodation. By mid-war, a survey of "ordinary" rental housing in Toronto discovered that about half of it was overcrowded, much of it badly so.[18]

Newspapers were full of "apartments wanted" advertisements, and obligatory key money (under-the-table kickbacks) and similar devices were common. So was makeshift housing. Toronto put up temporary housing around city parks. Other cities experimented with Quonset huts, rudimentary makeshift shelters, and even, in some cases, tent cities. Looking at the longer term, the dominion government strengthened its support of home ownership with the National Housing Act in 1944. At the same time, it recognized the emergency existing in the short term and actually made it illegal to move to Victoria, Vancouver, Ottawa, Hull, Toronto, or Montreal unless one could prove to government the wartime need to do so.[19]

The efforts were insufficient. Years of depression slump and wartime boom had taken their toll. For many, the plight of crowding and long-distance commuting turned to desperation, especially when young children were involved. "For countless numbers of children," lamented a postwar commission on youth, "home was a dilapidated makeshift dwelling, hopeless as far as healthful living was concerned, where life was insecure, and days were anxious. Lowered self-respect,

poor health, anxiety, strained family relationships, lack of privacy –
these were the consequences of poor housing that often created the
juvenile delinquent."[20]

By the end of the war, the idea of home thus contained very powerful connotations, ranging from material comfort and renewed relationships to the end of war itself. Underlying it all was a search for
stability by a generation that had known nothing but instability. The
home, coming home, and the formation of the family as a point of reference in an unstable world all merged into one vision. Soldiers overseas, according to one editorial, evinced a growing recognition of the
values of Canadian home life. "They felt a growing desire to give similar advantages to children of their own." The war had been fought for
the values of the family. "Christian and democratic countries have
made no mistake in emphasizing the value of family and home life.
Individuals who exemplify the art of being in a family circle are better
fitted thereby for usefulness in larger spheres and for gaining the
secret of true happiness."[21]

When the war ended, two things happened. First, in spite of the
Veterans Charter, insecurity continued. Towards the end of the war,
the dream of home and family had been threatened by uncertainty
about the future. Economists, politicians, and the average person
feared that the war had created a temporary economic boom, brought
on by artificial conditions, and that the end of the fighting would lead
to a short bout of rapid spending, rising inflation, and then a sharp
crash. This, as their parents reminded them, was what had happened
after World War I. It was also what government experts had planned to
cope with and had expected during the war itself.[22]

All of this was very much to the fore in the 1945 election as each
party tried to claim for itself the ability to avoid such a disaster.[23] The
economic gloom clashed sharply with the hopes of Canadians for
families, homes, and children. For this reason the Co-operative Commonwealth Federation (CCF), with its promises of social security,
had risen to new heights of popularity by mid-war. Government had
responded with a series of "social welfare" reports and studies, all of
which attempted to find a way to ensure that the end of the war would
not bring economic disaster. In the popular press, such plans received
a great deal of attention.[24]

The depression did not return, but we must be careful not to use
the benefit of hindsight to telescope history. For several years after the
war, the prosperity always seemed fragile. There were bouts of inflation and sharp if relatively short recessions between 1946 and 1955.
Even as it became apparent that prosperity was the dominant pattern,
the memories of recent years remained. There was, indeed, something

of a paradox in the postwar period. Although this was, overall, one of the most prosperous periods in Canadian history, only gradually did policy makers and the public overcome the wartime fear that the slightest misstep would recreate disaster.[25] It was not until the boom of the 1960s that governments and public alike began to turn their backs on the need for security and to chart policy and personal actions on a very different set of imperatives.

Fear of economic fragility was accentuated by the determined postwar effort of Canadians to acquire material possessions. In 1946 the *Star Weekly* observed, "There is a powerful demand for everything that one can eat, wear, read, repair, drink, ride, and rest in. The nylon line is the symbol of 1946."[26] Between 1945 and 1952, automobile registrations doubled. As one observer put it, "It took only seven years to duplicate the motor vehicle production and ownership achievement of the previous forty-five years."[27] In 1953 a turning point was reached, for more than 50 per cent of Canadian families now owned a car. By 1960, two-thirds of households had a car and 10 per cent had two or more.[28]

The same pattern occurred in housing. By the end of the 1940s, the combination of prosperity, low-rate mortgages, and new building techniques had helped alleviate the housing shortage of wartime. In the fifteen years after the war, more than a million Canadians moved to that borderland between city and country, the suburb. The suburb became the symbol of the young postwar family. Scholars descended on suburbs as if they were a strange and previously undiscovered society.[29] Magazines and newspapers of the era were replete with stories of that new curiosity, suburban life. As early as 1954, *Maclean's* called it the "great phenomenon of the twentieth century." In 1960, *Time* magazine dedicated a cover to the suburban housewife and had a bannered headline: "One-Third of a Nation, U.S. Suburbia 1960."[30]

Of course, not all postwar families lived in the suburbs. Hundreds of thousands grew up, as had their parents or grandparents, in city homes, rural farmhouses, or small villages. Still, *Maclean's* was right. The suburb was the great phenomenon of the age, and it came to typify the childhood of the baby boomer. The rise and triumph of low-density residentially oriented communities was the single most significant urban event of the postwar decades. As one American writer has aptly commented, "If the nineteenth century could be called the Age of Great Cities, post-1945 America would appear to be the Age of Great Suburbs."[31] In the United States, the suburbs grew 8.5 times as fast as the central cities from 1945 through the end of the 1960s, and by the 1970s more Americans lived there than in either the cities or the countryside. In Canada, the trend was the same. The 1961 census noted that the 1950s had brought growth that was consistently higher in the suburban areas than in the cities proper.[32] Communities that hardly existed before the war became major centres of growth for the postwar generation. Places such as Scarborough, North York, and Etobicoke in Toronto; Hamilton Mountain and Burlington near Hamilton; Burnaby and North Vancouver in Vancouver; and St-Laurent and the west-island communities of Pointe Claire and Beaconsfield in Montreal typified the new urban landscape that developed in the postwar drive for one's own space and home.

Both the consumption patterns of the postwar years and the move to the suburbs reinforced the desire for security. Of course, it is obvious that mortgages and small children are restraints on those who would take a wild and adventurous direction in life. There is more to it than simple financial liability, however. The pattern of consumption and domesticity that dominated after the war was self-reinforcing.

Historians have emphasized the stability of the 1950s, but in their own way these years were revolutionary. People were moving to new communities and purchasing their way to new technological comforts. Historians have not paid much attention to just how much housing changed during the boom of the 1950s and 1960s. Partly, this is because many of the devices we take for granted were available by the early twentieth century. Central heating (albeit by coal), hot and cold water, flush toilets, and baths or showers provided comfort and hygiene. In the interwar years the development of electrical appliances had meant that mechanical refrigeration and electric ovens were available. But there was a catch. These were still luxury goods, owned mainly by the more affluent urban resident. As late as 1941, most Canadians (four out of five) had iceboxes, and the vast majority (nine out of ten) used coal or wood as a heating source. Not many had central heating at all. A bare majority (six out of ten) had piped water in their houses, but fewer than half had a bath or shower. Even the flush toilet was far from universal, with just over half of all Canadian dwellings possessing one. Only the very rich had more than one.[33]

For decades, therefore, the average Canadian had seen many of these conveniences as things that, though technologically feasible, were for someone else. After the war, for the first time, this changed. This is what the critics of modern tract housing have not understood. The houses may have been small, unimaginative, and even tacky, but they made modern technology available to the average Canadian. By 1961, the vast majority of houses were centrally heated and seven out of ten used oil, natural gas, or electricity, thus removing the labour from heating. In all but the poorest or most remote rural areas, piped running water, mechanical refrigeration, and flush toilets had effectively become universal.[34] Already, new time savers were appearing. Automatic clothes washers and dryers began to appear by the end of the 1950s and within a few years were a common feature of middle-class life. Even dishwashers, though far from common, were increasingly seen in homes by the early 1960s.[35]

This revolution marked not only the adoption of new technologies but the broadening of a standardized North American middle-class lifestyle. The years of prosperity and nearly full employment, as well as the determination of parents, meant that a higher percentage of baby-boom parents owned houses than any previous generation in Canada, some 75 per cent by 1966.[36] They also tended to buy their houses earlier and to upgrade house size, available appliances, and automobile ownership through a continuous twenty-year period. The modern house with indoor plumbing and central heating, along with the car and the fridge and stove, was attained by the parents of the baby boom, and thus their adult years seemed truly affluent, standing in sharp contrast to earlier experiences.

Modernization also brought standardization. The similarities between the new suburbs of the large Canadian cities were striking. True, a few superficial regional variations remained. In the West, houses were covered with stucco or wood, whereas brick was more likely to be used in Ontario. On the West Coast, furnaces were not yet universal. On the Prairies, back alleys hid garages that were separated from the houses. But apart from such details, suburban households in Canada were pretty much the same. The average number of persons per household grouped closely around the national average of 3.9, varying from a low of 3.5 in Burnaby, British Columbia, to 4.0 in Dartmouth, Nova Scotia.[37] This may have occurred in part because housing size was so tightly circumscribed, varying between five and six rooms in all cases. There was also an 80 per cent chance that the house would be a bungalow.[38] Suburbia was a land of modern conveniences wherever one went. The already mentioned flush toilets, refrigerators, and central heating were effectively universal. Also nearly universal was the automobile, with at least eight (and, in most cases, nine) out of ten households possessing one. Only in francophone St-Laurent, where automobile ownership was less and multiple housing common, was there significant variation. Otherwise, the home of the Canadian suburbanite varied little across the country.

All of these circumstances encouraged people to search for security. First, the circumstances of war and disruption created a romantic vision of a postwar world in which the family would be reunited or the marriage knot tied. Second, economic insecurity hung over the postwar years, despite the prosperity emphasized in retrospective views. Third, families were going through tremendous change. There were new communities, new homes, new children.

Remember as well that all of this was occurring as people adjusted from wartime to home. Even peace and prosperity had their points of disruption. For some, returning "home" proved difficult. For society as a whole, the potential problems of the transition from the military to civvy street had emerged as an issue even before the war ended. In this, World War II really was different from all previous wars, at least in the sense that it saw the transition not merely in economic but in psychological terms. The interwar years had seen the rise of psychiatry as a legitimate and recognized, though always controversial, profession. In part, this was the result of the tremendous impact of Freudian and post-Freudian ideas, though perhaps on the public more than on practitioners. By the time the war began, both official and public perceptions were sufficiently aware of psychological issues that in both Canada and the United States the concepts of "psychological fitness" for duty and such mental difficulties as "battle exhaustion" gained a recognized place in military medical treatment.[39]

As the war neared its end, articles on the psychological difficulties of the returned soldier began to appear in medical journals. Even the normal soldier, the psychiatrists warned, faced stress in returning to civilian life. Popular magazines and newspapers picked up the stories and transmitted them in shorter versions to a wider audience. They all carried the same message: the very dreams of home that so affected everybody could create problems. "During long separation from his own family and civilian friends the soldier usually idealizes them and the home situation out of all recognition," warned Canada's senior military psychiatrist. "His return to the reality of his home environment may prove to be difficult and disturbing to him."[40]

There were indeed problems. Many veterans had serious difficulty adjusting to the unregimented life of the civilian. Others felt a tremendous loss of status as they changed from meaningful military roles to uncertainty and unemployment. This situation was depicted by Hollywood in *The Best Years of Our Lives*, in which one of the returning heroes, a decorated air force captain, had been a soda fountain attendant before the war. His wife, whom he had married just before shipping out, wanted him to continue to wear his uniform. He had to grapple with the fact that all his war activities meant little in civilian life. In less dramatic fashion, the return to civvy street was a shock for thousands. Inevitably, friends and relatives, through either tactlessness or indifference, did the wrong thing. They asked about war experiences when people did not want to be asked. They did not ask about war experiences when the veteran wanted to talk. If a pattern runs through the reminiscences of veterans, it is the astonishment of seeing day-to-day life going on. For the people at home, life continued on after victory. But for the soldier returning from overseas, one life had ended and another begun. This made even the happiest return a potentially wrenching event: "But suddenly it was all over. Done and gone forever. We all had lives to begin living and there was no time to think of that wonderful adventure. Now was the time we had to think of. The real adventure was ahead, and I knew I would miss terribly my friends for a while because they were the only friends I had."[41]

To put a couple or family back together was hard enough. For returning veterans to put it back together while trying to change what had really become a way of life was even harder. It is not surprising, therefore, that the first year or so after the war brought many difficulties. For family members who had to cope with the moody, irritable, and seemingly unappeasable returned serviceman, there were problems as well. Wives and girlfriends had to cope with the rumours about those overseas girls. There was a great deal of controversy about English, Scottish, and French women and what might have happened overseas. Special hatred was reserved for German women who, lurid stories reported, had set out to seduce many boyfriends and husbands.[42] Added to all this was a fear for the children of the war. Jeff Keshen has demonstrated how, during the war, family separation and the prevalence of working women raised fears that a generation of juvenile delinquents was being created.[43] The fear of family breakdown, though always more imagined than real, carried into the postwar years as a challenge to those who saw the commitment to family as the centrepiece of their new lives.

For the sake of stability, the family, and children, all the postwar messages sent a clear directive to the hundreds of thousands of women who had gone into war work. Both social mores, though undermined to a degree by war experience, and the need to find a place for the returning soldiers dictated that the wartime employment of women would alter when the war ended. It was even legislated to some extent by the provision that anybody who had sacrificed a paying job to join the services had the right to get that job back on discharge.[44] More than that, this was a culture that emphasized marriage and family and security. These things, people believed, were not compatible with the working wife. One message was transmitted continually: a successful marriage was one in which the wife stayed home. As an article entitled "How to Stay Married" ominously concluded, two-career families had "an alarming record in the divorce courts."[45] When a teenage girl was asked about work in the spring of 1945, her response indicated that the messages had got through: "We think that the day of the girl in any

job a man does will be gone when we're ready to work."[46] She was
right. Between 1944 and 1946 more than 300,000 women, or 25 per
cent of the total female workforce, left their jobs either voluntarily
or involuntarily. The percentages were undoubtedly higher in the
highly paid industrial professions, in which so much war work had
been concentrated. Not until a full generation had passed was the
presence of women in the workforce again as prevalent as it had been
during the war.

If the impact of the end of the war on female workers is clear, the
attitude of women towards the postwar shift is harder to discern. Some
had never seen work as anything but a temporary thing, a patriotic
duty to be borne. For them there was a sense of being "liberated to the
kitchen" at the end of the war. Part of the cult of marriage, after all,
was a belief that work in the home was not only inevitable but was the
desirable goal of a woman. "This is my generation," said one fictional
young woman to her shocked mother. "Yours earned the right to have
a career ... mine earned the right not to have one if we don't want
it."[47] Other women deeply resented what was happening. After years of
proving they could do the work, they were now being pushed aside.[48]
Most of them probably felt a mixed set of emotions – regret at the loss
of pay cheque and independence; relief at the opportunity to return
to a more normal existence.[49] The adjustment from paycheque to
domesticity, however, was yet another point of stress in the move from
wartime to peacetime.

One year after the end of the war, homecoming seemed a little
less glamorous, a little more troublesome. "In homes across Canada
there are tens of thousands of little battles brewing," concluded one
observer. Husbands constantly reminiscing about England or sneak-
ing off to drink with their army buddies created resentment and
friction on the part of wives. Wives who had no understanding or
interest in hubbie's wartime stories created bitterness and a sense of
isolation in the returned soldier. Many wives, in turn, missed the
financial independence bestowed by war work and were having to
cope with a husband so wrapped up in his own past that he could not
or would not see that they too were having to deal with change.
Home, as the psychiatrists had warned, was not the utopia the soldier
had dreamed about: "Canada, this is your nostalgia. It plants aches in
the hearts of men and women in homes from Pacific to Atlantic. It
makes the men who come back, and the women who waited for them,
bitter with resentment."[50] For many spouses, the war remained an un-
knowable gulf between them. The years healed the friction for most,
but the gap was still there – two lives that had gone separate ways, at
least for a while.

The quest for a stable home life seemed all the more important to the degree that it seemed under challenge. Marriage and family were built on specialized roles, and these roles had to be resumed if social stability was to return. For a year or so after the war, the return to the kitchen became something of an obsession. In 1945 the favourite theme in stories of this genre was some sort of romantic reunion. By 1946 and into 1947, the romance had faded somewhat and the tension had risen. The theme now was not the return home but life after the return, based usually on some variation of the theme of working wife/returning husband. In story after story, the tension was set around the wife's decision to retain her usually interesting, usually white-collar job. From that point, there were endless variations. Sometimes the husbands were supportive, either setting up a two-career family or staying home as a house husband. In such cases, the wife invariably discovered that the role reversal was not what she really wanted. It was wrong for "big, powerful men like Ritchie" to be working at "niggling domestic chores."[51] In other cases, the husband was emasculated by his working wife, and the marriage seemed likely to fail unless she left work. In still other cases, trickery was used. The pretty maid hired to care for him (men could not take care of the home in many of the stories) became a real or imagined love threat. Whatever the variation, the moral was always the same: the women returned home and ultimately were always happy and relieved to have done so.

The insistence on the importance of traditional gender roles was an extension of the profound insecurity that beset Canadians during these years. As the previous fifteen years had shown, family life was a fragile thing. It was made more fragile by the need for people to adjust to one another after being so long apart. The tensions of reunion and of hasty marriages soon showed up in separations and divorces. The year after the end of the war established a record not only for marriages but for divorces. The next year was even worse. Divorce was at an all-time high and generated a tremendous tide of concern among clergymen, marriage experts, and others about the apparent collapse of the institution of marriage.[52]

The cherished goal of stability and family seemed under challenge, and, in reaction, the public in general, both men and women, insisted on a return to "traditional values." Yet there is no evidence that working housewives actually created the strains that fictional stories and expert advisers implied they did. Rather, the working housewife became a symbol of the wartime and postwar turbulence in family life. She had to return home so that the family might return to stability. Most working housewives would have left their jobs anyway, but the shrill insistence that they do so left a residue of resentment that surfaced on occasion in later years.

All ages have had their insecurities. Even so, the situation of the young adults of the postwar years was exceptional. As a generation, they had lived the first twenty or thirty years of their lives under abnormal conditions. Economic insecurity, war, and rapid changes in the standard of living were all part of their experience. Even as the postwar years began to yield better opportunities, the move to the suburbs and a community of strangers, the addition of children, and the expansion of the middle class all signalled further change. Amid it all, these young people were told that the happy family unit was a fragile thing, dependent on a careful balance of psychological forces. Of course, the Cold War and fear of the bomb probably added to this general mood. On balance, however, Canadians seem to have derived their quest for security and stability from their own experience. That the members of this generation sought common values, familiar rules, and a certain domestic quietude is understandable even in the absence of any obsession with the Cold War, since they had been through so much.

NOTES

1 David Halberstam, *The Fifties* (New York: Villard Books 1993), 59.

2 Thomas Doherty, *Teenagers and Teenpics: The Juvenilization of American Movies in the 1950s* (Boston: Unwin, Hyman 1988), 144.

3 Elaine Tyler May, *Homeward Bound: American Families in the Cold War Era* (New York: Basic Books 1988).

4 Harold Innis, "Canada, the United States and Great Britain," in his *Essays in Canadian Economic History* (Toronto: University of Toronto Press 1956), 394–412.

5 F.H. Leacy, ed., *Historical Statistics of Canada*, 2nd ed. (Ottawa: Statistics Canada 1983), G 415–442.

6 Landon Jones, *Great Expectations: America and the Baby Boom Generation* (New York: Coward, McCann & Geoghegan 1980). See also Doug Owram, *Born at the Right Time: A History of the Baby Boom in Canada* (Toronto: University of Toronto Press 1996).

7 Owram, *Born at the Right Time*.

8 *Maclean's*, 15 June 1945, front cover; 15 October 1945, inside back cover.

9 "Morning," *Chatelaine*, June 1945, 26.

10 Adele White, "When That Man's Home Again," *Chatelaine*, February 1945, 23.

11 Community Silverware advertisement, "Back Home for Keeps," *Star Weekly*, 6 October 1945, 32.

12 C.P. Stacey, *Arms, Men and Governments: The War Policies of Canada 1939–1945* (Ottawa: Queen's Printer 1970), 48, 66 (i.e., those born between 1910 and 1925).

13 Leacy, *Historical Statistics of Canada*, B 75–81.

14 This phenomenon was also present in the United States. See May, *Homeward Bound*, 60.

15 Ruth Roach Pierson, "*They're Still Women After All*": *The Second World War and Canadian Womanhood* (Toronto: McClelland and Stewart 1986), details the experience of women in wartime work.

16 Canada, Privy Council, *Canadian War Orders and Regulations*, 1942 (Ottawa: King's Printer 1943), Department of Munitions and Supply, Transit Controller, 31 October 1942, transit order 3–B.

17 Maud Ferguson, "Wartime Living in Canada," *Canadian Affairs* 1, no. 4 (15 June 1943): 5.

18 National Archives of Canada (hereafter NA), Records of the Canadian Youth Commission, MG 28 I 11, vol. 42, file 6, "Report of the City Council's Survey Committee on Housing Conditions in Toronto, 1942–3," 27–8. The definition of overcrowding was more than one person per room in an apartment or house. See also, in the same volume, Triangle Forum Club, "A Brief to the Canadian Youth Commission on the Importance of an Adequate Housing Program in Canada," April 1944.

19 See advertisement in *Saturday Night*, 10 March 1945, 44. On the state of the housing crisis at the end of the war, see NA, Records of the Department of Finance, vol. 3980, file "Housing," Arthur MacNamara to W.C. Clark, 22 May 1945.

20 Canadian Youth Commission, *Youth, Marriage and Family* (Toronto: Ryerson Press 1948), 42.

21 *Star Weekly*, 10 November 1945, 6.

22 Doug Owram, *The Government Generation: Canadian Intellectuals and the State 1900–1945* (Toronto: University of Toronto Press 1986), 293–4.

23 J.L. Granatstein, *Canada's War: The Politics of the Mackenzie King Government 1939–1945* (Toronto: Oxford University Press 1975), 384–5, 389, 397, 405–6.

24 Owram, *Government Generation*, 290–2.

25 See, for an example of this at the federal level, Robert Campbell, *Grand Illusions: The Politics of the Keynesian Experience in Canada, 1945–1975* (Peterborough: Broadview Press 1987). Campbell argues that postwar finance ministers did not trust the surpluses that were piling up and feared that a sharp downturn would catch an unwary government off guard.

26 "The Great American Boom," *Star Weekly*, 27 July 1946.

27 Gordon Campbell, "An Analysis of Highway Finance and Road User Imposts in Canada" (PH D thesis, Purdue University, 1956), 59.

28 *Annuaire du Québec*, 1968–9, 677; Canada, Dominion Bureau of Statistics, *Household Facilities and Equipment* (Ottawa 1960).

29 One of the most famous suburban studies is a Canadian one: John Seeley, R. Alexander Sim, and E.W. Loosley, *Crestwood Heights: A Study in the Culture of Suburban Life* (Toronto: University of Toronto Press 1956).

30 John Gray, "Why Live in the Suburbs," *Maclean's*, 1 September 1954, 7; *Time* (Canadian edition), 20 June 1960, front cover.

31 Robert Fishman, *Bourgeois Utopias: The Rise and Fall of Suburbia* (New York: Basic Books 1987), 182.

32 Dominion Bureau of Statistics, *Census of Canada 1961*, vol. 99–526, 4–5.

33 John R. Miron, *Housing in Postwar Canada: Demographic Change, Household Formation, and Housing Demand* (Kingston and Montreal: McGill-Queen's University Press 1988), 183–7.

34 Ibid.

35 By 1971, 40 per cent of Canadian households had clothes dryers and 13 per cent had dishwashers. See *Census of Canada*, 1971, vols. 93–734, 93–742, "Housing."

36 Michael Doucet and John Weaver, *Housing the North American City* (Montreal and Kingston: McGill-Queen's University Press 1991), 314.

37 Frederick Elkin, *The Family in Canada* (Ottawa: Vanier Institute of the Family 1964), 21, notes the convergence in family size. The 1961 census showed a range from 3.5 per family in British Columbia to 4.2 in Quebec for the original nine provinces. Newfoundland stood apart with 4.7.

38 Typical housing design can be seen in the "Canada Housing Design Council 1958 Awards. Report of the National Jury," Royal Architectural Institute of Canada *Journal*, June 1958, 230–4. All nine awards were given to bungalows, and none of the houses was more than 1,500 square feet in size.

39 Terry Copp and Bill McAndrew, *Battle Exhaustion: Soldiers and Psychiatrists in the Canadian Army, 1939–1945* (Montreal and Kingston: McGill-Queen's University Press 1990).

40 Major-General G.B. Chisholm, "Psychological Adjustment of Soldiers to Army and to Civilian Life," *American Journal of Psychiatry* 101 (1944–45): 300–2. See also Brigadier J.C. Meakins, "The Returning Serviceman and His Problems," *Canadian Medical Association Journal* 51, no. 3 (September 1944): 195–202; D. Ewen Cameron, "The Reintegration of the War Veteran in Industry," ibid., 202–6.

41 Barry Broadfoot, *The Veterans' Years: Coming Home from the War* (Vancouver/Toronto: Douglas & McIntyre 1985), 38–9.

42 On sex and the armies overseas, see the American work by John Costello, *Virtue under Fire: How World War II Changed Our Social and Sexual Attitudes* (Boston: Little, Brown 1985), chaps. 13–15.

43 Jeff Keshen, "Wartime Jitters: Canada's Delinquency Scare and Its Consequences" (unpublished paper, University of Alberta, 1994).

44 See May, *Homeward Bound*, 76–8, on the generally similar American response.

45 C. Wesley Topping, "How to Stay Married," *Chatelaine*, February 1946, 11.

46 "Teenage Special: Looking Ahead to Your Job," *Chatelaine*, May 1945, 13.

47 Velia Ercole, "Woman Set Free," *Chatelaine*, October 1945, 6. For a real-life version of this attitude, see May, *Homeward Bound*, 81.

48 Elizabeth Hawes, "Women Will Not Go Back in the Kitchen," *Star Weekly*, 8 December 1945, and Katherine Kent, "Dames at Desks," *Maclean's*, 15 January 1945, 10–11.

49 See the interviews with working women by the Canadian Youth Commission, printed as appendix B of its *Youth, Marriage and Family*, 214–19.

50 Margaret Francis, "Nostalgia," *Chatelaine*, November 1946, 16. See also Douglas MacFarlane, "Operation Civvy," *Maclean's*, 1 April 1946, 20.

51 Ruth Fenisong, "The Job," *Star Weekly*, 2 February 1946, 1.

52 Leacy, *Historical Statistics of Canada*, B 75–81. For contemporary comment, see A. Foster, "Poets Sing of Great Loves but the Divorce Courts are Crowded," *Saturday Night*, 23 February 1946, 28–9.

A Half-Century On:
The Veterans' Experience

Thanks to the Canadian Broadcasting Corporation, I had the good fortune to be able to attend the fiftieth anniversary celebrations of D-day in Normandy and London in June 1994 and the fiftieth anniversary commemoration of VE-day in Apeldoorn and London in May 1995. These were both astonishing events, at once of supreme interest to a historian of Canada's part in World War II and also deeply, wrenchingly emotional. As I think back on them, it seems to me that I spent both trips in tears most of the time. To watch the old men, once young, marching through the streets of Courseulles and St Aubin, and through Apeldoorn, Amsterdam, Groningen, and fifty small Dutch towns was at once to realize how quickly time passes, how soon we all become old. The two trips, the two commemorative events, also made me aware again how little, in contrast to many Western Europeans, Canadians know of what their soldiers did a half-century ago.

To be sure, London paid very little attention to the Canadians or to other Commonwealth and Allied troops who had helped Britain survive and triumph in World War II. The focus in the huge celebrations and superbly staged ceremonies in 1994 and 1995 was on the Battle of Britain, on surviving the Blitz, on the long, hard road back from defeat in 1940, on the role of British troops, and on the songs and travails of wartime daily life. Perhaps the monochromatic focus was justified, but I could not help thinking that, just as Britain no longer means very much to Canadians, Canada and the Commonwealth matter not a whit to the United Kingdom.

Then there was France. The French, in truth, did not seem particularly grateful for their 1944 liberation, although fifty years later they clearly appreciated the surge in business brought by the thousands of celebrants who poured into Normandy in June 1994. World War II was a time of shame and glory for France, a time of collaboration as much as a time of resistance, and the memories of the collapse of May and June 1940 seem to be alive still (and to lead to such vainglory as President Chirac's nuclear tests, which aim to prove that France remains a great power with its own independent nuclear deterrent and global policy).

It was utterly different in May 1995 in the Netherlands, the one country in the world where Canadians are universally hailed as liberators. Every house was decorated in the colours of the House of Orange and with Canadian flags; and homemade banners, most obviously erected by ordinary citizens or neighbourhood associations and not by the state or municipalities, seemed to stretch across every street. The theme of gratitude, written in English on one banner I saw in Apeldoorn, was everywhere clear: "Bless You, Boys."

The Dutch remember the war. They remember the brutality of the Nazi occupation, the starvation winter of 1944–45, the executions of resistance fighters that went on into May 1945, and the collaboration of many of their men and women with the oppressors. They remember but no longer hate the Germans, with whom they willingly cooperate in a combined German-Dutch corps in the North Atlantic Treaty Organization. They remember, above all, those who fought and died to liberate them, the men of the First Canadian Army who came from afar to drive the Germans out of Holland, the Royal Canadian Air Force pilots who supported the armies and who dropped food to them in the hungry days just before liberation, and the sailors of the Royal Canadian Navy who cleared mines and ferried supplies.

You could see their acts of remembrance in the Canadian war cemeteries at Groesbeek and Holten, both of which are supremely beautiful places – if one can say such a thing of graveyards where thousands of your countrymen are buried so far from home. When I went to Holten several days before ve-day, there were perhaps a hundred ordinary Dutch families wandering among the endless rows of headstones, which beneath a carved maple leaf, list the rank, name, dates of birth and death, regiment or corps, and sometimes a message from parents, wives, or children. Small children looked solemn as their parents talked to them. Although I could not understand what they were saying, I had no doubt of the message that was being conveyed: These men, these boys (and so many of them were boys who had the demographic bad luck to be born in the 1920s and to grow up knowing little else but depression and war) had died to free your nation from oppression a half-century ago. Do not forget what they did for your country. Remember that you are free because of them.

Those Canadians who assume that the liberation of Holland was a cakewalk against a beaten Wehrmacht would be disabused of that notion by the thousands buried in these war cemeteries. I was especially struck at Holten by the twenty men of the Cape Breton Highlanders whose headstones reveal that they were killed in action on 1 May 1945 in liberating the little port of Delfzijl, a battle which the history of their regiment calls its hardest fight of the war. On 1 May – with Hitler already a suicide and the war inexorably drawing to its close! The Dutch families at Holten that day understood what their liberation had cost.

The same public display of memory was evident for all to see in the single most extraordinary event I have ever been privileged to attend, the amazing victory parade of Canadians through Apeldoorn a few days before the VE-day anniversary. Apeldoorn is a pleasant town of about a hundred thousand people in central Holland, quiet, staid in the reserved Dutch way. But that day, just the same as fifty years earlier when the Canadian Shermans rolled into their towns, the Dutch were far from staid. In May 1995, Apeldoorn's streets were lined by at least half a million men and women, children and babes in arms. The fifteen thousand or so Canadian vets who marched through the streets were mobbed, showered with kisses, and handed drinks, smokes, and flags in the most sincere and astonishing outpouring of love, affection, and gratitude I have ever seen. The parade, scheduled to run for about two hours, lasted for eight, so slow was the triumphal progress through the happy crowds. That the vets lasted that long was a tribute to the power of exhilaration to overcome the aches and pains inherent to seventy-five-year-old bodies.

I shall never forget the sight of young mothers in their twenties, weeping and cheering simultaneously while holding their babies up to get a sobbing veteran's kiss. Nor will I forget the Dutch mothers telling astonished and typically blasé Canadian reporters that they were doing this because they wanted their children to be able to say that they had been touched by one of the men who liberated the Netherlands a half-century before.

Obviously, the Dutch remember. They teach their children about the war in their schools; they teach that freedom is everything and that, if not defended, freedom can be lost. They take whole schools to the Canadian cemeteries each year to lay flowers on the graves and to make the point that the preservation of freedom has a price. And all of this attention to the past showed during that moving, wonderful, amazing day in Apeldoorn.

How different it is here in Canada today. World War II was a time of supreme national effort for Canadians, who produced a military, industrial, and agricultural contribution to victory that was frankly astonishing. Ten per cent of the population was in uniform. Our war production, starting from virtually nothing, became large enough for us to give away billions of dollars' worth of weapons and foodstuffs to our Allies on a proportionate scale greater than that of the United States. There was scarcely a family in the land that did not have someone in the service either as a volunteer, as were the vast majority, or as a conscript.

We all know that every ethnic group has the data, carefully massaged, to demonstrate that its sons enlisted in disproportionate numbers. The Toronto *Globe and Mail* noted on 5 October 1995, for example, that French Canadians had enlisted in "huge" numbers. A letter in the same newspaper a few weeks before had argued that Ukrainian Canadians had enlisted in numbers above their proportionate share, and Jewish groups make the same claim, as do other ethnic organizations. I do not believe these filiopietistic interpretations, I am afraid, and I continue to suspect that World War II was largely fought by Canadians of British extraction. The gravestones at Holten and Groesbeek certainly suggest this.

Let me personalize this sweeping generalization. My own immediate family's contribution to the war was lamentably small – one cousin in the Royal Canadian Air Force who did not leave Canada and one uncle who saw action in Northwest Europe with the United States Army. No one from my father's side was in the Canadian forces. This was a source of enormous and continuing shame for me as I grew up in postwar Canada. I believed then, and continue to do so, that the sons of Eastern European Jewish immigrants should have had a special urgency to help defeat Hitler, but neither my father nor his two brothers who were of appropriate age volunteered or were called up for service. I am sure the Granatsteins would have been dreadful soldiers, but they ought to have enlisted nonetheless in what was unquestionably a just and necessary war, especially for Jews. The result of my embarrassment at their lack of the voluntary spirit was a succession of family arguments, followed by my going into the army when I was seventeen years old – to expiate my family shame and, as teenagers are wont to do, to act in the way most certain to infuriate my parents. I suspect that I was a lousy soldier – but that is a question for another day.

If I am correct that Canada's war was largely fought by those of British origin, then this may partly explain the curious way we study the war in our schools. In this new multicultural Canada, the history of the world wars is seen as a divisive force, something that is almost too dangerous to teach in primary and secondary schools. What might a child of German or Slovakian or Croatian origin think, how might he or she feel, if World War II were discussed? Better to say nothing – which is the case in most public and high schools – or to look at the war only in its economic impact on women munitions plant workers, or to stress the cruel and unjust way Canada treated its Japanese Canadians or barred Jewish refugees from Hitler – which is the case in most university courses and the newest textbooks on Canadian history. The pride that Canadians should feel over their very substantial role in the war, the lessons that its events should hold for us, are brushed aside by the efforts to create a history that suits the misguided ideas of contemporary Canada which have been held by successive federal and provincial ministers of Canadian heritage and multiculturalism and education, and by far too many academics who, unlike the cabinet ministers, might at least be expected to know better.

"Freedom's just another word for nothing left to lose," as a once popular song put it, and certainly that is how Canadian schools and universities treat it in their avoidance of our war history. But the song is dead wrong. Freedom is the word for that which is most precious, for that which cannot be lost, a word and a concept for which so many Canadians fought and died. The children and grandchildren of the Dutch who lived through the war and brutal occupation understand this and remember what can happen if freedom is lost. Pathetically, terribly, the children and grandchildren of those who liberated them do not.

Our veterans still remember, however. They have become inured to public indifference to the sincere, well-meaning, but largely unattended ceremonies on Remembrance Day (a public service holiday, of course) and to the small crowds who, despite the valiant and underfunded efforts of "Canada Remembers," celebrated the events of a half-century ago. Still, the celebrations of the milestones of the war – the fiftieth anniversary commemorations of the Battle of Britain, Battle of the Atlantic, D-day invasion, and VE-day (the Italian campaign was largely neglected, just as it was during the war!), which have now come to their end – were critically important to the vets. For all these now old men and women, whose memories of those times are becoming ever more important, the fiftieth anniversaries were their swansong. How fortunate it is that the Dutch knew how to sing their praises even if most Canadians did not.

Why are we so ignorant, so diffident? The lamentable failure of our schools, as I have suggested, is a large part of it, but it may also have something to do with the subject of this book. It is almost as if the national effort to provide the Veterans Charter during the war excused Canadians from having to do anything for veterans after it. Certainly, the Veterans Charter was a great accomplishment, the best package of veterans legislation put together by any of the belligerents, and a model of wartime generosity, gratitude, and compassion that stands in marked contrast to the mean-spirited approach that seemed to dominate the legislative mind in the years after 1918. Perhaps that is why the veterans after World War II played a lesser part in politics than their fathers did after the Great War. We all know of the government's panic in 1919 that the returned men might side with the strikers at Winnipeg and elsewhere if the general strike spread. We remember the political efforts of the Great War Veterans' Association for better benefits and bigger pensions. We recall the efforts of the Canadian Legion and the Canadian Corps Association to demand conscription in World War II. And we know that two World War I veterans – John Diefenbaker and Lester Pearson – became prime minister.

It was very different after 1945. The demobilization of the armies went smoothly, and the reconstruction period was handled with great skill. There was scarcely anything for which the veterans could ask that was not given them. There was a large packet of crisp notes, a suit of clothes, money for a farm or schooling or a house, cash to start a business and to learn a trade, care for the wounded in body and mind, and a system of pensions that, while inevitably bureaucratic, was generous and tax free.

Of course, there were veterans in politics. Some, like Davie Fulton, George Hees, Cecil Merritt, Ernest Sansom, George Pearkes, Walter Harris, and Ernest Halpenny, came home from the war in uniform to run for Parliament in 1945. Some got elected; some did not. But no World War II veteran became prime minister. King and St Laurent, neither of whom was a veteran, passed power to Diefenbaker and Pearson, Great War vets, and the torch was then handed on to Trudeau who, while of an age to be a participant in World War II, was not. Clark, Turner, Mulroney, Campbell, and Chrétien were all either too young for war service or born after the war.

The absence of veterans from the highest office is in itself striking. Compare the United States, where Presidents Eisenhower, Kennedy, Johnson (after a fashion), Nixon, Ford, Carter, Reagan (in his own mind if not in reality), and Bush served. Even more striking is the fact that veterans as a class played almost no part in politics in this country after the war. The only great issue on which the Canadian Legion spoke out with force, the only issue that I can remember – and the only time that I believed the vets should remember why they had fought the war – was not *The Valour and the Horror* controversy but the struggle over the new Canadian flag, which occupied the early years of Mike Pearson's Liberal administration. When an early three-leaf design was shown to the Canadian Legion convention by Pearson in 1964, the vets booed and then campaigned as hard as they could to retain the Union Jack and the Red Ensign as Canada's flags. It was as if they had not worn maple leaves in their cap badges, as many did, or served under First Canadian Army's flag or that of the Royal Canadian Air Force, both of which had maple leaves on them, or sailed in Royal Canadian Navy ships with a maple leaf on the funnel; it was as if none had wandered through the cemeteries where every headstone had the maple leaf front and centre. The veterans were wrong in 1964–65, and they discredited themselves – not least because they seemed to have interpreted a distinctive Canadian flag as pandering to Quebec, and Quebec, in veterans' eyes, had not carried its share of the war's burdens.

Still, this sole example of political intervention is a relatively minor one, the exception that proves the rule. The political influence of veterans as a class was markedly less after 1945 than after 1919, and I suspect this was because Mackenzie King, so much wiser than Robert Borden, gave the nation's soldiers, sailors, airmen – and, as Peter Neary and Shaun Brown have pointed out, the members of its women's units – a Veterans Charter that generously fulfilled the promises that were made when the armies went overseas.

There is now no chance that veterans have the capacity to affect the great public issues of our time. The rollback of social services which our politicians and bankers are forcing on us might be one such area where the elderly veterans could exercise some influence, but no government has dared to tamper very much with veterans' benefits, and the Royal Canadian Legion has largely remained silent.

All that the veterans now care about is the rectification of past injustices. They have campaigned successfully for a Dieppe and Hong Kong bar to wear on their medals; the Merchant Navy veterans' still try, less successfully, to secure the full veterans' benefits they certainly merit; and the Hong Kong survivors continue to seek in vain for government support for their efforts to secure their due compensation from Japan for their endless years of suffering in prisoner-of-war cages.

There is very little bitterness left towards the Germans against whom our armies fought. The German government has accepted responsibility for the monstrous actions of the Nazis, and today's Germans overwhelmingly understand and do not condone the sins of their grandfathers. But the Japanese, as I have suggested, have offered neither totally sincere apologies nor appropriate compensation; nor have they educated their citizens about Japan's expansionist war. When the Queen spoke at the vj-day commemoration in London in mid-August 1995, she mentioned the reconciliation that had been achieved with Germany and pointedly did not refer to any such reconciliation with Japan. Her remarks were, for all practical purposes, a statement of British government policy – and certainly they reflect the bitterness that still lives in the minds of the few Canadian survivors of Hong Kong.

Well, what do we now owe the veterans who won World War II? We owe them, most importantly, our freedom, our right to live as we wish in a nation, however troubled, however divided at times, that was and still remains God's country. Beyond some fine tuning, we do not owe them new programs, so complete was the Veterans Charter and the other programs that came into operation after the war. We do owe the half-million surviving veterans continuing care and compassion. Above all, for putting their lives on the line to protect their country, we owe them gratitude and remembrance – and, regrettably, these are the two things their countrymen have not given them in the last generation.

I think back to that banner that hung over the street in Apeldoorn in May 1995, and I wish that even one such banner had flown over just one street in one city or town in this country. In Apeldoorn, "Bless You, Boys" seemed to me to be a particularly appropriate phrase. It still seems to me to be precisely what all Canadians should say. So, "Bless You, Boys." Some of us have not forgotten what you did. Some of us will always remember.

Appendices

Public Opinion Polls

The information in this appendix is taken from the polls of the Canadian Institute of Public Opinion (CIPO), a 1941 offshoot of the American Gallup organization. For each question, the date noted is the date the poll was released.

In your opinion, what is the most important problem the Canadian government must solve in the next few months? [29 November 1941][1]

1 Conscription – conscription of manpower and wealth,
   mobilizing manpower, etc.   35%
2 An increased war effort – increased production and
   "winning the war"   23
3 Financial measures – prices, the cost of living, avoiding
   inflation, taxes, etc.   15
4 Problems related to labour and employment – how to
   deal with defence strikes, distributing employment, etc.   5
5 Farm problems   5
6 Post-war readjustments   4
7 All others   13

Do you think the living allowance now being paid to families of private soldiers is too much, about right, or too little? [18 February 1942][2]

	Total	Men	Women
Too much	3%	3%	3%
About right	47	50	44
Too little	33	32	34
No opinion	17	15	19

Do you think the soldiers who return from this war should be treated more generously than the veterans of the last war? [4 July 1942][3]

More generously	66%
Would not treat more generously	21
Undecided	13

After the war, do you think women should be given equal opportunity with men to compete for jobs in industry, or do you think employers should give men the first chance? [21 April 1943][4]

	Total	Men	Women
Equal chance	24%	21%	27%
Give men first chance	72	75	68
Undecided	4	4	5

After the war is over, do you expect to be able to keep your present job, or will you have to look for a new job? [28 April 1943][5]

	Canada	U.S.	Britain
Keep job	78%	79%	58%
New job	9	13	21
Undecided	13	8	21

After the war would you like to see many changes or reforms made in Canada, or would you rather the country remain pretty much as it was before the war? [1 October 1943][6]

	Canada	Britain	U.S.
Reform	71%	57%	32%
No reform	23	34	58
Undecided	6	9	10

When the war is over, do you think there will be a period when many people will be without jobs, or do you think this will be avoided in Canada? [22 January 1944][7]

	Total	Lib.	PC	CCF
Will be jobless period	58%	54%	56%	62%
Will be avoided	29	34	34	29
Undecided	13	12	10	9

Suppose you could sit down with Prime Minister Mackenzie King and could ask him any questions you wished, what questions would you like to ask the Prime Minister about problems here in Canada? [22 April 1944][8]

Problems dealing with postwar matters, other than demobilization	15%
Plans for demobilization and rehabilitation of soldiers	13
Various questions dealing with social legislation	7
Income tax questions	5
Farm problems	5
Questions concerning Quebec	4
Questions concerning the war effort	4
Conscription	3
Labour problems	3
Election	3
Immigration	3
Foreign Relations	2
Liquor	2
Housing	1
Rationing	1
Miscellaneous	10
No questions to ask	19

Do you think the problem of making plans to provide jobs for everyone after the war should be up to the Federal Government in Ottawa, or up to the Government in each of the provinces? [6 May 1944][9]

Federal	38%
Provincial	21
Both	36
Neither	1
Undecided	4

If the government should start a national health plan, would you be willing to pay a small part of your (or your family's) income each year so that you and your family could receive medical and hospital care whenever you needed it? [8 April 1944][10]

	Apr. '42	Apr. '43	Apr. '44
Willing	75%	69%	80%
Unwilling	18	16	16
Undecided	7	15	4

	By region		
	Quebec	Ontario	Prairies
Willing	67%	83%	90%
Unwilling	28	13	8
Undecided	5	4	2

Would you approve or disapprove of a plan providing that members of the armed forces be given a certain amount of money by the government when they leave the service? [11 March 1944][11]

Approve	87%
Disapprove	8
Undecided	5

Of those who approved demobilization pay:

56% voted for deferred payments
37% favoured one lump sum
 7% were undecided or felt payments should be made in some other way

Asked of the 87% who approved of demobilization pay: Do you think men and women who have served overseas should be paid the same amount when they leave the service as men and women who have served in Canada?

Larger payment for overseas service	61%
Same payment for both	33
Undecided	6

Do you think that women who join the armed forces should or should not receive the same rate of pay as men who join the armed forces?
[31 May 1944][12]

Should get the same pay	57%
Should not get the same pay	34
Undecided	9

	Men	Women
For equal pay	53%	60%
Against equal pay	38	30
Undecided	9	10

Some soldiers back from overseas say too many people in this country do not take the war seriously enough. Do you think this is true or not? [5 July 1944][13]

	Total	Quebec	Rest of Canada
True	56%	35%	63%
Not true	34	48	30
Undecided	10	17	7

Have you any idea about how much money you would get each week if you became unemployed? [15 July 1944][14]

31%   Know the benefits they will receive if thrown out of a job
4%   Think they know but gave very inaccurate figures
65%   Couldn't even hazard a guess as to what they would receive

Home owners were asked: Have you put off making any repairs or improvements on your home because of the war or have you kept it up as well as you ordinarily could? [26 July 1944][15]

Put off	36%
Kept up	47
None needed	14
Undecided	3

Asked of home renters: Do you plan to build or buy your own home after the war, or do you prefer to continue renting? [26 July 1944][16]

Plan to build	24%
Plan to buy	18
Continue renting	40
No specific plans	17
Return to home already owned	1

It is suggested that the government should pay a family allowance of between $5 and $8 per child every month to families in the lower income group. Do you think this is a good idea or not? [2 August 1944][17]

	Quebec	Rest of Canada
Good idea	81%	57%
Not good idea	12	35
No opinion	7	8

Which of these things do you think is most likely to follow this war: a short period of depression, a long period of depression, a short period of prosperity, or a long period of prosperity? [12 July 1944][18]

Short prosperity	37%		Long depression	18%
Long prosperity	18		Short depression	16
Undecided	11			

After the war, do you expect to have a job which will pay you more money than you are now earning, the same amount of money you are now earning, or less money than you are now earning? [22 July 1944][19]

	Today	Dec. 1943
Earn more	17%	30%
Earn the same	45	34
Earn less	33	19
Undecided	5	17

Asked of young Canadians between the ages of 15 and 24 years: Do you think opportunities for young people in Canada after the war will be better or worse than they were before the war? [26 August 1944][20]

Better	53%		Worse	17%
About the same	16		Undecided	14

Do you think the Government should make it possible for all young people who have the ability but not the money to go to university? [2 September 1944][21]

Yes	92%
No	4
Undecided	4

Under present plans soldiers who have volunteered for active service will get a sum of money in addition to such things as the clothing allowance after they are discharged. Soldiers who have not volunteered for active service will not receive this additional money. Do you approve of this or not? [21 October 1944][22]

	Total	Quebec	Rest of Canada
Approve	62%	39%	69%
Disapprove	34	54	28
Undecided	4	7	3

Which of these do you think is the best way to keep up unemployment and avoid a depression after the war? [6 September 1944][23]

1   Remove wartime controls on business and industry
2   Keep wartime controls on business and industry
3   The government to start large programs of public works
4   The government to take over ownership of business and industry

Remove controls	17%
Keep controls	19
Public works	41
Government ownership	14
Undecided	9

Which of these do you think should take the lead in setting up and carrying out plans to provide post-war employment: industry and business, the federal government in Ottawa, or provincial and municipal governments? [18 October 1944][24]

Federal government	49%
Industry and business	23
Provincial and municipal governments	16
No opinion	12

To reduce unemployment after the war it has been suggested that we establish a 30-hour week in industry to spread work among more people. Do you think this is a good idea or do you think we should have a longer working week? [25 November 1944][25]

Favour 30-hour week	62%
Want longer week	27
Undecided	11

From what you have heard or read, do you think the government in this war is doing too much for returned men, or not doing enough for them? [27 January 1945][26]

About right	44%
Not enough	40
Too much	2
Don't know	14

When the war is over, do you think there will be a period when many people will be without jobs, or do you think this will be avoided in Canada? [1 August 1945]²⁷

	Jan. '44	Today
Will be jobless period	58%	61%
Will be avoided	29	25
Undecided	13	14

In the next two or three years do you think our government in Ottawa will need more money than in the years before the war started, less money than before the war, or about the same amount as before the war? [29 December 1945]²⁸

More money	72%
Less money	6
About the same	16
Undecided	6

Do you think that veterans being discharged right now have any cause for complaint about the way the government plans for them are being carried out? [1 December 1945]²⁹

Yes	24%
No	52
Undecided	24

The 24% who felt that veterans did have reason to complain were asked: What complaints have you heard of? The biggest percentage named "job security."

Do you think business firms in this country will be able to provide enough jobs for everyone during the next five years, or will the government have to step in and provide work? [5 January 1946]³⁰

	(Comparison with results in the U.S.)	
	Canada	U.S.
Business can provide jobs	20%	42%
Government must help	70	42
Undecided	10	16

It has been suggested that returned men should form their own political party in this country. Would you approve or disapprove if this were done? [13 February 1946]³¹

Disapprove	63%	Undecided	19%
Approve	18		

What is the most difficult problem you, yourself, face today? [4 May 1946]³²

Had problems	68%	Don't know	10 %
Had no problems	22		

The 68% who had problems cited the following:

Financial; wages; cost of living; family expenses	14%
Housing; a place to live	11
Domestic problems (food; rationing; poor coal; bringing up children in the absence of husbands)	9
Employment (trying to find a suitable job; veteran re-establishment; etc.)	7
Business problems (getting farm, office help; lack of materials; crop conditions)	7
Personal problems (the children's future; getting shirts; trying to buy a car; etc.)	5
Taxes	4
Economic security (old age pensions; "will I lose my job in a depression"; etc.)	4
Health matters	3
Miscellaneous	6

(Percentages add to more than 68 because some respondents gave more than one answer)

Do you think every able-bodied young man should be required to serve a year's training in the navy, army, or air force before he reaches the age of 25? [19 June 1948]³³

	(*In comparison with earlier dates*)			
	Mar.'43	*Nov.'44*	*Sep.'46*	*June'48*
Approve training	56%	60%	66%	62
Disapprove	34	32	27	29
No opinion	10	8	7	9

(The question asked in 1943 and 1944 was worded "After the war is over, do you think every able-bodied young man should be required to serve one year in the army, navy, or air force?")

	Veterans	*Non-veterans*
Approve	75	58
Disapprove	20	32
No opinion	5	10

Would you say that the shortage of housing in this district is very serious, fairly serious, or not serious? [21 July 1948][34]

	Communities under 10,000 population	*Communities 10,000–100,000 population*	*Communities over 100,000 population*
Very serious	32%	57%	75%
Fairly serious	40	35	19
Not serious	24	7	5
Undecided	4	1	1

Do you think married women should be given equal opportunity with men to compete for jobs, or do you think employers should give men the first chance? [22 April 1950][35]

	1945	*Today*
Equal chance	20%	19%
Men first chance	69	67
Qualified	8	11
No opinion	3	3

In general, do you approve or disapprove of the present recruiting of women for the three armed services in Canada? [29 August 1951][36]

	National	*Quebec*	*Rest of Canada*
Approve	53%	31%	61%
Disapprove	27	43	21
No opinion	20	26	18

NOTES

1 *Public Opinion Quarterly* 6, no. 1 (1942): 158.

2 *Public Opinion Quarterly* 6, no. 2 (1942): 312.

3 *Public Opinion Quarterly* 6, no. 4 (1942): 665.

4 *Public Opinion Quarterly* 7, no. 2 (1943): 339.

5 Ibid.

6 *Public Opinion Quarterly* 7, no. 4 (1943): 748.

7 *Public Opinion Quarterly* 8, no. 1 (1944): 158.

8 *Public Opinion Quarterly* 8, no. 2 (1944): 289.

9 Ibid., 290.

10 Ibid., 292.

11 Ibid., 299.

12 Ibid., 300.

13 *Public Opinion Quarterly* 8, no. 3 (1944): 453.

14 Ibid., 446.

15 Ibid., 456.

16 Ibid.

17 Ibid., 446.

18 Ibid., 455.

19 Ibid.

20 Ibid., 456.

21 *Public Opinion Quarterly* 8, no. 4 (1944–45): 581.

22 Ibid., 582.

23 Ibid., 601.

24 Ibid.

25 Ibid.

26 *Public Opinion Quarterly* 9, no. 1 (1945): 98.

27 *Public Opinion Quarterly* 9, no. 3 (1945): 375.

28 *Public Opinion Quarterly* 9, no. 4 (1945–46): 525.

29 Ibid., 530.

30 *Public Opinion Quarterly* 10, no. 1 (1946): 139.

31 Ibid.

32 *Public Opinion Quarterly* 10, no. 2 (1946): 273.

33 CIPO news release, 19 June 1948.

34 Ibid., 21 July 1948.

35 Ibid., 22 April 1950.

36 Ibid., 29 August 1951.

Back to Civil Life

(revised 1 April 1946)

BACK TO CIVIL LIFE

Prepared

TO INFORM MEMBERS OF THE ARMED
FORCES AND CANADIANS GENERALLY

of Steps Taken for

**CIVILIAN REHABILITATION
OF THOSE WHO SERVED**

=== **THIRD EDITION** ===

(Revised April 1, 1946)

Issued under the authority of
HON. IAN A. MACKENZIE
MINISTER OF VETERANS AFFAIRS

Foreword

The purpose of this booklet is twofold: it is essential that those at present in the armed services shall be fully informed of the steps which have been taken looking towards their rehabilitation in civil life, and it is of equal importance that the prospective employers of these people, and the Canadian public as a whole, shall know what has been done to fit them for their return to the Dominion's normal peace-time occupations.

Canada has been making plans for the civil re-establishment of its service personnel since a few months after the outbreak of the war and the steps which have been taken are in full operation. Thousands already discharged have received financial assistance, other thousands have been given training. Those discharged, up until the present time, have given us a testing basis and results of this testing have been encouraging.

Canada's rehabilitation belief is that the answer to civil re-establishment is a job, and the answer to a job is fitness and training for that job. Our aim is that these men and women who have taken up arms in defence of their country and their ideals of freedom shall not be penalized for the time they have spent in the services and our desire is that they shall be fitted in every way possible to take their place in Canada's civil and economic life. We believe this ambition and this desire can be achieved. Results up until the present indicate this belief is well founded.

[signature]

[Ian A. Mackenzie]
Minister of Veterans Affairs

INDEX

OBJECT OF THE PROGRAM

1. The object of Canada's plan for the rehabilitation of her Armed forces is that every man or woman discharged from the forces shall be in a position to earn a living. The policy has been carried out with that in mind. The plan consists of giving discharged personnel, where needed, the skill and training to help themselves. Financial assistance is available for veterans taking training or while seeking employment. Financial assistance is also given to those who embark on private enterprise during the period they are awaiting returns from that private enterprise. There is medical treatment for those in need of treatment with financial assistance during the period of this treatment and there is compensation by way of pension for those with physical handicaps as a result of war service.

2. **The Canadian program of rehabilitation for ex-service personnel can succeed only to the extent that ex-service personnel are prepared to help themselves and to the extent that employers will provide opportunity. It cannot help those who have no desire to help themselves, but the planning has been predicated on the belief that few of those who have enlisted will come into this category.**

3. The leaders of the future Canada must come, in large measure, from the young people who did not count cost when they volunteered to serve their country. Because of this the opportunities for training and completion of education are not stinted.

4. Canada wants its sailors, its soldiers and its airmen, and the members of the various women's services, to take the widest possible advantage of the facilities which have been made available to them.

5. When John Brown, ex-sailor, soldier or airman, or Mary Smith, ex-member of the women's services, is ready for civilian occupation again many courses are open. They may want to return to their old jobs, they may want to learn a new trade, they may want to complete their education, or may need some assistance after starting in business for themselves. The desire may be to have a part in Canada's great agriculture industry, or to own a home with an acre or two of land on the outskirts of the community where they are regularly employed. These things are available and towards them ex-members are eligible for departmental and, if necessary, financial assistance.

Women Are Fully Eligible

6. Generally speaking the program applies equally to men and women of the services, and reference in this booklet to ex-service men, unless otherwise noted, should be taken as applying equally to ex-service women.

7. The responsibility of re-establishing service personnel in civilian occupations is three-fold: it is the responsibility of Government to provide and administer legislative machinery designed to prevent them being penalized through their war service; it is the responsibility of ex-service personnel to help themselves, making the best use of the facilities which the Government has provided; it is the responsibility of the community to welcome the veteran, offer him opportunities for employment and social activity and, generally, help him in every way possible to "reintegrate" himself.

8. **Much can be done by the Government through legislation but much more can be done by the service people themselves and by those who will become their employers and community associates.**

DEPARTMENT OF VETERANS AFFAIRS

9. The principal Government agency for the re-establishment of ex-service personnel is the Department of Veterans Affairs. This Department was formed to deal exclusively with veterans because the task of re-establishing veterans successfully is one of Canada's major post-war works. Set up in October, 1944, it took over that portion of the old Department of Pensions and National Health which dealt with veterans affairs. The Department includes various divisions such as the Rehabilitation Branch, Treatment Branch, the Directorate of the Veterans' Land Act, and the War Veterans' Allowance Board. Attached to it is the Canadian Pension Commission and the Veterans' Bureau, the latter representing ex-service men and ex-service women in prosecuting their claims for pension.

10. To facilitate application of veterans for grants and benefits under the rehabilitation program, the work of the Department has been decentralized with a number of district offices across Canada. Each district is modeled on the head office, with internal sections capable of dealing with all requests for assistance. Addresses of the District Offices for the various branches of the Department will be found as an appendix to this booklet.

District Supervisors of Casualty Rehabilitation

11. Across Canada in a number of the major cities Rehabilitation Centres have been set up. These centres are designed to avoid giving the veteran the "runaround," and all services which he may require can be found

under the one roof. Provision has been made for assistance in things such as counselling, for dealing with applications for pension, for applications for re-establishment credits, for authorizing training, and for certain of the treatment services. Co-operating with the Department of Veterans Affairs, the Department of Labour has installed in these Rehabilitation Centres officers of that Department to give immediate assistance to the veteran who is seeking employment only.

12. **At the time of discharge veterans are advised to visit the Rehabilitation Centres so that they may make their plans for their careers in civilian life, and apply for those benefits which will be of assistance to them in their re-establishment.**

13. Officers of the Department of Veterans Affairs in the Rehabilitation Centres are all ex-service men, many of them veterans of the present war. They understand veterans' problems and have been through the process of becoming re-established. They are prepared to give sympathetic, speedy consideration to the needs of ex-service men.

Veterans Officers

14. As mentioned before, the Department of Labour is co-operating closely with the Department of Veterans Affairs, and in order to make this co-operation effective, the Department has appointed a Veterans Officer in each office of the Employment Service of Canada. These Veterans Officers have been fully trained in the rehabilitation legislation, and are competent to assist those veterans, whose homes are not close to Rehabilitation Centres, in making application for the various grants and benefits under the rehabilitation program.

District Supervisors of Casualty Rehabilitation

15. To provide a specialized service for those veterans with physical handicaps a special section of the Department of Veterans Affairs, known as the Casualty Rehabilitation Section, has been set up. This service is carried out by District Supervisors of Casualty Rehabilitation and their assistants who are located in each District, with their headquarters usually in the Department's hospitals.

16. As a result of their work, new and broader horizons have been opened up for the physically handicapped veterans. Their philosophy is that, properly placed in employment, physically handicapped veterans need not be economically handicapped, and that they can be one hundred per cent efficient in their jobs. They contact disabled veterans as soon as possible after their arrival in hospital, and from that time on provide an individual re-establishment service for the veteran.

17. In many cases they arrange commencement of training while the veteran is still in hospital. They explain to prospective employers the correct procedure of job analysis, and work with those employers finding positions that are suited to the remaining faculties of the physically handicapped. A large number of physically handicapped veterans have been placed in satisfactory employment through this system.

Voluntary Organizations

18. Across Canada, a number of voluntary groups have accepted the responsibility of assisting veterans in their community problems of re-establishment. Chief among these are volunteer Citizens' Committees, which have been organized in more than 700 communities. These groups have made a close study of veteran legislation and, in many cases, have made surveys of business and employment opportunities. They have worked to bring about an employment preference for veterans in positions which are available and which the veteran is qualified to fill. They also will assist in the veteran's personal problems during the re-establishment period.

19. **On discharge, veterans are supplied with the name and address of the Chairman and Secretary of the nearest Citizens' Committee, so that they may contact these people on return to their communities.**

20. In addition to Citizens' Committees, veterans' organizations such as the Canadian Legion, the Canadian Corps Association, the Army and Navy Veterans in Canada and the War Amputations of Canada, are taking a definite interest in the re-establishment of men and women from this war, while service clubs, churches, fraternal societies and others are also prepared to assist in the work.

21. Provincial authorities, too, have in many cases passed special legislation for the benefit of discharged service men and service women.

WHAT CAN BE DONE BEFORE DISCHARGE

He Can Prepare

22. The period before discharge can be much more than a waiting period. From the experiences of those who have already bridged the gap between service and civilian life, it is apparent that the veterans who make the smoothest and most satisfactory re-adjustment are those who have devoted considerable thought to their re-establishment, and decided upon their post-discharge careers. The men and women who do not know what they want, and cannot make up their minds, are the ones who find their re-establishment a very real problem. The last short period of service life may profitably be devoted to studying material available on the rehabili-

tation program, constructive discussion with service counsellors, educational officers, etc. which, combined with an honest assessment of the service man's own abilities, will enable him to leave the service with his own re-establishment program founded on a sound basis. Service men should take advantage also of every opportunity to take training courses which fit into their plans and which may be available. Knowledge gained now means both time and money saved after discharge.

23. Deleted.[1]

24. Even though a service man may have a job to return to he will undoubtedly find it profitable to do some of these things:

(a) Read books on his trade or profession or the one in which he is interested. These may be obtained through Naval School-masters and Army and Air Force educational officers.

(b) Take one of the correspondence courses available free to service men and women.

(c) Take advantage of any unit or service educational scheme.

(d) Study carefully printed material available on re-establishment, attend lectures, and take part in discussions on post-war affairs. Each unit will have well informed officers or other ranks who have been trained to advise and assist personnel to plan for re-establishment in civil life.

In-Service Counselling

25. This is given at strategic points in the demobilization stream, prior to discharge, to provide information and advice to enable the service man to consider at an early date factors relevant to his personal plans. At these points the service man will find that he has available the services of specially trained counsellors who are well informed on the legislation enacted for the benefit of veterans. **Their special training fits them to assist the serviceman to decide on the field offering his particular abilities the greatest chance of success after he is discharged, and to explain how the rehabilitation legislation can assist him to achieve that goal.**

DEMOBILIZATION

26–27. Deleted.[2]

28. As personnel become available for discharge they will go through the normal process of discharge as laid down by their own services, i.e., medical and dental examinations, receipt of clothing allowance, discharge certificate, back pay, deferred pay, rehabilitation grants, etc.

29. At the discharge centre personnel will have a final interview with the Service Counsellor who will complete a service interview summary. This summary, known as WD 12, records facts relating to the pre-enlistment

and service experience of the service man and any other information pertinent to his re-establishment.

30. The purpose of this summary is to provide the Department of Veterans Affairs with a comprehensive picture of the civilian potentialities of the veteran together with the recommendation of the In-Service Counsellor as to how they may best be utilized for the veteran's civilian re-establishment. Thus when the veteran approaches an officer of the Department of Veterans Affairs after discharge, that officer has before him an outline of the abilities and desires of the veteran which forms a basis for any action he may feel is required.

Personal Equipment

31. Personnel being discharged are permitted to keep their uniform and personal necessaries. Rifles, respirators and equipment must be turned in.

Clothing Allowance

32. All ranks retired or discharged after July 31, 1944, receive a clothing allowance of $100, free of income tax, to assist in the purchase of civilian clothing. **However, this allowance is not payable to any one retired or discharged by reason of a civil conviction involving penal servitude.**

Rehabilitation Grant

33. A rehabilitation grant will normally be paid, subject to the regulations, to a service man who has completed at least 183 days of service and receives an honourable discharge.

34. This grant provides for the payment of 30 days' extra pay and payment to dependents of one month's extra dependents' allowance. The purpose of this rehabilitation grant is to provide the serviceman and his dependents with some ready money while getting started in civilian life. It is not subject to income tax.

Transportation to Home

35. Arrangements have been made for free transportation and travelling expenses to the place in Canada where the service man was residing when he enlisted, or to any other point in Canada that can be reached at no greater cost. He may apply to be discharged in the district in which he has established a bona fide residence or has a bona fide intention of establishing such residence.

Repatriation to Countries Other Than Canada

36. If the service man came to Canada from some other country to enlist, transportation to the point where he was residing immediately prior to enlistment will be given at public expense. If he married while serving overseas transportation to that point will also be provided for his dependents.

Discharge Overseas

37. Discharge overseas will not normally be permitted, only very exceptional cases being considered. However, special provision has been made for the release of certain personnel, recommended by a specially constituted committee, for the purpose of continuing educational training designed to assist them to re-establish themselves in Canada. Upon completion of such training the Minister of Veterans Affairs may authorize transportation for such personnel to Canada.

Return of Dependents from Overseas

38. Arrangements have been made for the return to Canada of wives and children of members of the Canadian forces overseas. This also applies to widows and children of members of the Canadian forces who have died overseas.
39. Dependents allowance, not including assigned pay, is continued for the dependents of service men who have been repatriated and discharged, providing that they were in receipt of dependents allowance and assigned pay at the time of discharge and have made application for transportation to Canada. No application is required but dependents should be advised to write, if necessary, to the Canadian Wives Bureau, 6 Charles II St., London S.W.1.

Placement Facilities through National Employment Service

40. It is realized, of course, that many service men and women will want to go directly from the forces into jobs. The referral to employment is a function of the Dominion Department of Labour which, in order to smooth the return of veterans to civilian occupations, has set up special facilities within the Head Office, Regional Offices, and Local Offices of the National Employment Service.
41. At the Head Office of the Unemployment Insurance Commission at Ottawa, a supervisor of Veterans' Placement supervises and recommends upon the special placement of veterans, provided by the Local Offices,

and studies procedures with a view to affording improved placement facilities for discharged personnel.

42. In the five Regional Offices across Canada, regional supervisors of Veterans' Placements carry out similar functions for the region.

43. In all Local Offices – regardless of size, designated members of the staff have undergone special training in order to place the offices in a position to give preferred attention to veteran applicants, particularly those who are seeking employment for the first time following discharge.

44. Where Rehabilitation Centres have been established, officers from the National Employment Service are located in them, in order to give advice to those who are looking for jobs.

45. Service Counsellors prepare an "In-Service" history (Form w.d. 12) for personnel about to be discharged. This shows such matters as education, service trade training, special qualifications and so forth. A copy of this is made available to the Local Employment Office thereby eliminating duplication of effort and saving the veteran's time.

The Procedure

46. Service personnel being discharged at a discharge centre are interviewed by a staff member from the Local Employment Office. If they wish to be placed in a job an application is made out and forwarded to the Local Employment Office, and the applicant given an Introduction Card for presentation there. At this time a National Registration Certificate is also issued to him.

47. The serviceman is then advised to apply at his local Employment Office where he is referred to the Armed Forces Registration Unit. Here employment possibilities are further discussed. He is then referred to the appropriate Selection Section of the Employment Office, which has the responsibility of endeavouring to place him in employment.

48. The Armed Forces Registration Units, set up in the Local Employment Offices, assist service personnel upon discharge to locate jobs, and to inform them of benefits to which their service entitles them under the Unemployment Insurance Act – or under the Reinstatement in Civil Employment Act in cases where a veteran intends to return to his former employment. The Unit takes care of the necessary documentation and is competent to advise on employment opportunities from the point of view of the veteran.

49. All members of the Armed Forces Registration Units are themselves veterans with overseas service.

50. Procedures vary somewhat in the case of Navy Discharges. Naval personnel and service women are generally referred direct to the Employment Office upon discharge.

51. In the smaller centres, where the Department of Veterans Affairs has no local office, the Veterans Officer in the Employment Office gives information on all phases of rehabilitation.

Reinstatement in Former Jobs

52. Many service men and women left jobs in order to join the forces – jobs which they may wish to take up after discharge. One of the first Acts placed on the statute books looking towards re-establishment was the Reinstatement in Civil Employment Act. This Act is administered by the Dominion Department of Labour through the National Employment Service, and it is a wise precaution for any veteran who wishes to return to his or her old job, to consult the Reinstatement Officer in the nearest Employment Office **immediately** after discharge.

53. Under the terms of this Act a veteran is entitled to reinstatement with the employer whose services he left to enlist, providing he had been employed for at least three months by that employer immediately prior to enlistment and providing he applies for reinstatement within a specified period. **Generally speaking, it is the duty of that employer to give him employment on terms no less favourable than would have prevailed had the period of employment not been interrupted by war service.** He must be given pension and seniority rights for the period of his service and any wage increases which might normally go with such seniority or, where increases are based on employees skills, such useful skills as he may have acquired while in the service must be taken into account and wage rates adjusted accordingly.

54. Where it is the policy of the employer to give vacations with pay, time spent with the Forces is to be counted as time in the service of the employer in arriving at the amount of vacation to be given. In the calendar year in which reinstatement occurs, the reinstated employee must be in the employment for 90 days in order to qualify for any vacation he would ordinarily be entitled to under the employer's rules.

55. The Armed Services have adopted a policy of notifying the employer of the discharge of a former employee, so that the veteran may return to his former employer knowing that he is expected.

Certain Safeguards

56. While the Act is designed to require reinstatement of a former employee whenever such reinstatement is feasible, there are certain circumstances when an employer may not be required to reinstate a former employee.

57. **For instance, if a veteran were employed originally to replace an employee who had been accepted previously for service in the armed forces and if**

**the first employee has been reinstated in his employment, the Act does
not apply to the replacement. Reasonable changes of circumstances, other
than the engagement of some other persons, or an offer to reinstate in the
most favourable occupation and under the most favourable conditions
possible, may be offered by an employer as a defence in the case of proceedings under that Act.**

58. Nor does the Act require reinstatement if the ex-service man is incapable
of performing work which is available, through a physical or nervous condition except that in certain cases for reasons of health an ex-service man
may be granted a six months extension on the normal period during
which he may claim reinstatement. If seeking an extension, the veteran
should consult the Reinstatement Officer in the nearest Office of the
National Employment Service within three months of discharge if demobilized in Canada, or within four months if discharged overseas.

59. **The onus is on the ex-service man to apply to his former employer for
reinstatement within three months after discharge from the Armed Services in Canada or from hospital treatment following discharge in Canada
(or within four months if discharged overseas) with the exception noted
above for those whose health does not permit them to resume work within
that period.**

THE WAR SERVICE GRANTS ACT 1944

60. The War Service Grants Act, effective Jan. 1, 1945, since amended, and
the regulations thereunder, established a system of war service gratuities
for those honourably discharged ex-service men and women who served
on active service either without territorial limitation or in the Aleutian
Islands, or N.R.M.A personnel despatched to the United Kingdom, European or Mediterranean operational theatres. It is divided into two parts:
Part I consisting of gratuity, Basic and Supplementary, and Part II dealing
with Re-establishment Credit.

61. The amount of gratuity and credit depends on length and theatre of service. **In computing qualifying service, periods of absence or leave without
pay, absence without leave, penal servitude, imprisonment or detention
and periods when pay is forfeited are not included.**

Gratuities

62. (a) **Basic Gratuity.**
The Basic Gratuity is $7.50 for every 30 days service in the Western Hemi-
sphere (while enlisted or obligated to serve without territorial limitation)
and $15.00 for every 30 days service overseas. This is actually calculated as
follows: $7.50 for each completed 30-day period of qualifying service, plus

an additional 25c. for every day of overseas service which falls within such periods. These rates are applicable to all ranks.

(b) Supplementary Gratuity.

63. The Supplementary Gratuity is calculated on the basis of seven days pay and allowances for each six months of service overseas, or proportionately where the service includes periods of less than six months. "Pay and allowances" includes the pay and allowances which were being paid at the date of discharge or at the time of posting for discharge, and in any event includes lodging (or provision) allowance in the case of a member of the Naval forces, and subsistence allowance in the case of a member of the Military or Air Forces at standard rates payable in Canada.

64. **"Overseas Service" is defined in the act as follows: "Any service involving duties required to be performed outside the Western Hemisphere and includes service involving duties required to be performed outside of Canada and the United States of America and the territorial waters thereof in aircraft, or anywhere in a ship or other vessel, service in which is classed as sea time."**

65. **"The Western Hemisphere" is defined as: "The continents of North and South America, the islands adjacent thereto and the territorial waters thereof including Newfoundland, Bermuda and the West Indies but excluding Greenland, Iceland and the Aleutian Islands."**

66. The basic and supplementary gratuities are paid in equal monthly instalments not exceeding the amount of one month's pay and allowances in effect at the time of discharge. The veteran receives, then, at discharge any back pay and deferred pay, clothing allowance of $100 and his rehabilitation grant of 30 days pay and allowances. (Servicemen, whose discharge or retirement has been approved, may also receive, if they so elect, pay and allowances in lieu of any disembarkation or annual leave to which they may be entitled.)

67. The War Service Gratuity, or any unpaid balance thereof, is payable to the dependents of a sailor, soldier or airman who died while serving or before the gratuity was fully paid to him. **Application should be made by such dependents by letter to the headquarters of the service in which the serviceman last served. The letter should state the regimental number, rank and name of the serviceman and any details known concerning his length of service.**

68. Where no dependent qualifies for the gratuity of a deceased serviceman or veteran it becomes part of his "service estate" which is distributed, by the Estates Branch of the Department of National Defence, to those persons legally entitled to receive it.

69. A veteran of His Majesty's Forces other than Canadian who, at the time of enlistment and subsequent to September 10, 1939, was domiciled in Canada, is entitled to the benefits of the War Service Grants Act in the same

way as if his service had been in the Canadian Forces, but at the time he makes application he must be both domiciled and resident in Canada. A deduction will be made equal to any grant of a similar nature which he may have received, or to which he is entitled, from the Government of the country in whose Forces he served. Similar arrangements may now be made in respect to Canadians who served in the forces of His Majesty's Allies.

70. Service personnel, called up under the National Resources Mobilization Act, are not eligible under the War Service Grants Act for any period of service except service in the Aleutian Islands or the United Kingdom, European or Mediterranean operational theatres.

71. A Board of Review has been established to review all cases where the veteran has been adjudged not entitled to gratuity.

Re-establishment Credit

72. The Re-establishment Credit, which is a grant and not a loan, is primarily designed for those ex-servicemen and women who do not elect to take educational, vocational or technical training or benefits under the Veterans' Land Act. This credit is equal in amount to the basic gratuity referred to in para. 62 (a), i.e., it is calculated on the basis of $7.50 for each 30-day period of qualifying service plus 25c. for each of those days served overseas.

73. This credit, **which does not have to be repaid**, may be used, wholly or in part, at any time within a period of ten years from the date of discharge for one or more of the following purposes; **Provided the veteran is resident in Canada and intends to use his credit for his own re-establishment in Canada, except for certain insurance schemes outlined in (viii):**

   (i) The acquisition of a home, in an amount not exceeding two-thirds of the equity as determined under the Act;

   (ii) the repair or modernization of a home owned by a veteran or by a veteran and his or her spouse as joint tenants or solely by the spouse;

   (iii) to reduce or discharge a mortgage or other encumbrance on a home owned by a veteran or by a veteran and his or her spouse as joint tenants or solely by the spouse;

   (iv) the purchase of furniture and household equipment for his domestic use, in an amount not exceeding ninety per cent of the cost, or the payment of the full cost of repair to such articles;

   (v) working capital for his profession or business;

   (vi) the purchase of tools, instruments or equipment for his trade, profession or business, or the cost of repair of such articles;

   (vii) the purchase of a business either solely or in partnership, in an amount not exceeding two-thirds of the equity fund required for such purpose;

(viii) payment of premiums under an insurance scheme established by the Government of Canada, including Dominion Government Annuities;

(ix) the payment of fees and the purchase of special equipment required for educational or vocational training not otherwise provided for;

(x) for any other purpose authorized by the Governor-in-council.

74. Facilities now exist to permit veterans to purchase furniture, using their credit, before receiving their statement of gratuities. Veterans wishing to take advantage of this procedure should ascertain what articles of furniture they desire, where they wish to purchase them, the price of each article, and take this information to the nearest Supervisor of Re-establishment Credits who will issue, if the purchases are approved, a special authorization form and explain how this arrangement works.

75. If a veteran has been granted educational, vocational or technical training benefits or benefits under the Veterans' Land Act and the amount of those benefits, as determined by the Minister of Veterans Affairs, is less than the amount of re-establishment credit, which would otherwise have been available to him, the remainder of this credit may be authorized as outlined above. If, on the other hand, the re-establishment credit has been used wholly or in part and later an application is made for these benefits, such benefits may be granted but a compensating adjustment must first be made in an amount equivalent to the credit already received.

76. **Before making any commitments, involving the use of his re-establishment credit, the veteran should contact the Supervisor of Re-establishment Credits at the nearest District Office of the Department of Veterans Affairs.**

77. Both the gratuity and credit of a veteran are tax free and may not be attached or assigned for debt. Over payments of service pay and allowances, however, may be deducted from the gratuity.

Veterans residing outside Canada may now use their re-establishment credit to pay premiums, as they fall due, for Veterans Insurance.

Administration

78. The War Service Grants Act, Part I, is administered by the Department of National Defence for that Department has the necessary records to calculate and verify the periods of service for which a veteran is entitled to gratuities. Gratuities must be applied for and normally this application will be made as a part of the discharge procedure. Where such procedure is not followed, application should be made to the Headquarters of the Service

in which the Veteran last served on forms which are readily obtainable from any service depot or office of the Department of Veterans Affairs.

79. The War Service Grants Act, Part II, is administered by the Department of Veterans Affairs and applications may be made to the nearest office of that Department at any time after the veteran receives his "statement of gratuities," usually enclosed with the first gratuity cheque. Application from outside Canada should be made direct to Department of Veterans Affairs, Ottawa, Canada.

80. Evidence has come to light indicating that a few unscrupulous persons are prepared, by various means, to cheat veterans of their benefits under this Act. Veterans are therefore advised to seek the advice of Departmental Officials before committing themselves. Any evidence indicating fraud should be brought to the attention of the nearest office of the Department at once so that appropriate action may be taken.

VETERANS REHABILITATION ACT

81. The Veterans Rehabilitation Act which has replaced the Post-Discharge Re-establishment Order, authorizes the Department of Veterans Affairs to pay allowances to, or on behalf of, honourably discharged veterans if they are:

    1. Temporarily incapacitated through illness.
    2. Unemployed although fit and available for work.
    3. Awaiting returns from a farm or business on their own account.
    4. Taking vocational or educational training.

    Where courses of training are authorized, any fees connected with the course may be paid under the provisions of the Act. The Act also provides for the payment of the necessary contributions to make veterans eligible for full benefits under the National Unemployment Insurance Act, for the period of their service since June 30, 1941, when they have completed fifteen weeks in insured employment.

82. **Temporary Incapacitation Allowance:** This is to assist ex-members of the Forces who, after discharge, may become temporarily incapacitated and unable to work, although not to an extent great enough to enable them to benefit under the Treatment Regulations. If, in the opinion of departmental medical authorities, this condition exists these veterans, while building up their health, are entitled to an allowance for a period normally of two weeks, at any time within the eighteen months following discharge, except that this grant may not be paid for any period for which a rehabilitation grant was paid.

83. **Out-of-Work Allowance:** This provides for the period when discharged personnel are out of work, with the exception of the first nine days of unemployment and any period for which the veteran received a rehabilitation grant. It applies if the discharged person "is capable of performing and is available for work, and is unable to obtain suitable employment."

84. It is available for up to 52 weeks, but not exceeding the length of service, within the eighteen months following discharge. It is not the intention, however, that this allowance should become something in the nature of a dole. Under section 43 of the Unemployment Insurance Act the Out-of-Work Allowances may be terminated if such a course is held to be advisable.

85. Originally this allowance was paid through the offices of the Department of Veterans Affairs, but early in 1946 arrangements were completed whereby applications for this allowance are made at the local offices of the National Employment Service who pay the allowance weekly.

86. **Awaiting Returns Allowance:** This is designed to assist farmers, business and professional men and others wishing to embark on private enterprise on their own account. The Department has recognized the fact that in commencing a business, or in taking over a farm, invariably there is a period when the new owner must wait for returns to come in. During this period, which does not include any part of the thirty days for which the veteran received a rehabilitation grant, the ex-service man or woman who enters the field of private endeavour is eligible for a grant for a period of up to 52 weeks but not exceeding the period of service.

87. **Training Allowances:** These are paid to veterans for whom training, either vocational or educational, has been authorized. The basis upon which training is authorized is that it will directly assist the veteran to re-establish himself in civil life in a new career or on a higher level in his previous occupation. It is necessary, of course, that the veteran be adapted to the type of training desired. It is considered essential for the welfare of Canada, as well as for the re-establishment of veterans, that Canada's youth, who interrupted their education to enlist in the service of their country, be given an opportunity to continue that education, if it will further their re-establishment. Indeed, veterans who demonstrate exceptional ability and effort may be carried through, not only to university graduation, but in outstanding cases, right to the conclusion of postgraduate work, even though this may entail more months in college than served in the forces. In addition to paying allowances while veterans are taking training, the Act also makes provision for the payment of tuition and other fees connected with the courses approved, or payment of fees for correspondence courses in cases where such training is authorized. Both vocational and educational training are dealt with at greater length in the following pages.

88. Generally speaking all honourably discharged veterans of the Canadian Forces who came to Canada to enlist from some other country, are eligible for allowances while taking training outside Canada. They must, of course, be adapted to the training desired and it in turn must be such that it will directly assist in their re-establishment.

89. Educational courses must be taken in institutions approved or accredited by the Department of Veterans Affairs of the Canadian Government or its counterpart of the country concerned.

90. Training in industry is limited to organizations where there is a well established training program approved by the Department of Veterans Affairs. Applications for training assistance should be submitted to the Director of Training, Department of Veterans Affairs, Ottawa, Canada.

SCALE OF GRANTS

91. The scale of grants provides for payments of up to $60.00 monthly to single men or women and up to $80.00 monthly to a man and his wife when the ex-service man or woman is taking training or completing education. When out of work or temporarily incapacitated, the grant is up to $50.00 monthly to single persons and up to $70.00 monthly to a man and his wife. When awaiting returns from private endeavour, the grant is dependent on economic conditions, with a maximum of $50.00 monthly to a single person and $70.00 to a man and wife. Additional monthly allowances are made for dependents on the following scale:

Additional monthly allowance for one child $12.00
Additional monthly allowance for second child. 12.00
Additional monthly allowance for third child 10.00
Additional monthly allowance for each subsequent child
   (not in excess of three) 8.00
Additional maximum monthly allowance which may be authorized
   for dependent parent or parents. 15.00

92. In the case of discharged members of the Women's Services the "out-of-work benefit shall not be paid to a married woman whilst her husband, in the opinion of the Department, is capable of maintaining her either wholly or mainly and under legal obligation to do so."

Where Other Income Is Received

93. In determining the amount of an allowance to be paid to a veteran under the Veterans Rehabilitation Act, any prospective wages, salary, pension or other income of the veteran and his dependents, for the period in ques-

tion, may be taken into consideration and the allowance adjusted accordingly.

For veterans receiving allowances while taking training, either educational or vocational, the amount of "other income" permitted without the allowances being reduced is up to $75.00 per month. Married veterans whose wives are earning more than $75.00 per month receive allowances as single veterans, plus allowances for any children.

Pensioners Taking Training or Continuing Education

94. Under the provisions of the Order all pensioners continue to receive the full amounts of their pension and additional pension allowances from the Canadian Pension Commission, this amount being supplemented by a grant under the Veterans Rehabilitation Act, to bring the pensioner's income at least to the level of that of the non-pensioner and higher if he is taking training.

95. In the case of a pensioner who is receiving vocational training or continuing his education, a special training grant is paid, based on his pension rate. This has the effect of bringing the income of all pensioners taking vocational training or continuing education above that of non-pensioners and above the amount of their own pensions.

VOCATIONAL TRAINING

96. It is expected that many persons will be stimulated by counselling before leaving the service to take whatever steps may be necessary in order to decide what they intend to do on re-entering civil life. If a discharged person feels that his rehabilitation could be affected by vocational training, the person should go to the nearest Rehabilitation Centre of the Department of Veterans Affairs. Here he may apply for training or discuss the matter with the Department's counsellors. At this stage full information will be available as to the precise arrangements which may be made for the person's training. The general principle followed by district training boards in considering applications for vocational training under the Veterans Rehabilitation Act is that such vocational training as will lead to rehabilitation should be approved. Opportunities for training apply to men and women alike.

Facilities for Training

97. The Department of Veterans Affairs does not itself operate training schools of any sort. When vocational training has been approved, the person, who is to be trained, is turned over to a Dominion-Provincial organization

known as Canadian Vocational Training, which has been in existence for a number of years. Facilities already existing, such as schools which are privately or publicly owned, are being used, and c.v.t. is setting up special training centres where necessary. For many occupations training on-the-job is preferable and c.v.t. endeavours to locate suitable opportunities in industry itself where such training is indicated. Short trial courses are available to assist in choosing a proper vocation. In certain special cases training may be authorized outside Canada if such training is not available in this country and it is otherwise deemed suitable and necessary to the individual's re-establishment in Canada.

98. In the program, wherever training is provided in skilled trades, the co-operation of employers and of organized labour is obtained in working out the details, while special arrangements are being made for the training and employment of the handicapped. In these latter cases the Canadian National Institute for the Blind, the National Society of the Deaf and Hard of Hearing, the War Amputations of Canada and special clinics and advisory committees are co-operating and assisting in the work. Discharged persons in hospital for treatment may be permitted to take approved correspondence courses with fees paid by the Department. Such an arrangement may also be extended to discharged persons who are employed if part-time or evening classes are not available.

99. In all cases where training is granted, the prospects for permanent employment are taken into consideration and the policy is to guide ex-service personnel into training where opportunity for employment offers the best possibility of permanent, speedy re-establishment.

100. Many ex-service personnel already have completed training under the provisions of the Veterans Rehabilitation Act and have been employed in the industry or along the line in which they were trained.

Financial Assistance

101. Once training is approved and begun the discharged person becomes eligible for maintenance allowances and any fees connected with the course. In the case of a single man or woman, these allowances are up to $60.00 per month. A man and his wife receive up to $80.00 per month, and in addition dependents' allowances, listed in paragraph 91 may be paid. If it is necessary that a married person or a single person with dependents leave his usual place of residence in order to take training, a further grant of $5.00 a week may be made, or in certain similar cases the normal maintenance grant may be supplemented by a commuting allowance not exceeding $5.00 weekly.

102. The length of the period of training depends upon the nature of the training. In most cases vocational training grants will not be paid to a discharged person for a period in excess of fifty-two weeks. Where a longer

period of training is required, however, the grants may be extended beyond fifty-two weeks, but cannot ever be extended beyond the period of service except in the case of a pensioner. When a discharged person is training on the job, provision may be made by which the wages, which the employer is able to pay to a learner, may be supplemented by the Department.

UNIVERSITY TRAINING

103. Provision is made in the Veterans Rehabilitation Act for the continued education of students whose university careers were interrupted by enlistment. Assistance is intended for the following types of students: –

   (a) Those who must complete matriculation before going on to university;
   (b) Those who were in university at the time of enlistment and wish to complete their university courses;
   (c) University graduates who wish to begin or complete graduate training and whose attainments qualify them for such training in the Canadian public interest.
   (d) In special cases, assistance is available for refresher or brush-up courses in the professions.

104. University training, generally, is intended to provide, for the service of Canadian communities, highly trained people in the professions. Specifically, it gives veterans an opportunity to prepare themselves for careers to which they aspired prior to enlistment.

105. Universities throughout Canada have cooperated generously in making accommodation and staff available. They are sparing no effort to provide facilities for all persons who may qualify for training.

106. Students, who must complete matriculation before proceeding to university, should take seriously into consideration the length of the course and the period for which grants are available. Information on courses should be obtained from the nearest Rehabilitation Centre of the Department of Veterans Affairs.

107. However, the general regulations applying to all university training are briefly outlined in the following paragraphs.

108. Assistance is available to students whose qualifications are acceptable to an accredited university and whose rehabilitation can be effected through such training.

109. Qualification for admission to a university must be achieved within fifteen months of discharge unless this period is extended by the Department for good reasons. Such reasons include illness and the completion of matriculation studies.

110. University maintenance grants and fees are available to veterans for as many months as the veteran has served in the Forces. Thus a veteran with two years service is eligible for twenty-four months, or approximately three academic years, of training. However, length of service does not necessarily ensure continued training. Such assistance is provided only so long as the student continues to show satisfactory progress and effort.

111. No student may receive assistance while repeating a year's work for which benefits have been paid; nor may he exhaust benefits in university training and then receive vocational training.

112. If, on the other hand, a veteran demonstrates high scholarship within the period of his entitlement he may, upon the recommendation of the university scholarship committee, be granted extension of the assistance he has been receiving. Outstanding students may be assisted to the completion of their course and if it is considered to be in the national interest, may be granted post-graduate training.

113. The purpose of these regulations is to encourage able students to take the fullest possible advantage of Canada's educational facilities for their own rehabilitation and for the contribution they may make to Canadian development.

114. Deleted.[3]

THE VETERANS' LAND ACT

115. The main purpose of the Act is to assist qualified veterans to establish themselves (a) on full-time farms, (b) on small holdings with homes, main income to be derived from some source other than the operation of the holding, (c) on small holdings coupled with commercial fishing as the chief occupation.

116. The Act is not intended to provide city and town housing, nor to set up veterans in commercial, industrial, or professional occupations apart from farming and commercial fishing and the other purposes described in paragraph 128.

117. The government absorbs a substantial part of the cost of each establishment, namely $33\frac{1}{3}\%$ of the cost of land and buildings plus the total cost of livestock and equipment up to $1200.00.

TYPES OF ESTABLISHMENT

118. **Full-Time Farming.**
For veterans who have practical experience in farm operation and who are otherwise qualified assistance is available to engage in farming as a full-time occupation. Encouragement will be given to sustain the "family farm" as a Canadian institution.

119. **Small Holding (coupled with industrial or other employment).**
For veterans whose normal sphere in Canadian society is in industry or commerce or in the field of agricultural employment, assistance is available to operate a small block of land, preferably an acre or more outside the corporate limits of urban municipalities. Mechanics, carpenters, masons, electricians, factory workers and white-collar men may benefit. It is believed that seriously disabled veterans in receipt of substantial pensions whose condition is stabilized to a point where recurring institutional care is not likely to be necessary, may be specially interested in this type of semi-rural settlement.

120. **Small Holding (coupled with commercial fishing).**
For veterans whose normal occupation is in the commercial fishing industry provision is made for assistance to purchase comfortable homes and fishing equipment.

Financial Provisions

121. The Act provides a maximum of $6000 to cover cost of land, buildings and other permanent improvements, livestock and farm equipment or fishing equipment, of which not more than $1200 may be used for the purchase of livestock and equipment, or fishing gear.

Terms of Sale to a Qualified Veteran

122. The following is an illustration of the veteran's financial obligations and conditional benefits in a full-time farming establishment costing $4800 for land and buildings and $1200 for livestock and equipment.

123. At the time he makes application to purchase the veteran must deposit in cash 10% of the cost of farm buildings and other permanent improvements, namely $480. He then signs a contract to repay only two-thirds of the cost of land, buildings, and other permanent improvements or $3200 over a period up to twenty-five years with interest at 3½% amortized. The annual payment including principal and interest is $194.14. The entire $1200 cost of stock and equipment, plus $1120 – the difference between the cost of land, buildings and other permanent improvements and what the veteran pays – is borne by the state. In this case the state conditional grant is $2320, or 38% of the total cost of the farm establishment.

Conditions of Resale

124. The Act forbids the sale, assignment or other disposition of the property by the veteran within a period of ten years following the date of his establishment unless the full cost of the land, improvements, and chattels is

paid. In simpler terms, the conditional grant, referred to above, is earned only when the veteran has satisfactorily fulfilled the terms of his contract for ten years. Title to the property does not pass to the veteran until he has completed the contract. If he desires to dispose of it before ten years he must repay the total cost to the government of his establishment.

125. The conditions of sale, repayment, and resale in connection with small holding establishments are the same as above. Expenditure for chattels is made in accordance with actual need, and in the case of small holdings would be much less than for full-time farming and commercial fishing enterprises.

126. There is nothing to prevent a veteran securing a farm or small holding of greater value than $6000 provided he is in position to pay the excess cost in cash at time of establishment as well as the necessary 10% down payment.

127. The veteran may select his farm or small holding subject to the approval of the Director of the Act, and the farm must be such that, in the opinion of the Director of the Act, it offers a reasonable opportunity of successful rehabilitation.

Settlement on Provincial Lands and on Indian Reserves

128. Provision was made during 1945 for non-repayable grants up to $2320 to veterans settled on Provincial lands, and for Indian veterans settled within Indian reserves, for the purchase of building materials and other construction costs, clearing and preparation of land for cultivation, purchase of livestock and farm machinery, machinery or equipment essential to forestry, commercial fishing equipment, trapping, or fur farming equipment, but not breeding stock, and essential household equipment (and in the case of Indian veterans the acquisition of occupational rights to lands in Indian reserves). Agreements have been completed with the three Prairie Provinces and are under negotiations with most of the others.

Loans to Veterans Who Own Farms

129. Provision is made for the granting of loans at 3½% interest rate to veterans who own farm land and require funds to resume farming operations. Advances not exceeding 60% of the value of the land or a maximum of $4400 may be made to pay off a mortgage, effect improvements or buy livestock and equipment. Of this, not more than $2500 or 50% of the value of the land and buildings may be advanced for purchase of livestock and equipment. Mortgage loans are repayable in full, with interest at the rate of 3½% over period not exceeding twenty-five years.

Administration – Decentralized

130. The Office of the Director, The Veterans' Land Act, is in Ottawa. Central administrative offices have been set up under District Superintendents and each district is divided into regions with a Regional Supervisor in charge.

131. The ex-service man's point of contact with the Veterans' Land Act organization is the Regional Office, a list of which appears at the back of this booklet. There is a local Advisory Committee at each Regional Office to review with the veteran his qualifications and suitability for the type of establishment proposed and to review the quality and suitability of the land for settlement.

132. The Act does not set a terminating date and it is expected that settlement will be spread over a period of several years. Veterans have been urged, and are still urged in their own interest, not to rush into settlement. There is no second chance under the Act and each veteran should be sure he has settled down to a soundly planned scheme of life, before committing himself to a purchase contract which extends over a long term of years.

Relationship to Other Rehabilitation Benefits

133. Veterans desiring assistance under the Veterans' Land Act other than a mortgage loan, may not use Re-establishment Credit. No benefit other than Re-establishment Credit limits in any way a veteran's right to consideration under the Veterans' Land Act.

MEDICAL TREATMENT

Facilities

134. Facilities for every type of treatment, and covering the whole of Canada, already exist or will be set up by the Department for the benefit of the veteran. These are represented by:

(a) First class hospitals owned and operated by the Department.
(b) Health and Occupational Centres in most Districts. (For post-hospital care.)
(c) Hospitals with which the Department has a contract.
(d) Out-Patient clinics in connection with Departmental Hospitals and District Offices.
(e) Salaried medical officers in sub-District Offices.
(f) Licensed medical practitioners in every community in Canada where adequate practitioner services are established.

135. The regulations governing treatment are broad and generous, and cover the whole range of medicine and surgery. No matter what is wrong with the ex-service man or woman the Department of Veterans Affairs has the facilities and staff for complete diagnosis and treatment. Application for treatment, however, must be made through the facilities set up by the Department to provide this treatment. The Department may not assume responsibility for treatment obtained otherwise.

Classes of Treatment

136. Treatment is divided into twelve classes. This division concerns more the hospital allowances paid during treatment than the treatment itself. There is only one kind of treatment provided, and that is the best.

137. The veteran of the present war is likely to be interested only in three of the twelve classes referred to above.

138. The **first** of these, known as **Class 2**, was set up to provide for the service man or woman requiring continuous treatment on discharge from the service. To this group goes the maximum benefit of hospital allowances. Any ex-service man or woman who is discharged from the services with a disabling condition which requires treatment is admitted to a hospital or treated as an outpatient under the Department of Veterans Affairs and all necessary treatment carried to completion. Pay received is known as hospital allowance, but is exactly the amount which was paid during the service, including dependents allowance and trade pay if any. Hospital allowances to this amount may be continued in all cases for a period of one year, provided, of course, treatment has not been brought to completion in that period.

139. Before the completion of one year's treatment, the Canadian Pension Commission will have ruled on whether or not the disability was pensionable. If a favourable ruling is given, and the patient is required to continue under treatment, hospital allowances are payable for a second year. The ex-service man or woman does not necessarily have to remain in hospital all this time to obtain these benefits. If out-patient treatment is indicated and approved, and physical incapacity for work exists, similar monetary benefits outlined above apply.

140. Let us suppose an adverse ruling has been given by the Canadian Pension Commission. The individual would be entitled to hospital allowances at the pay of rank, etc., for a period of one year, and for any subsequent period of treatment entitled to hospital allowances on the same basis as those allowances paid to those temporarily incapacitated under the Veterans Rehabilitation Act. In other words, the individual would become a Class 3 patient. In both Class 2 and Class 3 active remedial treatment

must be required continuously. Class 2 treatment must be applied for within 30 days of discharge but it may be deferred up to one year if departmental facilities are not available or the veteran's physical condition prevents the carrying out of treatment at the time of application.

141. **Class 3.** Treatment is provided under this class by the Department for all veterans for the full post-discharge year. It has nothing to do with service related disabilities and has been set up as a re-establishment measure to provide treatment for any condition which may arise within the year following discharge. A man may break his leg months after discharge, and be entitled to treatment from the Department for this condition. Treatment itself will be carried to completion. Hospital allowances which may be subject to certain deductions are paid at a lesser rate than Class 2, and only for a period equal to the length of service, but not for a longer period than one year. They are essentially the same as those outlined in the scale of grants referred to in para. 91.

Pensioners (Class 5)

142. It is with the foregoing two groups that the ex-service man or woman will be most interested, because the greater number will likely be hospitalized in one or other of these categories. There is, however, another most important group, namely, the pensioners. Where an ex-service man or woman has been given entitlement to a pension by the Canadian Pension Commission for a service related disability he is entitled to free treatment by the Department for this disability for the rest of his life, not only in Canada, but in other parts of the world where suitable arrangements can be made for his treatment.

143. While in hospital for his pensionable disability, it is assumed that the individual concerned is 100% disabled, and hospital allowances are paid on the basis of 100% pension less $15 per month. This applies even if the individual's disability has been assessed at 5% or even less.

144. Pensioners are also entitled under certain conditions to treatment for non-pensionable disabilities, and this same privilege applies to non-pensioners with meritorious service, that is, service in a theatre of actual war. No payment is made for these periods of hospitalization, but if the patient is without other means, a small monthly sum is provided for comforts and clothing.

145. In order to correct any misunderstanding, it should be stated here that treatment privileges are only available to the ex-service man himself and not to his relatives or dependents.

146. Separate arrangements are made for the treatment of venereal disease and its complications.

Treatment

147. When reference is made in the foregoing to treatment, this means a complete treatment service, including the provision of artificial limbs where indicated, belts and supports, trusses, hearing aids, etc. The services of the best specialists in all fields are available to those requiring such services. Special centres have been set up in the large metropolitan areas and almost every outstanding physician or surgeon in Canada is in some way or other associated with the Department's services. Special Centres have been set up for the care of the paralyzed. Adequate arrangements have been made with St. Dunstan's and the Canadian National Institute for the Blind for the care and retraining of those who have lost their eyesight. Artificial eyes are provided for those who require them each designed to the individual requirement of the wearer and reproduced as an exact duplicate of the normal eye. A repair and replacement service is maintained for those who require adjustment or replacement of any of the prosthetic appliances with which they have been issued.

Convalescence

148. A new series of establishments known as Health and Occupational Centres are being set up across Canada in Halifax, Saint John, Montreal, Ottawa, Toronto, London, Winnipeg and Vancouver. The purpose of these centres is to bridge the gap between the discharge from hospital and the return to normal civilian life. They are set in beautiful surroundings, quarters are extremely comfortable, and most of the centres provide such facilities as gymnasium, swimming pool, workshop, etc.

Prosthetic Services

149. Physical disabilities incurred by members of the Forces are compensated to the greatest possible extent by prostheses supplied through the Prosthetic Services Branch of the Department. These include artificial legs and arms, artificial eyes, specially made shoes, braces, splints, hearing aids, and many minor types of orthopaedic aids. They are distributed through Centres situated in the larger Canadian cities where facilities are maintained to provide for personal measuring, manufacture and fitting. Appliances are thereafter adjusted, maintained, and renewed for life in service-related disability cases.

150. The highest grade woods, metals, leather and fabrics obtainable, shaped, assembled, and fitted by highly skilled fitters, ensure that Canada's war disabled are assisted for life by aids equal in quality to those obtainable anywhere.

DENTAL TREATMENT

151. The following ex-members of the Canadian Armed Forces are eligible for free dental treatment:

152. 1. All who are shown to have dental requirements listed on examination, by the Canadian Dental Corps, at the time of discharge or retirement. (Application to be made within 90 days of date of discharge or retirement.)

153. 2. All former members of the Forces are entitled to any necessary dental treatment provided same has been authorized and commenced upon a date not more than 365 days subsequent to discharge from the Forces.

154. 3. Those entitled to training or other benefits under the Post-Discharge Re-establishment Order, who must have dental treatment to fit them for training, or trainees who must have dental treatment in order that there shall not be any interference with their training because of an adverse dental condition.

155. 4. Pensioners for direct dental injury or disease, gastric ulcer, duodenal ulcer, gastritis, and allied conditions; hand, and hand and arm amputees.

156. 5. In addition to the above there are several classifications under which a veteran may qualify for dental treatment. Therefore, any veteran requiring such treatment should apply to the nearest office of the Department of Veterans Affairs where a decision regarding his eligibility for same will be given.

157. In cases of emergency any registered dentist has authority to render treatment for the relief of pain or repair of a broken denture. In all other cases an applicant must receive prior authority from the Department before accepting treatment, as the Department may not accept the responsibility for the payment of accounts for unauthorized treatment.

CANADIAN PENSIONS

158. The Canadian Pension Commission, under the provisions of the Pension Act, has exclusive jurisdiction to adjudicate upon all matters and questions relating to the award, increase, etc. of any pension awarded under the Act as the result of Naval, Military or Air Service.

159. The Head Office of the Commission is in Ottawa and Pension Medical Examiners represent the Commission in key centres throughout the Dominion. Advice regarding pensions can be obtained from these Examiners or from Pensions Advocates of the Veterans' Bureau employed in the District Offices of the Department.

Procedure Following Retirement or Discharge

160. Every member of the forces is medically boarded on retirement or discharge. A copy of the board proceedings is forwarded by the Records Office of the service concerned to the Secretary of the Canadian Pension Commission in Ottawa.

161. The Pension Act defines an applicant for pension as "any member of the forces in whom a disability is shown to exist at the time of his retirement or discharge." The board proceedings are reviewed by the Medical Advisory Staff of the Commission and, when there is record of disability, the case is automatically prepared and submitted to the Commissioners for a decision as to entitlement to disability pension.

162. When entitlement to pension is conceded by the Commission and the disability can be assessed from the available board proceedings an assessment is made which forms the basis for an award, payment of which is immediately instituted. When the decision is favourable and the available information is not adequate for assessment purposes, arrangements for examination are made through the local office of the Commission in the applicant's district.

163. In cases where entitlement is not granted by the Commission the dischargee is notified of the decision and the reasons therefor and is fully informed regarding the action he may take should he desire to proceed further in his claim to pension.

164. Disability pension is compensation for the loss or lessening of normal abilities as a result of war service and not for length of service. Entitlement may be conceded for a gunshot wound but if there was no assessable degree of disability there would be no payment of pension. Once the Commission has conceded entitlement and assessed the degree of disability, pension is awarded in accordance with the scale of awards set forth in the Pension Act. Disabilities are assessed on a percentage scale, total disability being 100% and awards are governed by the degree of pensionable disability found on medical re-examination from time to time.

Basis for Pension Awards – World War II

165. Pension is paid for disability or death resulting from injury or disease, or the aggravation thereof, which is attributable to or incurred during military service, except that, when such service has been wholly rendered in Canada, pension is awarded only if the injury or disease, or aggravation thereof, resulting in disability or death arose out of or was directly connected with military service.

166. Where service has been in Canada only, the Commission has discretionary power to grant awards in cases in which pension is not awardable

as of right, provided the injury or disease, or the aggravation thereof, resulting in serious disability or death, **was incurred during service** and the applicant **is in necessitous circumstances**. In such cases the rate of pension may vary in accordance with the applicant's financial circumstances. The rates quoted are, therefore, not standard for this type of award.

Disability Awards

167. EXCEPT WHERE TOTAL DISABILITY EXISTS, DISABILITY PENSION IS NOT INTENDED TO PROVIDE COMPLETE MAINTENANCE. DISABILITY PENSION IS COMPENSATION, FOR HANDICAP IN THE GENERAL LABOUR MARKET, WHICH IS PAID BY THE STATE TO ENSURE FOR THE PENSIONER AND HIS DEPENDENTS MAINTENANCE WHICH HE IS UNABLE TO PROVIDE. Consequently a totally disabled person receives 100 per cent pension. A 50 per cent disabled person receives a 50 per cent pension, and so on down the line to a last class of 5 per cent. Additional pension for dependents is provided for by the Pension Act and these allowances are graduated in accordance with the degree of disability suffered by the pensioner.

168. The rates for a one hundred per cent disability for all ranks up to and including that of Sub-Lieutenant (Navy), Lieutenant (Military) and Flying Officer (Air), are:

Man.............................$900.
Wife............................. 300.
First child .... 180.
Second child...................... 144.
Each subsequent child .... 120.

For ranks above those mentioned, higher rates are provided. The additional pension for wives and children, however, is the same for all ranks.

Death Awards

169. The rates of pension for widows and children of all ranks up to and including Sub-Lieutenant (Navy), Lieutenant (Military) and Flying Officer (Air), are:

Widows ....$720.
First child .... 180.
Second child...................... 144.
Each subsequent child.............. 120.

For ranks above those mentioned, higher rates are provided. The rates for children, however, are the same for all ranks.

Other Benefits

170. Orphan children receive double the rates for Children. A dependent parent may be pensioned at the rate for a widow or such lesser rate as may be deemed necessary by the Commission to provide maintenance, except when the deceased member of the forces left a widow, or widow and children, or orphan children entitled to pension. In such cases, a single parent may receive an amount not in excess of $360 per annum. If there are two parents, an amount to $720 per annum may be awarded.
171. A dependent brother or sister of a late member of the forces who was wholly or substantially supported by him at the time of his death may be awarded pension under certain statutory conditions.
172. The statute provides for a last sickness and burial grant not exceeding $150 when the estate of a disability pensioner is not sufficient to pay such expenses.
173. An additional allowance for helplessness (not less than $250 and not exceeding $750 per annum) may be paid to a disability pensioner if totally disabled, when the services of an attendant are required.
174. The Act also includes provision for the award of an allowance on account of wear and tear of clothing to pensioners whose clothes are subject to extra wear through use of artificial aids.

Pre-war Canadians Serving with United Kingdom Forces

175. The benefits of the Pension Act (subject to the following paragraph) have been conferred on all persons domiciled in Canada at any time during the four years next preceding the date of the commencement of World War II who subsequent to the 1st September 1939 served in the Naval, Military or Air Forces of the United Kingdom.
176. When a gratuity or pension has been awarded to such person under the laws and regulations of the United Kingdom such may be augmented to the equivalent benefits as provided by the Canadian Pension Act during periods of residence in Canada.

VETERANS' BUREAU

177. This branch of the Department of Veterans Affairs was created by the Dominion Government for the express purpose of assisting pension applicants, without expense to themselves, in the prosecution of their pension claims. Any applicant for pension may take advantage of the services

of the Veterans' Bureau which is independent of and does not come under the jurisdiction of the Commission in any way. This body has been in existence for a number of years, has a staff of advocates and other officials who are thoroughly conversant with the provisions of the Pension Act, and have had considerable experience and training in the preparation and presentation of pension claims.

178. District pensions advocates have offices in all large centres of the Dominion, from coast to coast. They are, in the main, former barristers or advocates of good standing at the bar of the provinces of Canada, and are well fitted for the task of assisting and advising pension applicants. A list of the addresses of District Pensions Advocates will be found in the appendix.

THE VETERANS INSURANCE ACT

179. When Canada entered the present war it was realized that men and women who went into uniform faced the possibility of returning to civilian life with their health impaired, or with some physical disability. It was realized also that as a result of this impairment in health or disability, many service men and women would be unable to provide protection for their families through the normal channels of commercial life insurance. To meet this situation, Parliament, at its 1944 Session, passed an Act known as The Veterans Insurance Act.

180. The plans of insurance available are 10 Payment Life, 15 Payment Life, 20 Payment Life, Life Paid-up at 65 and Life Paid-up at 85; that is, premiums may be paid for 10, 15, or 20 years or until age 65 or 85 respectively, is reached. The longer the term of payment, the smaller the premium required. Term and Endowment policies are not issued. The insurance is of the nonparticipating type, that is, no dividends are paid.

181. Any ex-service man or woman of the Canadian Forces of World War II is eligible as well as any person who has been discharged from service in the naval, military or air forces of His Majesty other than those of Canada and who was domiciled in Canada at the commencement of such service. In addition, other classes are eligible as follows: (1) the widow or widower of a veteran if the veteran was not insured under the Act; (2) Merchant Seaman entitled to receive a bonus under the Merchant Seamen Special Bonus Order; (3) members of the Corps of (Civilian) Canadian Fire Fighters and Auxiliary Services Supervisors with service overseas; and (4) any other person in receipt of a pension under the Pension Act by reason of his service in World War II.

182. Policies may be applied for in amounts ranging from $500 to $10,000. The amount of the policy is payable only in the event of the death of the insured.

183. After premiums have been paid for two full years, the policy may be surrendered for its Cash Surrender Value, or it may be transferred to reduced Paid-up Insurance or Extended Term Insurance. There is no provision for loans against the policy.

184. Examples of Monthly Premiums per $1000. Insurance.

AGE	PAYABLE FOR			Payable to	Payable to
	10 years	15 years	20 years	age 65	age 85
20	$2.89	$2.12	$1.74	$1.20	$1.14
25	3.18	2.34	1.93	1.39	1.30
30	3.53	2.60	2.15	1.64	1.51
35	3.93	2.91	2.42	1.98	1.78
45	4.98	3.73	3.16	3.16	2.59
55	6.45	5.01	4.40	6.45	4.03

185. Some of the salient points concerning Veterans Insurance are as follows: –
Premium rates are low and premiums may be paid in monthly instalments at no extra cost;
No medical examination except in a very few special cases;
Premiums may be paid from Re-establishment Credit or from pension;
There are no restrictions as to residence, travel or occupation, including naval, military and air service. No extra premiums are charged when the veteran's occupation is unusually hazardous – as, for example, mining, construction, commercial flying, etc. In the event of total and permanent disability before the age of 60, premiums are waived unless the veteran is entitled to a 100% disability pension under the Pension Act. There is no extra premium for this benefit. All policies are automatically non-forfeitable and have a liberal cash value after they have been in force for two years.

186. Applications for Veterans Insurance may be made within three years from the date of discharge from service or within three years from the effective date of the Act (20th February, 1945) whichever is the later.

187. Complete details may be secured in the booklet "What's Ahead?" or from in-service counsellors and officers of the Department of Veterans Affairs.

WAR VETERANS' ALLOWANCES AND DUAL SERVICE PENSIONS

188. Veterans' Allowances and Dual Service Pensions are provided under authority of the War Veterans' Allowance Act and the Dual Service Pension Order. These two legislative measures were enacted following the realization that certain ex-members of the Forces might no longer be

able to provide for their maintenance, for various reasons, although their incapacity or disabilities might not be due to or related to their war service.

189. Principally, the War Veterans' Allowance Act was enacted to provide for the veterans of World War I – and more recently for veterans of World War II. The Dual Service Pension Order was passed to provide for those veterans who, not being able to qualify by reason of their service in either war, have served in both.

190. Under the terms of the two legislative measures, provision is made for the widows, as well as for the orphans of all deceased veterans who during their lifetime would have been eligible for consideration in their own right.

191. In addition to the above, the provisions of the War Veterans' Allowance Act have been extended to the ex-members of the North West Field Force as well as to the veterans of the South African War. It also provides for ex-members of His Majesty's Imperial Forces on the condition that they were domiciled in Canada at the time at which they joined such Forces for purpose of war service.

192. The main conditions of eligibility under the War Veterans' Allowance Act are:

(a) Service in a theatre of actual war, or
(b) pensionability under the Canadian Pension Act.

193. In the case of the Dual Service Pension Order, applicants need not have served in a theatre of actual war or be in receipt of a Disability Pension; but must have served in both wars.

194. The ex-members of the Forces to whom these benefits may be granted are divided into three categories, as follows:

(a) Ex-members who have reached the age of sixty;
(b) Ex-members under the age of sixty who are permanently unemployable;
(c) Ex-members under the age of sixty, not permanently unemployable but incapable of maintenance because of industrial handicaps combined with physical or mental disabilities; but this classification only applies to those who served in a theatre of actual war.

195. The rates of allowances (or Dual Service Pensions) are authorized up to $365.00 or $730.00 in any one year, in favour of single veterans or married veterans respectively. These two amounts represent the maximum income of the veteran from all sources in either case. In computing the maximum income, however, there are certain exemptions such as $125.00 earnings in any one year from casual employment and a few others.

Procedure

196. Whilst any ex-member of the Forces may write to the Board direct, it is preferable, in their own interest – and to save time in the consideration of their applications – that veterans first communicate with one of the various district or sub-district offices of the Department of Veterans Affairs throughout Canada. In either case they will be advised as promptly as possible as to their eligibility for consideration and will be given an opportunity of completing an application form.

CIVIL SERVICE COMMISSION

197. Under the Civil Service Act and recent Orders in Council preference in appointment to positions in the Civil Service of Canada is granted to ex-service personnel, but to be eligible for such preference, persons must fall in one of the following classes: –

(1) Persons in receipt of pensions by reason of their services in the war of 1914–1918 or the war of 1939–1945, regardless of theatre of service, who (a) have from causes attributable to such service lost capacity for physical exertion to an extent which makes them unfit efficiently to pursue the avocations which they were pursuing before the war, and (b) have not been successfully re-established in some other avocation.

(2) (a) Persons who have been on active service overseas with the naval, military, or air forces, or who have served on the high seas in a sea-going ship of war in the naval forces, of His Majesty or of any of the Allies of His Majesty, during the war of 1914–1918 or the war of 1939–1945, who have left such service with an honourable record or who have been honourably discharged. (b) Members of the Royal Canadian Air Force who have been required in the course of operational duties to fly outside the territorial waters of the Western Hemisphere. (c) Members of the Canadian Army who have served outside the Western Hemisphere. This means service in Greenland, in Iceland, or in the Aleutian Islands, but not service in Newfoundland, in Bermuda, or in the West Indies. (d) Members of the Royal Canadian Navy who have served on the high seas in a ship or other vessel, service in which is classed as "sea time" for the purpose of advancement of naval ratings or which would be so classed were the ship or other vessel in the service of the Naval Forces of Canada. (e) Persons who served with the South African Military Nursing Services. Persons with service as above in connection with the war of 1939–1945 are given the preference only if they were residents of Canada at the time they became members of the Forces. The preference is not extended to persons who (a) in connection with the European war or (b) in

connection with the war in the Pacific, arrived after V-E-Day (May 8th, 1945) or V-J-Day (August 15th, 1945), respectively, in a country or zone of operations, service in which is recognized as overseas active service, or whose service on the high seas commenced after the dates specified.

(3) Widows of persons who have served as specified in (2) and who have died owing to such service.

198. **Veterans' Information Office**

To assist ex-service personnel entitled to this preference who are interested in securing Civil Service employment, there is a Veterans' Information Office in Ottawa and at each District Office of the Civil Service Commission, the addresses of which will be found in the address appendix on the back of this booklet. Telephone numbers are also given and it is advisable to arrange an appointment whenever possible.

199. These offices are staffed by veterans and are established to give service to veterans. Full particulars are available regarding Civil Service positions, qualifications, rates of pay, conditions of employment, examinations by means of which appointments are made, and any other information which may be of assistance to the veteran who desires employment in the Public Service. Veterans are invited to write or call the Veterans' Information Office of the Civil Service Commission whichever is most convenient to them.

THE NATIONAL HOUSING ACT

Home for Home Owners (Parts I and III)

200. The National Housing Act is not a part of the legislation making up the rehabilitation programme but is designed to assist all citizens of Canada who wish to own their own homes. Under this Act a prospective home owner may borrow money from an approved lending institution, such as an insurance company, to assist in financing the construction of his own house.

201. Loans are based on lending value which may be either the cost of the home or the appraised value, whichever is the lesser, and the amount that can be borrowed may not be less than 50% nor more than the following percentages of the lending value:

95% of the first $2000;
85% of the second $2000;
70% of the amount of lending value in excess of $4000.

202. The remainder of the lending value, which must be put up by the prospective home owner, is called the "equity" and veterans may use their re-
establishment credit to provide up to two-thirds of such equity. **Where a
veteran proposes to use all or part of his re-establishment credit for this
purpose he should consult his nearest Supervisor of Re-establishment
Credits before making any commitments.**

203. Loans under the Act are made by the lending institution at 4½%, generally
for twenty years, and are repayable in monthly instalments which include
principal, interest and also one-twelfth of the estimated annual taxes.

204. Under normal conditions it is not considered wise to apply for a loan
where the monthly repayments would exceed 20% of the net monthly
income. Broadly speaking this means that the amount borrowed should
not exceed twice the annual net income.

205. The point of contact for loans under the National Housing Act is an
approved lending institution and such contact should be made before
commitments are entered into with respect to the proposed house. Parts
I and III of the National Housing Act have been broadly outlined in a
booklet, entitled "Homes for Canadians," which is available from any
branch office of the National Housing Administration or upon request
to the Head Office, Department of Finance, Ottawa. A list of the approved lending institutions is included with each booklet. A number of
standard plans and designs may be obtained also from the Administration for the sum of $10 per set. A booklet of sketches of these standard
plans and designs is also available free upon request.

INCOME TAX

206. An income tax return for the calendar year must be completed and filed
on or before April 30th of the succeeding year by every person who had
a taxable income for the calendar year in excess of $660, if single, or in
excess of $1,200, if married.

207. The exemption which applies to the pay and allowances of service men
when they are overseas continues for the first six months of service after
they return to Canada. It is to be noted, however, that this further exemption applies only while the service man remains in the forces and
that it does not extend to any civilian earnings. On the other hand, a
discharged member of the forces whose service pay and allowances were
not taxable may, upon taking civilian employment, obtain exemption
from tax deductions for the balance of the calendar year by filing form
T.D.1A with his employer if it is evident that his civilian earnings for the
year are not going to be sufficient to give him a taxable income.

208. Individuals in business are required to pay their estimated income tax for the current year by quarterly instalments. Every employer must also make tax deductions from the salaries or wages he pays and must remit the amounts deducted within one week of each pay day.

209. Income tax return forms are available at post offices. Other forms and additional information may be obtained from the Office of any District Inspector of Income Tax. The responsibility for procuring the necessary forms and filing returns rests upon the taxpayer and the law provides penalties in the event of non-compliance.

NATIONALS OF OTHER COUNTRIES

210. All veterans of the Canadian Forces are eligible, subject to the provisions and limitations of the various pieces of legislation, for all the benefits of the Canadian Rehabilitation Program – providing they remain in Canada to take advantage of them.

211. However, should they take up residence outside Canada they may still apply for and receive the benefits of this program outlined below.

Clothing Allowance . . . . paragraph 32
Rehabilitation Grant . . . . paragraph 33–34
Repatriation to countries other than Canada . . . . paragraph 36
Return of dependents from Overseas. . . . . paragraph 38–39
War Service Grants Act . . . . paragraph 60–80
Training Allowances. . . . . paragraph 87–95
Vocational Training . . . . paragraph 96–102
University Training . . . . paragraph 103–113
Treatment and pensions for pensionable disabilities paragraph 142–143
Prosthetic Services. . . . . paragraph 149–150
Pensions . . . . paragraph 158–176
Veterans' Bureau . . . . paragraph 177–178
Veterans' Insurance. . . . . paragraph 179–187

212. Non-resident veterans of the Canadian Forces when applying for benefits of the Canadian Rehabilitation Program should write directly to the Department of Veterans Affairs, Ottawa. Such veterans are also eligible, in certain cases, for certain similar benefits from their own countries. To obtain the maximum assistance they should ascertain the extent of the benefits to which they may be eligible, in their own countries, before applying for similar benefits under the Canadian Rehabilitation legislation. Benefits may not be duplicated.

CIVIL SERVICE COMMISSION

LIST OF DISTRICT OFFICE ADDRESSES

City	Address	Telephone
Halifax	261 Quinpool Road	3-9321
Saint John	60 Prince William St.	3-2769
Quebec	Morin Building, 111 Mountain Hill	2-5225
Montreal	520 Transportation Bldg., 132 St. James St. West	Ha. 0257
Ottawa	Room 302, Jackson Bldg.	9-6916
Toronto	465 Bay Street	Ad. 5185
Winnipeg	436 Main Street	2-3848
Regina	615 McCallum Hill Bldg.	2-0289
Edmonton	10113 – 100th Street	2-2834
Calgary	Room 28, Canada Life Bldg.	M-2236
Vancouver	789 W. Pender Street, Room 616	PA. 5251
Victoria	Room 702, Belmont Bldg.	E-8522

THE VETERANS' LAND ACT
DISTRICT SUPERINTENDENTS

Vancouver, B.C. . . . . 518 Rogers Bldg., 470 Granville St.
Edmonton, Alta. . . . . Blowey-Henry Bldg., 9901 Jasper Ave.
Saskatoon, Sask. . . . . Room 611, Federal Bldg.
Winnipeg, Man. . . . . Dominion Public Bldg., Main and Water St.
Toronto, Ont. . . . . .Dominion Bldg., 465 Bay St.
Ottawa, Ont. . . . . Trafalgar Bldg., 207 Queen St.
Montreal, Que. . . . . Confederation Bldg., 1253 McGill College Ave.
Saint John, N.B. . . . . .144 Union St.

VETERANS' LAND ACT REGIONAL SUPERVISORS

Victoria, B.C. . . . . Belmont Bldg.
New Westminster, B.C. . . . . .Westminster Trust Bldg., 713 Columbia St.
Kelowna, B.C. . . . . .Kerr Bldg., 706 Pendozi St.
Kamloops, B.C. . . . . Bank of Commerce Bldg., 118 Victoria St.
Nelson, B.C. . . . . 373 Baker St.
Dawson Creek, B.C. . . . . Dawson Creek
Grande Prairie, Alta. . . . . .Donald Hotel Block
Peace River, Alta. . . . . .Peace River
Calgary, Alta. . . . . .515 Calgary Public Bldg.
Red Deer, Alta. . . . . Snell Block, 144 Ross St.
Edmonton, Alta. . . . . .Northern Bldg., 9859 Jasper Ave.
Lethbridge, Alta. . . . . Masonic Hall Bldg., 10th St. South

St. Paul, Alta. . . . . St. Paul
Saskatoon, Sask. . . . . .505 Canada Bldg., 101–123 21st St. E.
Prince Albert, Sask. . . . . Canada Bldg., Central Ave.
Regina, Sask. . . . . .Imperial Bank Bldg., 11th Ave. and Scarth St.
Yorkton, Sask. . . . . Massey-Harris Bldg., 41 Broadway W.
Dauphin, Man. . . . . Public Bldg.
Brandon, Man. . . . . Strand Bldg., 131 10th St.
Winnipeg, Man. . . . . Grain Exchange Annex
Port Arthur, Ont. . . . . 17 South Cumberland St.
Sault Ste. Marie, Ont. . . . . 622 Queen St. E.
Sudbury, Ont. . . . . .156 Elm St. E.
New Liskeard, Ont. . . . . Public Bldg.
Windsor, Ont. . . . . .Canada Building
London, Ont. . . . . .Richmond Bldg., 371–381 Richmond St.
Mount Forest, Ont. . . . . Public Bldg.
Dundas, Ont. . . . . .Public Building
Toronto, Ont. . . . . .21 Lombard St.
Campbellford, Ont. . . . . .Public Building
Kingston, Ont. . . . . Weber Bldg.
Ottawa, Ont. . . . . Room 611, Aylmer Building, Slater Street
Hull, Que. . . . . 88 Wellington Street
Montreal, Que. . . . . 516 Dominion Square Bldg.
Sherbrooke, Que. . . . . 4 Wellington St. S.
Quebec, Que. . . . . 15 Boulevard des Capucins
Gaspe, Que. . . . . Gaspe
Fredericton, N.B. . . . . Loyalist Bldg., 432–442 Queen St.
Moncton, N.B. . . . . 2nd Floor, Imperial Block, 849–853 Main St.
Charlottetown, P.E.I. . . . . .Riley Bldg., 103 Queen St.
Truro, N.S. .McPhail and Cox Building, 515 Prince St.
Kentville, N.S. . . . . Chisholm Block, 21 Webster St.
Halifax, N.S. . . . . .Administration Bldg., Camp Hill Hospital
Sydney, N.S. . . . . Naval Administration Bldg.

PROSTHETIC CENTRES

"A" District .379 Common Street, MONTREAL, Quebec.
"B" District . . . . Camp Hill Hospital, HALIFAX, N.S.
"C" District . . . . Trafalgar Bldg., 207 Queen Street, OTTAWA, Ontario
"D" District .Christie Street Hospital, TORONTO 4, Ont.
"E" District . . . . . .118 Dalhousie Street, QUEBEC, P.Q. (serviced by Montreal)
"F" District . . . . Westminster Hospital, LONDON, Ont.
"G" District . . . . .Deer Lodge Hospital, WINNIPEG, Man.
"H" District . . . . Old Post Office Building, REGINA, Sask.
"I" District . . . . 517–8th Avenue West, CALGARY, Alta.

"R" District . . . . Veterans' Pavilion, University Hospital, EDMONTON, Alta.

"J" District . . . . Shaughnessy Hospital, VANCOUVER, B.C.

Sub-District. . . . . Belmont Building, VICTORIA, B.C.

"K" District . . . . Lancaster Hospital, SAINT JOHN, N.B.

"L" District . . . . 6th Floor, Lister Block, 42 James Street N., HAMILTON,
Ontario (serviced by Toronto).

If personal attendance is not necessary, artificial limbs may be forwarded by express, charges collect, to above Superintendents, Prosthetic Services Branch, Department of Veterans Affairs.

DISTRICT OFFICES AND PENSION MEDICAL EXAMINERS CANADIAN PENSION COMMISSION

DISTRICT

"B" HALIFAX, N.S. . . . . Camp Hill Hospital

"W" CHARLOTTETOWN, P.E.I. . . . . 76 Great George St., P.O. Box 130

"K" SAINT JOHN, N.B. . . . . .Lancaster Hospital, P.O. Box 1406

"E" QUEBEC, P.Q. . . . . .15 Boulevard des Capucins

"A" MONTREAL, P.Q. . . . . . .Old Examining Warehouse, 379 Common Street

"C" OTTAWA, Ont. . . . . Aylmer Bldg., 13 Slater St.

"T" KINGSTON, Ont. . . . . Post Office Building

"D" TORONTO, Ont. . . . . .Prudential Bldg., 55 York Street

"L" HAMILTON, Ont. Lister Block, 42 James Street N.

"F" LONDON, Ont. . . . . Westminster Hospital

"G" WINNIPEG, Man. . . . . .Commercial Bldg., Notre Dame Ave. E.

"H" REGINA, Sask. . . . . New Regina Trading Company Bldg.,
Scarth St. at 12th Avenue

"S" SASKATOON, Sask. . . . . .Birks Building, 153 Third Ave. S.

"I" CALGARY, Alta. . . . . 217 – 7th Avenue West

"R" EDMONTON, Alta. . . . . Redwood Building, 11250 Jasper Avenue

"J" VANCOUVER, B.C. . . . . Shaughnessy Hospital

VICTORIA, B.C. . . . . Belmont Building

DISTRICT PENSIONS ADVOCATES

CHARLOTTETOWN, P.E.I. . . . . .86 Great George Street, P.O. Box 507

HALIFAX, N.S. . . . . Camp Hill Hospital

SAINT JOHN, N.B. . . . . .65 Prince William Street, P.O. Box 1406

QUEBEC, P.Q. . . . . .15 Boulevard des Capucins

MONTREAL, P.Q. . . . . .Old Examining Warehouse, 379 Common Street
(Cor. McGill)

OTTAWA, Ont. . . . . 411 Aylmer Building, 13 Slater Street

TORONTO, Ont. Prudential Building, 55 York Street
HAMILTON, Ont. . . . . 6th Floor, Lister Block, 42 James Street North
LONDON, Ont. . . . . .Westminster Hospital
FORT WILLIAM, Ont. . . . . .226 South May Street
WINNIPEG, Man. . . . . 803 Commercial Bldg., Notre Dame Ave. E.
REGINA, Sask. . . . . New Regina Trading Company Bldg., Scarth Street
at 12th Avenue
SASKATOON, Sask. . . . . Birks Building, 153 Third Avenue S.
CALGARY, Alta. . . . . .217 – 7th Ave. W.
EDMONTON, Alta. . . . . Redwood Building, 11250 Jasper Avenue
VANCOUVER, B.C. . . . . Shaughnessy Hospital
VICTORIA, B.C. . . . . .Belmont Building

REHABILITATION CENTRES

CHARLOTTETOWN, P.E.I. . . . . .134 Richmond Street
HALIFAX, N.S. . . . . Camp Hill Hospital
SAINT JOHN, N.B. . . . . 71–91 Prince William Street
QUEBEC, P.Q. . . . . 15 Boulevard des Capucins
MONTREAL, P.Q. .317 Common Street (Cor. McGill)
OTTAWA, Ont. . . . . .Aylmer Bldg., Slater Street
KINGSTON, Ont. . . . . .Post Office Building
TORONTO, Ont. . . . . .55 York Street
HAMILTON, Ont. . . . . 145 King Street West (Cor. Bay)
LONDON, Ont. . . . . .343 Richmond Street
WINDSOR, Ont. . . . . .346 Victoria Street
WINNIPEG, Man. . . . . .Commercial Building
REGINA, Sask. . . . . New Regina Trading Co. Bldg.
SASKATOON, Sask. . . . . London Building
CALGARY, Alta. . . . . 217 – 7th Avenue West
EDMONTON, Alta. . . . . Redwood Bldg., 11250 Jasper Avenue
VANCOUVER, B.C. . . . . .717 Granville Street
VICTORIA, B.C. . . . . 202 Belmont Building

District Superintendents of Rehabilitation and Supervisors of Re-establishment Credit, Training, Education and other rehabilitation officers are located at these addresses.

NOTES

These notes give the deleted sections as they appeared in the 15 October 1945 version of *Back to Civil Life*.

1   22. Although victory has been achieved full scale demobilization cannot yet be undertaken; discharge machinery cannot discharge all those in the discharge stream in a week or so; nor would such a policy be advantageous to servicemen themselves. It may therefore be taken for granted that many servicemen, reading this booklet, will be remaining in the services for varying periods. Some, of course, will have greater opportunities and facilities for thinking and preparing for their future than others.

23. **However, servicemen should take advantage of every opportunity to plan now for their post-war careers and where possible take advantage of any training courses which fit into their plans and which may be available.**

The 1 April 1946 version of *Back to Civil Life* was issued after the majority of service personnel had been discharged. It merged the old section 23 with section 22.

2   26. The policies and procedures relating to demobilization vary as to detail in each of the three services. Insofar as it is practicable, however, the overall policy in each of the services is to discharge first those who have seen the longest and hardest service.

27. Because of the urgency of certain essential civilian requirements, such as housing, the Industrial Selection and Release Board has been set up under the Department of Labour, to deal with applications from employers for the early release of certain specially qualified servicemen.

3   114. Such intention is applicable also to graduate students who wish to go on to higher degrees. In the field of graduate studies, particularly, emphasis will be placed on the relation of the applicant's specialized study to the national interest.

Further Reading

Two books cover the basics of Canada's World War II history: C.P. Stacey, *Arms, Men and Governments: The War Politics of Canada 1939–1945* (Ottawa: Queen's Printer 1970), and J.L. Granatstein, *Canada's War: The Policies of the Mackenzie King Government, 1939–1945* (Toronto: Oxford University Press 1975). Demobilization is covered in Dean F. Oliver, "When the Battle's Won: Military Demobilization in Canada, 1939–1946" (PH D thesis, York University, 1996). The indispensable work for understanding the origins of veterans policy in Canada is Desmond Morton and Glenn Wright, *Winning the Second Battle: Canadian Veterans and the Return to Civilian Life 1915–1930* (Toronto: University of Toronto Press 1987). The development of the Veterans Charter is the subject of Shaun R.G. Brown, "Re-establishment and Rehabilitation: Canadian Veteran Policy – 1933–1946" (PH D thesis, University of Western Ontario, 1995). See also Dean F. Oliver, "Public Policy in Canada: Federal Legislation on War Veterans, 1939–46," in Raymond B. Blake, Penny E. Bryden, and J. Frank Strain, eds., *The Welfare State in Canada: Past, Present and Future* (Concord, Ont.: Irwin 1997), 193–214. A work written during the war that greatly influenced policy towards veterans is Robert England, *Discharged: A Commentary on Civil Re-establishment of Veterans in Canada* (Toronto: Macmillan Company of Canada 1943); see also his *Twenty Million World War Veterans* (Toronto and New York: Oxford University Press 1950). The details of Canada's program for World War II veterans are in *Back to Civil Life*, the pamphlet that explained the benefit package to members of the armed forces, and *The Veterans Charter: Acts of the Canadian Parliament to Assist Canadian Veterans* (Ottawa: King's Printer 1946), a compendium of all the legislation and regulations relating to veterans affairs. *Back to Civil Life*, which was issued by the Department of Veterans Affairs and went through several revisions, is reprinted here as appendix 2. Another useful wartime account is C.N. Senior, *When the Boys Come Home: Their Post-War Opportunities in Canada* (Toronto: Collins 1944).

A mine of information about veterans and their needs can be found in the interim reports (no final report was published) of the Royal Commission on Veterans' Qualifications, which was chaired by Wilfrid Bovey. Even more important are the annual reports of the Department of Veterans Affairs. Not surprisingly, Canadian newspapers were full of articles about veterans in the immediate postwar years, and these bring the period back to life. One such account, published in *Maclean's*, 1 May 1945, is J.D. Ketchum, "Home Won't Be Heaven Soldier." This is reprinted in J.L. Granatstein and Peter Neary, eds., *The Good Fight: Canadians and World War II* (Toronto: Copp Clark 1995), 416–25. This same volume also reprints (from *The Street*) Mordecai Richler, "Benny, the War in Europe and Myerson's Daughter Bella" (426–30), a poignant reflection on the postwar experience. The subject of veterans' benefits has, of course, been a continuing preoccupation of *Legion*, the official publication of the Royal Canadian Legion.

Walter S. Woods, the principal architect of the Veterans Charter, wrote two books about the genesis and accomplishments of the Canadian program for the veterans of World War II: *Rehabilitation (A Combined Operation)* (Ottawa: Queen's Printer 1953) and *The Men Who Came Back* (Toronto: Ryerson Press 1956). In the same vein, see also Frederick Lyon Barrow, *A Post War Era: A Study of the Veterans Legislation of Canada, 1950–1963* (Ottawa: Queen's Printer 1964). Three widely read books that draw on reminiscences of the war and immediate postwar periods are Barry Broadfoot, *Six War Years: Memories of Canadians at Home and Abroad* (Toronto: Doubleday Canada 1974) and *The Veterans' Years: Coming Home from the War* (Vancouver/Toronto: Douglas & McIntyre 1985); and Ted and Alex Barris, *Days of Victory: Canadians Remember: 1939–1945* (Toronto: Macmillan Company of Canada 1995). The experiences of Canadian servicewomen in World War II are explored in Ruth Roach Pierson, *"They're Still Women After All": The Second World War and Canadian Womanhood* (Toronto: McClelland and Stewart 1986), and Carolyn Gossage, *Greatcoats and Glamour Boots: Canadian Women at War (1939–1945)* (Toronto: Dundurn Press 1991). The implications of the Veterans Charter for ex-servicewomen are analysed in Peter Neary and Shaun Brown, "The Veterans Charter and Canadian Women Veterans of World War II," *British Journal of Canadian Studies* 9, no. 2 (1994): 249–77, and J.L. Granatstein and Peter Neary, eds., *The Good Fight: Canadians and World War II*, 387–415. The story of the integration of Newfoundland veterans into the Canadian system is told in Peter Neary, "How Newfoundland Veterans Became Canadian Veterans: A Study in Bureaucracy and Benefit," in James Hiller and Peter Neary, eds., *Twentieth Century Newfoundland: Explorations* (St John's: Breakwater 1994), 195–237. For the impact of the

Veterans Charter on Canadian universities in general and on selected insti-
tutions, see: *Report of the National Conference of Canadian Universities on Post-War
Problems* (Toronto: University of Toronto Press 1944); W.P. Thompson, *The
University of Saskatchewan: A Personal History* (Toronto: University of Toronto
Press 1970); Stanley Brice Frost, *McGill University for the Advancement of Learn-
ing*, vol. 2, *1895–1971* (Kingston and Montreal: McGill-Queen's University
Press 1984); P.B. Waite, *Lord of Point Grey: Larry MacKenzie of U.B.C.* (Van-
couver: University of British Columbia Press 1987); and James D. Cameron *For
the People: A History of St Francis Xavier University* (Montreal and Kingston:
McGill-Queen's University Press 1996).

United States books and articles that invite Canadian comparison are Robert
J. Havighurst, *The American Veteran Back Home* (New York: Longmans, Green
1951); R.B. Pitkin, "How the First G.I. Bill Was Written," *American Legion Maga-
zine* 86, no. 1 (January 1969): 24–8, 51–3; ibid., no. 2 (February 1969): 22–6,
48–51; and ibid., no. 5 (May 1969): 33, 59; Davis R.B. Ross, *Preparing for
Ulysses: Politics and Veterans During World War II* (New York: Columbia University
Press 1969); Keith W. Olson, *The G.I. Bill, the Veterans and the Colleges* (Lexington: University Press of Kentucky 1974); Theodore R. Mosch, *The GI Bill: A
Breakthrough in Educational and Social Policy in the United States* (Hicksville, New
York: Exposition Press 1975); Thomas N. Bonner, "The Unintended Revolu-
tion in America's Colleges since 1940," *Change* 18, no. 5 (September/October
1986): 44–51; Richard Severo and Lewis Milford, *The Wages of War: When Amer-
ica's Soldiers Came Home – From Valley Forge to Vietnam* (New York: Simon and
Schuster 1989); Theda Skocpol, *Protecting Soldiers and Mothers: The Political
Origins of Social Policy in the United States* (Cambridge, Mass.: Belknap Press of
Harvard University Press 1992); Edward Kiester, Jr, "The G.I. Bill May Be the
Best Deal Ever Made by Uncle Sam," *Smithsonian* 25, no. 8 (November 1994):
128–32, 134, 136, 138–9; Michael J. Bennett, *When Dreams Came True: The GI
Bill and the Making of Modern America* (Washington and London: Brassey's
1996); John W. Jeffries, *Wartime America: The World War II Home Front* (Chicago:
Ivan R. Dee 1996); and Theda Skocpol, "Delivering for Young Families: The
Resonance of the GI Bill," *The American Prospect* 28 (September–October,
1996): 66–72.

The decade after World War II, perhaps because it was largely shaped by
the good, grey Liberal government of Louis St Laurent, remains remarkably
unstudied. The one indispensable book whose references should be mined by
all researchers is Doug Owram's *Born at the Right Time: A History of the Baby
Boom Generation* (Toronto: University of Toronto Press 1996). Owram's work
traces the impact that the children of the veterans studied in this collection
have had on the increasingly prosperous Canada for which their fathers and
mothers fought. Equally useful is Robert Bothwell et al., *Canada since 1945*
(Toronto: University of Toronto Press 1989), an able account (with heavy

emphasis on national politics and the economy) of the success story that was postwar Canadian history.

There are numerous biographical and autobiographical studies that deserve examination. J.W. Pickersgill, the public servant-turned-Liberal cabinet minister, is the major author. *The Mackenzie King Record*, vol. 3, *1945–1946*, and vol 4, *1947–1948* (Toronto: University of Toronto Press 1970) by Pickersgill and D. F. Forster are indispensable for their presentation of the diary kept by Mackenzie King, prime minister until 1948. All subjects, including veterans and social welfare, can be found here. The full text of King's enormous, invaluable diary is available on microfiche from the University of Toronto Press. Pickersgill is also the author of *My Years with Louis St Laurent: A Political Memoir* (Toronto: University of Toronto Press 1975), arguably the best account of King's successor, the quiet, competent Quebecer who made running the country look easy. Dale Thomson's *Louis St. Laurent: Canadian* (Toronto: Macmillan Company of Canada 1967) should also be consulted. One of the key ministers in the King and St Laurent governments, Paul Martin, Sr, left two fine volumes of memoirs under the title *A Very Public Life* (Ottawa: Deneagu 1983, 1985). Martin was the minister who pressed harder for social welfare than any other, and his account of the problems is extremely useful in explaining the slow development of cradle-to-grave security in Canada. It fell to Diefenbaker, Pearson, and Trudeau to complete the welfare state which Mackenzie King had advanced during the war.

There are many specialized accounts of the development of various social policies – though, regrettably, nothing of great value on the way such policies directly affected veterans in postwar Canada. For federal finance, see W.I. Gillespie, *Tax, Borrow and Spend: Financing Federal Spending in Canada, 1867–1990* (Ottawa: Carleton University Press 1991), and more narrowly, David W. Slater, *Finance and Reconstruction: The Role of Canada's Department of Finance 1939–1946* (Ottawa: privately published, 1996). On the social welfare state in general, see Keith G. Banting, *The Welfare State and Canadian Federalism* (Kingston and Montreal: McGill-Queen's University Press 1982), Dennis Guest, *The Emergence of Social Security in Canada* (Vancouver: University of British Columbia Press 1980), and the essays in Jacqueline Ismael, ed., *Canadian Social Welfare Policy: Federal and Provincial Dimensions* (Kingston and Montreal: McGill-Queen's University Press 1987).

Housing was a subject of great concern to veterans who returned to a country whose housing stock in 1945 was almost wholly inadequate. See Albert Rose, *Canadian Housing Policies 1935–1980* (Toronto: Butterworths 1980), and John C. Bacher's very critical account, *Keeping to the Marketplace: The Evolution of Canadian Housing Policy* (Montreal and Kingston: McGill-Queen's University Press 1993). Welfare policy in Ontario has been ably examined in James Struthers, *The Limits of Affluence: Welfare in Ontario, 1920–1970* (Toronto: University of Toronto Press 1994), while two useful books on the elderly, a group that now includes every surviving veteran, are Kenneth Bryden, *Old Age Pensions and Policy-Making in Canada* (Montreal and London: McGill-Queen's University Press 1974), and Victor W. Marshall, ed., *Aging in Canada: Social Perspectives* (Toronto: Fitzhenry & Whiteside 1980). Finally, several of the essays in Bettina Bradbury, ed., *Canadian Family History: Selected Readings* (Toronto: Copp Clark Pitman 1992), touch on postwar Canada.

Contributors

TERRY COPP is Professor of History at Wilfrid Laurier University. He is co-author (with Bill McAndrew) of the much-acclaimed *Battle Exhaustion: Soldiers and Psychiatrists in the Canadian Army, 1939–1945* (Montreal & Kingston: McGill-Queen's University Press 1990); the founder of the journal *Canadian Military History*; and the author and publisher of a multivolume history of the First Canadian Army's actions during World War II in Northwest Europe.

J.L. GRANATSTEIN, OC, is Distinguished Research Professor of History Emeritus at York University and Rowell Jackman Resident Fellow of the Canadian Institute of International Affairs. He is the author of many books on Canada's part in World War II.

DON IVES has worked for Veterans Affairs Canada since 1974. He now serves as Commemorations Officer.

JEFF KESHEN teaches in the Department of History at the University of Ottawa. He is the author of *Propaganda and Censorship during Canada's Great War* (Edmonton: University of Alberta Press 1996) and is completing a study of the Canadian home front in World War II.

DESMOND MORTON, OC, Director of the McGill Institute for the Study of Canada, is one of the country's leading military historians. His voluminous work includes (with Glenn Wright), *Winning the Second Battle: Canadian Veterans and the Return to Civilian Life 1915–1930* (Toronto: University of Toronto Press 1987).

PETER NEARY is Professor of History and Dean of the Faculty of Social Science at the University of Western Ontario. He is the author of *Newfoundland in the North Atlantic World, 1929–1949* (Kingston and Montreal: McGill-Queen's University Press 1988) and the editor of *White Tie and Decorations: Sir John and Lady Hope Simpson in Newfoundland, 1934–1936* (Toronto: University of Toronto Press 1996). He is the co-editor (with J.L. Granatstein) of *The Good Fight: Canadians and World War II* (Toronto: Copp Clark 1995).

DEAN F. OLIVER is a graduate of the Memorial University of Newfoundland and York University. His 1996 York PH D thesis is entitled "When the Battle's Won: Military Demobilization in Canada, 1939–1946." He is now a postdoctoral fellow at the Norman Paterson School of International Affairs, Carleton University, and is studying postwar defence policy.

DOUG OWRAM is Vice-President Academic of the University of Alberta and one of the major Canadian historians of his generation. His publications include *The Government Generation: Canadian Intellectuals and the State, 1900–1945* (Toronto: University of Toronto Press 1986) and *Born at the Right Time: A History of the Baby Boom Generation* (Toronto: University of Toronto Press 1996).

MICHAEL D. STEVENSON is a graduate of Laurentian University and the University of Western Ontario. His 1996 Western PH D thesis is entitled "National Selective Service and the Mobilization of Human Resources in Canada during the Second World War." He is now a postdoctoral fellow at Trent University and is studying the history of job-training programs in Canada.

JAMES STRUTHERS teaches in the Canadian Studies Program at Trent University. He is the author of *No Fault of Their Own: Unemployment and the Canadian Welfare State, 1914–1941* (Toronto: University of Toronto Press 1983) and *The Limits of Affluence: Welfare in Ontario, 1920–1970* (Toronto: University of Toronto Press 1994).

MARY TREMBLAY teaches in the School of Rehabilitation Science, Faculty of Health Sciences, McMaster University. She is writing a history of spinal cord injury rehabilitation in Canada.

Index